# INVESTMENT FUNDAMENTALS

**Also by Gitman and Joehnk**
FUNDAMENTALS OF INVESTING, *3rd edition*
PERSONAL FINANCIAL PLANNING, *4th edition*
MANAGERIAL FINANCE *(with George E. Pinches)*

**By Lawrence J. Gitman**
PRINCIPLES OF MANAGERIAL FINANCE, *5th edition*
BUSINESS WORLD, *2nd edition (with Carl McDaniel, Jr.)*
FINANCIAL MANAGEMENT: CASES, *2nd edition (with Edward A. Moses
   and Bernard J. Winger)*
PORSTRAT: A PORTFOLIO STRATEGY SIMULATION *(with Abderrahman
   Robana and William D. Biggs)*
BASIC MANAGERIAL FINANCE

# INVESTMENT FUNDAMENTALS

## A GUIDE TO BECOMING
## A KNOWLEDGEABLE INVESTOR

Lawrence J. Gitman

Michael D. Joehnk

*with*

Judy R. Block

1817

HARPER & ROW, PUBLISHERS, New York
Cambridge, Philadelphia, San Francisco, Washington
London, Mexico City, São Paulo, Singapore, Sydney

FIRST EDITION

*Designed by Lorraine Mullaney*

Library of Congress Cataloging-in-Publication Data

Gitman, Lawrence J.
  Investment fundamentals.

  Includes index.
  1. Investments—handbooks, manuals, etc.   I. Joehnk, Michael D.
II. Block, Judy Rachel, 1948–    .   III. Title.
HG4527.G58   1988      332.6'78        87–45642
ISBN 0–06–015861–1

88 89 90 91 92 RRD 10 9 8 7 6 5 4 3 2 1

# CONTENTS

# 3
## RETIREMENT PLANNING: THE CRUCIAL SECOND COMPONENT
24

# 4
## GAUGING THE RETURN FROM YOUR INVESTMENT DOLLAR
34

# 5
## MEASURING YOUR EXPOSURE TO RISK
53

# PART TWO:   THE MARKETS AND HOW THEY WORK

# 6
## THE SECURITIES MARKETS
65

# 7
## HOW THE SECURITIES
## MARKETS WORK
### 75

# 8
## YOU AND YOUR BROKER:
## PARTNERS IN
## THE SECURITIES MARKETS
### 82

# 9
## THE NUTS AND BOLTS
## OF TRADING
### 90

# 10
## DIFFERENT TYPES
## OF SECURITIES TRANSACTIONS
### 107

# 11

## INFORMATION:
## THE KEY
## TO INVESTMENT SUCCESS
121

# PART THREE:  PLAYING IT SAFE—STOCKS,
# BONDS, AND MUTUAL FUNDS

# 12

## UNDERSTANDING
## COMMON STOCKS
135

# 13

## INVESTING IN COMMON STOCKS:
## BEGINNING THE
## SELECTION PROCESS
147

# 14

## COMMON STOCK ANALYSIS:
## LOOKING AT THE PAST
155

# 20
## CONVERTIBLE SECURITIES: A HYBRID INVESTMENT VEHICLE
231

# 21
## PREFERRED STOCK: A HYBRID OF A DIFFERENT SORT
242

# 22
## THE REWARDING WORLD OF MUTUAL FUNDS
255

# 23
## INVESTING IN MUTUAL FUNDS
274

# PART FOUR: TAKING CHANCES—TAX SHELTERS, OPTIONS, COMMODITIES, AND FINANCIAL FUTURES

## 24
### TAX-SHELTERED INVESTMENTS
285

## 25
### OPTIONS: THE POWER OF LEVERAGE SWEETENS THE POT
300

## 26
### STOCK INDEX AND OTHER OPTIONS
321

## 27
### THE FAST TRACK OF COMMODITIES TRADING
329

## 28
### TRADING IN FINANCIAL FUTURES
343

THE MARKET FOR FINANCIAL FUTURES  343  FINANCIAL FUTURES COME IN THREE
BASIC FORMS  345  FINANCIAL FUTURES CONTRACTS  346  TRADING IN
FINANCIAL FUTURES  349  SHOULD YOU INVEST?  353

## PART FIVE:  WHERE YOU GO FROM HERE

## 29
### DEFINING YOUR
### INVESTMENT PORTFOLIO
357

DIVERSIFY TO REDUCE RISK  358  BUILDING A PORTFOLIO  360
SOME SAMPLE PORTFOLIOS  363

## 30
### MONITORING YOUR
### INVESTMENT PORTFOLIO
370

EVALUATING THE PERFORMANCE OF INDIVIDUAL SECURITIES  370
COMPARE PERFORMANCE TO INVESTMENT GOALS  374  ASSESSING PORTFOLIO
PERFORMANCE  378  TIMING TRANSACTIONS  382  CONCLUDING COMMENTS  387

# PREFACE

It wasn't that long ago that a 100-million-share day on the New York Stock Exchange was a newsworthy event. Today, no one even takes notice unless the daily share volume exceeds 250 million. And it wasn't that long ago that the Dow Jones industrial average was under 1,000. Since then, we've seen the market reach new heights and then, almost overnight, erase gains that took a year or more to produce.

Changes like these have made investments—and investing—front page news all over the country. When the Dow breaks new records—either up or down—when interest rates and bond prices fluctuate, when trading begins on yet another market index option, most of us know about it. If the news if good, we wonder how we can invest our money to get our small piece of the lucrative financial pie. And if it's not so good, we wonder what we can do to protect ourselves financially.

Interestingly, the monumental rise and fall in stock prices has made many investors more conscious of not only the pitfalls they face, but also the financial opportunities that are now open to them in other investment areas. Stock index and other options have exploded in popularity along with the stock market itself. Bonds are no longer seen as a conservative investment for retirees looking for dependable interest income. Rather, they are now viewed as a trader's vehicle with enormous capital gains as well as income potential. And mutual funds are considered by many to be the answer to the harried investor's prayer: Simply buy shares in a mutual fund and let the experts make your crucial investment decisions (oh, if it were only that simple . . . ).

Despite the high profile investing has achieved, successful investing is still a skill and it is as difficult as always to be successful at it. Witness the millions of institutional and individual investors who lose money every day and the millions more who could have made a lot more money had they come prepared with the knowledge and discipline to plan an intelligent investment program.

Our purpose in writing this book is not to guarantee you investment success—

no one can do that—but to give you the basic knowledge you need to be successful in different markets and under different market conditions. We will do that by exploring four basic investment areas:

- Equities (common stocks)
- Bonds and other fixed-income securities
- Mutual funds
- Options, commodities, and financial futures

For this information to make any sense, we believe it must be presented in the context of your unique investment needs. Thus, we'll examine liquidity—the need for money now—and retirement planning—the need for it later; tax-sheltered investments; and the necessity to put your total financial life together in the form of a well-managed investment portfolio. Perhaps most importantly, we'll also look at the concepts of risk and return, for without a clear understanding of how you measure these critical investment elements, you'll have no way of comparing investments and choosing the ones that are right for you.

We hope you will dip into *Investment Fundamentals: A Guide to Becoming a Knowledgeable Investor* on a regular basis to review basic investment concepts and to make sure your total investment plan makes sense. Although we do not come to you with yet another "winning" investment scheme, we feel we offer a lot more: an all-encompassing introduction to investments that is tailored to your unique investment needs.

Lawrence J. Gitman
Dayton, Ohio

Michael D. Joehnk
Scottsdale, Arizona

*January 1988*

# ONE
## DECIDING HOW TO INVEST

# 1

## INVESTING:
## ITS ROLE IN YOUR LIFE

On a single day in 1929, Winston Churchill's fortune would have been wiped out had it not been for the generosity of his friend, financier Bernard Baruch. When Churchill plunged into the wild American stock market and saw the value of his holdings plummet in the Great Crash, Baruch was there to protect him. According to author William Manchester, "Baruch had left instructions to buy equivalent stocks every time Churchill sold his and to sell whenever Churchill bought." The net result of Baruch's actions was to neutralize Churchill's losses by balancing them with an equivalent profit. This act of kindness probably altered the course of history, for without his fortune Churchill would have been forced to leave politics.

How many of us have guardian angels like Bernard Baruch watching over us every time we put money in the market and, more to the point, correcting our mistakes? This is the stuff dreams are made of, like crystal balls that forecast interest rates and corporate takeover candidates. When reality sets in, however, we realize that no one is about to hand us anything in the world of investments. We must make things happen through hard work—by setting investment goals and learning about the various investment vehicles and strategies.

# WHAT ARE INVESTMENTS?

Simply stated, an *investment* is any vehicle into which funds can be placed with the expectation that they will be preserved or increase in value and/or generate positive returns. Idle cash is not an investment, since its value is likely to be eroded by inflation and it fails to provide any type of return. The same cash placed in a bank savings account would be considered an investment, since the account provides a positive return. We will differentiate among various types of investments on the basis of a number of factors such as whether the investment is a security or property; whether you make it in a direct or indirect way; whether it is a debt, equity, or option; whether it is low or high risk; and finally, whether it is long or short term.

*Security or property.* Investments that represent evidence of debt, ownership of a business, or the legal right to acquire or sell an ownership interest in a business are called *securities.* The most common types of securities are bonds, stocks, and options. Investments in *property,* on the other hand, involve real property or tangible personal property. *Real property* is primarily land and buildings. *Tangible personal property* includes such items as gold, antiques, and art. Although there is much to be said about buying and selling real estate and tangible assets—and indeed thousands of books have been written on these subjects—we will focus here on financial securities alone. Securities investing is such a complex field that even after this book is done, there will be a lot more to say.

*Direct or indirect.* When you make a direct investment, you directly acquire a security such as a stock or a bond by buying it in the market. In contrast, you can buy securities indirectly by purchasing shares of a mutual fund, which is a diversified portfolio of securities issued by a variety of firms. In this case, you own a fraction of the entire portfolio, made up of numerous securities, rather than a security of a single firm.

*Debt, equity, or option.* Usually, an investment will represent a debt or an equity interest. *Debt* represents funds loaned in exchange for the receipt of interest income and the promised repayment of the loan at a given future date. When you buy a debt instrument like a *bond,* you are lending money to the issuer, who agrees to pay a stated rate of interest over a specified period of time, at the end of which the original sum will be returned. *Equity* represents an ownership interest in a specific business. Typically, you obtain an equity interest in a business by purchasing securities known as *stock. Options* are neither debt nor equity; rather, they are securities that provide you with an opportunity to purchase another security or property at a specified price over a stated period of time. You may, for example, pay $500 for an option to purchase a 2 percent interest in the Alex Company for $30,000 until December 31, 1992. If a 2 percent interest is currently valued at $24,000, you will not exercise this option. However, if it jumps in value to $35,000, you certainly will. Option investments, although not as common as debt and equity investments, are growing rapidly in popularity.

*Low or high risk.*   Investments are sometimes differentiated on the basis of risk. As used in the financial marketplace, *risk* refers to the chance that the value or return on an investment will differ from its expected value. It is the chance that something undesirable will occur. The broader the range of possible values or returns associated with an investment, the greater its risk, and vice versa.

You face a risk continuum that ranges from low-risk government securities to high-risk commodities. Although each type of investment vehicle has a basic risk characteristic, the actual level of risk depends on the specific investment. For example, although stocks are generally believed to be more risky than bonds, so-called junk bonds are far more risky than the stock of a financially sound firm such as IBM.

When you make a low-risk investment, you are fairly certain to receive the return you expect as well as your principal when you sell the investment. High-risk investments, on the other hand, are often considered speculative. The terms *investment* and *speculation* refer to different approaches to the investment process. When you invest, you purchase securities whose value and level of expected return (earnings) are somewhat stable and therefore predictable. When you speculate, on the other hand, the future value and expected earnings of the securities are highly uncertain. Simply stated, speculation is high-risk investment. As you might expect, because of the greater risk, the returns associated with speculation are also greater.

*Short or long term.*   The life of an investment can be described as either short or long term. *Short-term* investments typically are those with lives of a year or less. *Long-term* investments are those with longer maturities—or perhaps, like common stock, with no maturity at all. For example, a 6-month certificate of deposit would be a short-term investment, while a 20-year bond would be a long-term investment. Of course, by purchasing a long-term investment and selling it after a short period of time, say 6 months, you can use a long-term vehicle to meet a short-term need. Indeed, matching the life of an investment to the period of time over which you want to invest is one of the most important investment skills you can acquire.

## LEARN THE STEPS IN INVESTING

How do you go about putting together an investment program? If you're serious about wanting results, you take the following steps.

### MAKE SURE YOUR LIFE IS IN ORDER

Investing makes little sense if your life is in total disarray. If at the end of every month you're scrounging to make ends meet, then investing has no place in your financial life. Moreover, investments are not intended to meet your current needs. Rather, they are the mechanism for using current funds to satisfy future needs.

At the very least, you need money for day-to-day living expenses. You also need cash for emergencies, including losing your job, and insurance protection for yourself and your family in case you die, become sick or disabled, or suffer a major property loss. Only when these basic needs are covered should you consider investing.

## ESTABLISH INVESTMENT GOALS

Your next step is to establish your investment goals. For example, an investment goal might be to accumulate $15,000 for the down payment on a summer home to be purchased in 1997 or to accumulate $250,000 for use at retirement in 2004. Above all, your goals must be realistic. Because goal-setting is so important, we'll come back to it again and again.

## EVALUATE INVESTMENT VEHICLES

Before selecting specific investment vehicles, it is important to evaluate them in terms of your investment goals. You must carefully analyze the different choices open to you, making sure that they are both technically strong and consistent with these goals. This process typically involves *valuation,* which is the process of estimating the true worth of an investment in terms of its possible return and risk (topics which will be covered in detail in later chapters).

## SELECT SUITABLE INVESTMENTS

No matter how carefully you work out your investment plans, your investment program will fall flat on its face if you choose the wrong investment vehicles. If you want income, it's a mistake to choose a speculative stock even if the stock triples in value in a week. Remember that when you can gain so much in such a short time, you can also lose your total investment, just as quickly.

## CONSTRUCT A DIVERSIFIED PORTFOLIO

An investment portfolio is a collection of investment vehicles assembled to meet an investment goal. You should diversify your portfolio by including investment vehicles with different levels of risk and return. For instance, your portfolio might contain 20 shares of IBM stock, $20,000 in government bonds, and 10 shares of IDS Growth mutual fund. This gives you the advantage of earning higher returns or being exposed to lower risk than if you limit your investments to one or two vehicles.

A portfolio has the surprising quality of possessing a different risk-return characteristic from those of its individual investment vehicles. For example, gold and other precious metals are by themselves extremely risky investments—their prices fluctuate constantly and often dramatically in commodity markets. Yet when they are held with securities such as common stock in a diversified portfolio, over time the portfolio exhibits lower risk or a higher return than if only metals or common stock were held.

There are two types of diversification techniques—random and purposive. In *random diversification,* as the name implies, investment vehicles are selected at random, such as by drawing names from a hat. This may hardly seem like a sound investment strategy, but it can work. Portfolios constructed this way have sometimes performed better than those designed by professionals. *Purposive diversification* is the process of selecting vehicles to achieve a stated portfolio objective. For example, you might observe that whenever the new car industry is depressed and its sales and profits are low, the car replacement parts industry booms. By diversifying between firms in both industries, it might be possible to reduce your total risk while maintaining a return equal to what you could earn by investing in only one of the two industries.

## MANAGE YOUR PORTFOLIO

Once you have constructed a portfolio, you must continually evaluate its actual behavior in relation to expected performance. If, for example, the investment return, risk, or ultimate value is not consistent with your objectives or expectations, you may have to sell certain investments and buy others. Portfolio management therefore involves monitoring and restructuring the portfolio as required by the actual behavior of the investments in order to maintain a group of investments that meets your goals.

---

# SET INVESTMENT GOALS

Starting an investment program without having a clear idea of your investment goals is like starting a long car trip without a map. In either case, you're soon hopelessly lost. Worse yet, you may run into problems you're not prepared to handle.

With investments, there's nothing more important than knowing where you're going before you take the first step. To do this, you must zero in on your investment goals: Are you after current income—a regular return on your investment that you can depend on year after year? Are you saving for a major expenditure, like a down payment on a house? Are you setting aside money for retirement? Are you sheltering income from taxes? As we take a closer look at these goals, remember that the investment direction you take should reflect your own individual situation. Your standard for success must be how close you come to your own goals, not how your goals stack up against the goals of your close friends.

## CURRENT INCOME: SO YOU NEED MONEY *NOW*

If your goal is money in your pocket today, look for investments that offer high current income at low risk. You can get this by investing in stocks paying high dividends, and in bonds, certificates of deposit, and other instruments offering high interest.

These investments are especially attractive to retired people who may need extra money to supplement their pensions and Social Security. Although it may be a stereotype, the picture we have of a retired person clipping coupons from a high-yield bond is exactly what most seniors should be doing at this point in their lives. It's impossible to overestimate the psychological comfort that comes from having money in the bank after you retire.

Current income may be your goal even if retirement is years ahead. People with special family problems, such as a dependent with a chronic medical condition, often seek out investments providing high current returns.

## MAJOR EXPENDITURES: SAVING FOR THE BIG TIME

Families often put money aside for years for just one major expenditure. Here are the most common reasons people save:

- To accumulate funds for a down payment on a house
- To pay for children's college education
- To finance a business venture
- To splurge on a luxury item such as a fur coat, a sports car, or an expensive vacation

Once you decide exactly what you want, you can choose an investment direction. If, for example, your goal is putting aside enough money for college, you'll probably want a low-risk investment such as a high-grade bond or blue chip stocks. On the other hand, if your savings goal is a sailboat—which most of us would consider a nonessential item—you can afford to take more chances, and your investment choice might be growth stocks with the possibility of spectacular capital gains or junk bonds known for their high interest and even higher risk.

## RETIREMENT: THERE'S NO MORE IMPORTANT REASON TO INVEST

Although accumulating funds for retirement is the single most important reason for investing, too often it takes the back burner in an investment plan. Many of us make the mistake of thinking that our pensions and Social Security will take care of our retirement needs. Unfortunately, by the time we realize that there will be a major shortfall, it is often too late to do anything about it. Even though retirement planning may be the last thing on your mind when you're in your twenties, thirties, or even forties, the earlier in life you start a retirement investment program, the greater your chance for success.

## SHELTER FROM TAXES: KEEP YOUR MONEY OUT OF THE HANDS OF UNCLE SAM

There's a simple axiom in the financial marketplace that applies to every one of us: "It's not what you make that counts, but what you keep." Keeping money out of the hands of Uncle Sam by investing in legitimate tax shelters is an investment goal that can make a tremendous difference in your savings and lifestyle. Although sheltering income from taxes was made considerably more difficult with the passage of the Tax Reform Act of 1986, there are still investment decisions you can make that will increase the money you have left after your taxes are paid.

## AN INVESTMENT PLAN: TRANSLATING YOUR GOALS INTO ACTION

The more specific you can be in stating your investment goals, the easier it will be for you to reach them.

Once you've defined your goals, you're ready to start an investment program. The backbone of the program is an investment plan—the general strategy you will use to achieve each goal. For example, if your goal is to accumulate $80,000 over a 10-year period for retirement, you must know exactly where the money will come from. If you'll get $30,000 from a retirement pension, you must focus on accumulating the additional $50,000. You must evaluate available returns, the level of risk you're willing to take, and the effect of taxes on your investment. If you have $10,000 to invest toward your goal of $50,000, you might decide to divide it evenly between income and growth stocks providing a total annual return of 10 percent: 20 percent in current income and 80 percent in capital appreciation. By using the future value techniques you'll learn about later, you discover that you'll have $26,000 at the end of 10 years. So you have to devise a plan to accumulate an additional $24,000 to meet your original goal. At a 10 percent rate of return, you would have to invest approximately $1,500 at the end of each of the next 10 years in order to accumulate this $24,000. If this is feasible, your next step is to choose specific securities that will provide this high current income. If it's not, then you must reevaluate your goals.

As you can see, developing an investment plan involves a number of steps. *The first step:* determine what you now have. In this case, the givens are a $30,000 retirement plan and a sum of $10,000 that is available for investments. *The second step:* evaluate the rate of return available from investment vehicles. *The third step:* determine how much current income has to be invested to make up any shortfall.

Except for the givens, all the other figures are estimates that must be closely and constantly monitored. Although you may expect a 10 percent rate of return, you have no way of determining future interest rates. If they decline, so will the earnings available for reinvestment and your total accumulated capital at the end of 10 years. Therefore you must be prepared to adjust your goals and strategies as new economic facts become clear.

Adjustments may also be necessary if an investment sours. A company plagued by poor management may take years to correct itself—and while it does, stockholders will suffer losses in the form of decreased dividends and depressed stock prices. One way to minimize the effect of a bad investment is to diversify your holdings. A well-balanced portfolio lessens the risk that one bad investment will lead to financial ruin. We will consider all these matters in greater detail as we proceed.

## HOW DO I GET STARTED?

How do you actually get started on your investment plan? To begin with, you need *some* money. Not a lot; perhaps $500 to $1,000 will do, though $2,000 to $3,000 would be even better. In addition to money, you need knowledge and know-how. You should *never* invest in something you are not sure about—that is the quickest way to lose your money. Learn as much as you can about the financial marketplace, different types of securities, and various trading strategies. Become a *regular* reader of publications such as *Money, Changing Times, The Wall Street Journal, Barron's,* and *Business Week.* Keep up to date on developments in the market; start following the stock market, interest rates, and developments in the bond market.

We strongly suggest that, after you have learned a few things about stocks and bonds, you set up a portfolio of securities *on paper* and make *paper trades* in and out of your portfolio for 6 months to a year in order to get a feel for what it is like to make (and lose) money in the market. Start out with an imaginary sum of, say, $10,000 (as long as you are going to dream, you might as well make it worthwhile). Then keep track of the stocks and bonds you hold, record the number of shares bought and sold, dividends received, and so on. Throughout this exercise, be sure to use actual prices (as obtained from *The Wall Street Journal* or your local newspaper) and keep it as realistic as possible. If you are going to make mistakes in the stock market, you are much better off doing so on paper. If your relatives and friends have done a lot of investing, talk to them. Find out what they have to say about investing, pick up some pointers, and possibly even learn from their mistakes. Eventually you will gain a familiarity with the market and become comfortable with the way things are done there. When that happens, you will be ready to take the plunge.

At this point, you need a way to invest—more specifically, you need a broker and some investment vehicle in which to invest. The stockbroker is the party through whom you will be buying and selling stocks, bonds, and other securities. If your relatives or friends have a broker they like and trust, have them introduce you. Alternatively, visit several of the brokerage firms in your community; talk to one of their brokers about your available investment funds and your investment objectives.

As a beginning investor with limited funds, you should probably confine your investment activity to the basics—stocks, bonds, and mutual funds. Avoid getting fancy, and certainly do not try to make a killing each and every time you invest—that will lead only to frustration, disappointment, and, very possibly, heavy losses. Instead, go for "relatively high" returns; for example, those that exceed what you can get from a savings account. Further, *be patient!* Don't expect the price of the stock to double overnight; indeed, it may even drop a little now and then. Finally, remember that you do not need spectacular returns in order to make a lot of money in the market. Instead, be *consistent* and let the concept of compound interest work for you: just $1,000 a year invested at 15 percent will grow to over $100,000 in 20 years! While the type of security in which you invest is a highly personal decision, you might want to give serious consideration to some sort of mutual fund as your first investment. Mutual funds provide professional management and diversification that individual investors can rarely obtain on their own.

## INVESTING IN DIFFERENT ECONOMIC ENVIRONMENTS

Knowing when to invest is just as important as knowing where to invest. While it is easy to make money when the market is booming, it's hard—and sometimes impossible—to come out ahead during a recession. At times like this, even the best investment can turn into a disaster. You must then decide whether to hold your position or get out while you can with whatever you can. Like most investment decisions, the answer depends on what you think the future holds.

The question of when to invest is tough because it deals with market timing. The fact is that most investors, even professional money managers, cannot call the peaks and troughs in the market with much consistency. Knowing whether the market is in a state of expansion or decline is considerably easier than being able to pinpoint when it is about to change course.

As the figure on the next page shows, the market—and the economy as a whole—goes through cycles of recovery and expansion (economic improvement) and decline and recession (economic decline). While it is easy to see when things are moving up or down, it is often very difficult to recognize the shifts that occur at the peaks and troughs. The shaded areas in the figure represent the time of uncertainty. The toughest part of market timing deals with predicting these changes in market direction.

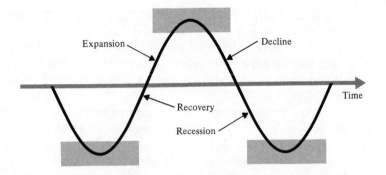

Expansion

Decline

Recovery

Recession

Time

If you're totally uncertain about which direction the market is going, then your best course of action is to do nothing; simply sit it out. If you have new money to invest, hold off until you get a better handle on the future course of the market. Under these conditions, the best thing you can do is put your money temporarily into some form of savings account or money market fund. When the market direction clarifies, you can move your money to a more permanent investment vehicle such as stocks, bonds, and mutual funds. If you already have money invested in stocks or bonds, then stay put. Don't move out of your investments until you're satisfied that the market has indeed changed course (or is almost certainly about to do so).

Even if you have a good sense of where the market is headed, you have to respond in different ways depending upon the type of investment you've made. Common stocks and other equity-related securities (like stock mutual funds, convertible securities, stock options, and stock index futures) are highly responsive to economic conditions. Stocks do best when business is expanding or is about to enter into a state of recovery and expansion. In general, stocks are strong when corporate profits rise. Growth-oriented and speculative stocks tend to do especially well during expansions and, to a lesser extent, so do blue chip and income-oriented stocks. In contrast, when the economy is in a state of decline, the returns on common stocks generally reflect the downswing.

Bonds and other forms of fixed income securities (such as preferred stocks and bond funds) are highly sensitive to movements in interest rates. In fact, interest rates are the single most important variable in determining bond price behavior and returns to investors. Because interest rates and bond prices move in opposite directions, it follows that rising interest rates are bad for bonds. If you feel that interest rates are going to continue to rise, then hold off buying long-term bonds. You'll benefit in two ways: first, you'll avoid the loss that is guaranteed to occur when rates rise, and second, by waiting, you'll be able to capture even higher bond yields. Thus, as long as interest rates are heading up, the best course of action is to hold such short-term money market investments as money market mutual funds or money market deposit accounts. This will enable you to preserve your capital and generate higher returns in the long run. On the other hand, when rates start heading down, buying long-term bonds will give you the opportunity to lock in high current yields and generate attractive capital gains.

DECIDING HOW TO INVEST

# INVESTING THROUGHOUT YOUR LIFE

Just as you should take different courses of action as you move through different stages of an economic cycle, you should also follow different investment philosophies as you move through different stages of the life cycle. Most investors tend to be more aggressive when they are young and more conservative as they get older. In a very general sense, investors tend to move through the following investment stages:

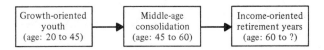

| Growth-oriented youth (age: 20 to 45) | → | Middle-age consolidation (age: 45 to 60) | → | Income-oriented retirement years (age: 60 to ?) |

Most young investors—those in their twenties and thirties—tend to prefer growth-oriented investments that stress capital gains rather than current income. Often these investors don't have much in the way of investable funds, so capital gains are generally viewed as the quickest—if not necessarily the surest—way to build up a sizable pool of investment capital. These investors are inclined to favor speculative and growth-oriented common stocks and mutual funds, convertible securities, puts and calls, stock index options, etc., that offer substantial price appreciation within relatively short time periods.

As investors move into their midforties, their investment programs start to change. During middle age, family responsibilities grow, forcing changes in investment approaches. In general, investing becomes far less speculative. Most investors combine quality growth investments with investments offering current income. Blue chip, growth and income stocks, preferreds, convertibles, high-grade bonds, and mutual funds are all widely used during this period. And because taxes are likely to be a bigger burden, municipal bonds and tax-sheltered investments take on a more prominent role as well. Thus, the whole portfolio undergoes a transition to higher quality securities and, at the same time, the foundation is set for the rapidly approaching retirement years.

Finally, as investors move into their retirement years, preservation of capital and current income are the principal concerns. A secure, high level of income is now paramount, and capital gains are viewed as merely a pleasant, occasional by-product of investing. The investment portfolio has become highly conservative and is now made up of blue chip income stocks, high-yielding government bonds, quality corporate bonds, bank certificates of deposit, and other money market investments. In most cases, the portfolio has also become a lot "shorter"; that is, more money is being placed into short-term savings accounts and money market funds. The objective at this point is to live as comfortably as possible off investment income, reaping the rewards of a lifetime of saving and investing.

# 2

## LIQUIDITY: THE FIRST COMPONENT OF A SUCCESSFUL INVESTMENT PROGRAM

In the language of money, *liquidity* is a measure of how quickly and safely you can convert an investment or savings vehicle into cash and come away with at least as much as you originally put in. The more easily you can do this, the higher the liquidity. A checking account is much more liquid than stocks and bonds. While you can write a check and usually collect your cash on the spot, you have to go through the more time-consuming process of selling your securities and collecting the proceeds before you see a dime. You may have to wait more than a week to get your hands on your money. Worse yet, you may not get back your total investment. In a declining market, there's no assurance that you will be able to sell long-term securities for as much as you originally paid.

### SHORT-TERM SECURITIES PROVIDE LIQUIDITY

Most financial experts agree that you should have at least 3 to 6 months of after-tax income in various forms of liquid reserve and that these reserves should be an integral part of your savings and investment program. There are three good reasons

14

to invest in short-term securities: First, they serve as a pool of ready cash for emergencies or for some specific purpose, like buying a car or paying college tuition. Second, they offer a temporary, income-producing resting place for money until a better, more permanent investment is located. And third, they sometimes offer higher returns than long-term securities, as was the case during the economic recession of the early 1980s. While stock and bond values plummeted, such short-term investments as money funds and certificates of deposit earned double-digit returns.

## ROLE OF SHORT-TERM SECURITIES

As you can see, short-term securities are for both saving and investing. As savings instruments, most of us use them as financial safety nets to protect us from economic ruin in case of illness, job or property loss, or some other personal financial disaster. It is no understatement to say that we all need at least some money in the bank to cover these financial contingencies if we are to sleep well at night and function effectively during the day. Savings also provide money for major expenditures. Because savings must be available to us no matter what, return is less important than safety, liquidity, and convenience. The most popular savings vehicles include Series EE savings bonds, money market deposit accounts, money market mutual funds, and passbook savings accounts.

When these short-term securities are used as investments instead, return is often just as important as liquidity and convenience, so they tend to be managed much more aggressively than in a savings program. Of course, the way you use them will depend on your level of investment knowledge and your willingness to take risks. Most investors hold at least part of their investment portfolio in short-term, highly liquid securities, if for no other reason than to be able to act on unanticipated investment opportunities. You may also view these securities as a temporary holding place in an unsettled or declining market. For example:

- After cashing in a 20-point gain on 1,000 shares of a blue chip stock, you need time to choose your next investment, so you instruct your broker to transfer your money into the brokerage firm's money fund—a safe and highly liquid short-term investment.
- You believe that interest rates are about to rise sharply, so you sell your long-term bonds and buy Treasury bills. You feel comfortable that you will receive a steady although relatively small rate of return, which is far better than losing money due to the decline in bond values caused by rising interest rates.

Other less aggressive investors, satisfied that these short-term securities provide the highest return for the lowest risk, use them as permanent investments. They remain satisfied as long as they continue to receive a steady income flow.

Short-term securities used for investment purposes offer higher yields than securities used for savings. These include money market deposit accounts, money market mutual funds, certificates of deposit, and commercial paper.

## HOW SHORT-TERM SECURITIES EARN INTEREST

Short-term investments earn interest in one of two ways. Some, like passbook and NOW accounts, pay a stated rate of interest. Others, like Treasury bills, earn interest on a *discount basis.* This means that the security is sold for a price that is less than its redemption value, the difference being the interest earned. This return can be expressed as an annual rate, using the following equation:

$$\text{annual rate of return on a discount security} = \left[\frac{360}{\text{number of days to maturity}}\right] \times \left[\frac{\text{redemption value} - \text{purchase price}}{\text{purchase price}}\right]$$

To illustrate, suppose you buy a T-bill for $9,860 that can be redeemed for $10,000 at the end of 91 days (13 weeks). The total interest on this security is $140 (redemption value − purchase price), and its annual rate of return is:

$$\text{annual rate of return} = (360/91) \times \left(\frac{\$10,000 - \$9,860}{\$9,860}\right)$$

$$= (3.956) \times (.01420)$$

$$= .05618 \text{ or } 5.6\%$$

This rate of return of 5.6% indicates that for each dollar invested, you will earn the equivalent of 5.6 cents per year.


## HOW RISKY ARE THEY?

In general, short-term investments have very little risk. Their most serious risk is that purchasing power will be lost when the rate of return falls short of the inflation rate. Fortunately, this does not happen too often. On the contrary, when viewed over time, most short-term investments achieve rates of return that are about equal to, and sometimes slightly higher than, the average inflation rate. Moreover, by rolling into new issues as the old issues mature, it is possible to capture high returns as interest rates move up. For example, although outstanding long-term bonds suffer income and capital losses due to their locked-in interest rates, as market rates rise, the return on new issues of short-term securities increases along with interest rates.

Short-term investments have almost no risk of default (nonpayment) since they are issued by such highly reputable institutions as the U.S. Treasury, large money center banks (banks located in major financial centers such as New York, Chicago, London, and Tokyo), and major corporations. What's more, deposits in federally regulated commercial banks, savings banks, savings and loans, and credit unions are insured up to $100,000 by federal deposit insurance agencies. (Savings institutions that lack federal insurance are often covered by state insurance.)

Finally, the value of short-term investments remains fairly stable even when interest rates change. When the maturity of an investment is measured in months, and sometimes even days, it is less susceptible to interest rate shifts than longer term issues. So in general, the shorter the maturity, the less volatile the market price. As a result, your chances of losing money through a capital loss are extremely small. For example, if over time you analyze the prices of different issues of 6-month Treasury bills you'll see that although their yields may vary over a wide range, their prices change relatively little.

Perhaps the biggest disadvantage of short-term issues is their relatively low return. In general, you should expect the return you receive on short-term investments to be lower than the return on long-term investments. This is no surprise since low risk is almost always synonomous with low return. You should also expect your return to drop when interest rates fall.

Your decision to invest in short-term securities depends on how you view these issues of risk and return and how you assess your liquidity and investment needs. The greater your need for immediate access to at least part of your money and the greater your understanding of the role short-term investments can play in your overall investment plan, the more likely you are to include them in your investment portfolio.

## POPULAR SHORT-TERM INVESTMENTS

The world of short-term investments changed dramatically in 1980 when Congress passed the Depository Institutions Deregulation and Monetary Control Act, also known as the Banking Act of 1980. This act gradually lifted the barriers to competition that had previously existed among the various financial institutions, with the result that investors had many more short-term savings options open to them. For the first time, all deposit institutions—not just commercial banks—could offer checking accounts (known as NOW accounts). In addition, interest ceilings on many different accounts were lifted, and new types of accounts were created.

While this was happening, other financial institutions were becoming more interested in the short-term investor. Mutual funds pushed their money market accounts, brokerage firms their universal and sweep accounts. In addition, investors could use U.S. Treasury bills and Series EE bonds as well as commercial paper as short-term depositories for their cash.

This dramatic increase in the number of short-term investment alternatives created confusion as well as opportunity. With more options available, it has become more difficult to decide where to invest your money. This is true whether you want to use these short-term vehicles as a temporary resting place for your money or as part of a long-term investment strategy. We will try to clarify the choices here so that your short-term investments provide attractive returns. (Note: For convenience, we will use the term *bank* to refer to commercial banks, savings and loans, mutual savings banks, and credit unions. Technically, the term refers to commercial banks alone.)

## PASSBOOK SAVINGS ACCOUNTS

It wasn't long ago that the only short-term savings vehicle considered by most investors was the passbook savings account, which got its name from the passbook used to record account activity. Today, although this account is still in use, it has lost its popular appeal. Indeed, many investors see it as a relic of the time before banking deregulation. The main reason so many savers have turned away from passbook accounts is their extremely limited return. Although interest rate ceilings on these accounts were lifted on April 1, 1986, they continue to pay a relatively low rate, typically 5 percent or less.

Of course, passbook accounts have some pluses: There are no minimum balance requirements, and you can make as many withdrawals as you choose (although you'll have to pay a small bank fee if you make too many withdrawals during a month or quarter). And if convenience is important—or in cases of emergency—passbook accounts give you immediate access to your money. (Unfortunately, you'll have to travel to the bank to get your cash since checking is not offered.)

Although by almost anyone's definition, these advantages are quite meager, passbook accounts still draw a significant number of depositors who like the convenience of maintaining a savings account at their local bank, lack the resources to invest in other short-term vehicles, or are simply unaware that higher yielding and equally safe outlets are available. On balance, passbook accounts should play little or no role in your short-term savings program.


## NOW ACCOUNTS

A NOW (Negotiated Order of Withdrawal) account is simply a checking account that pays interest at any rate the financial institution chooses. In effect, it gives you a way to earn interest on the cash you need to pay your monthly bills. This may be no small thing. Depending upon your average monthly balance, your idle cash can bring in hundreds of dollars a year.

Most banks set minimum deposit requirements of between $500 and $1,000 for NOW accounts. In some cases, the interest you receive is tied to your monthly balance. You might receive a higher rate if your balance exceeds $2,500 than if it falls below this amount. There are no restrictions on the number of withdrawals you can make by check or in person. And if service charges are levied, they are no greater than those attached to regular checking accounts.

The NOW account's appeal is that it can serve as both a checking and a savings vehicle. Its convenience may entice you to use it as a storehouse for all your short-term cash. Before you do, however, see how NOW account rates compare with the rates of other short-term vehicles. It might be to your advantage to maintain a conventional checking account while investing your excess funds elsewhere. Human nature being what it is, if the difference is only a few dollars, opt for convenience. However, don't get too complacent. While your NOW account may be a good place to park your money when interest rates are low, you'll get a much better return elsewhere when interest rates rise.

## MONEY MARKET DEPOSIT ACCOUNTS (MMDAs)

These accounts were introduced in 1982 to give banks a way to compete with money market mutual funds (described below). They succeeded mainly because of competitive rates and federal deposit insurance. (Money market mutual funds are not federally insured.)

Generally, you'll do just about as well in an MMDA as you would in a money market mutual fund and better than you would in a NOW account. Indeed, while NOW accounts are really little more than convenience accounts, MMDAs are legitimate savings outlets. Most MMDAs restrict the number of transfers you can make to six each month, including three checks, and require that you maintain a minimum balance of around $2,500.

## MONEY MARKET MUTUAL FUNDS (MMMFs)

These funds, also known simply as money funds, are mutual funds that invest exclusively in higher-yielding short-term securities, including Treasury bills, corporate commercial paper, and jumbo certificates of deposit issued by commercial banks—both domestic and foreign. Since these securities are sold in denominations of $10,000 to $1 million or more, they would be out of the reach of most investors were it not for money funds.

The return on these funds is determined by the return on all the short-term investments in the fund's portfolio. Some funds are able to bolster their returns by including higher risk, foreign, short-term securities in their portfolios. Generally, money fund returns rise and fall with money market interest rates. While rates peaked above 15 percent in the early 1980s, some dropped below 5 percent in 1986 and 1987.

Money market mutual funds fall into several different categories including general purpose money funds, tax-exempt money funds, and government securities money funds. These are explained in detail in Chapter 22. As with all investments, your choice depends on your investment objectives.

Money funds can be purchased directly through a mutual fund or through a broker or investment dealer. Just about every major brokerage firm has a money fund of its own, and hundreds of others are sold by investment companies as no-load funds (see Chapter 23). Initial investment requirements can be as low as $500, although $1,000 to $5,000 is more typical. You can write checks on your money fund account as long as the amount is above a specified minimum—commonly $500. In addition, if you invest in a money fund that is part of a large fund family, you can transfer your money from one fund to another as investment conditions change. Some funds, however, charge a small fee for such transfers.

The main competitor of the money market mutual fund is the money market deposit account. Although many people choose MMDAs because they are federally insured, it is important to keep in mind that no money market mutual fund has ever failed. Because of the kinds of securities included in their portfolios, they are extremely safe, and diversification lowers the risk even more. This excellent track record is likely to continue as long as the general economy avoids a nose-dive. If you're worried about that possibility, then you certainly should choose a money market deposit account—even if you can get a better return through a money fund. Otherwise, analyze both options to find the one with the highest return.

## CERTIFICATES OF DEPOSIT (CDs)

Commonly called CDs, these savings instruments differ from those we've already discussed in one important way: they tie up your money for a specified period of time, which can range from 7 days to a year or more. Although it is possible to withdraw funds prior to maturity, an interest penalty (of 31 to 90 days' interest, depending upon the original maturity of the CD) usually makes withdrawal somewhat costly.

CDs are issued by banks, which are free to offer any rate and maturity they want. Since the competition is stiff, you'll find relatively attractive rates if you take the time to shop around. All bank CDs are federally insured, making them good choices for those who want to avoid the risk of default. Their major drawback is lack of liquidity. Of course in a falling interest rate market, this drawback can work in your favor, since you will continue to receive the relatively high return guaranteed by your CD. However, when interest rates rise, long-term CDs will make it impossible for you to get in on the improved rates unless you are willing to pay a hefty penalty.

## COMMERCIAL PAPER

Commercial paper is a short-term unsecured promissory note (in plain language, an IOU) issued by a corporation with a very high credit standing. These notes are typically sold in denominations of $100,000 to businesses, banks, brokerage firms, money market mutual funds, and individuals. (Smaller denominations of $25,000 and $50,000 are sometimes available.) Since the secondary (resale) market in commercial paper is extremely limited, investors must usually hold onto their paper until it matures. Typical maturities range from a few days to 270 days, which is the maximum maturity allowed before the Securities and Exchange Commission requires registration. Independent agencies rate the quality of commercial paper, which in part affects its return. In general, the poorer the quality, the greater the risk and the higher the return. For the most part, the return on commercial paper is comparable to that on large CDs.

Perhaps the best way to get into this market is through money market mutual funds, which typically include large quantities of commercial paper in their investment portfolios. In addition, banks and brokerage firms break down commercial paper and sell small portions of it ($10,000 denominations are typical) to individual investors at slightly below their stated yield. If you choose this direct route, look for returns that are competitive with high-yielding CDs. Since commercial paper is not federally insured, it is a good idea to stick with high-rated vehicles with a maturity date suited to your investment needs.

## U.S. TREASURY BILLS (T-BILLS)

These obligations of the U.S. Treasury, also known as T-bills, are issued as part of the ongoing process of funding the national debt. T-bills are sold on a discount basis in minimum denominations of $10,000, with $5,000 increments. They are issued with 3-month (13-week), 6-month (26-week), and 1-year maturities. You can purchase T-bills indirectly through local commercial banks or securities dealers who charge a commission on the sale. Or you can buy them directly through the Federal Reserve Bank by specifying both the amount and maturity you want.

T-bills are also traded on the secondary market where the activity is brisk. You can usually find a wide selection of maturities ranging from less than a week to as long as a year. In part, the attractiveness of T-bills is due to their exemption from state and local income taxes, which in some areas are as high as 20 percent. Because they are issued by the U.S. Treasury, they are regarded as the safest short-term investment. Be aware that because they are so safe, they offer relatively low returns.

## UNIVERSAL (SWEEP) ACCOUNTS

Universal accounts, also known as sweep accounts, are not separate investment vehicles but a means of servicing a wide range of checking, investing, and borrowing activities by automatically sweeping excess funds into various short-term investment vehicles. For example, Merrill Lynch's Cash Management Account automatically channels excess funds into a money fund, and if securities are purchased for an amount greater than the current balance, the needed funds are supplied automatically through a margin loan. The same principle is at work in a bank sweep account that combines a NOW and an MMDA. At the end of each day, if the NOW account balance exceeds $2,500, the excess is swept automatically into the higher yielding MMDA. These accounts are extremely popular among investors. Their only major drawback is a stiff minimum balance requirement. Merrill Lynch is typical: it requires an initial balance of $20,000 in cash or securities—an amount that puts this account out of reach for many small investors.

## SERIES EE SAVINGS BONDS

Series EE savings bonds have been a traditional part of many investment portfolios since the bonds were first introduced in 1941. (At that time they were known as Series E bonds.) These bonds are *accrual-type securities*, which means that interest is paid when the bond is cashed, on or before maturity, rather than periodically over the life of the bond. All government-issued savings bonds are backed by the full faith and credit of the U.S. government and can be replaced without charge in case of loss, theft, or destruction. They can be purchased at banks or through payroll deduction plans. They are issued in denominations of $50 through $10,000, although you pay only half of the bond's face value at the time of purchase. Thus, you pay $50 for a $100 bond but receive the full $100 at maturity.

The actual maturity date on EE bonds is unspecified, since they pay a variable rate of interest. Thus, the higher the interest, the shorter the time it takes for the bond to accrue from its discounted purchase price to its maturity value. All EE bonds held 5 years or longer receive interest at the higher rate of 6 percent or 85 percent of the average return on 5-year Treasury securities, as calculated every 6 months. The yield, therefore, changes every 6 months in accordance with prevailing Treasury note yields, though it can never drop below a minimum guaranteed rate of 6 percent. EEs held for less than 5 years (they can be redeemed any time after the first 6 months) earn interest at a fixed graduated scale that increases with the length of time the bonds are held.

The interest on Series EE bonds is exempt from state and local taxes. In addition, you need not report this interest on your federal tax return until you redeem the bonds. Although interest can be reported annually (this might be done, for example, if the bonds are held in the name of a child who has limited interest income) most investors choose to defer it. In effect, this means that the funds are being reinvested at an after-tax rate of no less than the guaranteed minimum of 6 percent. What's more, it is possible to defer the tax shelter beyond the redemption date of your Series EE bond: instead of cashing in the bonds, you exchange them for Series HH bonds, which have a 10-year maturity and are available in denominations of $500 to $10,000. Unlike EE bonds, they are issued at their full face value and pay interest at the current fixed rate of 6 percent semiannually. The accumulated interest on the Series EE bonds remains free of federal income tax until the HH bonds reach maturity or until you cash them in. Thus, in contrast to their predecessors, not only do today's Series EE bonds represent a safe and secure form of investment, they also provide highly competitive yields and attractive tax incentives.

## MATCH WITH YOUR PERSONAL FINANCIAL GOALS

With all these options open to you, choosing one short-term security over another is no easy task. It's a job that involves evaluating the availability, safety, liquidity, and yield of each security to find the one most suited to your savings and investment needs.

This summary of key characteristics of the short-term investments we've discussed will help you start this process. The letter grade we've assigned to each characteristic reflects our estimate of the investment's quality in that area. For

## A SCORECARD FOR SHORT-TERM ACCOUNTS AND SECURITIES

| Savings or Investment Vehicle | Availability | Safety | Liquidity | Yield (Average Rate in Early 1987) | |
|---|---|---|---|---|---|
| Passbook savings account | A+ | A+ | A | D | (4.0%) |
| NOW account | A | A+ | A+ | D | (5.0%) |
| Money market deposit account (MMDA) | B | A+ | A | B− | (5.3%) |
| Money market mutual fund (MMMF): general purpose and government security funds | B | A/A+ | B+ | B | (5.6%) |
| Certificate of deposit (CD): 6-month certificate | B | A+ | C | A | (5.8%) |
| Commercial paper | B− | A− | C | A | (5.8%) |
| U.S. Treasury bill (3-month) | B− | A+ + | A− | A− | (5.4%) |
| Series EE savings bond | A+ | A+ + | C− | B | (6.0%) |

example, we gave money market mutual funds a B+ on liquidity since they often restrict withdrawals to amounts of $500 or more. Money market deposit accounts, on the other hand, received an A since they have fewer withdrawal restrictions. As you look at the various yields, keep in mind that as an investment scores lower in the areas of availability, safety, and liquidity, its yield generally rises.

# 3

# RETIREMENT PLANNING: THE CRUCIAL SECOND COMPONENT

It's hard to think about retirement when you're 20, 30, or even 40 years old. And it's even harder to plan for it by putting money away year by year. This is especially true if the money you need for retirement is already earmarked for current expenses such as the down payment on a house and college tuition. But no matter how hard it is to plan for retirement when you're young, it's infinitely harder to make ends meet when you retire without money in the bank or a source of regular income.

The younger you are when you start planning for retirement, the more productive your funds will be. The power of compound interest makes this so: If you invest $1,000 today, you will have accumulated $17,449 in 30 years, assuming a 10 percent rate of return over the entire 30-year period. The same $1,000 grows to $45,258 in 40 years—a sum two and one half times as great. (The method used to determine these future values is described in the next chapter.) Even if rates drop and you can't invest your money at the 10 percent rate over the life of the investment, and even if inflation reduces at least part of the value of your money, you'll still come out way ahead by investing early. The crucial point is that the sooner you invest for retirement, the more you will accumulate, regardless of the rate of return.

# THE HEART OF YOUR INVESTMENT PROGRAM

Planning for retirement should never be an afterthought. On the contrary, it should be an integral part of your investment program. Moreover, you should spend as much time and effort managing your retirement investments as you do the other parts of your investment portfolio.

Retirement planning begins with an honest appraisal of what your needs and income will be after you retire. We will help you take this look by focusing on the retirement planning done by a hypothetical family, Bob and Shirley Mason. The Masons are in their midthirties, have two children, and have a combined annual income of about $45,000 before taxes. For the first time they are thinking about setting aside money for retirement. This table shows the Masons' estimates of their retirement income and expenses in current and future dollars.

|  | Current Dollars | Inflation Factor | Future Needs |
|---|---|---|---|
| ESTIMATED EXPENDITURES |  |  |  |
| Housing and utilities | $ 5,600 |  |  |
| Food—at home and dining out | 6,000 |  |  |
| Transportation | 2,200 |  |  |
| Travel and entertainment | 5,200 |  |  |
| Medical | 2,000 |  |  |
| All other | 7,000 |  |  |
| Total expenditures | $ 28,000  × | 4.322*  = | $121,016 |
| ESTIMATED INCOME |  |  |  |
| Social Security | $ 12,000  × | 4.322*  = | $ 51,864 |
| Employer retirement plan | 7,000  × | 5.743**  = | 40,201 |
| Subtotal | $ 19,000 |  | $ 92,065 |
| Additional required income | 9,000 |  | 28,951 |
| Total income | $ 28,000 |  | $121,016 |
| ASSET REQUIREMENT |  |  |  |
| Anticipated return on assets held during retirement |  |  | 0.10 |
| Assets required ($28,951/.10) |  |  | $289,510 |

*Inflation rate (or growth rate) of 5% per year for 30 years.
**Growth rate of 6% per year for 30 years.

As you can see, Bob and Shirley first determine what their expenditures would be if they retired immediately. This enables them to base their retirement planning on today's dollars. They turn next to retirement income. Unfortunately, the payments they will receive from Social Security and Bob's retirement plan fall $9,000 short of their estimated expenditure of $28,000 a year.

Since this shortfall is in today's dollars and not in the dollars that will exist when their retirement actually takes place, the Masons must estimate the future value of their income and expenditures. To do this, they first project the rate of inflation over the next 30 years—an average 5 percent a year. Based on this estimate, calculated by using the future value techniques described in Chapter 4, their expenditures will grow from $28,000 to $121,016.

Bob and Shirley also believe that Social Security increases will match the inflation rate and that Bob's retirement plan will grow at 6 percent a year, putting them slightly ahead of inflation. Thus, the Mason's total annual income in 30 years will be approximately $92,000, which is $28,951 short of the money they will need to meet their expenditures.

The Masons turn next to the rate of return they expect to earn on their investments *after* they retire. This will tell them how big their nest egg must be *by retirement* in order to eliminate the expected annual shortfall of $28,951. If they earn 10 percent on their money after they retire, they'll need a total of $289,510 by retirement. This figure is determined by dividing the annual amount needed by the rate of return: $28,951/.10 = $289,510. This nest egg will yield $28,951 a year given a 10 percent rate of return ($289,510 × .10 = $28,951). As long as the capital ($289,510) remains untouched, it will generate the same annual amount for as long as the Masons live and will eventually become part of their estate.

Since the Masons do not expect any financial windfall in the form of an inheritance, they realize that they have to put a certain amount of money away each year in a *systematic savings plan*. Assuming they can earn a 10 percent rate of return, they will have to save $1,760 each year for the next 30 years in order to accumulate the $289,510 they need to retire.

Unfortunately, the success of this plan is dependent, in part, on factors beyond the Masons' control. If they fail to earn a 10 percent rate of return on their investment, they won't achieve their targeted goal. If, for example, interest rates over the 30-year period remain stable at 8 percent, they will have only $199,376 by retirement—$90,000 short of their retirement target. They'll experience a similar shortfall if they fail to put aside $1,760 each year. For example, if the most they can save is $1,200 each year, they'll have only $197,389 by retirement, assuming a 10 percent rate of return. In either case, they can reduce their standard of retirement living or start tapping their capital earlier than expected.

Actually, we have simplified the Masons' retirement plan somewhat by leaving out a few important complications. First, inflation will probably continue after they retire. Although Social Security income will continue to grow at the annual rate of inflation, the benefits from Bob's retirement plan as well as the income from their investment assets will not. This means that during each year of retirement, they will have to dip into their capital to meet day-to-day living expenses. The table on the next page illustrates this process for the first 3 years of retirement.

The Masons fear that if this drain continues for too long, they will be left with almost nothing in their final years. Even though they realize that this is not likely to happen, they also realize that there are no guarantees. To provide a hedge against this type of uncertainty, they decide to increase the size of their annual retirement contribution to about $2,200, which will give them a much larger retirement nest egg.

|                                      |          | YEARS     |           |
|--------------------------------------|----------|-----------|-----------|
|                                      | 1        | 2         | 3         |
| Expenditures*                        | $121,016 | $127,067  | $133,420  |
| Income                               |          |           |           |
|   Social Security*         | $ 51,864 | $ 54,457  | $ 57,180  |
|   Employer retirement plan | 40,201   | 40,201    | 40,201    |
|   Supplemental income      | 28,951   | 28,951    | 28,605    |
|    Total income       | $121,016 | $123,609  | $125,986  |
| Budget deficit                       | $      0 | $  3,458  | $  7,434  |
| Retirement assets at end of year     | $289,510 | $286,052  | $278,618  |

*Assumes a rate of growth of 5% for years 2 and 3.

Our example also ignored the impact of federal income taxes on the Masons' retirement income. Under current law, a portion of their Social Security income may be taxable. Depending on how Bob's retirement plan is structured, a portion or all of their retirement income may also be taxable. And in all likelihood, all their investment income will be taxable. If everything else remained the same, this additional tax burden would mean that they would have to come up with more than $9,000 a year in additional income, which would make their $289,510 nest egg too small.

# SOURCES OF RETIREMENT INCOME

The only hope most people have of achieving their retirement goals is early planning. This starts with a thorough understanding of the three basic sources of retirement income: Social Security, employer-sponsored retirement programs, and individual self-directed retirement plans.

## SOCIAL SECURITY: THE MAINSTAY OF MANY RETIREMENT PROGRAMS

Social Security is a fact of life for nearly every working and retired American. What Social Security taxes take away from you while you're working, Social Security benefits return to you after you retire. Even though the tax bite is heavy (if you earned $20,000 in 1987, you paid $1,430 in Social Security taxes; the maximum tax for the same year was $3,132), most people actually receive far more from the Social Security system than they put in.

People who retired in 1985 at age 65, and whose benefits are based on maximum earnings, receive $760 a month from Social Security. If they are married, their spouse is also eligible for benefits, the exact amount of which depends on the spouse's own contribution to the system. A nonworking spouse is eligible to receive half of the working spouse's benefits, which in this case brings the combined payment to $1,140 a month.

The Social Security Administration determines the actual amount of benefits you will receive by considering such factors as the amount you've paid into the system, your age, your spouse's eligibility and work history, and cost-of-living adjustments. If you are going to retire sometime in the near future, you can contact the Social Security Administration to find out your exact benefits. There is no point in doing this too early since your benefits package changes considerably over time.

Social Security benefits are taxable if, once you retire, the total of your adjusted gross income and half your benefits exceeds $25,000 for an individual and $32,000 for a couple filing a joint return. In this case, up to half of your benefits will be taxed based on a graduated scale. For the purpose of determining this tax, the government includes any income you receive from tax-free securities as part of your adjusted gross income.

Although Social Security will provide you with regular monthly income, it won't give you enough to live on—especially if you were in a high tax bracket before you retired, lived a lifestyle such a bracket affords, and expect to sustain that lifestyle after retirement. On average, if you are married and fit into the broad category of middle class, you can expect your Social Security benefits to equal 40 to 60 percent of your wages in the year before retirement. The more you earn, the smaller the percentage—a fact that makes it necessary to supplement your Social Security benefits with other sources of retirement income.

## LOOK TO YOUR BOSS FOR EMPLOYER-SPONSORED PROGRAMS

Employers may offer two types of retirement programs: basic plans and supplemental plans.

*Basic plans.* Many employers provide retirement programs as part of the total compensation package they offer employees. These plans provide at least some of the income needed to supplement Social Security. The major advantage of most of these plans is that the initial contributions and reinvested earnings accumulate tax-free. (The government grants this special tax-exempt status to employer-funded plans.) If you were forced to fund the same retirement plan on your own with after-tax dollars, you would have to come up with considerably more money. For example, if you were in the 28 percent tax bracket, you would have to start with $139 to end up with the same $100 your employer puts in. Looking at it another way, you could only contribute $72 in after-tax income for every $100 of untaxed income your employer contributes. A difference this large compounded over many years will add many thousands of dollars to your retirement fund.

Employer plans are *noncontributory* if the employer bears all the cost or *contributory* if the employees share in the cost. Employee contributions usually amount to between 3 and 8 percent of total wages. At some point, benefits accumulated from employer contributions under a pension plan are nonforfeitable. That is, employees are entitled to the full amount of these benefits even if they leave the company before retirement. *Vesting,* as this right is known, was first guaranteed by the Employee Retirement Income Security Act (ERISA) of 1974. Under current law, employees are generally vested after 5 years of service. However, some plans gradually vest employees over a 4-year period, starting after the employee has worked for the company for 3 years and ending with full vesting in year 7.

Two basic methods are used to determine retirement benefits. The law requires that your employer tell you in writing how your determination is made:

- In a *defined benefit plan,* benefits are determined through a formula that generally includes such factors as level of earnings and length of employment. A typical plan might pay 1 percent of the average annual salary over your last 3 years of employment for every year you worked. If you averaged $35,000 over this period and worked for the company for 20 years, your annual retirement income would be $7,000 (0.01 × $35,000 × 20). This plan tells you exactly what your benefits will be at retirement.
- A *defined contribution plan* does not spell out your retirement income but rather defines precisely the amounts you and your employer contribute to the plan. Thus, your actual retirement income depends on how much is accumulated for you at retirement—an amount you cannot know with certainty until you retire. This plan makes it more difficult to plan your retirement income and manage your overall investment portfolio to meet your retirement needs.

*Supplemental plans.*    In addition to a basic retirement plan, many employers offer supplemental plans that allow employees to accumulate tax-deferred savings until retirement. Especially popular are the so-called *401(k) deferred compensation plans,* which were first introduced in 1978. (While our discussion here will center on 401(k) plans, similar programs are available for employees of public, nonprofit organizations; known as 403(b) plans, they offer basically the same features and tax shelter as 401(k) plans.)

Basically, a 401(k) plan gives you the option of diverting a portion of your salary into a company-sponsored tax-sheltered savings account. Both the original contribution and the interest it earns accumulate tax-free until the money is drawn out at retirement, when presumably you are in a lower tax bracket.

The law allows you to contribute up to 25 percent of your annual pay to this plan, to a maximum of $7,000. For employees covered under 403(b) plans, the maximum contribution is $9,500. (The Tax Reform Act of 1986 sharply reduced the appeal of the 401(k) plan by lowering the maximum tax deferred *employee* contribution to $7,000 from $30,000.) However, most companies set maximum contributions at a much lower level. Caps between 1 and 12½ percent of an employee's base pay are not unusual. Some firms sweeten the 401(k) pot even more by matching all or part of the employee's contribution. In the most common plan, the company kicks in 50 cents for every dollar the employee contributes—note that employer contributions do *not* affect the $7,000 limit set on employee contributions. These matching programs provide considerable tax and savings incentives to individuals and clearly enhance the appeal of this retirement plan.

To encourage savings for retirement, all 401(k) plan contributions are locked into the account until the employee turns 59½ or leaves the company. However, you can get to your money, without penalty, if you can prove financial hardship.

Let's look at a specific example to see how valuable this tax-deferred retirement plan can be. Suppose you earn $35,000 a year and can contribute up to 6 percent of your pay to a 401(k) plan. This would enable you to reduce your taxable income by $2,100 ($35,000 × .06) to $32,900. If you were in the 28 percent bracket, this would lower your federal tax bill by nearly $600, a tax savings that offsets a good portion of your contribution to the plan. In effect, you have added $2,100 to your retirement program with only $1,500 of your own money. The rest comes from the federal government in the form of a reduced tax bill.

In addition to the contribution tax deferral, all the interest on this money accumulates tax-free. Assuming your annual $2,100 401(k) contribution earned 7 percent a year, at the end of 10 years your principal and interest would total $26,770 after taxes. Had the earnings on the $2,100 annual deposit been taxable upon receipt at a 28 percent rate, the total at the end of 10 years would have been $26,463. In this case the tax-free accumulation resulted in more than $300 of additional after-tax earnings.

## SET UP A SELF-DIRECTED RETIREMENT PROGRAM

In a self-directed retirement program, you have almost complete control over which investments to buy and sell. Even though the financial institution you designate acts as custodian of your funds, you decide *how* the money is invested. Self-directed retirement programs include Keogh plans and Individual Retirement Accounts.

*Keogh plans.* Introduced in 1962 as part of the Self-Employment Individuals Retirement Act—also known as HR10, or simply the Keogh Act—these plans allow self-employed individuals to establish tax-deferred retirement plans for themselves and their employees. Like contributions to 401(k) plans, payments to Keogh accounts are deductible from taxable income, and all income earned in the account accumulates tax-free. The maximum contribution is $30,000 a year, or 20 percent of *net* earnings, whichever is less. (Net earnings are earnings after all expenses are paid except taxes and retirement contributions.)

If you are self-employed, either full or part time, you are eligible to set up a Keogh account. Thus, if you work for someone full time but have a part-time business of your own, you can contribute to a Keogh plan. If, for example, you earn $10,000 a year from a part-time consulting business, you can contribute 20 percent of that income ($2,000) to your Keogh account—a move that reduces your taxable income and thus the amount you pay in taxes. Keogh contributions for part-time work are completely separate from the retirement benefits you receive through your primary employer. At retirement, you will receive income from both sources.

Keogh accounts can be opened through banks, insurance companies, brokerage houses, mutual funds, and other financial institutions. Annual contributions must be made by the time you file your tax return. Therefore, the latest you can contribute to this account is the tax filing deadline of April 15. For example, you have until April 15, 1989, to contribute to your 1988 Keogh.

All Keogh contributions and investment earnings must remain in the account until you reach age 59½, unless you become seriously ill or disabled. If you take money out before age 59½, you'll have to pay 10 percent additional income tax as a penalty at the time of withdrawal. Keep in mind that you are not required to start withdrawing your funds at age 59½. They can stay in the account, continuing to earn tax-free income, until you are 70½, at which time you have 10 years to withdraw all the money. In fact, as long as you continue to be self-employed, you can make tax-deferred contributions to your Keogh account until you reach the maximum age of 70½.

All withdrawals are treated as ordinary income and are fully taxable. Like other tax-deferred accounts, Keogh plans enable you to put off paying taxes until retirement when your tax bracket will probably be lower.

*Individual Retirement Accounts (IRAs).* Individual Retirement Accounts (IRAs) are tax-deferred retirement programs. The maximum annual contribution to an IRA is $2,000 for an individual and $2,250 for an individual and a nonworking spouse. If both spouses work, the maximum family contribution is $4,000. The Tax Reform Act of 1986 places limits on IRA participation for employees who are eligible for employer-sponsored retirement plans.

In general, if you are a participant in an employer plan and if your income is above a certain level, you cannot deduct your IRA contribution from your taxes. The maximum adjusted gross income for a fully deductible IRA is $25,000 for a single return and $40,000 for a joint return. The maximum deduction is reduced according to a specific formula for income above these amounts and phases out entirely at $35,000 for single returns and $50,000 for joint returns.

Under the new tax law, even if you are not eligible to make a tax-deferred IRA contribution, you can still set up an IRA with after-tax dollars. In this case, the interest income you earn from the IRA accumulates tax-free until you begin withdrawing the funds at retirement.

The following rules apply whether your IRA contributions or just your IRA income is tax-deferred:

- You can deposit as much or as little as you want, up to the applicable limit. This can be as much as 100 percent of your compensation. For example, if your earned income is only $1,800, you can contribute up to 100 percent of it to your IRA.
- After age 59½, you can withdraw funds as you see fit. You can even withdraw the total amount in one lump sum, although this may not be practical from a tax standpoint.
- Any tax-deductible contributions withdrawn from an IRA prior to age 59½ are subject to a 10 percent penalty on top of the regular tax you pay at the time of withdrawal. Any after-tax or nondeductible contributions are exempt from this withdrawal penalty.

- You do not have to stay with the same IRA every year. In fact, you may have as many different IRAs as you wish.
- You can switch from one IRA account to another—either by having the trustee make the transfer or by withdrawing the funds yourself and depositing them in the new account—subject to certain rules.
- You must begin withdrawing money by age 70½
- You cannot borrow from your IRA account.

Like the other retirement plans we have discussed here, IRAs defer rather than eliminate taxes. Even so, the impact of tax deferral is substantial. As the following table indicates, in 25 years you can accumulate about twice as much money in an IRA as you can in a fully taxable account. This difference increases with time: after 45 years, you'll have 2.6 times more. This example assumes that you have $1,000 of earned income each year that is also available for investment and that you can make a tax-deferred IRA contribution. After the first year, you'll have $1,080 in your IRA account, assuming the money is invested at a rate of 8 percent. If you allot the same pretax money to a non-IRA account, you must first pay $280 in taxes (assuming a 28 percent tax rate), leaving you with only $720 to invest. The subsequent earnings of $58 ($720 × .08) are also taxed at 28 percent, leaving you with an after-tax income of only $42: $58 − .28 ($58) = $58 − $16 = $42. Thus, in the first year you accumulate only $762—$318 less than you would have in an IRA.

| Years Held | IRA | Non-IRA |
|---|---|---|
| 1 | $ 1,080 | $ 762 |
| 5 | 6,335 | 4,272 |
| 10 | 15,645 | 9,926 |
| 15 | 29,323 | 17,405 |
| 20 | 49,421 | 27,359 |
| 25 | 78,951 | 40,471 |
| 30 | 122,341 | 57,821 |
| 35 | 186,097 | 80,778 |
| 40 | 279,774 | 111,153 |
| 45 | 417,417 | 159,502 |

*Funding Keoghs and IRAs.* Since Keoghs and IRAs are self-directed retirement accounts, you can choose to manage your account as conservatively or aggressively as you want. Not surprisingly, considering the nature of these investment programs, most people take a conservative approach. Since such high-return investments as real estate or growth stocks involve equally high risk, most investors steer clear of them for their retirement programs. It is important to keep in mind that although Keogh plans and IRAs are attractive tax shelters, this in no way affects the underlying risk of the securities that make up the account.

Conventional wisdom suggests funding your Keogh and IRA with *income-producing assets*; this would also suggest that if you are looking for capital gains, it is best to do so outside of your retirement account. The reasons for this are twofold: (1) growth-oriented securities are by nature more risky and (2) you cannot write off losses from the sale of securities held in a Keogh or IRA account. This does *not* mean it would be altogether inappropriate to place a good-quality growth stock or mutual fund in a Keogh or IRA—in fact, many advisors contend that growth investments should *always* have a place in your retirement account. The reason is their performance: such investments may pay off handsomely, since they can appreciate totally free of taxes. In the end, it is how much you have in your retirement account that matters rather than how your earnings were made along the way.

Investors can select from a wide variety of vehicles to fund Keogh and IRA accounts, including stocks and bonds and such short-term instruments as bank and mutual fund money market accounts. Not surprisingly, as the size of an account begins to grow, many investors diversify their holdings.

Although very few vehicles are prohibited outright, there are some that should be avoided simply because they are inappropriate. Tax-exempt municipal bonds, for example, are not a wise choice since they duplicate the tax shelter already part of the Keogh or IRA.

Most Keogh and IRA accounts were set up initially with banks and thrift institutions. Later, as investors became more comfortable with the concept, many began to invest through brokerage firms, insurance companies, and mutual funds. The fees to open and administer these accounts vary considerably among these institutions. Brokerage firms are generally the most expensive, charging between $25 and $100 to open an account and about the same amount to maintain it each year. Banks and mutual funds are generally less expensive. It pays to shop around.

# 4

## GAUGING THE RETURN
## FROM YOUR INVESTMENT DOLLAR

------

When buying a product or service, most of us have preconceived notions of value. When an item is relatively inexpensive, we generally will pay the marked or quoted price. However, as the price increases, most of us spend more time considering value, which to a great extent depends on our level of expected satisfaction. Because price and value are not necessarily the same, we try not to pay a price in excess of value.

When making investment decisions, the same logic applies in an even stricter sense. An investment can be viewed as a financial commodity, the price of which results from the interaction of supply and demand. Although you can't see the value of an investment in the same way you see the value of a physical commodity such as a car, investment value is just as real and just as measurable. Its defining characteristics are return and risk. By understanding how to measure these dimensions, you'll be able to put the right dollar sign on an investment and pay a fair price for it. In this chapter, we'll analyze the concept of return and in the next, we'll focus on risk.

# RETURN: THE REWARD FOR INVESTING

Although a return on an investment is not necessarily guaranteed, it is expected return that motivates people to invest. The return can be seen as the reward for investing. Suppose, for example, you have $1,000 in a savings account paying 5 percent annual interest, and a business associate has asked you to lend her that much money. If you lend her the money for 1 year, at the end of which time she pays you back, your return would depend on the amount of interest you charged. If you made an interest-free loan, your return would be zero. If you charged 5 percent interest, your return would be $50 (.05 $\times$ $1,000). Since prior to making the loan you were earning a safe 5 percent on the $1,000, it seems clear that you should charge a minimum of 5 percent interest. This strategy allows you to receive the same reward you would receive had you not made the loan.

Unfortunately, not all investment vehicles guarantee a return. For example, while the $1,000 deposited in a federally insured savings account provides a certain return, the $1,000 loan does not. You have no way of knowing for sure if you'll ever get all or even part of your $1,000 from your business associate. She may not be able to pay it back because of financial difficulty, or she may not want to pay it back because she knows you're not likely to sue her. Assume that at the end of a year you are able to recover only $950. In this case, your return would be minus $50 ($950 − $1,000) or minus 5 percent (−$50/$1,000). Thus, the size of your expected investment return is an important factor in deciding whether the investment is worthwhile.

# RETURN COMES IN DIFFERENT FORMS

Your return on an investment can come from two different sources. The most common source of return is *current income,* which comes from such periodic payments as interest and dividends. The other source of return is *capital gains,* which occur when you can sell an investment for more than you originally paid. When you lose money, capital gains turn into capital losses.

### CURRENT INCOME

The money you receive periodically as a result of owning an investment is current income. Interest received on a bond, dividends received from a stock, and rent received from real estate are three major forms of current income. To be considered income, these payments must come in the form of cash or must be readily convertible into cash.

In the following table, compare the current income generated by the two different investments over a period of a year. If you invest in A, your current income will be $80; B, on the other hand, provides a $120 return, which on the surface is much greater.

|  | INVESTMENT | |
| --- | --- | --- |
|  | A | B |
| Purchase price (beginning of year) | $1,000 | $1,000 |
| Cash received | | |
| 1st quarter | $ 10 | $ 0 |
| 2nd quarter | 20 | 0 |
| 3rd quarter | 20 | 0 |
| 4th quarter | 30 | 120 |
| Total (for year) | $ 80 | $ 120 |
| Sale price (end of year) | $1,100 | $ 960 |

## CAPITAL GAINS (OR LOSSES)

As you can see at the bottom of the table, however, there's more to the story. Before deciding which investment is best, you have to determine whether you come out ahead or behind when you sell the investment at the end of the year.

You can determine this by calculating your capital gain or loss, or the change in market value of the investment between the time of purchase and the time of sale. When you make an investment, you expect your invested funds to be returned sometime in the future. In the case of a bond, this return occurs at maturity, or earlier if the bond is traded before it matures. As you will see later, in the chapters on bonds, the market price of the bond when you sell it depends mainly on interest rates; when interest rates drop, the value of the bond—and your potential capital gains—increases; when interest rates rise, bond values drop—as does your chance of realizing a capital gain when you sell the bond. The change in value of stocks, real estate, and many other investment vehicles not having a specified maturity date depends upon a variety of factors that make it more difficult to predict their future worth.

The table above shows how a capital gain or loss can affect the bottom line of an investment. If you put money in investment A, your capital gain would be $100 ($1,100 sale price − $1,000 purchase price). If, on the other hand, you chose investment B, you would have a capital loss of $40 ($960 sale price − $1,000 purchase price).

By combining this information with the current income you receive on each investment, you can calculate your *total return:*

| | INVESTMENT | |
|---|---|---|
| Return | A | B |
| Current income | $ 80 | $120 |
| Capital gain (loss) | 100 | (40) |
| Total return | $180 | $ 80 |

Thus, even though investment B's current income was much higher than investment A's, investment A turned out to be a better investment because of its capital gains. If you look at these return figures as a percentage of your initial investment, you can see that you earned 18 percent on investment A ($180/$1,000) and 8 percent on investment B ($80/$1,000). Given everything we've told you so far about investments A and B, investment A is the better choice. Investing is rarely this simple, however. To determine if investment A really is the better of these two choices, you have to consider the relative risk of each as well as the effect of taxes on the amount of money you actually earn. These factors and their implications for your investment strategies will be covered in detail in later chapters.

# WHY RETURN IS IMPORTANT

The concept of return is important because it enables you to compare the amount of actual or expected gain provided by various investments. You can calculate a historical return by looking at the past and an expected return by estimating future performance.

## ANALYZING HISTORICAL DATA

Although we all know that the future does not necessarily reflect the past, most of us would agree that the past provides valuable information that can help us formulate our expectations about future performance. This view is generally accepted among investors, who look to the past performance of an investment for clues to its future.

In the table on the next page, past performance is analyzed on a yearly basis. When return is analyzed over an extended period as it is here, you can readily determine the average level of return during the period. Just as important, you can determine the trend of the return. In this case, the average total return over the past 10 years, expressed as a percentage, was 8.10 percent (see column 6). Looking at the yearly returns, we can see that after a negative return in 1979, the investment had a positive and generally increasing return over the next 4 years until it went into the red once more in 1984. Between 1985 and 1988, the returns were positive and steadily increasing once more.

| | (1) | MARKET VALUE (PRICE) | | | TOTAL RETURN | |
|---|---|---|---|---|---|---|
| | | (2) Beginning of the Year | (3) End of the Year | (4) [(3) − (2)] Capital Gain | (5) [(1) + (4)] ($) | (6) [(5) ÷ (2)] (%)* |
| Year | Income | | | | | |
| 1979 | $4.00 | $100 | $ 95 | −$ 5.00 | −$ 1.00 | −1.00% |
| 1980 | 3.00 | 95 | 99 | 4.00 | 7.00 | 7.37 |
| 1981 | 4.00 | 99 | 105 | 6.00 | 10.00 | 10.10 |
| 1982 | 5.00 | 105 | 115 | 10.00 | 15.00 | 14.29 |
| 1983 | 5.00 | 115 | 125 | 10.00 | 15.00 | 12.00 |
| 1984 | 3.00 | 125 | 120 | — 5.00 | — 2.00 | −1.60 |
| 1985 | 3.00 | 120 | 122 | 2.00 | 5.00 | 4.17 |
| 1986 | 4.00 | 122 | 130 | 8.00 | 12.00 | 9.84 |
| 1987 | 5.00 | 130 | 140 | 10.00 | 15.00 | 11.54 |
| 1988 | 5.00 | 140 | 155 | 15.00 | 20.00 | 14.29 |
| Average | $4.10 | | | $ 5.50 | $ 9.60 | 8.10% |

*Percent return on beginning-of-year market value of investment.

## CALCULATING FUTURE PROSPECTS

These historical return data give you the tools you need to project future perform-ance. If you expect the upward trend of 1985–88 to continue, your expected future return would be in the range of 12 to 15 percent. On the other hand, if future prospects seem poor or if the investment is cyclical—moving up and down over a predictable period of time—an expected return of 8 to 9 percent may be more reasonable. Looking more closely at the pattern of the past 10 years, you can see that the returns have cycled from one poor year (occurring in 1979 and then again in 1984) to 4 good years of generally increasing returns (1980–83 and 1985–88). Based on this pattern, we might expect a poor return in 1989 followed by increasing returns in the 1990–93 period.

## FACTORS THAT AFFECT RETURN

The level of return you actually achieve or expect to achieve from an investment depends on a variety of factors, including the internal characteristics of the invest-ment, environmental factors, and inflation.

## LOOK CLOSELY AT THE INVESTMENT VEHICLE

The return you can expect from an investment is tied to the special characteristics of the investment, including its type (e.g., municipal bonds vs. stock options), the way it is financed, the caliber and style of corporate management, and, just as importantly, the corporate clients. For example, the common stock of a large, well-managed steel manufacturer whose major customer is General Motors and whose major financing comes from company stock is likely to provide a much better return than that of a small, poorly managed clothing manufacturer whose customers are small specialty stores and whose financing comes mainly from debt.

## ANALYZE OUTSIDE FORCES

Investment return is often influenced by factors that have nothing directly to do with the investment itself. Such external forces as war, shortages of raw materials, price controls, the actions of the Federal Reserve, and political events may affect the level of return. Because each investment vehicle is affected differently by these forces, it is not unusual for two extremely similar vehicles to produce different levels of return. For example, while the threat of war in the Middle East might adversely affect the return on common stock of a commercial aircraft manufacturer, it could boost the return on a company manufacturing military aircraft.

## CONSIDER INFLATION

Inflation, which has been relatively common in the United States for many years, tends to have a favorable impact on some investments like real estate, and a negative impact on other investments like stocks and fixed income securities. Inflation brings with it rising interest rates, which in turn influence investment success. The return on each type of investment vehicle exhibits its own unique response to inflation. For example, the bull market for stocks during the mid-1980s was largely fueled by the low levels of inflation (4 to 5 percent) and interest rates (7 to 10 percent) at that time.

---

# THE TIME VALUE OF MONEY

If at age 25 you begin making annual cash deposits of $1,000 into an account that pays 5 percent annual interest, your deposits will total $40,000 40 years later, assuming you make no withdrawals. However, because of the interest your money is earning, you will actually have the far larger figure of $121,000. The $81,000 your money earns is considered the money's time value.

When your money is earning money for you, the sooner you receive a given investment return the better. For example, two $1,000 investments that are expected to return $100 over a 2-year holding period with no capital gain are not necessarily equal. If the first investment returns the $100 at the end of 1 year and the second investment returns it at the end of 2 years, the first investment will provide the better return. In general, it is best to receive an investment return in as short a time as possible.

## INTEREST: THE BASIC RETURN TO SAVERS

Interest comes in the form of simple interest and compound interest. There are important differences between the two.

*Simple interest.* Simple interest is interest paid only on your actual balance for the actual amount of time your money is on deposit. For example, if you have $100 on deposit for 1½ years in an account paying 6 percent interest, you will earn $9 in interest (1½ × .06 × $100) over this period. Had you withdrawn $50 at the end of half a year, the total simple interest earned over the 1½ years would be $6, since you would earn $3 interest on $100 for the first half year (½ × .06 × $100) and $3 interest on $50 for the next full year (1 × .06 × $50).

Using the simple interest method, the stated rate of 6 percent interest represents the true rate of return. Because simple interest reflects the rate at which current income is earned regardless of the size of the deposit, it is a useful measure. The return on such investments as certificates of deposit and bonds is calculated according to the simple interest method.

*Compound interest.* Compound interest is paid not only on the initial deposit, but also on any interest accumulated from one period to the next. It is the method most often used by savings institutions. When interest is compounded annually, compound and simple interest calculations provide the same result.

The following table illustrates the concept of compound interest. In this case, the interest earned each year at a 5 percent rate is left on deposit rather than withdrawn. Therefore the $50 interest earned on the $1,000 on deposit during 1987

| Date | (1) Deposit or (Withdrawal) | (2) Beginning Account Balance | (3) [0.05 × (2)] Interest for Year | (4) [(2) + (3)] Ending Account Balance |
|------|------|------|------|------|
| 1/1/87 | $1,000 | $1,000.00 | $50.00 | $1,050.00 |
| 1/1/88 | (300) | 750.00 | 37.50 | 787.50 |
| 1/1/89 | 1,000 | 1,787.50 | 89.38 | 1,876.88 |

becomes part of the balance on which interest is paid in 1988, and so on. Note that the simple interest method is used in the compounding process; that is, interest is earned only on the initial balance each year.

*True vs. stated interest.* In general, the more frequently interest is compounded at a stated rate, the higher the true rate of interest. You can see this in the following table, which compounds the same savings account balance semiannually. To obtain the interest for each 6-month period, multiply the balance for the 6 months by half the stated 5 percent interest rate (see column 3).

| Date | (1)<br>Deposit or<br>(Withdrawal) | (2)<br>Beginning<br>Account<br>Balance | (3)<br>$[0.05 \times \frac{1}{2} \times (2)]$<br>Interest for<br>Period (6 mo.) | (4)<br>$[(2) + (3)]$<br>Ending<br>Account Balance |
|---|---|---|---|---|
| 1/1/87 | $1,000 | $1,000.00 | $25.00 | $1,025.00 |
| 7/1/87 | | 1,025.00 | 25.63 | 1,050.63 |
| 1/1/88 | (300) | 750.63 | 18.77 | 769.40 |
| 7/1/88 | | 769.40 | 19.24 | 788.64 |
| 1/1/89 | 1,000 | 1,788.64 | 44.72 | 1,833.36 |
| 7/1/89 | | 1,833.36 | 45.83 | 1,879.19 |

When you compare the amount of money you have at the end of the 3-year period when the interest is compounded annually with the amount you have when it is compounded semiannually, you see that you earn slightly more money with the more frequent compounding. Clearly, with semiannual compounding the true rate of interest is greater than the 5 percent rate associated with annual compounding. The following table summarizes how the true rate of interest associated with a 5 percent stated rate increases as the compounding periods become more frequent:

| Compounding<br>Period | True Rate<br>of Interest |
|---|---|
| Annually | 5.000% |
| Semiannually | 5.063 |
| Quarterly | 5.094 |
| Monthly | 5.120 |
| Weekly | 5.125 |
| Continuously | 5.127 |

When your money is compounded, the stated and true interest rates are equal only when interest is compounded annually. *Continuous compounding,* or compounding over the smallest imaginable interval of time—a microsecond—reflects the maximum true rate of interest that can be achieved with a stated rate of interest.

Because of the effect these different compounding periods have on return, you should evaluate the true rate of interest you'll get from an investment prior to making a deposit.

## FUTURE VALUE: AN EXTENSION OF COMPOUNDING

Future value is the amount to which a current deposit will grow over a period of time when it is placed in an account paying compound interest. Take a deposit of $1,000 that is earning 8 percent compounded annually. In order to find the future value of this deposit at the end of 1 year, the following calculation would be made:

$$\text{amount of money at end of year 1} = \begin{pmatrix} \text{amount of deposit} \\ \text{at beginning of} \\ \text{year} \end{pmatrix} \times \begin{pmatrix} \text{interest rate} \\ 1 + \text{expressed as} \\ \text{a decimal} \end{pmatrix}$$

$$= \$1{,}000 \times (1 + .08)$$
$$= \$1{,}080$$

If the money were left on deposit for another year, 8 percent interest would be paid on the account balance of $1,080. At the end of the second year, there would be $1,166.40 in the account. This $1,166.40 would represent the beginning-of-year balance of $1,080 plus 8 percent of the $1,080 ($86.40) in interest. The future value at the end of the second year is calculated below:

$$\text{amount of money at end of year 2} = \$1{,}080 \times (1 + .08)$$
$$= \$1{,}166.40$$

In order to find the future value of the $1,000 at the end of year $n$, the procedures illustrated above would have to be repeated $n$ times. Because this process can be quite tedious, tables of compound interest factors are available, as shown below. The factors in the table represent the amount to which an initial $1 deposit would grow for various combinations of years and interest rates.

## COMPOUND-VALUE INTEREST FACTORS FOR $1

| Year | INTEREST RATE | | | | | |
|------|-----|-----|-----|-----|-----|-----|
|      | 5%  | 6%  | 7%  | 8%  | 9%  | 10% |
| 1    | 1.050 | 1.060 | 1.070 | 1.080 | 1.090 | 1.100 |
| 2    | 1.102 | 1.124 | 1.145 | 1.166 | 1.188 | 1.210 |
| 3    | 1.158 | 1.191 | 1.225 | 1.260 | 1.295 | 1.331 |
| 4    | 1.216 | 1.262 | 1.311 | 1.360 | 1.412 | 1.464 |
| 5    | 1.276 | 1.338 | 1.403 | 1.469 | 1.539 | 1.611 |
| 6    | 1.340 | 1.419 | 1.501 | 1.587 | 1.677 | 1.772 |
| 7    | 1.407 | 1.504 | 1.606 | 1.714 | 1.828 | 1.949 |
| 8    | 1.477 | 1.594 | 1.718 | 1.851 | 1.993 | 2.144 |
| 9    | 1.551 | 1.689 | 1.838 | 1.999 | 2.172 | 2.358 |
| 10   | 1.629 | 1.791 | 1.967 | 2.159 | 2.367 | 2.594 |

Note: All table values have been rounded to the nearest 1/1,000th; thus calculated values may differ slightly from the table values.

DECIDING HOW TO INVEST

For example, a dollar deposited in an account paying 8 percent interest and left there for 2 years would accumulate to $1.166. Using the compound-value interest factor for 8 percent and 2 years (1.166), the future value of an investment (deposit) that can earn 8 percent over 2 years is found by multiplying the amount invested (or deposited) by the appropriate interest factor. In the case of $1,000 left on deposit for 2 years at 8 percent, the resulting future value is $1,166 (1.166 × $1,000), which agrees (except for a slight rounding error) with the value calculated earlier.

When you use a compound-value table, keep in mind that the values in the table determine the future value of $1 at the end of a given year. Note also that as interest rates increase, the compound-value interest factor also increases. Thus, the higher the interest rate, the greater the future value. Finally, note that for a given interest rate, the future value of a dollar increases with the passage of time.

## FUTURE VALUE OF AN ANNUITY

An annuity is a stream of equal annual cash flows. These cash flows can be inflows of returns earned from an investment or outflows of funds invested (deposited) in order to earn future returns. Investors interested in finding the future value of an annuity are typically concerned with what is called an *ordinary annuity*, which has a cash flow at the end of each year. The future value of this type of annuity can be determined mathematically, using a calculator, computer, or appropriate financial tables. Here we will use tables of compound interest factors for an annuity (see the sample table shown below). The factors in the table represent the amount to which *annual* end-of-year deposits of $1 would grow for various combinations of years and interest rates.

For example, $1,000 deposited at the end of each year for 8 years into an account paying 6 percent interest would accumulate to $9,897. Using the compound-value interest factor for an annuity at 6 percent for 8 years (9.897), the future value of this annuity investment is found by multiplying the annual investment (deposit) by the appropriate interest factor ($1,000 × 9.897 = $9,897).

## COMPOUND-VALUE INTEREST FACTORS FOR A $1 ANNUITY

| Year | \multicolumn{6}{c}{INTEREST RATE} |
|------|------|------|------|------|------|------|
|      | 5%   | 6%   | 7%   | 8%   | 9%   | 10%  |
| 1    | 1.000  | 1.000  | 1.000  | 1.000  | 1.000  | 1.000  |
| 2    | 2.050  | 2.060  | 2.070  | 2.080  | 2.090  | 2.100  |
| 3    | 3.152  | 3.184  | 3.215  | 3.246  | 3.278  | 3.310  |
| 4    | 4.310  | 4.375  | 4.440  | 4.506  | 4.573  | 4.641  |
| 5    | 5.526  | 5.637  | 5.751  | 5.867  | 5.985  | 6.105  |
| 6    | 6.802  | 6.975  | 7.153  | 7.336  | 7.523  | 7.716  |
| 7    | 8.142  | 8.394  | 8.654  | 8.923  | 9.200  | 9.487  |
| 8    | 9.549  | 9.897  | 10.260 | 10.637 | 11.028 | 11.436 |
| 9    | 11.027 | 11.491 | 11.978 | 12.488 | 13.021 | 13.579 |
| 10   | 12.578 | 13.181 | 13.816 | 14.487 | 15.193 | 15.937 |

*Note:* All table values have been rounded to the nearest 1/1,000th; thus calculated values may differ slightly from the table values.

# PRESENT VALUE: AN EXTENSION OF FUTURE VALUE

Present value is the inverse of future value. That is, while future value measures the value of a present amount at some future date, present value measures the current value of a future sum. By applying present value techniques, the value today of a sum to be received at some future date can be calculated.

In essence, when you determine the present value of a future sum, you are answering the following question: "How much would I have to deposit today into an account paying y percent interest in order to earn a specified sum by a specified number of years in the future?" In this case, the interest rate is known as the *discount rate,* or *opportunity cost.* It represents the annual rate of return that you could currently earn on a similar investment.

For example, say you are offered an investment that will provide you with exactly $1,000 in 1 year's time. Assuming you could earn 8 percent from other investments with similar risk, you have to determine the most you should pay for this opportunity. In other words, what is the present value of $1,000 to be received 1 year from now discounted at 8 percent? The following equation describes this situation. In this case Z equals the present value you are calculating:

$$Z \times (1 + .08) = \$1,000$$

Solving the equation for Z, we get:

$$Z = \frac{\$1,000}{(1 + .08)} = \$925.93$$

What the answer tells you is that if you deposit $925.93 into an account paying 8 percent interest today, it will grow to $1,000 in one year.

Because present-value calculations become more complex as the length of the investment period expands, present-value tables have been developed to simplify your calculations (see below). The factors in the table represent the present value of $1 for various combinations of years and discount rates. For example, the present

## PRESENT-VALUE INTEREST FACTORS FOR $1

| Year | DISCOUNT (INTEREST) RATE | | | | | |
|------|------|------|------|------|------|------|
|      | 5%   | 6%   | 7%   | 8%   | 9%   | 10%  |
| 1    | 0.952 | 0.943 | 0.935 | 0.926 | 0.917 | 0.909 |
| 2    | 0.907 | 0.890 | 0.873 | 0.857 | 0.842 | 0.826 |
| 3    | 0.864 | 0.840 | 0.816 | 0.794 | 0.772 | 0.751 |
| 4    | 0.823 | 0.792 | 0.763 | 0.735 | 0.708 | 0.683 |
| 5    | 0.784 | 0.747 | 0.713 | 0.681 | 0.650 | 0.621 |
| 6    | 0.746 | 0.705 | 0.666 | 0.630 | 0.596 | 0.564 |
| 7    | 0.711 | 0.665 | 0.623 | 0.583 | 0.547 | 0.513 |
| 8    | 0.677 | 0.627 | 0.582 | 0.540 | 0.502 | 0.467 |
| 9    | 0.645 | 0.592 | 0.544 | 0.500 | 0.460 | 0.424 |
| 10   | 0.614 | 0.558 | 0.508 | 0.463 | 0.422 | 0.386 |

Note: All table values have been rounded to the nearest 1/1000th; thus calculated values may differ slightly from the table values.

DECIDING HOW TO INVEST

value of $1 to be received 1 year from now discounted at 8 percent is $0.926. Using this factor (.926), the present value of $1,000 to be received 1 year from now at an 8 percent discount rate is found by multiplying .926 by $1,000, which equals $926. This table enables you to shortcut the equation we just used and come up with the same figure. (The small difference between these two figures is the result of rounding.)

Here's another situation: you want to know the present value of $500 to be received 7 years from now, discounted at 6 percent. The calculation is:

$$\text{present value} = .665 \times \$500 = \$332.50$$

where .665 represents the present-value interest factor for 7 years discounted at 6 percent.

When you're working with present-value tables, keep in mind that the present-value interest factor for a single sum is always less than 1; only if the discount rate were zero would this factor equal 1. Second, the higher the discount rate for a given year, the smaller the present-value interest factor. In other words, the greater your opportunity cost (the interest rate you could be earning), the less an amount to be received in the future is worth today. Finally, the further in the future a sum is to be received, the less it is currently worth.

## PRESENT VALUE OF A STREAM OF INCOME

Because the returns from a given investment are likely to be received at various future dates rather than as a single lump sum, you must be able to find the present value of a stream of returns. You will need this information in order to value various investment vehicles such as stocks, bonds, and real estate. A stream of returns can be viewed as a package of single-sum returns and may be classified as a mixed stream or an annuity. A *mixed stream* of returns is one that exhibits no special pattern; as noted earlier, an *annuity* is a pattern of equal annual returns. The following table illustrates each of these return patterns. In order to find the present value of each of these streams at the beginning of 1988, the present value of each component return must be calculated and totaled. Because certain shortcuts can be used in the case of an annuity, the calculation of each return stream will be illustrated separately.

### MIXED AND ANNUITY RETURN STREAMS

| End of Year | RETURNS | |
|---|---|---|
| | Mixed Stream | Annuity |
| 1988 | $30 | $50 |
| 1989 | 40 | 50 |
| 1990 | 50 | 50 |
| 1991 | 60 | 50 |
| 1992 | 70 | 50 |

*Mixed stream.* Assuming a 9 percent discount rate, the calculation of the present value of the mixed stream is illustrated in the following table. The resulting present value of $187.77 represents the amount today (beginning of 1988) invested at 9 percent that would be equivalent to the stream of returns given in column 1 of the table. Once the present value of each return is found, the values can be added, since each is measured at the same point in time.

### MIXED STREAM PRESENT-VALUE CALCULATION

| End of Year | (1) Return | (2) 9% Present-Value Interest Factor | (3) [(1) × (2)] Present Value |
|---|---|---|---|
| 1988 | $ 30 | 0.917 | $ 27.51 |
| 1989 | 40 | 0.842 | 33.68 |
| 1990 | 50 | 0.772 | 38.60 |
| 1991 | 60 | 0.708 | 42.48 |
| 1992 | 70 | 0.650 | 45.50 |
| | | Present value of stream: | $187.77 |

Note: Column (1) values are from the preceding table. Column (2) values are from the table of present-value interest factors presented on page 44.

*Annuity.* A simpler approach exists for finding the present value of an annuity, since tables of present-value interest factors for annuities are available, as shown below. The factors in the table represent the present value of a $1 annuity associated with various combinations of years and discount rates. For example, the present value of $1 to be received each year for the next 5 years discounted at 9 percent is $3.890. Using this factor, the present value of the $50 5-year annuity at a 9 percent discount rate can be found by multiplying the annual return by the appropriate interest factor. The resulting present value is $194.50 ($50 × 3.890).

### PRESENT-VALUE INTEREST FACTORS FOR A $1 ANNUITY

| Year | DISCOUNT (INTEREST) RATE | | | | | |
|---|---|---|---|---|---|---|
| | 5% | 6% | 7% | 8% | 9% | 10% |
| 1 | 0.952 | 0.943 | 0.935 | 0.926 | 0.917 | 0.909 |
| 2 | 1.859 | 1.833 | 1.808 | 1.783 | 1.759 | 1.736 |
| 3 | 2.723 | 2.673 | 2.624 | 2.577 | 2.531 | 2.487 |
| 4 | 3.546 | 3.465 | 3.387 | 3.312 | 3.240 | 3.170 |
| 5 | 4.329 | 4.212 | 4.100 | 3.993 | 3.890 | 3.791 |
| 6 | 5.076 | 4.917 | 4.767 | 4.623 | 4.486 | 4.355 |
| 7 | 5.786 | 5.582 | 5.389 | 5.206 | 5.033 | 4.868 |
| 8 | 6.463 | 6.210 | 5.971 | 5.747 | 5.535 | 5.335 |
| 9 | 7.108 | 6.802 | 6.515 | 6.247 | 5.995 | 5.759 |
| 10 | 7.722 | 7.360 | 7.024 | 6.710 | 6.418 | 6.145 |

Note: All table values have been rounded to the nearest 1/1,000th; thus calculated values may differ slightly from the table values.

## DETERMINING A SATISFACTORY INVESTMENT

The present-value concept can be used to define what is an acceptable investment and what is not. Ignoring risk at this point, a satisfactory investment is one for which the present value of benefits equals or exceeds the present value of costs. Since the cost, or purchase price, of the investment would be incurred initially at time zero, the cost and its present value are viewed as one and the same. If the present value of the benefits just equals the cost, your rate of return equals the discount rate. If the present value of benefits exceeds the cost, your return is greater than the discount rate. And finally, if the present value of benefits is less than the cost, your return is less than the discount rate. Thus, you want only investments whose benefits have a present value that equals or exceeds your cost. In these cases, the return is equal to or greater than the discount rate.

The following table illustrates how you can apply the present-value concept to actual investment cases. Assuming an 8 percent discount rate, you can see that the present value of the benefits over a 7-year period (1988–94) is $1,175.28. If the cost of the investment is less than or equal to $1,175.28, the investment is acceptable because your return will be at least 8 percent. If your cost is greater than $1,175.28, you can do better elsewhere since your return will be less than 8 percent.

### PRESENT VALUE APPLIED TO AN INVESTMENT

| End of Year | (1) Benefits | (2) 8% Present-Value Interest Factor | (3) [(1) × (2)] Present Value |
|---|---|---|---|
| 1988 | $90 | 0.926 | $ 83.34 |
| 1989 | 100 | 0.857 | 85.70 |
| 1990 | 110 | 0.794 | 87.34 |
| 1991 | 120 | 0.735 | 88.20 |
| 1992 | 100 | 0.681 | 68.10 |
| 1993 | 100 | 0.630 | 63.00 |
| 1994 | 1,200 | 0.583 | 699.60 |
| | | Present value of benefits: | $1,175.28 |

## HOW TO MEASURE RETURN

Our discussion so far has intentionally oversimplified the computations involved in determining return. In order to compare returns from different investment vehicles, you need to apply a consistent measure that incorporates differences in the timing of investment income and capital gains (or losses) and also allows you to place a current value on future benefits. Three different measures give you this information: holding period return, yield, and approximate yield.

## HOLDING PERIOD RETURN (HPR)

Because we are concerned with a broad range of investment vehicles, most of which are reasonably marketable, we need a measure of return that captures both periodic benefits and changes in value. This measure is called holding period return.

A *holding period* is the time during which return on an investment is measured. By using the holding period concept, you can compare the return over the same period of time for a variety of investment vehicles. The figures you come up with will allow you to choose the investment with the highest return. It would be impossible, for example, to compare the return on a stock you held for 6 months and sold on December 31, 1987, with the return on a bond you held for a year and sold on June 30, 1987, without applying the holding period measure. In essence, the HPR measure allows you to apply an annualized, or standardized, holding period to all the investments you are comparing.

*Understanding the components of return.*   Remember the two components of investment return, current income and capital gains (or losses). The portion of return considered current income is a *realized return*, since you generally receive it during the period. Capital gains returns, on the other hand, may not be realized; that is, you may not collect them during the holding period if you do not actually sell your investment. Even when the capital gain return is not realized during the holding period, however, it must be included in the return calculation.

For example, if you bought a stock for $50 a share, and 1 year later its market value was $70 a share, your capital gains return over the period would be $20. You would *realize* this return if you bought the stock at the beginning of the year and sold it at the end of the year. If, on the other hand, you purchased the stock 3 years earlier and plan to hold it for another 3 years, you would have the same $20 capital gain for the year even though you saw no actual change in your cash flow.

Most of our discussion throughout this book assumes that you make money on your investments. In the best of all possible worlds, this happens all the time. But back in the real world, there will be times when your investments just come out even, or worse yet, end up in the red. When an investment's current income is negative, you may have to take money out of your pocket to meet your obligations. This situation frequently occurs in real estate. You may find, for example, that an apartment complex you just purchased does not generate an adequate rental income to meet its monthly operational costs. In contrast, capital losses occur when the market value of your investment declines over a given holding period. Almost every investment is susceptible to capital loss, including stocks, bonds, options, commodities, and mutual funds.

*Computing holding period return.*   Holding period return (HPR) is the total return earned from holding an investment for a specified period of time (the holding period). It represents the sum of current income and capital gains (or losses) achieved over the holding period, divided by the beginning investment value. This measure is customarily used with holding periods of 1 year or less. The following equation is used:

$$\text{holding period return} = \frac{\text{current income} + \text{capital gain (or loss)}}{\text{beginning investment value}}$$

where

$$\begin{array}{l} \text{ending investment value} \\ - \text{ beginning investment value} \\ \hline = \text{ capital gain (or loss)} \end{array}$$

HPR provides a convenient way of comparing the total return realized or expected from given investments. For example, the following table summarizes the key financial variables for four investments made over a period of 1 year. The total current income and capital gain or loss for each investment during the 1-year holding period is given in lines 1 and 3. By adding these two sources of return together, you can calculate the total return for the year, shown in line 4. Dividing the total return (line 4) by the beginning-of-year investment value (line 2), gives you the holding period return, shown in line 5.

| | INVESTMENT VEHICLE | | | |
| | Savings Account | Common Stock | Bond | Real Estate |
| --- | --- | --- | --- | --- |
| CASH RECEIVED | | | | |
| 1st quarter | $15 | $10 | $ 0 | $0 |
| 2nd quarter | 15 | 10 | 50 | 0 |
| 3rd quarter | 15 | 10 | 0 | 0 |
| 4th quarter | 15 | 15 | 50 | 0 |
| (1) Total current income | $60 | $45 | $100 | $0 |
| INVESTMENT VALUE | | | | |
| End-of-year | $1,000 | $2,100 | $ 970 | $3,200 |
| (2) Beginning-of-year | 1,000 | 2,000 | 1,000 | 3,000 |
| (3) Capital gain (loss) | $ 0 | $ 100 | ($ 30) | $ 200 |
| (4) Total return [(1) + (3)] | $ 60 | $ 145 | $ 70 | $ 200 |
| (5) Holding period return [(4) ÷ (2)] | 6.00% | 7.25% | 7.00% | 6.67% |

Over the 1-year holding period, the common stock had the highest HPR, 7.25 percent, and the savings account the lowest, 6 percent. It should be clear from these calculations that all you need to find the HPR are beginning- and end-of-period investment values as well as the total current income you receive during the period.

Note that the HPR values calculated in line 5 would be the same regardless of whether the holding period was less than or greater than one year. Had the same data been drawn from a 6-month period rather than a 1-year period, the resulting HPRs would still be valid.

*Using HPR in investment decisions.*　　Holding period return gives you a convenient way to calculate the return on various investments. Because it relates both current income and capital gains to the investment value at the beginning of the period, it tends to overcome any problems that might be associated with comparing investments of different sizes. For example, if you look at the total returns (line 4) calculated for each of the four investments presented in the previous table, it appears that the real estate investment is the best since it has the highest dollar return. However, if you look more closely, you'll see that the real estate investment required the largest dollar outlay (the beginning-of-year figure of $3,000)—a fact that reduces its holding period return.

In order to choose the investment that provides the highest total return, simply compare the various HPRs in line 5. As you can see, the common stock's HPR of 7.25 percent is the highest. Since the return per invested dollar tends to reflect the efficiency of the investment, HPR provides a logical method for evaluating and comparing investment returns.

You can use HPR to calculate negative as well as positive values and to compare the positive return from one investment with the negative return from another. In addition, you can use HPR to calculate either historical return (as in the preceding example) or expected return.

## YIELD: THE TRUE RATE OF RETURN

While holding period return is a useful way to measure the return on investments held for a period of 1 year or less, it is generally inappropriate for longer holding periods, because it fails to consider the time value of money. For longer term investments, the present-value-based measure of yield is used instead.

Technically, investment yield is defined as the discount rate that produces a present value of benefits that equals the investment's cost. In fact, the yield calculation will tell you the true rate of return you earn on a given investment. As long as the yield on an investment is greater than or equal to the discount rate, the investment is acceptable. When the yield is below the discount rate, it is not.

To calculate the yield of most investments, you must use either future-value or present-value interest factors. In this case, we'll refer once more to the present-value interest factors given in the table on page 44. Assume you invest $1,000 today and expect to get back $1,400 at the end of a 5-year holding period. To determine the yield, you must find the discount rate that translates the $1,400 you receive 5 years from now into a present value of $1,000: First divide the present value ($1,000) by the future value ($1,400); this results in a value of .714 ($1,000/$1,400). Second, find in a table of present-value interest factors for $1 the factor for 5 years that is closest to .714. Our table shows that the closest factor is .713, which occurs at a 7 percent discount rate. Therefore, the yield on this investment is approximately 7 percent. If the investment yield must be 6 percent or higher in order to be competitive with other possible investments, this investment is an acceptable choice.

## APPROXIMATE YIELD

The yield for a stream of income is more difficult to determine. Like the yield calculation for a single cash flow demonstrated above, the yield for a stream of income is the discount rate that causes the present value of benefits to just equal the cost of the investment. One popular approximate yield formula, which can be used to estimate yield for both single cash flows and streams of income, is:

$$\text{approximate yield} = \frac{\text{average annual benefit} + \dfrac{\begin{array}{c}\text{future price} \\ \text{of investment}\end{array} - \begin{array}{c}\text{current price} \\ \text{of investment}\end{array}}{\text{number of years investment is held}}}{\dfrac{\begin{array}{c}\text{future price} \\ \text{of investment}\end{array} + \begin{array}{c}\text{current price} \\ \text{of investment}\end{array}}{2}}$$

*Single cash flow.* Let's look once more at the $1,000 investment that will be worth $1,400 in 5 years. Since the investment involves a single future cash flow, the average annual benefit is zero. Substituting this value along with a future price of $1,400, the current price of $1,000, and an investment period of 5 years into the approximate yield formula we get:

$$\text{approximate yield} = \frac{\$0 + \dfrac{\$1,400 - \$1,000}{5}}{\dfrac{\$1,400 + \$1,000}{2}}$$

$$= \frac{\$0 + \$80}{\$1,200}$$

$$= \frac{\$80}{\$1,200}$$

$$= 0.0667 = 6.67\%$$

The approximate yield of 6.67 percent is reasonably close to the actual yield of 7 percent calculated earlier.

*Stream of income.* We can use the data in the table on page 47 to illustrate the application of the approximate yield formula to a stream of income. Suppose that in the year 1994 the investment is sold for the future price of $1,200 shown in the table, and that it is the only benefit in that year. Assume further that the current price of the investment is $1,175.28. (Note: Setting the investment up this way should lead to an exact 8 percent yield, since that is the present-value interest factor used to discount the benefits to obtain the $1,175.28 value.) The average annual benefit is calculated by dividing the total annual benefits from years 1988 through 1993 of $620 (the sum of annual benefits of $90, $100, $110, $120, $100, and $100) by 7 (the number of years, 1988 through 1994, for which the investment is held). An average annual benefit of $88.57 ($620 ÷ 7) results. Substituting into the approximate yield formula:

$$\text{approximate yield} = \frac{\$88.57 + \dfrac{\$1,200 - \$1,175.28}{7}}{\dfrac{\$1,200 + \$1,175.28}{2}}$$

$$= \frac{\$88.57 + \$3.53}{\$1,187.64}$$

$$= \frac{\$92.10}{\$1,187.64}$$

$$= 0.0776, \text{ or } 7.76\%$$

The approximate yield of 7.76 percent is reasonably close to the actual yield of 8 percent. The approximate yield formula is used throughout this book to simplify what would otherwise be even more tedious yield calculations.

# 5

## MEASURING YOUR EXPOSURE TO RISK

———

When you're considering an investment, you can't look at return alone. You must also look at the investment risk, which in its simplest terms is the chance that the investment's actual return may differ from its expected return. In general, the more variable (or the broader the range of) possible returns from an investment, the greater its risk, and vice versa.

The risk associated with an investment is directly related to its expected return; the higher the return, the higher the risk. In general, your goal is to minimize risk for a given level of return or maximize the return for a given level of risk. This inverse relationship between risk and return is known as the *risk-return trade-off*.

# FORMS OF RISK

Investment risk comes in a number of different forms. Since these sources are interrelated, it is virtually impossible to measure the portion of risk attributable to any one source alone.

## BUSINESS RISK

Business risk concerns the ability of a corporation to pay investors interest, dividends, and all other returns owed them and the effect this has on investment earnings. When a company in which you've invested has inadequate earnings, or worse yet, fails, you may wind up with no return on your investment. If you're a stockholder—a part owner of this company—the value of your stock may plummet and the dividends you rely on for regular income may be reduced or canceled. If you're a bondholder—a financier of company debt—you're likely to receive some, but not necessarily all, of the amount you're owed, because the company has a legal obligation to pay its debt.

Business risk varies from business to business. For example, the business risk associated with investing in the common stock of a public utility differs from the business risk associated with investing in the stock of a struggling airline. In general, investments in similar types of firms have similar business risk, although differences in management, costs, and location can have an important impact on the bottom line.

## FINANCIAL RISK

The risk associated with the way a firm is financed is called financial risk. The larger the proportion of debt used to finance a firm and the smaller the proportion of equity (stock) financing, the greater its financial risk. Debt financing means that the company is obligated to make interest payments as well as repay the debt. These fixed payment obligations must be met before any earnings are distributed to company stockholders. When a company is unable to meet its debt obligations, it may go bankrupt or, in less serious cases, it may work out an arrangement to pay bondholder debt over an extended period of time. In either case, company stockholders will receive no dividend income and probably see the market value of their holdings drop.

## PURCHASING POWER RISK

In periods of inflation, when prices rise, the purchasing power of money declines. This means that your money buys less—and sometimes considerably less—than it did in the past. When, on the other hand, prices decline, the purchasing power of money increases.

In general, investments whose values move with general price levels (real estate, for example) are most profitable during periods of rising prices, while common stock and fixed return investments, such as savings accounts, bonds, and preferred stocks, do better when price levels drop.

## INTEREST RATE RISK

Securities that offer a fixed periodic return are especially affected by interest rate risk. As interest rates change, the prices of these securities fluctuate, decreasing with increasing interest rates and increasing with decreasing interest rates. As you will see in greater detail in Chapters 17 and 18, the prices of fixed income securities drop when interest rates rise in order to provide the same rate of return that is available on similar-risk securities. When interest rates drop, the return on fixed income securities is adjusted downward to a competitive level by an upward adjustment in the market price. Although fixed income securities are most directly affected by movements in interest rates, other vehicles such as common stocks are also influenced by them.

## LIQUIDITY RISK

The risk that you will not be able to liquidate an investment conveniently and at a reasonable price is called liquidity risk. Liquidity is especially important if you want to move in and out of various investments with little or no financial loss. In general, investments traded in thin markets, where supply and demand are small, tend to be less liquid than those traded in broad markets, where both supply and demand are strong.

Liquidity implies that you can sell an investment at a reasonable price. Although you can generally enhance the liquidity of an investment by cutting its price, you sacrifice a great deal to do so. For example, if you recently purchased a bond for $1,000 but can now only sell it conveniently for $500, the investment is not highly liquid. Bonds and stocks of major companies listed on the New York Stock Exchange are generally highly liquid, while the stocks of small companies trading over-the-counter often are not.

## MARKET RISK

Market risk tends to be caused by factors that have nothing to do with the investment itself. Changes in the political, economic, and social environment create market risk, as do changes in investor taste and preference. For example, in spite of the fact that a high-technology company has solid earnings, the stock value may drop if high-tech companies as a group lose favor in the market.

The impact these market factors have on investment returns differs from one investment to another in both the degree and the direction of change. A threat of war in the oil-rich Middle East may increase the value (and therefore the return) of a defense contractor's stock while, at the same time, causing the price of oil company stocks to plummet.

## BETA: A MODERN MEASURE OF RISK

Over the past 20 years, a theory has been developed that assesses investment return in terms of investment risk. This theory has two key parts: beta, which is a measure of risk, and the capital asset pricing model (CAPM), which relates the risk measured by beta to the level of required or expected return.

### DIVERSIFIABLE VS. NONDIVERSIFIABLE RISK

When you invest, you face two separate kinds of risk. *Diversifiable risk* (also known as *unsystematic risk*) results from such uncontrollable or random events as labor strikes, lawsuits, and regulatory actions and can generally be eliminated through diversification. Some investments are extremely sensitive to this risk while others are not affected by it at all. *Nondiversifiable risk* (also called *systematic risk*), on the other hand, affects all investments to one degree or another. War, inflation, international events, and political events are examples of this type of risk. The relationship between total risk, diversifiable risk, and nondiversifiable risk is given in the following equation:

$$\text{total risk} = \text{diversifiable risk} + \text{nondiversifiable risk}$$

Studies have shown that by including 8 to 15 carefully selected securities in your portfolio, you can eliminate or greatly reduce diversifiable risk. Assuming you hold a diversified portfolio, you should only concern yourself with nondiversifiable risk, which is like the market risk we discussed earlier, and which is inescapable. Each security possesses its own unique level of this market risk, which we can measure with beta.

### HOW TO FIND BETA

Beta is a measure of nondiversifiable risk; it shows how the price of a specific stock responds to market forces. It is found by relating the historical returns of the stock to the historical returns of the market as a whole. The measure of market return is typically the average return of all (or a large sample of) securities, such as all stocks in the Standard & Poor's 500 stock composite index or some other broad stock index. The beta for the market is set equal to 1; all other betas are viewed in relation to this value. Betas may be positive or negative. Nearly all betas are positive and fall between 0.2 and 2. The following table gives some beta values and their interpretations:

| Beta | Comment | Interpretation* |
|------|---------|-----------------|
| 2.0 | Move in same | Twice as responsive as the market. |
| 1.0 | direction as market. | Same response or risk as the market. |
| 0.5 | | Only half as responsive as the market. |
| 0 | | Unaffected by market movement. |
| −0.5 | Move in opposite | Only half as responsive as the market. |
| −1.0 | direction to market. | Same response or risk as the market. |
| −2.0 | | Twice as responsive as the market. |

*A stock that is twice as responsive as the market will experience a 2 percent change in its return for each 1 percent change in the return of the market portfolio; the return of a stock that is half as responsive as the market will change by ½ of 1 percent for each 1 percent change in the return of the market portfolio.

In general, the higher the beta, the riskier the investment. The positive or negative sign merely indicates whether the stock's return moves in the same direction as the general market (a positive beta) or in the opposite direction (a negative beta). The importance of beta in developing and monitoring portfolios of securities will be discussed in more detail in Chapters 29 and 30. Many of the large brokerage firms and subscription services publish betas for a broad range of securities, which has made betas an extremely popular way to assess investment risk.

## HOW TO USE BETA

Beta measures a security's market risk by revealing the type of response a security has to market forces. For example, if the market is expected to experience a 10 percent increase in its rate of return over the next period, then a stock having a beta of 1.5 would be expected to experience a return increase of approximately 15 percent (1.5 × 10%) over the same period of time. Because the beta of this particular stock is greater than 1, it is more volatile than the market as a whole.

If you own a stock with a positive beta, you're likely to make money when the market is up and lose it when the market is down. Take the preceding example: If the market is expected to drop by 10 percent, a stock with a beta of 1.5 is likely to drop by 15 percent. Because the stock has a beta of greater than 1, it is more responsive than the market, experiencing a 15 percent decline in its return as compared to the 10 percent decline in the market as a whole.

Stocks with betas of less than 1 are less responsive to changing returns in the market and are therefore less risky. For example, a stock with a beta of 0.5 is only half as responsive as the market as a whole. Thus, if the market goes down by 8 percent, this stock is likely to experience only a 4 percent decline.

## USING BETA TO ESTIMATE RETURN

The capital asset pricing model (CAPM) links together risk as measured by beta and the return on an asset. It therefore enables you to assess the impact of a proposed security on your portfolio's balance of risk and return and to understand the basic risk-return trade-offs involved in all types of financial decisions.

*The equation.*    Using beta as the measure of risk, the capital asset pricing model (CAPM) is given in the following equation:

   required return = risk-free rate + [beta × (market return − risk-free rate)]

where

> required return = the return required on the investment given its risk as measured by beta
>
> risk-free rate = the return that can be earned on a risk-free investment, commonly measured by the return on a U.S. Treasury bill
>
> market return = the average return on all securities, typically measured by the average return on all securities in the Standard & Poor's 500 stock composite index or some other stock index

The required return for a given security increases with increases in its beta. Quite simply, the higher the risk, the higher the required return, and vice versa.

For example, if you are considering a security with a beta of 1.25 at a time when the risk-free rate is 6 percent and the market return is 10 percent, you can determine the required return in the following way:

$$required\ return = 6\% + [1.25 \times (10\% - 6\%)]$$
$$= 6\% + [1.25 \times 4\%]$$
$$= 6\% + 5\%$$
$$= 11\%$$

Thus, you should expect an 11 percent return on the security, given its beta of 1.25. If the beta were lower, say 1, the required return would also be lower—in this case, 10 percent, or 6% + [1 × (10% − 6%)]. If the beta were higher, say 1.5, the required return would be 12 percent, or 6% + [1.5 × (10% − 6%)]. Clearly, CAPM reflects the positive mathematical relationship between risk and return; the higher the risk (beta), the higher the required return.

*The graph: the security market line (SML).*    When the capital asset pricing model is depicted graphically, it is called the security market line, as shown at the top of the next page. This line reflects the required return in the marketplace for each level of nondiversifiable risk (beta). It is always a straight line.

Risk, as measured by beta, is plotted on the horizontal axis of the graph, and required returns are plotted on the vertical axis. Using the risk-free rate of 6 percent, which is associated with a beta of zero, and the market return of 10 percent, which

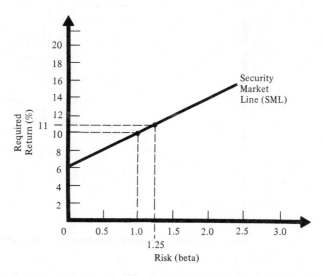

is associated with a beta of 1, the SML is plotted by connecting the two points. The required return of 11 percent for a security having a beta of 1.25 is also charted on this graph. It is clear from the SML that, as risk (beta) increases, so does the required return and vice versa.

## HOW TO EVALUATE RISK

As you can see, investment risk is often quantifiable. That is, you can tell how much risk you are taking each time you invest. This information is only valuable if you go one step further and relate the risk to your own disposition toward risk. You must ask yourself these questions: Is the amount of risk worth taking in order to get the expected return? Can I get a higher return for the same level of risk or a lower risk for the same level of return? You can answer these questions by looking at the general risk-return characteristics of alternative investments, by deciding what is an acceptable level of risk for you, and by making each investment decision in light of both risk and return.

### WEIGHING RISK AGAINST RETURN FOR EACH INVESTMENT

Different risks and different returns are possible for each type of investment vehicle. For example, while some common stocks offer low returns and low risk, others provide high returns and high risk. Despite these variations, we can make some general statements about risk-return characteristics of each of the major investment vehicles, as shown in the graph at the top of the next page.

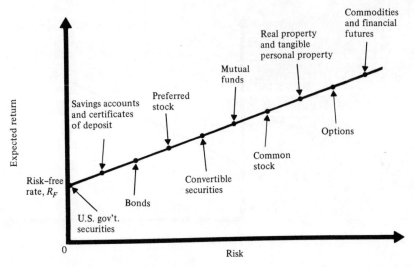

As you can see, the safest investment is U.S. government securities. But their return is also the lowest. At the other end of the spectrum, commodities and financial futures offer the highest return and the highest risk.

Let us repeat, this general pattern does not mean that all vehicles within a specific investment category behave in the same way. On the contrary, the risk-return relationship for each specific investment must be evaluated on its own. Only then can you be sure that the investment risk and return are acceptable to you.

## WHAT IS AN ACCEPTABLE LEVEL OF RISK?

Because people respond differently to risk, an acceptable level of risk to one investor may not be an acceptable level to another. As you can see in the following graph, there are three basic ways to respond to risk—by being risk-averse, risk-indifferent, and a risk-taker.

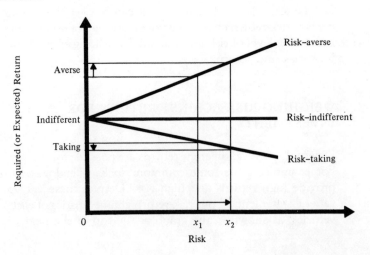

As risk goes from point $x_1$ to point $x_2$, the risk-indifferent investor requires no change in return even though the level of risk increases. The risk-averse investor, on the other hand, needs a greater return to compensate for increased risk. Most investors fall into the risk-averse category. Finally, the risk-taker is willing to give up some return while increasing investment risk. Most investors tend to accept only the risks with which they feel comfortable and, in general, tend to be more conservative than aggressive.

## TAKE THE FOLLOWING STEPS TO MAKE AN INVESTMENT DECISION

Making an intelligent investment decision requires that you put all this risk-return information together. The process of choosing one investment over another involves the following steps:

1. Using historical or projected return information, estimate the expected return over a given holding period. Use yield or present-value techniques to incorporate the time value of money in your analysis.
2. Using historical or projected return data, assess the risk associated with the investment. You can do this by comparing the beta of a stock to the market as a whole and by subjectively assessing the past return behaviors of comparable investment vehicles.
3. Evaluate the risk-return behavior of each alternative investment to make sure that the expected return is reasonable given its level of risk. If you find other vehicles with equal or lower levels of risk and greater returns, invest in them instead.
4. Select the investment vehicles that offer the highest returns associated with the level of risk you are willing to take. If, like most investors, you are risk-averse, you must be satisfied with a relatively low return. In all cases, as long as you are getting the highest return for the level of risk you're willing to accept, you've made a good investment choice.

Other factors such as taxes, liquidity, and portfolio management will also affect your investment decision. We'll take a close look at each of these in other chapters.

# TWO
## THE MARKETS
## AND HOW THEY WORK

# 6

## THE SECURITIES MARKETS

The food you eat, the clothes you wear, the books you read, all come to you through a marketplace that brings the suppliers of these products together with the people who want to buy them. Our economy could not function without these marketplaces, for there would be no way to match supply with demand. The securities markets work in much the same way as the markets for food, clothing, and books. They provide a mechanism through which the purchasers and sellers of different forms of securities come together to transact business quickly and at a fair price.

The securities markets deal in money and capital. The *money* market is where short-term securities—those with maturities of one year or less, usually valued at $100,000 or more—are bought and sold. The *capital* markets deal in stocks, bonds, and other long-term securities—those with maturities of more than one year. Since the capital markets are the focus of many of the investments we will talk about in this book, we will devote our attention to them here. These markets are classified as either primary or secondary.

# THE PRIMARY AND SECONDARY MARKETS

When a company wants to raise money by issuing new stocks, bonds, or other securities, it makes a public offering on the *primary market*. This is an extremely complicated process with fairly stringent government regulation that usually requires the services of an *investment banking firm*. Investment bankers are *underwriters*—that is, they guarantee to a corporation that it will receive at least a specified minimum amount from the securities it issues. Investment bankers also provide corporations with invaluable advice about the pricing and timing of an issue as well as other factors that might affect how the issue is received in the market. When a public offering is extremely large, the investment banker brings in other firms as partners in the deal. Together, these firms form an *underwriting syndicate*, which spreads the risk associated with selling new securities among many different firms.

The originating underwriter, with the assistance of syndicate members, puts together a *selling group*, which is responsible for distributing the new issue to the investing public. The selling group is normally made up of a large number of brokerage firms, each of which accepts responsibility for selling a certain portion of the issue.

The relationships among the participants in this process are made clear in the layout of the public offering announcement (see example on the next page). The firms that appear separately from the larger group and in a larger typeface are members of the investment banking syndicate. The remaining firms make up the selling group.

Members of the underwriting syndicate and selling group typically get paid in the form of a discount on the sale price of the securities. For example, an investment banker may pay the issuer $24 a share for stock to be sold for $25 a share. The investment banker may then sell the shares to members of the selling group for $24.75 a share. In this case, the original investment banker makes $0.75 a share ($24.75 sale price less $24 purchase price), and the members of the selling group make $0.25 a share ($25 sale price less $24.75 purchase price). Although some primary security offerings are sold directly by the issuer, the majority of new issues are sold through the mechanism we have described here.

Trading in securities does not end once the public offering of a new issue has been sold to investors. The investors in turn may wish to sell shares, while others may wish to buy them. These transactions, which are one step removed from the original offering, take place on the *secondary market*, also known as the *aftermarket*. This market, which is the most familiar market to investors, is made up of all the organized securities exchanges plus the over-the-counter market.

# THE ORGANIZED SECURITIES EXCHANGES

When you pick up your phone and tell your broker to buy 100 shares of IBM or sell 200 shares of Bank of America, you are instructing your broker to do business on your behalf on one of the organized securities exchanges. The two main ex-

## 500,000 Shares

# Warner Computer Systems, Inc.

## Common Stock

---

## Price $5 a Share

---

*Copies of the Prospectus are obtainable in any State from such of the under-
signed and such other dealers as may lawfully offer these securities in such State.*

**Drexel Burnham Lambert**
INCORPORATED

**Morgan Keegan & Company, Inc.**

} Investment Banking Syndicate

**Advest, Inc.**   **A. G. Edwards & Sons, Inc.**      **Ladenburg, Thalmann & Co. Inc.**

**Moseley Securities Corporation**                **Oppenheimer & Co., Inc.**

**Thomson McKinnon Securities Inc.**            **Tucker, Anthony & R. L. Day, Inc.**

**Robert W. Baird & Co.**   **Blunt Ellis & Loewi**   **The Chicago Corporation**   **Dain Bosworth**
INCORPORATED            INCORPORATED                                        INCORPORATED

**R. G. Dickinson & Co.**      **First of Michigan Corporation**      **Keeley Investment Corp.**

**McDonald & Company**            **The Ohio Company**            **Parker/Hunter**
SECURITIES, INC.                                                     INCORPORATED

**Piper, Jaffray & Hopwood**                    **Stifel, Nicolaus & Company**
INCORPORATED                                        INCORPORATED

} Selling Group

*September 15, 1986*

*Source: The Wall Street Journal, September 15, 1986.*

changes for stock and bond transactions are the New York Stock Exchange and the American Stock Exchange, which together account for approximately 88 percent of the total annual volume of shares traded on all organized U.S. exchanges. The remaining 12 percent of annual share volume is traded on one of 14 regional exchanges scattered throughout the country. Separate exchanges also exist for trading in options, commodities, and financial futures. In addition, foreign stock exchanges trade securities on foreign markets. As an investor, you should understand the basic structure, rules, and operation of each of these organized exchanges. Your goal is to be comfortable enough with the exchanges to conduct business on them when investment opportunities arise.

## THE NEW YORK STOCK EXCHANGE (NYSE)

The New York Stock Exchange is the biggest and most important of all the organized securities exchanges. More than 8 out of 10 shares traded on organized U.S. exchanges are traded on the NYSE.

*Membership.* A firm or individual cannot do business on the New York Stock Exchange without owning or leasing an exchange seat. Currently, there are 1,366 seats on the exchange, each of which provides its owner with exchange membership. Most NYSE members are brokerage firms, and some of these own more than one seat. Merrill Lynch, Pierce, Fenner & Smith, for example, the nation's largest brokerage firm, owns more than 20 seats.

Members fall into two broad groups based on their activities. The majority of members purchase and sell securities on behalf of their customers. A small number, however, transact business for other exchange members or for their own accounts. The following table classifies member activities. As you can see, commission brokers and specialists perform the majority of activities on the exchange.

## NYSE MEMBER ACTIVITIES

| Type of Member | Approximate % Total Membership* | Primary Activities |
|---|---|---|
| **A. MAKE TRANSACTIONS FOR CUSTOMERS** | | |
| Commission brokers | 52% | Make stock and bond purchase and sale transactions as requested by customers. |
| Bond brokers | 2 | Commission brokers who only make bond transactions for their customers. |
| **B. MAKE TRANSACTIONS FOR OTHER MEMBERS** | | |
| Independent brokers (Two-dollar brokers) | 10 | Execute orders for other brokers who are unable to do so due to excessive market activity. |
| Specialists | 29 | Make a continuous, fair, and orderly market in the issues assigned to them. They also make odd-lot purchase and sale transactions for members of the exchange. |
| **C. MAKE TRANSACTIONS FOR THEIR OWN ACCOUNT** | | |
| Registered traders | 4 | Purchase and sell securities for their own account. Must abide by certain regulations established to protect the public. |

*Because approximately 3 percent of the members are inactive, the percentages given total 97 percent.

*Listing policies.* To become listed on the NYSE, a firm must meet stringent requirements. It must have at least 2,000 stockholders each owning 100 shares or more; a minimum of 1.1 million shares of publicly held stock; a demonstrated earning power of $2.5 million before taxes at the time of the listing and $2 million before taxes for each of the preceding two years; net tangible assets of at least $16 million; and a total of at least $18 million in market value of publicly traded shares. It must also meet additional requirements of the U.S. Securities and Exchange Commission (SEC). Firms must also continue to meet these requirements after they are listed. If they do not, they may be "delisted" from the exchange. Currently over 1,500 firms, accounting for more than 2,300 stocks and 3,700 bonds, are listed on the NYSE. These include such corporate giants as IBM, General Motors, Exxon, AT&T, and General Electric. Because of their ability to meet the exchange's stringent listing requirements, these 1,500 corporations are considered the premier firms in American business. As a result, a firm may seek membership on the exchange to increase its visibility, trading activity, prestige, and status among investors. In fact, the value of stocks that shift from a lesser exchange or the over-the-counter market to the NYSE frequently rises.

## THE AMERICAN STOCK EXCHANGE (AMEX)

The American Stock Exchange is the second largest organized security exchange in the United States. It operates in a similar way to the New York Stock Exchange except that its listing requirements are not as stringent. There are approximately 660 seats on the AMEX, over 930 listed stocks, and 290 listed bonds. The AMEX includes listings for such well-known companies as BIC Pen, the *New York Times*, and Hormel Meat Packing.

## REGIONAL STOCK EXCHANGES

There are 14 regional stock exchanges in the United States:

| | |
|---|---|
| Boston Stock Exchange | National Stock Exchange |
| Cincinnati Stock Exchange | Pacific Stock Exchange |
| Colorado Stock Exchange | Philadelphia Stock Exchange |
| Detroit Stock Exchange | Pittsburgh Stock Exchange |
| Honolulu Stock Exchange | Richmond Stock Exchange |
| Intermountain Stock Exchange | Spokane Stock Exchange |
| Midwest Stock Exchange | Wheeling Stock Exchange |

The most important of the regionals are the Midwest, Pacific, and Philadelphia Exchanges. Most are modeled after the NYSE, but as you might expect, membership and listing requirements are considerably more lenient. Each regional exchange lists between 100 and 500 securities. For the most part, listed securities represent small firms operating within the region, although many major NYSE and AMEX corporations are also listed here.

*Dual listings* have the effect of increasing a security's trading activity. The *Intermarket Trading System (ITS)*—an electronic communications network—gives investors the opportunity to buy and sell dual-listed stocks at the best price. This system links a number of the regional stock exchanges to the NYSE, AMEX, and the over-the-counter market.

## FOREIGN STOCK EXCHANGES

The foreign stock exchanges create a marketplace for the buying and selling of foreign securities. The largest foreign exchanges are the Tokyo and London exchanges, which follow immediately behind the New York Stock Exchange in dollar volume of traded shares. Other important foreign exchanges are located in Zurich, Sydney, Paris, Frankfurt, Hong Kong, and South Africa. Canada has three stock exchanges of its own: the Montreal, Toronto, and Canadian Exchanges. Many of the securities traded on foreign exchanges are issued by foreign subsidiaries of American companies.

Investors who want to buy and sell the stock of foreign companies can do so in two different ways. They can purchase the foreign security through a foreign broker or a foreign branch office of a U.S. broker—a method that is often complicated by various administrative, tax, and transfer problems. Or they can purchase the stock directly on a major U.S. security exchange or in the over-the-counter market. This can be done by purchasing *American Depository Receipts (ADRs),* which are negotiable receipts for the stock of a foreign corporation that are held in trust in a foreign branch of a U.S. bank. ADRs are available in two different forms. *Company sponsored ADRs* are fully registered with the Securities and Exchange Commission and are often traded on the New York and American stock exchanges. The securities of such foreign firms as British Petroleum (Great Britain) and Sony Corporation (Japan) fall into this group. *Unsponsored ADRs* are not fully registered with the SEC and trade over-the-counter. Popular unsponsored ADRs include DeBeers Mines (South Africa) and Toyota Motors (Japan). Investors can buy and sell either type of ADR with the assistance of their broker.

## OPTIONS EXCHANGES

Options, which allow the holder to purchase or sell a financial asset at a specified price over a stated period of time, are listed and traded on the Chicago Board Options Exchange (CBOE), as well as on the American Stock Exchange, the Pacific Stock Exchange, and the Philadelphia Stock Exchange. The dominant options exchange is the CBOE, which was established in 1973. The CBOE, like other exchanges, has membership, listing, and trading requirements. Usually an option for the purchase (a call) or sale (a put) of a given financial asset is listed on only one exchange, although dual listings sometimes occur. Options exchanges deal only in security options; options to purchase or sell property are not traded in this marketplace. (Stock and other security options will be covered in detail in Chapters 25 and 26.)

## FUTURES EXCHANGES

Futures, which are contracts guaranteeing delivery of some commodity, foreign currency, or financial instrument at a specified price at a given future date, are purchased and sold on a variety of exchanges. The dominant exchange is the Chicago Board of Trade (CBT), which provides an organized forum in which members can make transactions in any of the listed commodity and financial futures contracts. A number of other futures exchanges specialize in certain commodities rather than offering the broad spectrum of commodities listed on the CBT. These include the Kansas City Board of Trade, the Minneapolis Grain Exchange, the Winnipeg Grain Exchange, the Chicago Mercantile Exchange, the New York Coffee, Sugar, and Cocoa Exchange, the New York Cotton Exchange, and the Commodities Exchange, Inc., in New York. The major currency futures exchange, on which financial futures are also traded, is the International Monetary Market (IMM), which is actually part of the Chicago Mercantile Exchange. Another futures exchange, the New York Futures Exchange (NYFE), is a subsidiary of the NYSE and deals primarily in stock index futures. (Commodities and financial futures are further covered in Chapters 27 and 28).

---

# THE OVER-THE-COUNTER MARKET

The over-the-counter market (OTC) is not a specific institution; rather it is a way of trading what are sometimes called *unlisted securities*. This market accounts for about 35 percent of the dollar volume of all shares traded in the United States. Active OTC traders are linked by a sophisticated telecommunications network in which prices are determined by both competitive bids and negotiation. The actual process depends on the general activity of the security. More than 30,000 issues are traded over-the-counter, including a majority of all stocks and corporate bonds and most government bonds. Approximately 5,000 of these issues have an active market in which frequent transactions are made. Some of the best-known OTC stocks are Intel Corporation, Apple Computer, Adolph Coors Company, Liz Claiborne, and MCI.

## THE ROLE OF DEALERS

The market price of OTC securities is determined by security traders known as *dealers*. Each *makes markets* in certain securities by offering to buy or sell at stated prices. Thus, unlike the organized exchanges, where the buyer and seller of a security are brought together by a broker, these dealers are always the second party to a transaction. For example, a dealer making a market in Lomax Enterprises might offer to buy shares from investors at $29.50 and sell shares to other investors at $31. The *bid price* is the highest price offered by the dealer to purchase a given security; the *ask price* is the lowest price at which the dealer is willing to sell the security. In the marketplace, one investor could *sell* stock in Lomax Enterprises at the (lower) bid price of $29.50 while another could buy it at the (higher) ask price of $31. The dealer makes a profit from the spread between the bid and the ask price.

## NASDAQ

OTC dealers are linked with the purchasers and sellers of securities through the *National Association of Securities Dealers Automated Quotation (NASDAQ)* system, an automated system that provides up-to-date bid and ask prices on over 4,700 highly active OTC securities. NASDAQ insures continuity in the OTC market by making it easy for buyers and sellers to locate one another. (To trade securities not quoted on NASDAQ, purchasers and sellers must find one another through references or known market-makers in the securities.) Over 2,100 of the largest and most important NASDAQ stocks are traded on the NASDAQ/National Market System (NASDAQ/NMS).

## NEW ISSUES AND SECONDARY DISTRIBUTIONS

In order to create a continuous market for unlisted securities, the OTC market also provides a forum in which new public issues, both listed and unlisted, are sold. Subsequent transactions of listed securities are made on the appropriate organized securities exchange; unlisted securities continue to trade in the OTC market. The OTC market also handles *secondary distributions*—the sale of large blocks of securities by major shareholders. In this case, organized exchanges are bypassed in order to minimize the potentially negative impact these transactions could have on the price of the securities.

## THIRD AND FOURTH MARKETS

The *third market* is the name given to over-the-counter transactions made in securities listed on one of the organized exchanges. It exists to serve the needs of large institutional investors, such as mutual funds, pension funds, and life insurance companies, by allowing them to make large transactions at a reduced cost. These transactions are typically handled by firms or dealers that are not members of an organized securities exchange. Their commission for bringing together large buyers and sellers is below what is normally charged for similar transactions on the securities exchanges. Thus this system provides sizable savings to institutional investors and minimizes the impact of the transaction on the price of the security. Since the introduction of negotiated commissions on the organized exchanges, in 1975, the importance of this market has been somewhat reduced.

The *fourth market* is the name given to transactions made directly between large institutional buyers and sellers. Unlike the third market, fourth-market transactions bypass the dealer. However, an institution may hire a dealer to help search for a suitable buyer or seller.

## REGULATING THE SECURITIES MARKETS

The Securities and Exchange Commission (SEC), an agency of the federal government, was established to enforce the Securities Exchange Acts of 1933 and 1934. These acts were aimed at regulating not only securities exchanges and securities markets but also the disclosure of information on both new and outstanding listed securities. In addition to the SEC regulations, most states have laws regarding the sale of securities within their borders. These *blue sky laws* protect investors by preventing firms from attempting to sell nothing but "blue sky." The exchanges themselves also perform a self-regulatory function through their governing bodies.

The OTC market is regulated by the National Association of Securities Dealers (NASD), which is made up of all brokers and dealers who participate in the OTC market. The NASD is a self-regulatory organization that polices the activities of brokers and dealers in order to insure that its standards are upheld. The SEC supervises the activities of NASD, thus providing investors with further protection from fraudulent activities.

## GENERAL MARKET CONDITIONS: BULL OR BEAR

Conditions in the securities markets are commonly classified as bull or bear, depending on whether the general level of prices is rising (a bull market) or falling (a bear market). Changing market conditions generally stem from changes in investor attitudes, changes in economic activity, and government actions aimed at stimulating or slowing down the level of economic activity. *Bull markets* are favorable markets normally associated with investor optimism, economic recovery, and governmental stimulus; *bear markets* are unfavorable markets normally associated with investor pessimism, economic slowdowns, and government restraint. Over the past 60 or so years, the behavior of the stock market has been generally bullish, reflecting the growth and prosperity of the economy. After a period of somewhat bearish behavior, a record-breaking bull market began in August of 1982, peaked in August 1987, and two months later, on Monday, October 19, crashed, as the market fell by over 22 percent on that day. Since then, the market has exhibited bearish behavior. In general, the investor experiences higher (or positive) returns on common stock investments during a bull market. During bear markets many investors turn to alternative vehicles to obtain higher and less risky returns. It is not unusual to find securities that are bullish in a bear market or bearish in a bull market. Market conditions are difficult to predict, and usually can be identified only with the benefit of hindsight.

# 7

## HOW THE SECURITIES
## MARKETS WORK

---

It almost seems like an impossible feat: you call your broker on the phone, place an order to buy or sell a security, and within minutes the order is complete. Even though we're all used to dealing with high-speed computers that produce these kinds of results, it's hard to take this system for granted, considering the millions of trades that take place every day.

Our aim in this chapter is to show you exactly what happens to your order after you hang up the phone. Specifically, we'll take a close look at how two securities markets work: the New York Stock Exchange, which is the most important organized securities exchange in the world, and the NASDAQ system for trading over-the-counter stocks.

Getting to know how orders are executed on these markets will make you more comfortable with the securities trading process. However, it should not reduce your awe at what is truly a remarkable system.

# THE NEW YORK STOCK EXCHANGE

Look at any picture ever taken of the trading floor of the New York Stock Exchange during business hours. What you see—or at least what you appear to see—is sheer chaos. Exchange members and clerks are scurrying to and fro and everyone seems to be shouting. With all this going on, it's difficult to imagine that anything of real value is being accomplished.

This perception is as wrong as it could be, for the New York Stock Exchange, on the corner of Wall and Broad Streets in New York City, is the most important organized securities exchange in the world. It's where the giants of U.S. industry trade, including IBM, General Motors, AT&T, General Electric, and Exxon. Many would call it the heart of the U.S. free enterprise system.

In 1985, 27.5 billion shares traded on the NYSE, 49 percent of the total common stock share volume. The dollar value of these securities far exceeded that of other markets, totaling $970.5 billion, or nearly 69 percent of the dollar value of all shares traded on all organized exchanges and the over-the-counter markets. This despite the fact that there are far fewer companies and issues on the New York Stock Exchange than in NASDAQ:

|  | NYSE | NASDAQ |
|---|---|---|
| Companies | 1,540 | 4,136 |
| Issues | 2,319 | 4,723 |

The dollar volume is easily explained by the importance and capitalization of companies doing business on the New York Stock Exchange: they are the nation's biggest and richest.

The New York Stock Exchange provides a marketplace in which you can buy and sell securities. It brings traders together by matching the best bid price (the offering price to buy) with the best ask price (the offering price to sell). In its simplest terms, the exchange is nothing more than an auction in which investors who want to sell come together with those who want to buy and exchange securities at an agreed-upon price.

## TRACING AN ORDER ON THE NYSE

Let's trace an order from the time you make it to see how the system works. (The American Stock Exchange and the regional stock exchanges are all patterned after the NYSE, so the system we describe here applies to the other exchanges as well.)

When you give the order to your broker, he or she is responsible for executing it at the highest possible price if you are selling and at the lowest if you are buying.

Suppose you decide to buy 100 shares of IBM at the market price. You call your broker to place the order. Your broker then communicates it via computer to the specialist on the exchange floor whose job it is to handle the buying and selling of IBM common stock. This specialist is located at a specific post on the trading floor. (Currently, there are some 400 specialists on the New York Stock Exchange operating out of 15 trading posts.)

Orders are transmitted by means of the Designated Order Turnaround (DOT) system, which electronically links member firms to the specialists in various stocks. This instantaneous order transmittal system brings your order into contact with all other buy and sell orders for IBM, thus allowing the forces of supply and demand to determine the market price at which the stock will trade.

Orders that are received before the stock market opens are processed by another electronic system called the Opening Automated Report Service (OARS). This system matches all backlogged buy and sell orders before the market opens, allowing the specialist to determine the stock's opening price. These electronic systems give you immediate access to traders wanting to sell IBM, and guarantee that you will buy the stock at the best possible price.

*The role of the specialist.*    Specialists are at the heart of the organized market trading system. They are matchmakers who make sure that all orders are filled. In essence, specialists act as both brokers and dealers for particular securities: They are brokers—that is, agents for others—when they take responsibility for the proper execution of a trade brought to them by someone else. When, on the other hand, they buy and sell stock from their own account in order to maintain a "fair and orderly market," they are principals in the transaction along with you.

To maintain a ready supply of a stock, specialists are willing to pay a premium for it. Say IBM just sold at 120. The next buy offer is 119¼, while the next offer to sell is 120¼. In order to close the gap between these buy and sell offers, a specialist steps in and bids 119¾ for 100 shares, using his or her own account to make the bid, thus narrowing the gap between the buy and sell offers from 1 full point to half a point. The specialist then stands ready to purchase the stock at 119¾—a move that gives the seller a better price than had the specialist not intervened. In the process, specialists maintain a smooth market by eliminating big jumps in market price. They sell stocks from their own accounts to maintain the market as well.

Specialists never move from their spots on the trading floor and are experts on one or more securities. In 1986, the average specialist handled 27 different stocks. Specialists "keep the books" in their stocks and act in the place of brokers who cannot wait at the trading booth until the customer's specific price is reached. No matter what kind of order you place, part of the commission you pay your broker goes to the specialist.

*Doing business in odd or round lots.*    An odd lot is less than 100 shares of a security. A round lot is a 100-share unit or a multiple of 100 shares. Thus, you are dealing in an odd lot if you buy 25 shares of stock, but a round lot if you buy 200 shares. A trade of 225 shares is a combination of the two.

Since all transactions made on the floor of the major stock exchanges are made in round lots, the purchase or sale of odd lots requires the assistance of a specialist. Frequently, an additional fee is charged for the specialist's services. This fee, which usually amounts to between 12½ and 25 cents a share, is known as an *odd-lot differential.* Individual investors in the early stages of their investment programs make mostly odd-lot trades.

*Completing the trade.*   Once your order is executed on the trading floor, you receive confirmation of it from your broker. If you bought a security, you are required to pay for it within 5 business days. If you sold it, the broker is required to deliver your money within the same period of time.

The millions of transactions that take place every year on the NYSE, the AMEX, and NASDAQ are processed through the National Securities Clearing Corporation which debits and credits all investor accounts after transactions are made.

## BASIC SECURITIES ORDERS

There are three basic types of securities orders: limit orders, stop-loss orders, and the most common type, market orders. It is important to note that there is no charge for placing any of these orders, only to execute them. Brokerage fees are levied only after the order has actually been transacted.

*Limit order.*   An order to buy at or below a specified price, or sell at or above a specified price, is known as a *limit order.* When you place a limit order, your broker transmits it to a specialist dealing in the security on the floor of the exchange. The specialist executes the order as soon as the specified market price (or a better one) exists and all other orders with precedence have been filled. Orders with precedence include similar orders received earlier and orders with better specified prices (buy orders at a higher specified price and sell orders at a lower specified price). You can specify that the order remain in effect until a certain date or until canceled; the latter type is called a GTC or *good till canceled* order. The GTC order remains on the specialist's books until executed or canceled by your broker.

Assume, for example, that you place a limit order to buy 100 shares of a stock currently selling at 30½ at a limit price of $30. Once the specialist has cleared all similar orders received before yours and once the market price of the stock has fallen to $30 or less, your order is executed. It is possible, of course, that your order might expire (if it is not a GTC order) before the stock price drops to $30.

Although a limit order can be quite effective, it can also keep you from making a transaction. If, for instance, you put in a buy order at $30 or less and the stock price moves from its current $30.50 to $42 while you are waiting, your limit order prevents your order from being filled. As a result, you lose the opportunity to earn $11.50 a share ($42 − $30.50).

Limit orders for the sale of a stock can also get you into trouble when the stock price comes close to—but never reaches—that limit before dropping substantially. Generally, limit orders are most effective when a stock price fluctuates a great deal, since you have a better chance that the order will be executed.

*Stop-loss order.*   An order to sell a security when its market price reaches or drops below a specified level is called a *stop-loss* or *stop order.* Stop-loss orders are placed on securities you already own. The stop-loss order is placed on the specialist's book and becomes active once the stop price has been reached. When activated, the stop order becomes an order to sell the security at the best available price. Unfortunately, stop orders do not guarantee that you'll get the price you want. If the price of the security is plummeting, the sale could take place well below the price at which the stop was initiated.

You can use this mechanism to protect yourself to some extent against a rapid decline in share price, however. For example, assume you own 100 shares of Willard Industries, which is currently selling for $35 a share. Because you believe the stock price could decline rapidly at any time, you place a stop order to sell at $30. If the stock price does in fact drop to $30, the specialist will sell the 100 shares of Willard Industries at the best price available at that time. But if the market price declines to $28 prior to the sale, you will receive less than the $30. Of course, if the market price stays above $30 you will have lost nothing as a result of placing the order, since the stop order will not be filled.

The principal risk in using stop-loss orders is *whipsawing,* which refers to a situation where a stock temporarily drops in price and then bounces back upward. If, for example, Willard Industries dropped to 30, then 29½, and then rallied back to 37, your stop-loss at 30 would have forced a sale—and you would lose the chance to benefit from the price increase.

Stop orders can also be placed to buy a stock, though they are far less common than sell orders. For example, you may place a stop order to buy 100 shares of MJ Enterprises, currently selling for $70 a share, once its price rises to, say, $75—the stop price. These orders are commonly used to limit losses on short sales (discussed later) and to get into a stock as its price appears to be rising.

Stop orders are sometimes preferred over limit orders even though they don't guarantee execution at the specified price or better. The preference for them stems from the fact that once the specified price is hit the order is executed. In the case of limit orders, execution is not guaranteed if other orders are ahead of yours on the specialist's book.

*Market order.*   In contrast, *market orders* are orders to buy or sell stock at the best price available at the time the order is placed. This is the fastest way to have an order filled, since market orders are executed as soon as they reach the exchange floor. Because of the speed with which market orders are executed, the buyer or seller of a security can be fairly certain that the price at which the order is transacted will be very close to the market price prevailing at the time the order was placed.

# THE NASDAQ MARKET FOR OVER-THE-COUNTER STOCKS

While it's easy to recognize the New York Stock Exchange as a bustling marketplace, there's little about the NASDAQ market for over-the-counter stocks that even suggests a traditional securities market—at least on the surface. There's no common trading floor or even a common trading city. And there are no specialists making markets in specific stocks. On the contrary, some 500 NASDAQ market-makers are dispersed in 38 states and the District of Columbia and never come together to meet one another.

This all makes sense when you realize that the NASDAQ over-the-counter market isn't a place at all, but rather a way of doing business. The NASDAQ system is a computerized stock market that puts you in touch with other traders through what is really nothing more than an extremely sophisticated electronic bulletin board.

## MARKET-MAKERS: THE HUB OF THE NASDAQ SYSTEM

At the heart of the NASDAQ system is continuous competition among multiple market-makers, or dealers, who are connected to one another by way of a sophisticated computer network. Market-makers are securities firms that are always able to buy or sell specific securities for or from their own inventories. Because market-makers are in constant competition with one another to make transactions, they eliminate the need for the specialist who is at the heart of the organized exchange system. The job of the specialist—to match buy and sell orders that come onto the trading floor and to insure an orderly market by filling unmatched orders—is made obsolete by the continuous competition among market-makers who are linked via computer to tens of thousands of brokers across the country. Looking at it another way, the participation of numerous market-makers in the sale and purchase of each stock creates what many experts consider to be the ultimate free marketplace. Your broker's job is simple: to review the bid and ask prices on the computer screen and choose the best one for you.

Any dealer who can satisfy NASDAQ's capital requirements can become a market-maker in a particular stock. How many choose to take a position in a stock depends largely on the forces of supply and demand. In 1987, the 500 market-makers in the NASDAQ system held more than 40,000 positions in various stocks. As many as 49 market-makers took a position in a single issue—a situation that guaranteed tremendous competition and the most favorable prices for investors.

At times, the competition is so fierce that if one market-maker lowers or raises the price by as little as ⅛ of a point (12½ cents), the others will follow suit, not willing to lose the deal. The average NASDAQ issue has 8 market-makers, while issues traded on NASDAQ's National Market System (NMS) have 11. The NMS lists more than 2,100 of the most actively traded OTC issues, including such corporate giants as MCI, Apple Computer, and Intel.

The system protects investors against abuses by requiring market-makers to trade at the price they display on the NASDAQ computer system and by requiring that this price be closely related to the stock's current market value. With so many market-makers ready to buy and sell, the system also insures a flow of continuous trading—a claim the specialist-centered exchanges often cannot make. On the organized exchanges, when there is a large volume of orders for a particular listed stock, specialists may halt the trading until they can balance the buy and sell orders—a situation that gives investors no choice but to wait until the backlog is resolved.

## TRACING AN ORDER THROUGH NASDAQ

The best way to describe how the NASDAQ system works is to trace a trade. Suppose you want to buy 100 shares of Liz Claiborne, Inc., an OTC stock, at the market. You contact your broker, who immediately inputs the NASDAQ symbol for Liz Claiborne (LIZC) into a desktop computer terminal. The readout tells your broker at what price various market-makers are willing to sell the stock. Your broker picks the best price and passes it on to you. In this case, the best price is $20 a share.

At the same time, your broker learns the daily high, low, and last sale prices for the stock and, for actively traded stocks like Liz Claiborne, the daily volume of trades. All this readily available information helps you decide the best trading strategy.

When you actually place your order, it is handled in one of two ways. If the brokerage firm you deal with makes a market in Liz Claiborne, it will sell the stock to you from its own inventory, meeting the best price on the computer system. About half of all retail orders are filled in this way.

If the firm does not make a market in the stock, your broker finds the best price listed on the computer screen. This process is simplified even more by the Small Order Execution System (SOES), which guarantees that you will get the best bid or ask price if you trade 1,000 shares or fewer of National Market System securities or 500 or fewer of all other NASDAQ stocks. This automatic execution system expedites about half of all NASDAQ transactions and frees telephone and teletype systems to handle larger orders.

Within seconds your trade is complete and you receive notification of it from your broker.

This system of competitive market-makers has proven so attractive that NASDAQ is seriously challenging the supremacy of the organized exchanges—at least in terms of share volume. In 1985, NASDAQ's share volume accounted for 37 percent of all stocks trading on domestic markets. This was 10 times the volume of the American Stock Exchange and ¾ the volume of the New York Stock Exchange.

# 8

## YOU AND YOUR BROKER: PARTNERS IN THE SECURITIES MARKETS

---

Investing is a team effort. One of the worst mistakes you can make is to think of investing as something you must do on your own without advice. Although, in the end, no one can make your investment decisions for you—and the rewards or disappointments that come from them are yours as well—you should have a staunch ally in the person of your stockbroker.

Think of your broker as someone who can help you cut through the overwhelming amount of investment information that you're exposed to every day and help you get what you're after. You'll appreciate that a good broker is nothing short of indispensable. Your broker will not only guide you through the maze of rules and regulations that govern the various securities markets, but also give you valuable advice that can mean the difference between investment success and failure.

### STOCKBROKERS: YOUR LINK TO THE MARKET

To buy and sell securities you need a stockbroker, also known as an account executive or financial consultant. Stockbrokers are licensed by the exchanges on which they place orders. They are bound by the ethical guidelines of the exchanges and the SEC.

Stockbrokers work for brokerage firms that own seats on the exchanges. When your broker receives your order, he or she transmits it to a member of the securities exchange who executes it for you. For example, the largest brokerage firm, Merrill Lynch, Pierce, Fenner & Smith, has offices in most U.S. cities. Orders from these offices are transmitted to the main office of Merrill Lynch in New York City and then to the floor of the stock exchange where they are executed. Confirmation of the order is sent back to the broker placing the order, who then relays it to the customer. This process is carried out in a matter of minutes with the use of sophisticated telecommunications networks.

All brokers provide the following services:

- Holds your security certificates for safekeeping. Stocks kept by the broker are said to be held in the firm's *street name,* since the broker can liquidate them for you without your signature.
- Provides protection against the loss of securities or cash through the *Securities Investor Protection Corporation (SIPC),* an agency of the federal government established by the Securities Investor Protection Act of 1970. SIPC was established to protect customer accounts against the consequences of brokerage firm failure. It insures each customer's account for up to $500,000 except that claims for cash are limited to $100,000 per customer. SIPC insurance does not guarantee that the dollar value of the securities will be recovered; only that the securities themselves will be returned. Some brokerage firms insure certain customer accounts for amounts in excess of the SIPC coverage.
- Sends you a statement at the end of each month describing all your transactions for the month and showing commission charges, interest charges, dividends and interest received, and your account balance.

Orders for over-the-counter securities must be executed through market-makers, who are dealers specializing in that security. The NASDAQ system, along with the available information on who makes markets in certain securities, allows the brokers to execute orders in OTC securities. Normally, OTC transactions can be executed rapidly, since market-makers maintain inventories of the securities in which they deal. Although the procedure for executing orders on organized exchanges may differ from that in the OTC market, you always place orders with a broker in the same manner, regardless of the market in which the security is traded.

## FULL-SERVICE BROKERS VS. THE DISCOUNTERS

Stockbrokers spend most of their time buying and selling securities for their clients; that is, executing their clients' orders at the best possible market price. Since the passage of the Securities Acts Amendments of 1975, brokers have been permitted to charge commissions based on what the market will bear. Most firms use fixed commission schedules for the small transactions made mostly by individual investors, and negotiated commissions for their large institutional clients. Individuals who maintain a sizable account—typically in the range of $25,000 or more—can also negotiate the cost of commissions. Thus, brokerage firms compete not only on the basis of services offered, but also on the basis of cost.

Full-service brokers, who charge more—and sometimes substantially more—for transactions than discount brokers, justify their premium price by the range of services they offer, including research and summary reports that can pinpoint specific investment opportunities. A brokerage house like E. F. Hutton or Prudential-Bache has a large, extremely sophisticated research staff that periodically issues analyses of economic, market, industry, and company behavior and recommends specific securities to buy and sell. You can expect your full-service broker to individualize these recommendations for you by matching specific securities to your short- and long-term investment goals.

Although discount brokers offer neither research information nor investment advice, they draw millions of customers looking for lower commission fees. Depending on the size and the type of transaction you make, discount brokers can save you between 30 and 70 percent of the commissions charged by full-service brokers. Since these savings are so substantial, you must weigh the added commissions you pay your full-service broker against the value of the advice you receive.

Discount brokers also offer convenience. Charles Schwab & Co., the nation's largest discounter, with 20 percent of the discount business, has over 90 branches throughout the country and 1 million customers. The firm offers 24-hour service and access to a variety of accounts, including IRAs, asset management accounts, and mutual funds.

Many investors use both a full-service and a discount broker—a strategy that makes a great deal of sense. If you know exactly what you want to buy or sell, use your discounter to save on commission fees. When you need advice about the direction of the economy, the market, or a specific security, then turn to your full-service broker.

The rapidly growing volume of business done by discount brokers like Charles Schwab has encouraged banks and insurance companies to enter the discount brokerage field. It has also put pressure on full-service brokers to lower commission fees and expand client services. Many full-service brokers now offer special discounts to high-volume customers, favorable interest rates on margin accounts, special research reports, lower minimum investment requirements for universal accounts, and interest on all uninvested balances.

Full-service brokers also attract clients with personal service. You can go to your broker's office and follow your stocks on the quotation board, a large screen that electronically displays all NYSE and AMEX security transactions within minutes of their execution. A telequote system, which provides a capsule description of almost all securities and their prices via a computer terminal—is also available in many cases.

## SELECTING A STOCKBROKER

If you feel you need a full-service stockbroker, you should select a person who understands your investment goals and who has the know-how to help you reach them. Choose a broker who has many of the same basic feelings about investing that you do. If you're conservative, for example, don't choose someone who talks about the pot of gold at the end of the speculative growth company rainbow.

Probably the best way to find a broker is to ask friends or business associates for recommendations. It's not important—and often not a good idea—to know your broker personally. A strictly business relationship eliminates the possibility that social concerns will get in the way of your investment goals.

This does not mean that your broker's sole interest is commissions. On the contrary, responsible brokers do everything they can to get to know your personal financial needs inside out and to establish a long-term broker-client relationship based on what they can do for you. If you feel your broker is "churning" your account—recommending buy and sell transactions simply to generate commissions—find another broker fast. Your goal is to choose someone who understands your investment goals and provides the services you need at the lowest possible cost.

# HOW TO OPEN AN ACCOUNT

Your relationship with your broker starts when you open your account. The information you provide on the personal data card gives your broker a good idea of your personal financial situation, including your investment goals and the amount of money you want to invest.

When you open an account, you form a legal relationship with your broker. For example, you provide instructions relating to the transfer and custody of securities and the borrowing of funds through a margin account. (Margin accounts are described in detail in Chapter 10.) If you are acting as a trustee, an executor, or are a corporation, additional documents are needed to establish the account. No laws or rules prohibit you from establishing accounts with more than one broker. Indeed, that's exactly what many astute investors do in order to benefit from a variety of research reports and buy and sell recommendations.

## CHOOSING THE RIGHT ACCOUNT

You can establish a number of different types of accounts with a stockbroker. We will look briefly at several of the more popular types.

*Single or joint.*  A brokerage account may be either single or joint. Joint accounts are most common between husband and wife or parent and child. The account of a minor (a person less than 18 years of age) is a *custodial account.* In this case, a parent or guardian must be part of all transactions. Sometimes a married couple will have two or more accounts—each spouse will have a single account and together they will have a joint account. Regardless of which account form you maintain, the names of the account holders are used to identify the account.

*Cash or margin.* In a cash account, the most common type of account, you can make only cash transactions. That is, you must cover the total cost of every purchase with cash. Despite this requirement, you can place buy orders even though you do not have enough cash in your account to cover the cost of the transaction, because you are given 5 business days to deliver the cash to the brokerage firm. Similarly, the firm is given 5 business days to deposit the proceeds from the sale of securities into your account.

A margin account allows you to borrow money from the brokerage firm in order to make purchases. Before allowing you to open this kind of account, the brokerage firm will determine whether you are a good credit risk in the same way a bank does when you take out a loan. As in a bank, you pay interest on the money you borrow.

*Discretionary.* You can choose to establish a discretionary account, which gives your broker the right to make purchase and sale transactions for you without your specific approval. The organized exchanges generally oppose this practice because they fear that unscrupulous brokers will manipulate these accounts for their own profit. To make sure this doesn't happen, the exchanges require that an officer of the brokerage firm supervise all discretionary accounts.

A more limited type of discretionary account permits a broker to buy or sell an amount of a given security specified by the customer at a time or price the broker believes to be in the customer's best interest. Your decision to extend discretionary privileges to your broker depends on how much confidence you have in him or her as well as on the amount of time you can devote to trading. These accounts are usually established by wealthy investors.

# INVESTMENT ADVISORS

Many individual investors turn to investment advisors for help. No matter how much or how little service you need, you'll find many advisors ready to give it to you for what is often a substantial fee.

The products provided by investment advisors range from broad general advice to specific and extremely detailed analyses and recommendations. You might, for example, receive an analysis of how recent swings in the Producer Price Index will affect the general market, or suggestions to buy and sell specific securities.

## TYPES OF ADVISORS

Investment advice can come from a number of different sources including stock-brokers, bankers, subscription services, and individual advisors and advisory firms. Often these advisors are recommended by, or work in conjunction with, a financial planner.

*Financial planners.*   Financial planners work with individual clients to develop personal financial plans. They analyze assets, liabilities, and sources of income and suggest ways of manipulating these different factors in order to achieve lifetime financial goals. The planning process involves collecting and analyzing all relevant data, identifying financial objectives, developing a written plan, helping to implement the plan, and periodically reviewing and revising it. In exchange for these services, the planner receives a fee. In addition, he or she may receive commissions on the sale of insurance, real estate, and other investments. Today, most professional financial planners are either Certified Financial Planners (CFPs) or Chartered Financial Consultants (ChFCs). (We'll discuss these designations later in the chapter.)

*Stockbrokers.*   The primary role of the stockbroker is to buy and sell securities for clients. In exchange for this service, brokers are paid a commission that is their primary source of income. Stockbrokers also provide clients with information and advice including portfolio analysis. This analysis—which may include specific recommendations to improve portfolio performance—is generally provided on a fee basis.

*Bankers.*   Bankers, like stockbrokers, often give customers investment advice. This advice typically comes from trust officers who are involved in investing funds held in trust for customers. The advice they give ranges from strict bookkeeping, in which the bank may act as custodian for the investor's securities, to managing (often as part of a trust agreement) an individual's complete investment portfolio.

Typically, banks require a minimum portfolio of $40,000 to $50,000 before they will agree to handle your account. Because banks tend to recommend higher quality investments, their advice is generally conservative. Over the past few years, a growing number of banks have established investment advisory departments, which, for a fee, will manage the investment portfolios of small investors. Many brokerage firms have set up similar operations.

*Subscription services.*   You can also get investment advice through subscription services and investment letters. These publications offer advisory services to subscribers ranging from advice on the economy, markets, and specific securities to periodic portfolio reviews and even portfolio management. The amount of personal advice you can expect as part of the basic service is clearly stated in advance, as are services available on a fee basis.

*Individual advisors and advisory firms.*   Qualified individuals will handle your portfolio for you for a substantial fee. These individuals are experts in such vital areas as changing tax laws and the various securities markets. They use their specialized knowledge to help clients achieve their short- and long-term financial goals. Some advisors will only handle portfolios on a discretionary basis—that is, they will only agree to manage your account if you give them complete control of your entire portfolio. For the most part, however, advisors do not demand this control and instead make portfolio recommendations directly to clients. Because of the nature of their service, most individual investment advisors have relatively few clients and are extremely selective in choosing them. One of their most important requirements is portfolio size; most will not handle clients with portfolios smaller than $100,000.

Investment advisory firms provide the same service on a larger scale. These firms have staffs of researchers and advisors specializing in certain types of portfolios. Some may specialize in managing large, growth-oriented portfolios while others may concentrate on more conservative, income-oriented portfolios. Clients are assigned to staff members on the basis of the size and objectives of their portfolios. Although these firms prefer to manage portfolios on a discretionary basis, they will agree in many cases to consult with clients before transactions are made. Most investment advisory firms are extremely sophisticated operations that rely on computer-based models to develop investment strategies. The minimum portfolio size is usually $100,000.

## REGULATION OF ADVISORS

The Investment Advisors Act was passed in 1940 in order to make sure that investment advisors give clients complete information about their backgrounds, disclose potential conflicts of interest, and so on. The act requires professional advisors to register and file periodic reports with the SEC. A 1960 amendment extended the SEC's powers to permit it to inspect the records of investment advisors and to revoke the registration of those who violate the act's provisions. Persons such as financial planners, stockbrokers, bankers, and accountants, who provide investment advice in addition to their main professional activity, are not regulated by the act.

In order to provide additional protection, many states have passed similar legislation requiring investment advisors to register and abide by the guidelines established by the state law. The federal and state laws regulating the activities of professional investment advisors do *not* guarantee competence; rather, they are intended to protect investors against fraudulent and unethical practices. It is important to recognize that, at present, *no* law or regulatory body controls entrance into the field. Therefore, investment advisors range from highly informed professionals to totally incompetent amateurs.

In order to increase your chances of receiving competent advice, choose an advisor who is professionally certified. Look for the letters CFA (Chartered Financial Analyst), CFP (Certified Financial Planner), ChFC (Chartered Financial Consultant), CLU (Chartered Life Underwriter), or CPA (Certified Public Accountant) after the advisor's name. Although these certifications do not guarantee anything, they tell you that these advisors have completed coursework in specific investment areas—a fact that generally indicates that they are not faking their expertise.

## THE COST OF INVESTMENT ADVICE

Professional investment advice typically costs between ¼ of 1 percent and 2 percent annually of the amount of money being managed. For large portfolios, the fee is typically in the range of ¼ to ¾ percent. For small portfolios (less than $100,000) an annual fee ranging from 1 to 2 percent of the amount managed is not unusual. These fees generally cover complete portfolio management, excluding, of course, purchase or sale commissions. The cost of periodic investment advice not provided as part of a subscription service may be based on a fixed fee or an hourly consultation charge.

## INVESTMENT CLUBS

If you are just beginning to invest or if you firmly believe that two or more heads are likely to be better than one, you might want to consider joining an investment club. Investment clubs are legal partnerships binding a group of investors (partners) to a specified organizational structure, operating procedures, and purpose. The goal of most clubs is to make investments with moderate risk in order to earn favorable long-term returns; only rarely do investment clubs aim for speculative short-term capital gains.

The typical investment club is made up of a group of people with similar goals who want to pool their knowledge and money to create a jointly owned portfolio. Each club member is responsible for obtaining and analyzing data on specific investment vehicles or strategies. At periodic meetings, members present their findings and recommendations to the group as a whole. This generally leads to an extensive discussion, after which the group decides whether or not to pursue the proposed idea. Most clubs require members to make scheduled contributions to the club's treasury in order to steadily increase the pool of investable funds. Although most clubs concentrate on security investments, they are occasionally formed to invest in options, commodities, and real estate.

The National Association of Investors Corporation (NAIC), which has approximately 6,300 affiliated clubs, publishes a variety of useful materials and also sponsors regional and national meetings on club organization and activities and investment techniques and strategies. If you're thinking of forming a club or joining an existing one, you can either call the NAIC (313-543-0612) or write (1515 E. 11th Mile Road, Royal Oak, MI 48067) or ask your stockbroker for advice.

# 9

## THE NUTS AND BOLTS
## OF TRADING

---

We'll look closely now at the transaction costs for many of the investment vehicles we talk about in this book and at the price quotations for these securities. You should be able to improve your returns by keeping on top of current prices and by knowing exactly how much it will cost you when you buy and sell. This is especially important since commission costs can eat up most or all of your profit.

## COMMON STOCKS

### PRICE QUOTATIONS FOR COMMON STOCKS

Investors in the stock market have come to rely on a highly efficient information system that quickly disseminates market prices. The stock quotes that appear daily in the financial press are a vital part of that information system. To see how price quotations work and what they mean, consider the following NYSE stock quotations from *The Wall Street Journal* of September 23, 1987, for trading activity that occurred the previous business day. For purposes of our example, we'll focus on the Walt Disney Company.

| 52-Week High | 52-Week Low | Stock | Div | Yld % | PE Ratio | Sales 100s | High | Low | Last | Chg. |
|---|---|---|---|---|---|---|---|---|---|---|
| 13¾ | 10 | DianaCp | .30 | 2.5 | 13 | 5 | 12 | 11⅞ | 11⅞ | − ⅛ |
| 60¾ | 37½ | Diebold | 1.20 | 2.4 | 20 | 219 | 49⅜ | 49 | 49⅛ | ... |
| 198¼ | 88½ | Digital | | ... | 22 | 10451 | 190 | 182¼ | 190 | + 7½ |
| 82½ | 36 | Disney | .32 | .4 | 26 | 5594 | 74½ | 71½ | 74½ | + 1¾ |
| 29⅞ | 21 | DEI | 1.48 | 5.2 | 23 | 137 | 28⅞ | 28¼ | 28⅝ | + ⅛ |
| 7⅜ | 4¾ | DivrsIn | | ... | ... | 42 | 5⅞ | 5⅝ | 5⅞ | + ⅛ |
| 49⅞ | 39½ | DomRs | 2.96 | 7.0 | 9 | 1551 | 42¼ | 41⅜ | 42¼ | + 1 |
| 45 | 32½ | Donald | .66 | 1.6 | 17 | 1657 | 41 | 40½ | 40½ | − ¼ |
| 45⅜ | 29½ | Donley s | .70 | 1.7 | 19 | 1166 | 40½ | 38⅝ | 40½ | + ⅞ |
| 76½ | 39⅞ | Dover | 1.12 | 1.5 | 29 | 542 | 73¾ | 71¼ | 73¾ | + 1¾ |
| 104⅝ | 51⅛ | DowCh | 2.20 | 2.2 | 22 | 11411 | 102 | 96½ | 101⅛ | + 3⅜ |
| 56¼ | 31⅞ | DowJns | .64 | 1.3 | 24 | 1229 | 48 | 45⅛ | 47¾ | + 2 |
| 22⅞ | 17 | Downey | .36 | 1.9 | 5 | 22 | 18¾ | 18½ | 18¾ | + ⅛ |
| 21⅞ | 15½ | Dravo | .25i | ... | 37 | 244 | 19 | 18⅞ | 18⅞ | − ⅛ |
| 35⅝ | 17⅝ | Dresr | .40 | 1.2 | ... | 1574 | 33⅞ | 32¼ | 33 | + ⅝ |
| 25½ | 18⅝ | DrexB | 1.86 | 9.1 | ... | 18 | 20¾ | 20¼ | 20½ | + ¼ |
| 45½ | 23⅞ | Dreyfus | .48 | 1.5 | 15 | 3532 | 32¼ | 30½ | 32¼ | + 1 |
| 131 | 77¾ | duPont | 3.40 | 3.0 | 18 | 7978 | 115⅞ | 110 | 115¼ | + 4½ |
| 66 | 56 | duPnt pf | 4.50 | 7.6 | ... | 59 | 59 | 58¼ | 59 | + ¾ |
| 10⅞ | 8¼ | DufPh n | .55e | 6.5 | ... | 2095 | 8½ | 8¼ | 8½ | + ¼ |
| 51¾ | 39⅜ | DukeP | 2.80 | 6.1 | 11 | 1199 | 45¾ | 44¼ | 45¾ | + 1¼ |
| 106½ | 91⅛ | Duke pf | 8.70 | 9.4 | ... | z800 | 92½ | 92½ | 92½ | + 1⅜ |
| 103½ | 84⅞ | Duke pf | 8.20 | 9.4 | ... | z1250 | 87 | 85½ | 87 | + 1 |

*Source: The Wall Street Journal*, September 23, 1987.

Stock prices are quoted in eighths of a dollar, with each eighth of a point worth 12½ cents. We'll now analyze the various columns:

The first two columns in the quotation, labeled *High* and *Low*, contain the highest and lowest prices at which the stock sold during the past 52 weeks. Note that Disney traded between 82½ and 36 during the period from September 23, 1986 to September 23, 1987.

The figure immediately following the abbreviated company name is the annual cash dividend paid on each share of stock. In the case of Disney, it was \$.32. This is followed by the stock's dividend yield and P/E ratio (explained later).

The daily volume is listed next in lots of 100 shares. Thus, the figure 5594 means that 559,400 shares of Disney stock were traded on September 22 ($5594 \times 100 = 559{,}400$).

The *High*, *Low*, and *Close* columns that follow contain the highest, lowest, and last (closing) price at which the stock sold that day.

As the *Net Chg* (net change) column shows, Disney closed up 1¾, which means that the price of the stock rose by almost \$2 a share from the closing price the day before.

Although the same basic quotation system is used for AMEX stocks, a slightly different system is used for OTC stocks. In all, about 4,700 stocks are included in the NASDAQ quotation network. For quotation purposes, these stocks are divided into three groups: NASDAQ National Market Issues, NASDAQ Bid and Asked Quotes, and Additional OTC Quotes. The National Market stocks are major, actively traded companies that are quoted just like NYSE issues. The OTC stocks that fall into the remaining two categories are generally smaller companies that are listed on the basis of their bid and ask prices (recall that the bid price is the price at which you can sell a stock, while the ask price is the price at which you can buy it).

Here is an example of a NASDAQ Bid and Asked Quote.

| Stock & Div. | Sales (100s) | Bid | Asked | Change |
|---|---|---|---|---|
| CrownAm  .40 | 115 | 12¼ | 13 | —¼ |

As you can see, the listing includes the name of the company, the amount of cash dividends paid per share, and the sales volume in round lots (115 = 11,500 shares of stock traded), then the highest bid price for the day is listed along with the lowest ask price. Finally, the change shown represents the change (from the previous business day) in the bid price of the stock.

In addition to these quoted OTC stocks, there are thousands of small, thinly traded stocks whose prices are not regularly reported in the financial press. These are the so-called "pink sheet" stocks. The only way to find the price of these issues is to call your broker.


## TRANSACTION COSTS FOR COMMON STOCKS

As a rule, brokerage fees equal between 1 and 3 percent of most stock transactions. The following table shows a commission schedule used by one major brokerage house:

| Share Price | NUMBER OF SHARES | | | | | | |
|---|---|---|---|---|---|---|---|
| | 5 | 10 | 25 | 50 | 100 | 200 | 500 |
| $  1 | $  1.66 | $  2.24 | $  4.00 | $  6.94 | $ 12.82 | $  24.57 | $  59.81 |
| .5 | 3.79 | 6.52 | 12.65 | 16.09 | 22.98 | 44.90 | 101.13 |
| 10 | 6.46 | 11.86 | 15.83 | 22.45 | 33.92 | 66.77 | 129.73 |
| 25 | 12.43 | 15.66 | 25.36 | 37.52 | 58.71 | 103.63 | 225.03 |
| 35 | 13.71 | 18.21 | 31.06 | 45.79 | 70.15 | 132.11 | 284.83 |
| 50 | 15.61 | 22.02 | 37.26 | 58.18 | 84.77 | 168.00 | 354.60 |
| 75 | 18.79 | 28.38 | 47.58 | 72.48 | 88.52 | 175.97 | 434.33 |
| 100 | 21.97 | 32.96 | 57.91 | 84.23 | 88.52 | 175.97 | 438.33 |
| 125 | 25.15 | 37.10 | 65.06 | 87.99 | 88.52 | 175.97 | 438.33 |
| 150 | 28.32 | 41.22 | 72.21 | 87.99 | 88.52 | 175.97 | 438.33 |

Source: A major full-service brokerage house.

THE MARKETS AND HOW THEY WORK

Not surprisingly, the commission you pay increases as the number and price of the shares traded increase. Thus, the cost of selling 50 shares of stock trading at $35 a share amounts to $45.79 while the cost of trading 200 shares of a $75 stock is $175.97. Although the real cost increases with the size of the transaction, on a share-by-share basis the relative cost declines. For instance, the brokerage fee for the 50-share transaction equals 2.6 percent of the transaction value, while the fee for the 200-share trade represents a cost of only 1.1 percent.

Dealing in odd lots adds 12½ to 25 cents a share to the cost of a stock transaction. When you buy or sell large round lots—several thousand shares, for example—you are charged less on a per share basis than when you make a small round-lot trade.

When you sell a stock, you must also pay a transfer fee and taxes. Fortunately, these charges are modest compared to brokerage commissions.

If you use a discount broker to buy and sell stock, your commission costs will be reduced substantially. The following table gives you a good idea of how large these savings can be. To discourage small orders, most discounters charge a minimum transaction fee of $18 to $35.

| | SIZE OF STOCK TRANSACTION | | | | |
|---|---|---|---|---|---|
| | $3,000 (100 shs. at $30) | $5,000 (500 shs. at $10) | $10,000 (1000 shs. at $10) | $15,000 (300 shs. at $50) | $25,000 (500 shs. at $50) |
| Typical full-service broker | $65 | $130 | $240 | $235 | $355 |
| Typical discount broker | $30 | $ 50 | $ 80 | $ 60 | $ 80 |
| Discount broker commissions as % of full-service broker commission | 46% | 38% | 33% | 25% | 22% |

## PREFERRED STOCKS

Preferred stock is like common stock except that it has a stated dividend rate, the payment of which is given preference over common stock dividends. (Preferred stock is discussed in Chapter 21.)

### PRICE QUOTATIONS FOR PREFERRED STOCKS

Although the quotes of preferred stock are intermingled with those of common (they are listed after a firm's common stock), preferreds are easy to pick out. Simply look for the letters *pf* after the name of the company. *Preference stock,* which is prior preferred stock that has seniority over other preferred stock, uses the letters *pr* instead of *pf* in the stock quotations. For example, as you can see in the following example, Commonwealth Edison (CWE) offers both preference and regular preferred issues.

| 52 Weeks High | Low | Stock | Div. | Yld % | P-E Ratio | Sales 100s | High | Low | Close | Net Chg. |
|---|---|---|---|---|---|---|---|---|---|---|
| 118½ | 106½ | CSO pr n | 15.25 | 13.0 | ... | z110 | 117½ | 117½ | 117½ | + 1¼ |
| 65½ | 42 | Combln | 2.24 | 3.9 | 9 | 88 | 57¾ | 57 | 57¾ | + ¾ |
| 36¾ | 26½ | CmbEn | 1.00 | 3.1 | ... | 155 | 32⅛ | 31⅞ | 32 | + ⅛ |
| 14⅞ | 9¾ | Comdta | .20 | 1.9 | 18 | 1205 | 10¾ | 10¼ | 10¾ | + ⅜ |
| 25 | 12 | Comds s | .16 | 1.0 | 9 | 310 | 17 | 16½ | 16⅝ | − ⅜ |
| 22½ | 12⅞ | CmMtl s | .32 | 1.9 | 11 | 14 | 17½ | 17¼ | 17¼ | − ¼ |
| 11¾ | 4¾ | Comdre | | ... | ... | 426 | 7⅝ | 7⅜ | 7⅜ | − ¼ |
| 35¾ | 27¼ | CmwE | 3.00 | 9.5 | 7 | 1212 | 31⅞ | 31⅝ | 31⅝ | − ⅛ |
| 22⅛ | 15⅞ | CwE pr | 1.90 | 9.0 | ... | 50 | 21 | 20¼ | 21 | + ¾ |
| 23¼ | 16¾ | CwE pr | 2.00 | 9.4 | ... | 28 | 21⅜ | 21¼ | 21⅜ | + ⅛ |
| 96¾ | 68⅛ | CwE pf | 8.38 | 9.8 | ... | z100 | 85¾ | 85¾ | 85¾ | − 1 |
| 26⅜ | 23¾ | CwE pr | 2.37 | 9.2 | ... | 6 | 25⅝ | 25½ | 25⅝ | + ⅛ |
| 28⅜ | 25 | CwE pf | 2.87 | 10.5 | ... | 19 | 27¾ | 27⅜ | 27⅜ | ... |
| 84 | 60 | CwE pr | 7.24 | 9.5 | ... | z260 | 76½ | 76½ | 76½ | ... |
| 45¾ | 26¼ | ComES | 2.72 | 6.7 | 10 | 15 | 40¾ | 40¼ | 40⅝ | + ⅛ |
| 40½ | 27⅞ | Comsat | 1.20 | 3.9 | ... | 385 | 30⅞ | 30⅛ | 30⅝ | − ¼ |
| 34⅜ | 22 | CPsyc | .32 | 1.0 | 19 | 624 | 32½ | 32⅛ | 32½ | + ⅛ |
| 18¼ | 8¼ | Compaq | | ... | 13 | 848 | 15½ | 15¼ | 15⅜ | ... |
| 28½ | 15½ | Compgr | .60 | 3.2 | 21 | 14 | 20 | 18⅞ | 18⅞ | − 1⅜ |
| 25¼ | 9⅝ | CmpAs s | | ... | 27 | 425 | 23 | 22⅞ | 22⅞ | ... |
| 39¾ | 23 | CompSc | | ... | 19 | 288 | 32½ | 31⅞ | 31⅞ | − ⅝ |
| 18⅝ | 9⅛ | Cptvsn | | ... | ... | 241 | 13⅛ | 13 | 13 | − ⅛ |
| 62⅞ | 34⅜ | ConAgr | 1.00 | 1.8 | 18 | 212 | 56¼ | 55 | 56¼ | + 1 |
| 27 | 17 | ConnE | 1.68 | 7.3 | 13 | 18 | 23¼ | 23 | 23⅛ | − ¼ |
| 24½ | 14⅜ | CnnNG s | 1.30 | 5.8 | 14 | 24 | 22¾ | 22⅜ | 22½ | + ¼ |
| 18 | 11⅛ | Conrac | .40b | 2.8 | 13 | 43 | 14¼ | 14 | 14¼ | + ⅛ |
| 12¼ | 11¼ | Consec n | | ... | ... | 23 | 11¾ | 11½ | 11½ | − ⅛ |
| 52⅞ | 33½ | ConsEd | 2.68 | 5.9 | 11 | 2874 | 45⅝ | 45⅛ | 45½ | + ½ |
| 62¾ | 46 | ConE pf | 5.00 | 8.2 | ... | 5 | 60¾ | 60½ | 60¾ | ... |
| 36½ | 21 | CnsFrt s | .82 | 2.3 | 15 | 2601 | 35½ | 34⅜ | 35¼ | + ⅝ |
| 35⅛ | 20¾ | CnsNG s | 1.32 | 4.3 | 13 | 516 | 31 | 30¾ | 31 | ... |
| 23⅝ | 5 | CnStor s | | ... | 27 | 382 | 16¼ | 16 | 16 | − ⅛ |
| 14¼ | 6½ | ConsPw | | ... | ... | 599 | 13 | 12¾ | 12¾ | − ¼ |
| 44 | 30 | CnP pfB | 4.50 | 10.6 | ... | z200 | 42⅞ | 42½ | 42½ | − ½ |
| 74 | 50 | CnP pfD | 7.45 | 10.2 | ... | z560 | 73¾ | 72¼ | 73 | − ¼ |
| 77 | 51¼ | CnP pfE | 7.72 | 10.2 | ... | z500 | 76¼ | 74 | 75½ | − ⅛ |
| 77⅜ | 52 | CnP pfG | 7.76 | 10.2 | ... | z730u | 77½ | 76 | 76 | + 1¼ |

*Source: The Wall Street Journal.*

The quotes are interpreted exactly like those of common stock. In this case, however, no price/earnings ratio is listed. Here we see that Commonwealth Edison has six issues of preferred stock outstanding paying annual dividends of anywhere from \$1.90 to \$8.38 a share. (The higher the annual dividend, the higher the price of the stock.) Current yields range from 9 to 10½ percent. Observe also the relatively low unit cost of the stock; four of the preferreds are priced at less than \$30 and the other two are moderately priced within the \$75 to \$85 range.

In some cases, you'll see the small letter *z* in the volume (or sales) column. This symbol signifies the actual number of shares traded rather than the round-lot volume. For example, while there were 5,000 shares (or 50 round lots) of the \$1.90 preferred traded, there were only 100 shares of the \$8.38 preferred stock traded.

## TRANSACTION COSTS FOR PREFERRED STOCKS

Preferred stocks are subject to the same transaction costs as common stocks. Transfer fees and taxes are also identical.

# WARRANTS

Warrants provide their holder with an opportunity to purchase a specified number of shares of common stock at a stated price per share over a given period of time. (Warrants are described in Chapter 25.)

## PRICE QUOTATIONS FOR WARRANTS

Warrants are usually listed with the common and preferred stock of the issuer. Their quotes are easy to pick out since the letters *wt* appear in the dividend column; see the quote for the Eli Lilly warrant in the following example. Notice that the market information for warrants is listed just like that of common or preferred stock.

| 52 Weeks High | Low | Stock | Div. | Yld % | P-E Ratio | Sales 100s | High | Low | Close | Net Chg. |
|---|---|---|---|---|---|---|---|---|---|---|
| 9⅞ | 2 | viLTV | | ... | ... | 1371 | 2⅝ | 2½ | 2⅝ | ... |
| 14½ | 3 | viLTVA | | 9.6 | ... | 2 | 5 | 4½ | 4½ | –1 |
| 19¼ | 3⅞ | viLTV pfB | | ... | ... | 106 | 5⅛ | 4⅞ | 5 | ... |
| 14 | 3¼ | LTV pfD | | ... | ... | 9 | 3⅞ | 3¾ | 3¾ | ... |
| 5⅜ | 1⅞ | LVI Gp | | ... | ... | 408 | 4¼ | 4⅛ | 4⅛ | –⅛ |
| 16¾ | 11⅜ | LQuint | | ... | 30 | 4851 | 13 | 12 | 12⅜ | –⅝ |
| 39¾ | 21½ | LaclGs | 1.90 | 5.2 | 10 | 34 | 36⅝ | 36⅜ | 36⅝ | +⅛ |
| 12⅛ | 6¾ | Lafarge | .20 | 2.0 | 20 | 53 | 10¼ | 10⅛ | 10⅛ | –⅛ |
| 30½ | 21¼ | Lafrg pf | 2.44 | 9.2 | ... | 8 | 26⅝ | 26½ | 26½ | ... |
| 16½ | 7¼ | Lamaur | .24 | 1.8 | 25 | 248 | 13½ | 13¼ | 13¼ | –¼ |
| 4⅞ | 2⅝ | LamSes | | ... | ... | 67 | 3 | 2⅞ | 2⅞ | –⅛ |
| 15⅜ | 10⅜ | LawtInt | .56 | 3.8 | ... | 450 | 14⅞ | 14⅜ | 14⅞ | +¼ |
| 14 | 4⅛ | LearPt | .05j | ... | ... | 220 | 5⅜ | 5¼ | 5⅜ | ... |
| 22½ | 9⅛ | LearP pf | .72j | ... | ... | 11 | 11¼ | 11 | 11 | –⅜ |
| 62¼ | 45¾ | LearSg | 2.00 | 3.6 | 18 | 137 | 55½ | 55 | 55¼ | +½ |
| 153 | 115 | LearS pf | 2.25 | 1.6 | ... | 1 | 137½ | 137½ | 137½ | +½ |
| 16½ | 11¾ | LeaRnl s | .40 | 2.8 | 17 | 73 | 14⅛ | 14⅛ | 14⅛ | –⅛ |
| 49¾ | 29 | LswyTr | 1.50 | 3.3 | 9 | 20 | 46 | 45⅝ | 46 | –⅛ |
| 27⅝ | 18⅞ | LeeEnt | .58 | 2.2 | 21 | 15 | 26¾ | 26⅜ | 26⅜ | –⅜ |
| 31¾ | 15¼ | LegMas | .20 | .8 | 14 | 36 | 25½ | 25 | 25½ | +½ |
| 36⅜ | 15⅝ | LegPlt s | .40 | 1.3 | 16 | 194 | 30¾ | 30¼ | 30⅜ | –½ |
| 16⅞ | 13¾ | Lehmn | 2.02e | 12.3 | ... | 291 | 16⅝ | 16⅜ | 16⅜ | –⅛ |
| 21⅝ | 10⅛ | Lennar | .20 | 1.3 | 13 | 117 | 16¼ | 16 | 16 | +¼ |
| 17⅞ | 15⅝ | LeslFy n | | ... | ... | 532 | 16⅛d | 15 | 15½ | –⅝ |
| 31¼ | 18⅛ | LeucNt | | ... | 9 | 59 | 31 | 30⅞ | 31 | ... |
| 45⅜ | 28¾ | LibtyCp | .72 | 1.7 | 13 | 65 | 43½ | 42¼ | 42¼ | –1¼ |
| 83½ | 41½ | Lilly | 1.80 | 2.2 | 21 | 2160 | 82⅜ | 79 | 82⅜ | +2⅞ |
| 29¼ | 8 | Lilly wt | | ... | ... | 1329 | 27⅜ | 26 | 27⅜ | +1⅜ |
| 34¼ | 14¾ | Limitd s | .16 | .5 | 32 | 2956 | 30⅜ | 29⅝ | 30⅛ | +¼ |
| 16 | 14⅞ | LncNtC n | | ... | ... | 166 | 15⅞ | 15⅝ | 15¾ | ... |
| 62¾ | 39¼ | LincNtl | 2.00 | 3.7 | 11 | 792 | 54½ | 53¾ | 54¼ | +½ |
| 249¼ | 168 | LincN pf | 3.00 | 1.4 | ... | 1 | 217¼ | 217¼ | 217¼ | +4 |
| 27½ | 22⅝ | LincPl | 2.28 | 8.6 | ... | 10 | 26⅞ | 26⅝ | 26⅝ | +⅛ |
| 93½ | 66 | Litton | 1.50j | ... | 38 | 1186 | 75¾ | 75 | 75¾ | –¼ |
| 32 | 21¾ | Litton pf | 2.00 | 8.0 | ... | 2 | 25 | 25 | 25 | +⅜ |

*Source: The Wall Street Journal*, August 21, 1986.

## TRANSACTION COSTS FOR WARRANTS

Warrants are purchased through brokers and are subject to commission and transaction costs similar to those for common stock.

# BONDS

## PRICE QUOTATIONS FOR BONDS

Except for municipal issues, which are usually quoted in terms of yield, all bonds are quoted on the basis of their dollar price. These quotes are always interpreted as a percentage of *par*, or *stated, value* expressed on the face of the bond and paid at maturity. Thus, a quote of 97½ does not mean $97.50, but instead that the issue is trading at 97.5 percent of par. If a bond has a par value of $1,000, then a quote of 97½ translates into a dollar price of $975 (.975 × $1,000). At par value of $5,000, in contrast, a quote of 97½ means a dollar price of $4,875 (.975 × $5,000).

As you can see in the examples on the next page, price quotations follow one system for corporate bonds and another for government issues.

To understand the corporate bond quotation system, look at the Alabama Power (AlaP) issue:

- The group of numbers immediately following the abbreviated company name gives the *coupon* (the stated annual interest rate) and the year in which the bond matures. For example, 7¾ 02 means that the bond carries a 7¾ percent annual coupon and will mature sometime in the year 2002.
- The current yield column that follows provides the issue's yield based on the current market price. (The current yield is found by dividing the bond's annual coupon by the closing price of the issue.)
- The daily volume column lists the number of bonds traded on the given day—35 bonds for Alabama Power.
- The next four columns provide the high, low, and closing price for the day along with the net change in the closing price from the day before.

Also appearing in the corporate quotes are some zero coupon bonds issued by Allied Chemical Corp. (AlldC). These bonds have the letters *zr* in place of their coupons. For instance, the zr09 Allied bond means that the issue is a zero coupon bond that matures in 2009. The price of most zeros is quite low compared to regular coupon bonds—thus the quote of 12 is not a misprint; rather it means that you could buy this bond at $120 (12% of par) and in the year 2009 receive $1,000 in return. (Chapter 18 explains zero coupon bonds.)

Corporate bonds are usually quoted in eighths of a point (87⅞, for example). In contrast, government bonds (Treasuries and agencies) are listed in thirty-seconds of a point. The figure to the right of the decimal in the quotation indicates the number of thirty-seconds in the fractional bid or ask price. For example, the bid price of the 7 percent Treasury issue is quoted at 97.24, which can also be written as 97²⁴⁄₃₂ or 97.75 percent of par. Thus, if you want to buy $15,000 of this issue, you can expect to pay $14,662.50 for it ($15,000 × .9775).

## CORPORATES

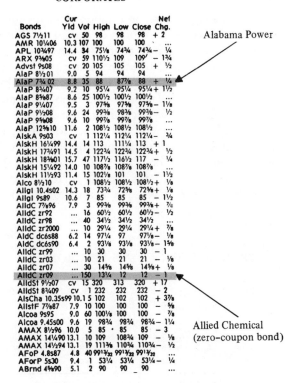

| Bonds | Cur Yld | Vol | High | Low | Close | Net Chg. |
|---|---|---|---|---|---|---|
| AGS 7½11 | cv | 50 | 98 | 98 | 98 | + 2 |
| AMR 10¼06 | 10.3 | 107 | 100 | 100 | 100 | ... |
| APL 10¾97 | 14.4 | 34 | 75⅛ | 74¾ | 74¾ | – ¼ |
| ARX 9⅜05 | cv | 59 | 110½ | 109 | 109′ | – 1¾ |
| Advst 9s08 | cv | 20 | 105 | 105 | 105 | + ½ |
| AlaP 8½01 | 9.0 | 5 | 94 | 94 | 94 | ... |
| AlaP 7¾02 | 8.8 | 35 | 88 | 87⅞ | 88 | + ¼ |
| AlaP 8¾07 | 9.2 | 10 | 95¼ | 95¼ | 95¼ | + 1½ |
| AlaP 8⅝87 | 8.6 | 25 | 100½ | 100½ | 100½ | ... |
| AlaP 9¼07 | 9.5 | 3 | 97⅝ | 97⅝ | 97⅝ | – 1⅛ |
| AlaP 9½08 | 9.6 | 24 | 99⅜ | 98⅜ | 99⅜ | – ½ |
| AlaP 9⅝08 | 9.6 | 10 | 99⅞ | 99⅞ | 99⅞ | ... |
| AlaP 12⅝10 | 11.6 | 2 | 108½ | 108½ | 108½ | ... |
| AlskA 9s03 | cv | 1 | 112¼ | 112¼ | 112¼ | – ¾ |
| AlskH 16¼99 | 14.4 | 14 | 113 | 111¼ | 113 | + 1 |
| AlskH 17¾91 | 14.5 | 4 | 122¾ | 122¾ | 122¾ | + ½ |
| AlskH 18⅜01 | 15.7 | 47 | 117½ | 116½ | 117 | – ¼ |
| AlskH 15¼92 | 14.0 | 10 | 108⅞ | 108⅞ | 108⅞ | ... |
| AlskH 11½93 | 11.4 | 15 | 102⅛ | 101 | 101 | – 1½ |
| Alco 8½10 | cv | 1 | 108½ | 108½ | 108½ | + ⅛ |
| Allgl 10.4s02 | 14.3 | 18 | 73¾ | 72⅝ | 72⅝ | + ⅛ |
| Allgl 9s89 | 10.6 | 7 | 85 | 85 | 85 | – 1½ |
| AlldC 7⅞96 | 7.9 | 3 | 99⅜ | 99⅜ | 99⅜ | + ⅞ |
| AlldC zr92 | ... | 16 | 60½ | 60½ | 60½ | – ½ |
| AlldC zr98 | ... | 40 | 34½ | 34½ | 34½ | ... |
| AlldC zr2000 | ... | 10 | 29¼ | 29¼ | 29¼ | + ⅞ |
| AldC dc6s88 | 6.2 | 14 | 97¼ | 97 | 97⅛ | – ⅛ |
| AldC dc6s90 | 6.4 | 2 | 93⅛ | 93⅛ | 93⅛ | – 1⅝ |
| AlldC zr99 | ... | 10 | 30 | 30 | 30 | – 1 |
| AlldC zr03 | ... | 10 | 21 | 21 | 21 | – ⅛ |
| AlldC zr07 | ... | 30 | 14⅝ | 14⅝ | 14⅝ | + ⅛ |
| AlldC zr09 | ... | 150 | 13¼ | 12 | 12 | – 1 |
| AlldSt 9½07 | cv | 15 | 320 | 313 | 320 | + 17 |
| AlldSt 8¾09 | cv | 1 | 232 | 232 | 232 | – 2 |
| AlsCha 10.35s99 | 10.1 | 5 | 102 | 102 | 102 | + 3⅞ |
| AllstF 7⅞87 | 7.9 | 10 | 100 | 100 | 100 | – ⅝ |
| Alcoa 9s95 | 9.0 | 60 | 100⅛ | 100 | 100 | – ⅞ |
| Alcoa 9.45s00 | 9.6 | 19 | 98¾ | 98¾ | 98¾ | – 1¼ |
| AMAX 8½96 | 10.0 | 5 | 85 | 85 | 85 | – 3 |
| AMAX 14¼90 | 13.1 | 10 | 109 | 108¾ | 109 | – ⅛ |
| AMAX 14½94 | 13.1 | 19 | 111⅜ | 110¾ | 110¾ | – ½ |
| AFoP 4.8s87 | 4.8 | 40 | 99 13/32 | 99 13/32 | 99 13/32 | ... |
| AForP 5s30 | 9.4 | 1 | 53¼ | 53¼ | 53¼ | – ¼ |
| ABrnd 4⅝90 | 5.1 | 2 | 90 | 90 | 90 | ... |

Alabama Power

Allied Chemical (zero-coupon bond)

## GOVERNMENTS
(U.S. Treasury Issues)

| Rate | Mat. Date | | Bid | Asked | Bid Chg. | Yld. |
|---|---|---|---|---|---|---|
| 11¾s, | 1993 | Nov | 122.18 | 122.26 | + .13 | 7.55 |
| 9s, | 1994 | Feb | 108.13 | 108.21 | + .15 | 7.45 |
| 4⅛s, | 1989-94 | May | 94.26 | 95.26 | ..... | 4.79 |
| 13⅛s, | 1994 | May p | 131.9 | 131.17 | + .15 | 7.60 |
| 8¾s, | 1994 | Aug | 107.14 | 107.22 | + .12 | 7.44 |
| 12⅝s, | 1994 | Aug p | 129.4 | 129.12 | + .13 | 7.60 |
| 10⅛s, | 1994 | Nov | 115.6 | 115.14 | + .15 | 7.55 |
| 11⅝s, | 1994 | Nov | 123.31 | 124.7 | + .13 | 7.58 |
| 3s, | 1995 | Feb | 95.20 | 96.20 | + .4 | 3.47 |
| 10½s, | 1995 | Feb | 117.14 | 117.22 | + .10 | 7.61 |
| 11¼s, | 1995 | Feb p | 122.2 | 122.10 | + .11 | 7.60 |
| 10⅜s, | 1995 | May | 117.5 | 117.13 | + .17 | 7.59 |
| 11¼s, | 1995 | May p | 122.16 | 122.23 | + .14 | 7.60 |
| 12⅝s, | 1995 | May | 131.4 | 131.12 | + .8 | 7.60 |
| 10½s, | 1995 | Aug p | 118.13 | 118.21 | + .15 | 7.57 |
| 9½s, | 1995 | Nov p | 112.11 | 112.19 | + .13 | 7.56 |
| 11½s, | 1995 | Nov | 125.5 | 125.13 | + .12 | 7.59 |
| 8⅞s, | 1996 | Feb p | 108.14 | 108.22 | + .10 | 7.56 |
| 7⅜s, | 1996 | May p | 99.16 | 99.24 | + .18 | 7.41 |
| 7s, | 1993-98 | May | 97.24 | 98.8 | + .16 | 7.23 |
| 3½s, | 1998 | Nov | 95.5 | 96.5 | + .4 | 3.90 |
| 8½s, | 1994-99 | May | 104.2 | 104.18 | + 1.3 | 7.70 |
| 7⅞s, | 1995-00 | Feb | 100.2 | 100.18 | + .24 | 7.70 |
| 8⅜s, | 1995-00 | Aug | 103.8 | 103.24 | + .25 | 7.78 |
| 11¾s, | 2001 | Feb | 130.20 | 130.28 | + 1.10 | 8.08 |
| 13⅛s, | 2001 | May | 141.24 | 142 | + 1.15 | 8.16 |
| 8s, | 1996-01 | Aug | 100.27 | 101.11 | + .24 | 7.80 |
| 13⅜s, | 2001 | Aug | 143.20 | 143.28 | + 1.5 | 8.21 |
| 15¾s, | 2001 | Nov | 164.14 | 164.22 | + 1.14 | 8.21 |
| 14¼s, | 2002 | Feb | 151.20 | 151.28 | + .24 | 8.24 |

7% Treasury bond

*Source: The Wall Street Journal.*

Government bond quotes not only include the coupon (the 7 percent figure shown in the first column of the quote), but also the year and month of maturity. In this case, the 7 percent Treasury bond matures in May of 1998. When there is more than one date in the maturity column (for example, 1993–98), the second figure indicates the issue's maturity date while the first indicates when the bond becomes fully callable, or when the issuer at its option can buy back the bond at a prespecified call price. Thus, our 7 percent bond matures in 1998 and carries a call deferment provision that extends through 1993. Unlike corporates, these bonds are quoted in bid/ask terms, where the bid price signifies the highest price at which you can sell the bond and the ask price is the lowest price at which you can buy it. The final column is not the current yield of the issue, but the bond's promised yield to maturity. This is a measure of return that captures both current income and capital gains or losses.

## TRANSACTION COSTS FOR BONDS

The following table provides some representative transaction costs for bond purchases and sales:

| | Brokerage Fee |
|---|---|
| **CORPORATES** | |
| First 5 bonds, or $5,000 par value | $10 each bond, or per $1,000 of par value |
| Next 20 bonds, or $20,000 par value | $7.50 each bond, or per $1,000 of par value |
| For everything above 25 bonds, or $25,000 par value | $5 each bond, or per $1,000 of par value |
| **GOVERNMENTS** | |
| For transactions involving par value of $50,000 or less | Net bid or ask price* plus $20 odd-lot charge (per trade) |
| For transactions involving par value of $50,000 or more | Net bid or ask price* |

*The "net" bid or ask price differs from the bid or ask price quotations by the amount of the brokerage fee charged on the transaction.

*Source:* A major brokerage house.

The cost of executing small transactions is fairly expensive, but as the size of the transaction increases, the relative cost declines quickly. Consider the cost of acquiring 40 corporate bonds worth $40,000:

| | | |
|---|---|---|
| For the first 5 bonds | 5 × $10.00 = | $ 50.00 |
| For the next 20 bonds | 20 × 7.50 = | 150.00 |
| For the next 15 bonds | 15 × 5.00 = | 75.00 |
| Total commissions | | $275.00 |

In relation to the $40,000 worth of bonds being purchased, commission costs amount to less than 1 percent, which is low compared to the transaction costs of most other securities.

Although these commission costs are quite appealing, you may have trouble completing your bond transactions. There are several reasons for this. First, many bonds have relatively thin markets; some issues may trade only 5 or 10 bonds a week, and many have no secondary market at all. Although there are many high-volume issues, take the precaution of checking the bond's trading volume before you buy—especially if you are looking for a lot of price action and need your order executed promptly.

Bond trading is also difficult because price information is often scarce. Except for Treasury, agency (issued by political subdivisions of the U.S. government), and some corporate bonds, it is very difficult to obtain current information on bond prices and other market developments.

Finally, you often have to look to both brokers and bankers to complete your transactions. Most brokerage houses tend to confine their activities to new issues and to secondary market transactions of listed Treasury obligations, agency bonds, and corporate bonds. Commercial banks are still the major dealers in municipal bonds (issued by states, counties, cities, and other nonfederal political subdivisions) and are fairly active in government securities as well.

# CONVERTIBLE BONDS AND CONVERTIBLE PREFERREDS

Convertible bonds and convertible preferreds are special types of bonds and preferred stocks, respectively, that permit their holder to convert them into a specified number of shares of common stock.

## PRICE QUOTATIONS FOR CONVERTIBLE BONDS

Convertible bonds are listed along with corporate bonds in the daily price quotation tables. They are distinguished from straight debt issues by the *cv* in the current yield column of the quote.

Note in the example on the next page the tendency for some convertibles (the Great Western Financial 8½ percent issue of 2010, for example) to trade at very high prices. These situations are justified by the correspondingly high values attained by the underlying common stock. Convertible preferreds, in contrast, are not isolated from other preferreds. They are listed with the *pf* markings, but carry no other distinguishing symbols. As a result, you must find out from some other source whether or not a preferred is convertible.

| Bonds | Cur Yld | Vol | High | Low | Close | Net Chg. |
|---|---|---|---|---|---|---|
| GM 8⅝s05 | 8.9 | 10 | 96½ | 96½ | 96½ | + ¼ |
| GTE 6⅝91 | 6.9 | 5 | 96⅝ | 96⅝ | 96⅝ | + ⅝ |
| GTE 10⅛95 | 9.7 | 4 | 104½ | 104½ | 104½ | + ½ |
| GTCal 8⅞96 | 8.8 | 5 | 100¾ | 100¾ | 100¾ | − 1 |
| Gene 14¼94 | 14.5 | 3 | 98 | 98 | 98 | − 2 |
| GaPac 5¼96 | cv | 3 | 120¼ | 120¼ | 120¼ | − 1¾ |
| GaPw 8⅞00 | 9.4 | 70 | 94½ | 94⅛ | 94⅛ | ... |
| GaPw 8⅛01 | 9.2 | 10 | 87⅞ | 87⅞ | 87⅞ | + ¼ |
| GaPw 7⅝01 | 8.9 | 10 | 85⅝ | 85⅝ | 85⅝ | + ⅛ |
| GaPw 8⅝04 | 9.4 | 29 | 92 | 91¾ | 92 | + ¼ |
| GaPw 11⅝00 | 11.0 | 8 | 106 | 106 | 106 | − ½ |
| GaPw 11¾05 | 11.1 | 5 | 106 | 105¾ | 105¾ | + ¼ |
| GaPw 9⅞06 | 9.9 | 37 | 99⅝ | 99¼ | 99¼ | + ⅛ |
| GaPw 9⅝08 | 9.9 | 22 | 97⅜ | 97¼ | 97⅜ | + ¼ |
| GaPw 9¾08 | 9.9 | 7 | 98¼ | 98¼ | 98¼ | + ¼ |
| GaPw 11s09 | 10.6 | 20 | 103⅝ | 103½ | 103½ | − ⅛ |
| GaPw 14½10 | 13.0 | 17 | 111¾ | 111¾ | 111¾ | + ¼ |
| GaPw 16⅛11 | 14.4 | 31 | 112¼ | 112 | 112 | − ⅜ |
| GaPw 16¼11 | 14.4 | 23 | 112½ | 112½ | 112½ | ... |
| GaPw 17½91 | 15.8 | 89 | 111 | 110 | 111 | + ⅞ |
| GaPw 16¼12 | 14.3 | 80 | 113¼ | 112⅞ | 113¼ | + ⅜ |
| GibFn 9¼08 | cv | 57 | 109 | 108½ | 109 | + ½ |
| viGloMr 16⅛02f | ... | 30 | 20¼ | 19¾ | 19¾ | − ¼ |
| GdNgF d8⅜93 | 9.4 | 23 | 89½ | 89¼ | 89¼ | − ¼ |
| Gdrch 8¼94 | 8.6 | 20 | 96⅜ | 96⅜ | 96⅜ | + 1⅜ |
| GWstFn 8½10 | cv | 10 | 130 | 130 | 130 | − 2 |
| GreyF zr94 | ... | 13 | 46 | 45½ | 45½ | ... |
| Grolr 9½05 | cv | 10 | 140 | 140 | 140 | − 1 |
| GrowGp 8½06 | cv | 20 | 107 | 107 | 107 | ... |
| Grumn 9¼09 | cv | 26 | 106½ | 106½ | 106½ | + ½ |
| Gruntl 7½11 | cv | 6 | 93¼ | 92 | 92 | + ½ |
| GlfWn 6s88 | 6.2 | 5 | 96⅝ | 96⅝ | 96⅝ | ... |
| GlfWn 7s03A | 9.0 | 26 | 78⅛ | 78 | 78 | + ⅛ |
| GlfWn 7s03B | 9.0 | 14 | 79 | 78⅛ | 78⅛ | − ⅞ |
| Harns dc12s04 | 11.9 | 34 | 100½ | 100 | 100½ | + ¾ |
| Hartmx 8½96 | 8.7 | 8 | 97½ | 97½ | 97½ | + 2¼ |

*Source: The Wall Street Journal,* October 7, 1986.

## TRANSACTION COSTS FOR CONVERTIBLE BONDS

Convertible bonds are subject to the same brokerage fees and transfer taxes as straight corporate debt. Similarly, convertible preferreds have the same transaction costs as straight preferreds and common stock.

# MUTUAL FUNDS

## PRICE QUOTATIONS FOR MUTUAL FUNDS

Mutual funds are operated by investment companies that raise money from shareholders and invest it in stocks, bonds, options, commodities, and money market instruments. They issue an unlimited number of shares and will buy back shares at a stated price.

The quotation system used with mutual funds distinguishes the no-load from the load funds. That is, all mutual funds are quoted according to their net asset value (NAV) and this information is included in the customary mutual fund quotations, as you can see in the example on the next page.

## MUTUAL FUNDS

Thursday, May 15, 1986
Price ranges for investment companies, as quoted by the
National Association of Securities Dealers. NAV stands for
net asset value per share; the offering includes net asset
value plus maximum sales charge, if any.

| | NAV | Offer NAV Price | Chg. | | | NAV | Offer NAV Price | Chg. |
|---|---|---|---|---|---|---|---|---|
| Spcl Eqt | 6.97 | 7.62− | .02 | | Growth | 19.29 | N.L.− | .18 |
| US GvSc | 9.47 | 10.35− | .05 | | Grw Inc | 14.29 | N.L.− | .08 |
| Tax Ex | 10.71 | 11.70− | .01 | | High Yld | 11.17 | N.L.+ | .02 |
| USGG | 10.71 | 11.70− | .06 | | Income | 9.05 | N.L.− | .04 |
| Kauf Fund | 1.13 | N.L.+ | .01 | | Intl Fd | 23.34 | N.L.− | .11 |
| **Kemper Funds:** | | | | | New Am | 13.97 | N.L.− | .07 |
| Cal Tax | 14.02 | 14.68− | .03 | | New Era | 19.09 | N.L.− | .25 |
| Income | x8.97 | 9.49− | .11 | | Nw Horz | 16.70 | N.L.− | .03 |
| Growth | 13.17 | 14.39− | .18 | | S-T Bond | 5.19 | N.L.− | .01 |
| High Yld | x11.33 | 11.99− | .11 | | TxFr Inc | 9.57 | N.L.− | .01 |
| Int'l Fd | 22.42 | 24.50 | ... | | TxFr HY | 11.35 | N.L.− | .01 |
| Muni Bd | x9.34 | 9.78− | .06 | | TxFr SI | 5.18 | N.L. | ... |
| Optn Inc | 10.82 | 11.83− | .09 | | **Principal Preserv:** | | ........... | |
| Summit | 6.05 | 6.61− | .05 | | S&P 100 | 10.18 | 10.89− | .16 |
| Technol | 13.46 | 14.71− | .15 | | TX EX | 8.73 | 9.14+ | .06 |
| Total R | 16.86 | 18.43− | .14 | | GOVT PI | 9.82 | 10.28− | .01 |
| US GvSc | x9.70 | 10.16− | .16 | | **Pro Services Funds:** | | | |
| KY Tax Fr | 6.80 | N.L. | ... | | Med Tec | 14.69 | N.L.− | .10 |
| **Keystone Mass Group:** | | | | | Pro Fnd | 12.91 | N.L.− | .08 |
| Cust B1 | 17.69 | N.L.− | .05 | | Pro Inco | 9.17 | N.L.− | .04 |
| Cust B2 | 20.33 | N.L. | ... | | **Prudential Bache:** | | | |
| Cust B4 | 8.43 | N.L. | ... | | Adjust R | 24.59 | N.L.− | .03 |
| CustK1 | 9.92 | N.L.− | .09 | | CalMn r | 11.45 | N.L.− | .02 |
| CustK2 | 8.79 | N.L.− | .07 | | Equity r | 9.69 | N.L.− | .10 |
| Cust S1 | 23.68 | N.L.− | .35 | | Global r | 20.00 | N.L. | ... |
| Cust S3 | 9.91 | N.L.− | .08 | | GNMA | (z) | (z) | ... |
| Cust S4 | 7.28 | N.L.− | .07 | | GovtPl r | (z) | (z) | ... |
| Intl Fd | 6.92 | N.L.− | .04 | | Govt Sec | (z) | (z) | ... |
| PrecM | 11.14 | N.L.− | .02 | | Grwth r | 15.23 | N.L.− | .10 |
| TaxEx | 10.77 | N.L. | ... | | HiYld r | 10.81 | N.L. | ... |
| Tax Fr | 8.68 | N.L. | ... | | HY Mfi r | 15.87 | N.L.− | .04 |
| **Kidder Group:** | | ........... | | | InVer r | 11.13 | N.L.− | .08 |
| KPEQI | 17.31 | N.L.− | .07 | | MnNY r | 11.61 | N.L. | ... |
| Govt Inc | 15.13 | N.L.− | .20 | | OptnGr r | 8.78 | N.L.− | .07 |
| Spcl Grw | 15.25 | N.L.− | .01 | | Resrch r | 12.51 | N.L.− | .13 |

Source: *The Wall Street Journal*, May 15, 1986.

The *NAV* (net asset value) column shows the price at which you can sell fund shares (or, from the fund's point of view, the price it will pay to buy back your shares). Next to the NAV is the offer price, the price you would have to pay in order to buy the shares. A difference between the NAV and the offer price indicates a *load mutual fund*—a fund that requires the purchaser to pay transaction costs, which are called "loads." For example, the Kemper Growth fund has a higher offer price ($14.39) than net asset value ($13.17); this difference of $1.22 per share represents the load charge. For the Kemper Growth fund, the load charge amounts to 8.5 percent of the offer price. However, the load rate is actually *more* when the commission is related to a more appropriate base—the NAV of the fund. When stated as a percent of NAV, the load charge for this fund rises to 9.3 percent.

Relative to what it costs to buy and sell common stocks, the costs of load funds are indeed very high, even after taking into account the fact that you don't have to pay a commission on the sale of most funds.

While the legal *maximum* load charge is 8½ percent of the purchase price, not all funds charge the maximum. Some funds, known as low-loads, charge commissions of only 1 to 3 percent. (Even this figure may seem high when you realize that many of these funds have no sales force and therefore do not pay sales commissions.)

Look at the listing once more and you'll see the letters *N.L.* in the offer price column of many funds, including the Keystone International Fund. These letters indicate that the fund is no-load, or that the shares are bought and sold at the net asset value (in the case of the Keystone International Fund, this value is $6.92). The final column indicates the change in the net asset value from the previous business day. The Keystone International Fund, for example, suffered a loss of 4 cents a share.

## PUT AND CALL OPTIONS

An option is an agreement that provides the opportunity to purchase or sell a specific stock at a specified price over a stated period of time. A *put* is an option to sell, and a *call* is an option to buy.

### PRICE QUOTATIONS FOR PUT AND CALL OPTIONS

Listed options have their own marketplace and quotation system. Finding the price (or premium) for a listed stock option is fairly easy, as the options quotations on the next page indicate.

Note that quotes are provided for calls and puts separately and that three expiration dates are listed for each option (in this case, December, March, and June). The dates along with the *striking price*—the contractual price at which the underlying stock can be bought or sold—are the most important features differentiating one option from another.

For example, there are numerous puts and calls outstanding on the Philip Morris (Ph Mor) stock, each with its own expiration date and striking price. Looking at the call with a striking price of 70, you can see that the option's expiration date dramatically affects its price. In December, a little more than a month away from the time these quotations were written, the price of the call is 2⅝ ($262.50 for 100 shares of stock—options premiums are quoted on a per-share basis, so the actual price of the standard 100-share contract is found by multiplying the quoted premium by 100). The farther out you go the more expensive the call. In March, it is 4½ ($450) and in June 5⅞ ($587.50).

The quotes are standardized and are read in the following way:

- The company and the closing price of the underlying stock are listed first. In this case, Philip Morris closed at 70⅝ on November 7, 1987.
- The striking price is listed next.
- Finally, the closing prices of the calls and puts are quoted relative to the three expiration dates.

# LISTED OPTIONS QUOTATIONS

Friday, November 7, 1986

**Closing prices of all options. Sales unit usually is 100 shares. Stock close is New York or American exchange final price.**

| Option & NY Close | Strike Price | Calls—Last | | | Puts—Last | | |
|---|---|---|---|---|---|---|---|
| | | Dec | Mar | Jun | Dec | Mar | Jun |
| Hecla | 10 | 2¾ | 3⅛ | r | 1/16 | r | r |
| 12⅝ | 12½ | ⅞ | r | 2 | 9/16 | r | r |
| 12⅝ | 15 | ⅛ | 9/16 | r | r | r | r |
| Hercul | 50 | 9½ | 10¼ | r | ⅛ | r | r |
| 59⅞ | 55 | 5 | 6½ | 7⅝ | ⅝ | r | r |
| 59⅞ | 60 | 1⅞ | 3½ | 4⅞ | 2⅜ | r | r |
| Kellog | 45 | r | r | r | ⅜ | r | 1⅝ |
| 50¼ | 50 | 2¼ | r | r | 1½ | r | r |
| 50¼ | 55 | r | 2 | r | r | r | r |
| 50¼ | 60 | ⅛ | ⅞ | s | r | r | s |
| L T V | 5 | r | ⅛ | s | r | 2⅞ | s |
| PacGE | 22½ | r | r | r | r | r | 9/16 |
| 24½ | 25 | ⅜ | 13/16 | 1⅛ | r | r | 1¾ |
| Pfizer | 55 | 7⅛ | 8¼ | 9 | r | 1 1/16 | 1¾ |
| 62⅛ | 60 | 3 | 5 | 6⅜ | 1⅛ | 2½ | 3¼ |
| 62⅛ | 65 | 15/16 | 2⅝ | 3¾ | 3¾ | 5¼ | r |
| 62⅛ | 70 | ¼ | 1 3/16 | s | r | r | s |
| Ph Mor | 55 | 15⅝ | s | s | r | s | s |
| 70⅝ | 60 | 11 | r | r | r | r | r |
| 70⅝ | 65 | r | 7⅝ | r | ½ | 1⅝ | 2⅛ |
| 70⅝ | 70 | 2⅝ | 4½ | 5⅞ | 2 | 3⅜ | 4¼ |
| 70⅝ | 75 | ⅞ | 2½ | r | 5¼ | r | r |
| 70⅝ | 80 | r | 1¼ | 2⅛ | r | r | r |
| 70⅝ | 85 | r | 11/16 | s | r | r | s |
| PrimeC | 15 | 2 | 2¾ | 3⅜ | 3/16 | r | 1 |
| 16⅝ | 17½ | 11/16 | 1½ | r | 1½ | 2 | 2⅛ |
| 16⅝ | 20 | 3/16 | ⅝ | 1⅝ | 3¼ | 3½ | r |
| 16⅝ | 22½ | 1/16 | r | ¾ | r | r | r |
| SFeSP | 25 | r | r | 8⅝ | r | r | r |
| 33¼ | 30 | 3⅝ | 4½ | 5½ | 5/16 | 13/16 | r |
| 33¼ | 35 | 1 1/16 | 1⅞ | 2⅝ | r | 2 13/16 | r |
| 33¼ | 40 | 5/16 | ¾ | s | r | r | s |

*Note*: r = option was not traded.
s = no options outstanding.

Thus, you can see that a Philip Morris call with a $75 striking price and a March expiration date is quoted at 2½. In contrast, a Philip Morris put with a $70 striking price and a June expiration date is trading at 4¼.

## TRANSACTION COSTS FOR PUTS AND CALLS

Option traders are subject to commission and transaction costs when they buy and sell an option. In relation to the number of shares of common stock controlled (100 shares per option), the transaction costs for executing put and call trades are relatively low. However, compared to the size of the transaction, the costs are fairly high.

As you can see from the table on the next page, which shows commission costs on a variety of listed options, buying one $5 option involves an investment of $500 and a transaction cost of only $26.75. Although this may seem low compared to

# COMMISSION COSTS ON LISTED OPTIONS

| Option Premium | NUMBER OF OPTIONS | | | | | | | | | | | | | | |
|---|---|---|---|---|---|---|---|---|---|---|---|---|---|---|---|
| | 1 | 2 | 3 | 4 | 5 | 6 | 7 | 8 | 9 | 10 | 11 | 12 | 13 | 14 | 15 |
| 1/16 | 3.88 | 4.55 | 5.22 | 5.89 | 6.56 | 7.22 | 7.90 | 8.56 | 9.23 | 9.90 | 10.57 | 11.24 | 11.91 | 12.57 | 13.25 |
| 1/8 | 4.55 | 5.89 | 7.22 | 8.56 | 9.90 | 11.24 | 12.57 | 13.91 | 14.45 | 14.45 | 15.78 | 17.12 | 18.46 | 19.80 | 21.13 |
| 3/16 | 5.22 | 7.22 | 9.23 | 11.24 | 13.25 | 14.45 | 15.12 | 17.12 | 19.13 | 21.13 | 23.14 | 25.15 | 27.16 | 29.16 | 31.17 |
| 1/4 | 5.89 | 8.56 | 11.24 | 13.91 | 14.45 | 17.12 | 19.80 | 22.47 | 25.15 | 27.82 | 30.50 | 33.17 | 35.85 | 38.52 | 41.20 |
| 5/16 | 6.56 | 9.90 | 13.25 | 14.45 | 17.79 | 21.13 | 24.48 | 27.82 | 31.17 | 34.51 | 37.86 | 41.20 | 44.54 | 47.88 | 51.23 |
| 3/8 | 7.22 | 11.24 | 14.45 | 17.12 | 21.13 | 25.15 | 29.16 | 33.17 | 37.18 | 41.20 | 45.21 | 49.22 | 53.23 | 57.25 | 61.26 |
| 7/16 | 7.90 | 12.57 | 15.12 | 19.80 | 24.48 | 29.16 | 33.84 | 38.52 | 43.21 | 47.88 | 52.57 | 57.25 | 61.93 | 66.61 | 71.29 |
| 1/2 | 8.56 | 13.91 | 17.12 | 22.47 | 27.82 | 33.17 | 38.52 | 43.87 | 49.22 | 54.57 | 59.92 | 65.27 | 70.62 | 75.97 | 81.32 |
| 9/16 | 9.23 | 14.45 | 19.13 | 25.15 | 31.17 | 37.18 | 43.21 | 49.22 | 55.24 | 61.26 | 67.28 | 73.30 | 79.32 | 85.33 | 91.36 |
| 5/8 | 9.90 | 14.45 | 21.13 | 27.82 | 34.51 | 41.20 | 47.88 | 54.57 | 61.26 | 67.95 | 74.63 | 81.32 | 88.01 | 94.70 | 101.38 |
| 11/16 | 10.57 | 15.78 | 23.14 | 30.50 | 37.86 | 45.21 | 52.57 | 59.92 | 67.28 | 74.63 | 81.99 | 89.35 | 96.71 | 104.06 | 109.74 |
| 3/4 | 11.24 | 17.12 | 25.15 | 33.17 | 41.20 | 49.22 | 57.25 | 65.27 | 73.30 | 81.32 | 89.35 | 97.37 | 105.40 | 110.75 | 114.76 |
| 13/16 | 11.91 | 18.46 | 27.16 | 35.85 | 44.54 | 53.23 | 61.93 | 70.62 | 79.32 | 88.01 | 96.71 | 105.40 | 111.08 | 115.43 | 119.78 |
| 7/8 | 12.57 | 19.80 | 29.16 | 38.52 | 47.88 | 57.25 | 66.61 | 75.97 | 85.33 | 94.70 | 104.06 | 110.75 | 115.43 | 120.11 | 124.79 |
| 15/16 | 13.25 | 21.13 | 31.17 | 41.20 | 51.23 | 61.26 | 71.29 | 81.32 | 91.36 | 101.12 | 107.35 | 113.59 | 119.78 | 124.79 | 129.80 |
| $1 | 26.75 | 32.38 | 40.97 | 49.56 | 58.15 | 66.75 | 75.34 | 83.93 | 92.52 | 101.12 | 107.35 | 113.59 | 119.83 | 126.07 | 132.31 |
| $5 | 26.75 | 44.62 | 59.33 | 74.04 | 88.76 | 101.12 | 113.47 | 125.83 | 138.19 | 150.55 | 167.81 | 178.26 | 188.73 | 199.18 | 209.65 |
| 1/8 | 26.75 | 45.00 | 59.91 | 74.81 | 89.42 | 101.92 | 114.40 | 126.89 | 139.38 | 158.73 | 169.33 | 179.92 | 190.51 | 201.13 | 211.72 |
| 1/4 | 26.75 | 45.39 | 60.49 | 75.57 | 90.08 | 102.71 | 115.34 | 127.95 | 140.58 | 160.11 | 170.86 | 181.59 | 192.32 | 203.05 | 213.80 |
| 3/8 | 26.75 | 45.77 | 61.05 | 76.34 | 90.75 | 103.50 | 116.26 | 129.01 | 141.76 | 161.51 | 172.37 | 183.25 | 194.12 | 205.00 | 215.86 |
| 1/2 | 26.75 | 46.15 | 61.63 | 77.10 | 91.41 | 104.29 | 117.19 | 130.07 | 142.96 | 162.89 | 173.90 | 184.91 | 195.92 | 206.94 | 217.95 |
| 5/8 | 26.75 | 46.53 | 62.20 | 77.87 | 92.06 | 105.09 | 118.11 | 131.13 | 150.65 | 164.27 | 175.42 | 186.57 | 197.71 | 208.87 | 220.02 |
| 3/4 | 26.75 | 46.92 | 62.78 | 78.63 | 92.74 | 105.89 | 119.04 | 132.19 | 151.91 | 165.65 | 176.95 | 188.23 | 199.52 | 210.81 | 222.10 |
| 7/8 | 26.75 | 47.30 | 63.34 | 79.40 | 93.39 | 106.68 | 119.96 | 133.25 | 153.15 | 167.04 | 178.45 | 189.89 | 201.32 | 212.75 | 224.18 |
| $9 | 28.96 | 56.86 | 76.75 | 93.35 | 109.94 | 132.24 | 149.60 | 166.94 | 184.30 | 201.64 | 216.54 | 231.42 | 246.31 | 261.20 | 276.09 |
| 1/8 | 29.16 | 57.25 | 77.15 | 93.88 | 110.61 | 133.08 | 150.56 | 168.05 | 185.54 | 203.03 | 218.06 | 233.08 | 348.10 | 263.15 | 278.17 |
| 1/4 | 29.35 | 57.63 | 77.55 | 94.41 | 111.27 | 133.90 | 151.53 | 169.16 | 186.79 | 204.41 | 219.59 | 234.75 | 249.91 | 265.07 | 280.24 |
| 3/8 | 29.54 | 58.02 | 77.94 | 94.94 | 111.93 | 134.73 | 152.50 | 170.27 | 188.03 | 205.80 | 221.09 | 236.41 | 251.71 | 267.02 | 282.31 |
| 1/2 | 29.74 | 58.39 | 78.35 | 95.47 | 112.60 | 135.57 | 153.47 | 171.37 | 189.27 | 207.18 | 222.62 | 238.06 | 253.50 | 268.96 | 284.40 |
| 5/8 | 29.92 | 58.78 | 78.74 | 96.00 | 113.25 | 136.40 | 154.44 | 172.48 | 190.51 | 208.56 | 224.14 | 239.72 | 255.30 | 270.89 | 286.47 |
| 3/4 | 30.11 | 59.16 | 79.14 | 96.52 | 113.92 | 137.23 | 155.41 | 173.59 | 191.78 | 209.94 | 225.67 | 241.39 | 257.11 | 272.83 | 288.55 |
| 7/8 | 30.30 | 59.55 | 79.53 | 97.06 | 114.58 | 138.06 | 156.37 | 174.70 | 193.02 | 211.34 | 227.18 | 243.05 | 258.91 | 274.77 | 290.62 |
| $10 | 30.50 | 59.92 | 79.93 | 97.58 | 115.24 | 138.69 | 157.34 | 175.80 | 194.26 | 212.72 | 227.71 | 244.71 | 260.71 | 276.70 | 292.70 |

Source: A major brokerage firm.

what it would take to buy 100 shares of the underlying stock outright, on a relative basis, the transaction cost is extremely high. In this case you are paying a 5.4 percent commission fee ($26.75 ÷ $500 = 0.054). Furthermore, the commission must be paid both when you buy the option and when you sell it. As the table shows, options have their own unique structure of commissions based on the number of options in the transaction and the size of the option premium.

# COMMODITIES

Commodities are traded by means of contracts (called *futures*) to deliver a certain amount of some specified commodity (such as grain, metals, wood, or meat) at some specified date in the future. The seller of the contract agrees to make the specified future delivery and the buyer agrees to accept it.

## PRICE QUOTATIONS FOR COMMODITIES

Although every commodity has its own specifications regarding amounts and quality of the product being traded, and although some commodities (wheat and gold, for instance) are traded on more than one exchange, each commodity contract is made up of the same five parts, and all prices are quoted in an identical fashion. Every contract specifies: (1) the product; (2) the exchange on which the contract is traded; (3) the size of the contract (in bushels, pounds, tons, or whatever); (4) the method of valuing the contract, or pricing unit (like cents per pound, or dollars per ton); and (5) the delivery month. Using a corn contract as an illustration, we can see each of these parts in the example below:

| | Open | High | Low | Settle | Change | Lifetime High | Lifetime Low | Open Interest | KEY |
|---|---|---|---|---|---|---|---|---|---|
| Corn (CBT)—5,000 bu.; cents per bu. | | | | | | | | | |
| May | 253½ | 253¾ | 252¼ | 252½ | −1¾ | 286½ | 230½ | 42,796 | ① the product |
| July | 258 | 258 | 256½ | 256¾ | −1¾ | 288 | 233 | 60,447 | ② the exchange |
| Sept | 260 | 260½ | 259 | 259 | −1½ | 263 | 236 | 7,760 | ③ the size of the |
| Dec | 263½ | 264 | 262½ | 263 | −1¼ | 267¼ | 244 | 41,638 | contract |
| Mar | 271¾ | 272 | 270¼ | 271 | −1¼ | 276 | 254¾ | 11,098 | ④ the pricing unit |
| May | 277¼ | 278 | 276¼ | 277 | −1 | 281 | 273¼ | 1,326 | ⑤ the delivery months |

The quotation system used for commodities is based on the size of the contract and the pricing unit. The financial media generally report the open, high, low, and closing prices for each delivery month (with commodities, the last price of the day, or the closing price, is known as the *settle price*). Also reported, at least by *The Wall*

*Street Journal*, is the amount of *open interest* in each contract—that is, the number of contracts presently outstanding. Note in the example on the previous page that the settle price for May corn was quoted at 252½. Since the pricing system is cents per bushel, this means that the contract was being traded at $2.52½ per bushel. Since each contract involves 5,000 bushels and each bushel is worth $2.52½, the market value of the contract was $12,625 (5,000 × $2.525 = $12,625).

## TRANSACTION COSTS FOR COMMODITIES

All trades are subject to round-trip commissions of about $50 to $80 for each contract traded. A *round trip commission* includes the costs on both ends of the transaction—when you buy and when you sell. The exact size of the commission depends on the number and type of contracts being traded.

## STOCK INDEX OPTIONS AND FINANCIAL FUTURES

These specialized forms of options and futures respectively are too complex for brief treatment here. They are discussed in detail in Chapters 26 and 28.

# 10

# DIFFERENT TYPES
# OF SECURITIES TRANSACTIONS

Most people know that you can make money in the market when prices climb, but did you know that you can also make money when prices fall? Here we'll discuss the basic transactions you can make to take advantage of both bull and bear markets and show you how to magnify your profits by investing with someone else's money.

## GOING LONG: THE MOST COMMON KIND OF TRANSACTION

When you buy a security in the hope that it will increase in value, you are trading *long.* The vast majority of investors buy securities because they expect the price to rise. In fact, more than 9 out of 10 stock transactions made on the New York Stock Exchange fall into this category.

It's no exaggeration to say that these transactions express confidence in the U.S. economy. In effect, these investors are telling other investors they are convinced company profits will increase and dividends will remain the same or rise. The country's entire economic system is built on this confidence, and all but short sellers benefit from it. (Short selling will be discussed in depth later in this chapter.)

Here's a simple example of how this strategy works. (As you will see from the price swings we describe, it is as easy to lose money as it is to make it.) After reading a number of medical journals, you are convinced that a biotechnology company is about to come out with a new—and very promising—cancer-fighting drug. Since the drug is not yet on the market, the company is selling at $20 a share, the price it has held (give or take a point or two) for about a year. You purchase 500 shares in the hope that eventual sales will boost corporate profits. You also hope that just the news of the drug's impending release will push the stock price up.

Your hunch is right. Within 2 weeks trading in the stock increases dramatically, and the price climbs to $30. You now have a paper profit, excluding commissions, of $5,000 (500 × [$30 − $20]). Even though this is a substantial gain, you decide to hold onto your stock at least until the drug hits the market. Although on the surface your decision is sound, you soon regret it. On news that several leading medical experts are skeptical about the drug's efficacy, the stock price plummets to $17. Your $5,000 paper gain has turned into a paper loss of $1,500 (500 × [$17 − $20]). Despite this setback, you decide that the drug's actual release may shift the tide of investor sentiment. Six months after the federal Food and Drug Administration approves the drug for use in the United States, the trend is promising. Although the price remains below its previous high of $30, it inches past $26 on news that the drug has helped some patients. However, since it is now clear that the drug is no breakthrough, the stock price remains fairly stable at this level. Realizing this, you decide to sell after about a year, content with a profit of $3,000 (500 × [$26 − $20]).

Even though dividends were not a factor in this example, they sometimes are a good reason to invest in equities—especially now that tax rates have been lowered by the 1986 Tax Reform Act. As you wait for the price of the stock to rise, you can collect a regular—and sometimes substantial—flow of income. Dividends are discussed in greater detail in Chapter 12.

## MARGIN TRADING: THE POWER OF LEVERAGE

Making profits with someone else's money is part of the American dream. It's how the rich get richer and how many smart investors succeed in the first place. Most of us use leverage to purchase a home: we put a small amount of money down and use the bank's money—in the form of a mortgage—to finance the rest. If you put a $40,000 down payment on a $200,000 house and 3 years later sell it for $240,000, you earn what is in effect a 100 percent profit on your $40,000 down payment.

You can create the same kind of leverage in the stock market if you trade on margin. The principle behind margin trading is buying securities with borrowed funds to reduce the amount of capital you have to put up yourself. The term *margin* refers to the amount of equity you have in an investment, or the amount that is *not* borrowed. That is, if your account is 75 percent margined, you have covered 75 percent of your investment position with your own money; only 25 percent is borrowed.

The Federal Reserve Board, which oversees our banking system, sets the margin requirements that govern the amount of borrowing you can do to buy stock. A 50 percent requirement has been in effect for stock since January of 1974. By raising or lowering this percentage, the Fed can depress or stimulate activity in the securities market, since the greater the percentage of each margin purchase investors must pay, the smaller the number of purchases they can make and vice versa. This is just one of the ways the Fed loosens or tightens funds.

Some brokerage firms have in-house margin requirements that are even stricter than the Fed's. Whatever the requirement, you'll need your broker's approval to open a margin account. This is entirely reasonable since your broker is financing part of your investments and has to be sure you can pay for any losses you might incur. Of course, you must pay for the money you borrow at the prevailing interest rate.

Margin trading can be used with most kinds of securities, including common and preferred stocks, all types of bonds, warrants, commodities, financial futures, and even mutual funds. Municipal bond investors usually avoid margin trading, since the interest paid on margin loans used to buy these tax-exempt bonds is not deductible for income tax purposes. (In 1988 individuals can deduct $4,000 more in investment interest expense than the investment income they receive. The excess amount is scheduled to drop to $2,000 in 1989, $1,000 in 1990, and zero after 1990.)

A simple example will help to clarify the basic margin transaction. Suppose you purchase 70 shares of General Motors common stock, which is currently selling for $63.50 a share. Since the prevailing margin requirement is 50 percent, you will have to put up only half of the total purchase price of $4,445 ($63.50 a share × 70 shares), or $2,222.50 in cash. You borrow the remaining $2,222.50 from your broker. Although you will have to pay brokerage commissions on all 70 shares—not just the 35 you bought with your own money—your interest payments are based only on the borrowed amount. This transaction allows you to purchase more securities than you could afford on a strict cash basis, which in turn magnifies your possible returns.

## WHAT ARE THE RETURNS AND RISKS OF MARGIN TRADING?

If you pick the right security and buy it on margin, your gains may turn out to be nothing short of spectacular. The table on the next page shows how margin trading can magnify your return.

| Percentage Change in Price of Security | PERCENTAGE CHANGE IN RETURN ON INVESTOR'S MONEY WITH MARGINS OF | | | | |
|---|---|---|---|---|---|
| | 90% | 75% | 50% | 25% | 10% |
| 20% | 22.2% | 26.6% | 40% | 80% | 200% |
| 50 | 55.6 | 66.7 | 100 | 200 | 500 |
| 75 | 83.3 | 100.0 | 150 | 300 | 750 |
| 100 | 111.1 | 133.3 | 200 | 400 | 1,000 |
| 200 | 222.2 | 266.6 | 400 | 800 | 2,000 |

As you can see, the money you earn depends on both the price behavior of the security and the amount of margin you use. For example, if you margin 90 percent of a purchase (remember, that means that you only borrow 10 percent), and the price increases by 50 percent, your return is 55.6 percent. The more you margin, the more you make. With a 50 percent margin and a 50 percent price rise, you come away with a 100 percent return.

Of course, margin trading can also get you into a great deal of trouble. If you're expecting a stock to climb and it drops instead, your losses will be magnified. To make matters worse, as you're losing money you're also paying interest on your *margin loan,* which is the official vehicle through which the borrowed funds are made available in a margin transaction. (Margin loans are used with all margin transactions except those involving commodities, financial futures, and short sales.) The interest you pay on the loan depends on prevailing market rates and the amount of money you borrow. This cost grows each day and reduces the profits—or magnifies the losses—you finally achieve.

The table at the top of the next page gives you a closer look at the potential profits and pitfalls of margin trading. Since the security you margin is always the ultimate source of return, it is critical that you take a great deal of time and effort in choosing it. Remember: any mistake you make will be magnified in the form of bigger losses.

## MARGIN REQUIREMENTS

The Federal Reserve sets two types of margin requirements: initial margin and maintenance margin.

*Initial margin.*   Initial margin is used to prevent overtrading and excessive speculation; it stipulates the minimum amount of money (or equity) investors must provide *at the time of purchase.* Generally, it is this margin requirement investors refer to in discussing margin trading. Any security that can be margined has a specific initial requirement. As the table at the bottom of the next page shows, these requirements vary by type of security.

| | Without Margin (100% Equity) | WITH MARGINS OF | | |
|---|---|---|---|---|
| | | 80% | 65% | 50% |
| Number of $50 shares purchased | 100 | 100 | 100 | 100 |
| Cost of investment | $ 5,000 | $ 5,000 | $ 5,000 | $ 5,000 |
| Less: borrowed money | 0 | 1,000 | 1,750 | 2,500 |
| Equity in investment | $ 5,000 | $ 4,000 | $ 3,250 | $ 2,500 |
| A. INVESTOR'S POSITION IF PRICE RISES TO $80/SHARE | | | | |
| Value of stock | $ 8,000 | $ 8,000 | $ 8,000 | $ 8,000 |
| Less: cost of investment | 5,000 | 5,000 | 5,000 | 5,000 |
| Capital gain | $ 3,000 | $ 3,000 | $ 3,000 | $ 3,000 |
| Return on investor's equity (capital gain/equity in investment) | 60% | 75% | 92.3% | 120% |
| B. INVESTOR'S POSITION IF PRICE FALLS TO $20/SHARE | | | | |
| Value of stock | $ 2,000 | $ 2,000 | $ 2,000 | $ 2,000 |
| Less: cost of investment | 5,000 | 5,000 | 5,000 | 5,000 |
| Capital *loss* | $ 3,000 | $ 3,000 | $ 3,000 | $ 3,000 |
| Return on investor's equity (capital loss/equity in investment)* | (60%) | (75%) | (92.3%) | (120%) |

*With a capital loss, return on investor's equity is *negative*.

The more stable investment vehicles, such as Treasury bonds, generally enjoy substantially lower margin requirements and therefore offer greater magnification opportunities. OTC stocks that are traded on the NASDAQ National Market System (NASDAQ/NMS) can be margined like listed securities; over 2,100 OTC stocks qualify—including most of the major firms traded over-the-counter (issues of banks, insurance companies, industrial and retail firms, etc.). All other OTC stocks are considered to have no collateral value and therefore cannot be margined.

### INITIAL MARGIN REQUIREMENTS FOR VARIOUS TYPES OF SECURITIES (NOVEMBER 1987)

| Security | Minimum Initial Margin (Equity) Required |
|---|---|
| Listed common and preferred stock | 50% |
| Regulated OTC stock | 50 |
| Convertible bonds | 50 |
| Warrants | 25 |
| Investment-grade corporate bonds | 25 |
| Treasury and agency bonds | 5% of principal |

Initial margin requirements also provide a check on the current status of your margin account. As long as the margin in the account remains at a level equal to or greater than prevailing initial requirements, you are free to use the account in any way you see fit. Should the value of your holdings decline, the margin in your account will also drop, leading to what is known as a *restricted account*. A restricted account is one that carries a margin level less than prevailing initial margin requirements. For example, if initial margin requirements are, say, 50 percent, an account would become restricted when its margin fell to 49 percent or less. A restricted account does not mean that you have to put up additional cash or equity. However, one of the important restrictions placed on the account is that, should you sell securities while the account is restricted, the amount that can be withdrawn is limited until the account is brought back up to initial margin levels.

*Maintenance margin.*  Maintenance margin is used to protect the creditors in margin transactions. It specifies the minimum amount of equity you must carry in your margin account at all times. If your account falls below this level, your broker is authorized to sell enough of your securities to bring the account back up to standard. However, before this is done, you will receive a *margin call*. That is, your broker will ask you to bring the equity in your account into line. Usually, this must be done within 72 hours of the time you receive the margin call.

The maintenance margin on equity securities is currently 25 percent and rarely changes, although it is often set slightly higher by brokerage houses for the added protection of both brokers and their customers. For straight debt securities like Treasury bonds, there is no real maintenance margin except that set by the brokerage houses themselves.

A margin account is considered restricted as long as its equity remains below the initial margin requirement; it will stay restricted until it finally falls below the maintenance level. At that point, the account will become *undermargined*. An undermargined account is serious because you have only one course of action: to bring the equity back up to the maintenance margin level. Clearly, before using margins to purchase securities you should make sure that adequate funds will be available to meet potential margin calls.

## CALCULATING MARGIN

The amount of margin in a transaction (or account) is always measured in terms of its relative amount of equity. Except when you're selling short, you can use a simple formula to determine the margin you have. You'll need two pieces of information for this calculation:

- The prevailing market value of the securities being margined
- The amount of money being borrowed or the size of the margin loan, which is known as the *debit balance*

This information allows you to use the following formula:

$$\text{margin (\%)} = \frac{\text{value of securities} - \text{debit balance}}{\text{value of securities}}$$

To illustrate its use, consider the following example. Assume you want to purchase 100 shares of stock at $40 a share using a 50 percent margin. The first thing to determine is how this $4,000 transaction will be financed. Since you know that 50 percent (the stated prevailing initial margin requirement) must be financed with equity, the balance (50 percent) can be financed with a margin loan. Therefore, you must borrow $2,000 ($4,000 $\times$ .50 = $2,000), which is the debit balance. The remainder ($2,000) represents your equity in the transaction, measured as the difference between the value of the securities being margined ($4,000) and the amount being borrowed ($2,000). In other words, *equity* is represented by the numerator in the margin formula.

If over time the price of the stock moves to $65, the margin will then be:

$$\text{margin (\%)} = \frac{\$6,500 - \$2,000}{\$6,500}$$

$$= 69.2\%$$

As you can see, while the value of securities in the equation changes with the market price of the stock, the size of the debit balance does not change—and it will not *unless* you pay off or take out more margin loans. As you can also see, your margin increases as the price of the stock goes up.

When the price of the security goes down, so does the amount of margin. For instance, if the price of the stock in our illustration drops to $30 a share, the new margin will be only 33 percent—in which case your account would be restricted, since the margin level has dropped below the prevailing initial margin.

You can use the same margin formula to determine the amount of margin you have in your account as a whole. Simply determine the value of all securities held in the account and the total amount of margin loans, and plug this information into the basic margin formula.


## WAYS TO PROFIT FROM YOUR MARGIN ACCOUNT

Margin trading can be used in three different ways: to increase transaction returns, to pyramid profits, and to increase current income. Since all involve a great deal of risk, they should be approached with caution. First and foremost, you should use them only if you completely understand how they work.

*Increasing transaction returns.* This strategy represents the most basic use of margin trading. In order to enjoy maximum capital gains from a specific transaction, you must first find a security that offers promising price appreciation and then buy it on as much margin as you can get. This stretches your resources as far as they will go. For example, suppose you discover a stock presently trading at $20 a share, and you are convinced it will move to $30 within 6 months. Because you feel so strongly that the stock will shoot up in price, you decide to margin it to the limit—the prevailing initial margin rate of 50 percent. Your capital is limited to $4,000, you borrow another $4,000 on margin, thus your total investment is $8,000 (i.e., 400 shares at $20 per share).

If, in fact, the price of the stock does climb to $30 within the 6-month time frame, you will receive $12,000 from the sale. You will recover your initial capital investment of $4,000; the brokerage house will get back the $4,000 it loaned you (plus $200 in interest); and you will receive $3,800 in net profit, representing a 95 percent return on your invested capital. This nearly doubles the 50 percent holding period return you would have received had you not margined the trade.

*Pyramiding profits.* The idea of pyramiding is to use the margin account to build up investment holdings. When investors hold securities that go up in value, but do not sell these securities, they earn what are known as *paper profits.* Pyramiding uses these paper profits to finance the acquisition of additional securities. This allows transactions to be made at margins below—and sometimes substantially below—prevailing initial margin levels. It is even possible to buy securities with no cash at all, financing them entirely with margin loans. You can do this because the paper profits in your margin account have created *excess margin*—that is, you have more equity in your account than you actually need.

For instance, if a margin account holds $60,000 worth of securities and is financed by a margin loan of $20,000, the account's margin level is 66⅔ percent, which is substantially above the 50 percent initial margin requirement. Pyramiding begins when you use this excess margin to buy additional securities. The key to pyramiding is keeping the account at or above the prevailing required initial margin level after the additional securities are purchased.

Here's an example of how pyramiding works. Let's continue the previous illustration and suppose that your stock actually rises to $30 a share. Since you are convinced that it will continue to grow, you want to hold onto it; but you also want to buy another issue which you feel has equal, if not greater, growth possibilities. Since your investment capital is almost gone, you decide to use the excess margin that now exists in your account to purchase shares of the new stock, which is trading at $10. The table on the next page summarizes what happens when you use pyramiding to buy the additional shares.

Step A shows the original margin transaction in which you purchased 400 shares of a $20 stock on margin. In this case, you put up $4,000 in cash and borrowed $4,000 from the broker. At step B, because of paper profits, your account held excess margin—66⅔ percent versus the prevailing initial margin requirement of 50 percent. Even after the second transaction was completely financed with margin loans (see step C, which shows that *no* new equity capital was used), the account still met the required 50 percent initial margin level (as shown in step D). This type of pyramiding can continue as long as there are additional paper profits in the margin account and as long as the margin level exceeds the prevailing initial requirement.

*Step A:*
## THE ORIGINAL MARGIN TRANSACTION

| | | |
|---|---|---|
| 400 shares purchased at $20/share using 50% margin (first transaction) | Value of securities | $ 8,000 |
| | Debit balance | 4,000 |
| | Equity | 4,000 |

*Step B:*
## SOME TIME LATER

| | | |
|---|---|---|
| Price of the 400 shares rises to $30 per share | Value of securities | $12,000 |
| | Debit balance | 4,000 |
| | Equity | 8,000 |

$$\text{new margin} = \frac{\text{value of securities} - \text{debit balance}}{\text{value of securities}}$$

$$= \frac{\$12,000 - \$4,000}{\$12,000}$$

$$= \underline{66\frac{2}{3}\%}$$

*Step C:*
## YOU PYRAMID YOUR MARGIN ACCOUNT

| | | |
|---|---|---|
| 400 shares of *another* stock purchased at $10/share (second transaction) | Value of securities | $ 4,000 |
| | Debit balance | 4,000 |
| | *New* equity capital | 0 |

*Step D:*
## THE NEW MARGIN ACCOUNT

| | | |
|---|---|---|
| Total of the two transactions *after* the pyramiding | Value of securities | $16,000* |
| | Debit balance | 8,000** |
| | Equity | 8,000 |

$$\text{new margin} = \frac{\$16,000 - \$8,000}{\$16,000} = \underline{50\%}$$

*400 shares at $30/share (first transaction) *plus* another 400 shares at $10/share (second transaction) = $12,000 + $4,000 = $16,000.

**Debit balance from first transaction *plus* debit balance from second transaction = $4,000 + $4,000 = $8,000.

*Increasing current income.*   This is the least common use of margin trading and can be done only when the interest cost for margin loans is relatively low and the current income you receive from securities in the form of dividends or coupon interest payments is relatively high. For example, a stock with an 8 percent rate of return might be a candidate for this strategy when interest rates on margin loans are 6 percent.

To illustrate, suppose you have $2,000 to invest and can borrow another $2,000 on margin at an interest rate of 6 percent to purchase 100 shares of stock at $40 a share. Because annual dividends on the stock amount to $3.20 a share, it earns an 8 percent rate of return ($3.20 ÷ $40.00 = .08), which exceeds the cost of margin funds. In the course of a year, you would realize $320 in dividends and pay only $120 in interest ($2,000 × .06); this would provide net dividend income of $200 a year for a rate of return of 10 percent on the $2,000 you originally invested. Had you not margined the purchase, you would have realized only the 8 percent rate of return, or $160 in dividend income.

Although this improvement in dividend income is real, it certainly does not amount to very much. Since you are exposing yourself to magnified losses if the market goes down, you have to consider carefully whether the small amount of additional return you receive in the form of added dividends is worth the risk.

## HOW TO MAKE MARGIN TRADES

To execute a margin transaction, it is necessary to set up a *margin account*. This is a special type of account set up at a broker's office to handle all margin transactions, regardless of the type of security being margined. It is opened with a minimum of $2,000 in equity, in the form of either cash or securities. Margin transactions are executed like any others; they can be used with any type of order and are subject to normal commissions and transfer taxes. Once margin transactions have been made, interest begins to accumulate on any margin loans taken out, and the broker will retain any securities you purchase on margin as collateral for the loan. Margin credit can be obtained from bankers as well as brokers, but nearly all margin trading is done through brokers because of their greater convenience.

# SHORT SELLING: HOW TO MAKE MONEY IN A DOWN MARKET

When you sell a security in the hope that it will decrease in value rather than rise, you are going *short* instead of long. This is how it works. You borrow the security from your broker and sell it in the marketplace, even though you do not actually own it. If you are right and the price of the security drops, you go into the market once again and buy the security back at a lower price. The difference between the sale price you receive for the borrowed security and the price you pay when you buy the security back is your profit.

In effect, short sellers reverse the investment process by starting the transaction with a sale and ending it with a purchase. Despite this, their goal is to make money in the same way as other investors: to buy low and sell high. Let's look at an example. Suppose you borrow 100 shares of stock from your broker and sell them at $50 a share, in the expectation that the price of these shares will drop. When this actually happens, you purchase the same 100 shares at the lower price—say, $25 a share. While you received $5,000 from the original sale, your cost to buy the stock back was only $2,500. Thus, you generate a profit of $2,500 minus commissions (see the table on the next page). Clearly, the profit or loss generated in a short sale depends on the price at which you buy back the stock. You make money only as long as the proceeds from the sale are greater than the buy-back cost.

## STEPS IN A SHORT SALE TRANSACTION

*Step 1:*
Borrow stock from broker: 100 shares
*Step 2:*
Sell stock: 100 shares at $50 a share = $5,000
*Step 3:*
Buy same stock in open market when price drops: 100 shares at $25 a share = $2,500
*Step 4:*
Calculate your profit: (subtract step 3 from step 2) = $2,500

## IS SHORT SELLING WORTH THE RISK?

The major advantage of selling short is the chance to convert a price decline into a profit. If your sole motivation is profits, you face a great deal of risk and only limited return by selling short. While the price of the security can fall only so far (to or near zero), there is no limit to how far the price can rise. (Remember, when a security goes up in price, the short seller loses.) The higher the price rises, the greater your loss. If, for example, the 100 shares of stock you shorted at $50 climbs to $60, your loss is $1,000 ($10 × 100); if it climbs to $70, your loss is $2,000; and so on.

Another disadvantage to selling short is that you do not earn dividends (or interest income) and in fact must pay any dividends earned by the security to the lender.

When this technique is used to protect profits that have already been earned, however, it is a highly conservative investment strategy, as you will see.

## HOW SHORT SALE TRANSACTIONS WORK

Although almost every type of security can be shorted—including common and preferred stocks, all types of bonds, convertible securities, warrants, puts and calls, and listed mutual funds—most investors limit their short sale activities to common stocks and puts and calls (options). Slightly more than 2 billion shares of stock were sold short on the New York Stock Exchange in 1984, accounting for about 9 percent of total share volume. The great bulk of these transactions were made by exchange specialists and other floor members, but individual investors accounted for nearly 3.6 million shares.

Short sale transactions are strictly regulated by the SEC in order to curb the abuses of the strategy that were partially responsible for the great market crash of 1929. (Interestingly, short selling was in no way responsible for the market crash of October 1987.) Today, short sales can be executed only when the price of the stock has risen or remained unchanged. This upward movement is known as an *uptick.* For example, you can short a stock at 51⅛ if the preceding transaction was 51. If the preceding transaction was 51¼, the short sale could not be completed. Although you can place a short sell order at any time, your broker will not be able to execute it on a *downtick,* or when the price of the security is lower than it was in the last transaction.

Contrary to what many new investors believe, you have to invest a certain amount of money to initiate a short sale even though the transaction begins with a sale rather than a purchase. The amount of capital you need is defined by a special margin requirement for short sale transactions. In the case of common stocks and other equities, you must meet an initial margin requirement of 50 percent before the transaction can begin. For example, if you want to short $5,000 worth of stock, you have to deposit $2,500 with your broker, or the equivalent amount in securities.

***Who lends the securities?*** If you have a margin account, shorting a stock involves nothing more than a phone call to your broker with instructions on the specifics of the sale. Borrowed securities almost always come from brokers. As a service to their clients, brokers lend securities held in their own portfolios or in their *street name accounts.* These are accounts containing stock certificates issued in the name of the brokerage house but held in trust for clients. Since many investors do not want to be bothered with handling and safeguarding stock certificates, it is common for securities to be issued to the broker, who then records the details of the transaction and is responsible for keeping track of all dividends, notices, and so on.

***Margin requirements.*** All shorts are executed on margin, but when margin trading is used in short transactions, it is defined in a slightly different way than when it is used in long transactions. No borrowed funds—and therefore no interest charges—are involved when you margin a short sale. The term *margin* simply indicates the size of the equity deposit you must make in order to initiate the transaction. Margined short sales are executed in the same margin account as margined long transactions. They are subject to initial margin requirements; have maintenance margin levels; and if the price of the security being shorted goes up too much, the account can become restricted or even subject to a margin call.

Because short sales are executed on margin, the amount of invested capital is limited to your equity deposit. This amount is used to determine your rate of return. The only complication in this return measure is that short sellers are responsible for making up any security-related income generated while the short transaction is outstanding. That is, if a dividend is paid during the course of a short sale, the short seller must pay an equal amount to the lender of the stock. (The mechanics of this transaction are handled automatically by the short seller's broker.) Since no additional dividend or interest income is received and no interest is paid, the return formula is fairly straightforward:

$$\frac{\text{return on invested capital from a short sale}}{} = \frac{\text{proceeds from sale} - \frac{\text{cost to purchase securities}}{} - \frac{\text{dividends paid by short seller}}{}}{\text{equity deposit}}$$

To illustrate, assume you want to use 50 percent margin to short a $60 stock you believe is going to drop to $40 within 6 months. Because the company pays annual dividends of $2 a share, you estimate that you will be liable for about $1 a share over the expected 6-month holding period. Computing the return on a per share basis (this figure will be the same regardless of how many shares are involved in the transaction), we see that the expected return on invested capital for this short sale is 63 percent:

$$\text{return on invested capital from a short sale} = \frac{\$60 - \$40 - \$1}{\$30} = \frac{\$19}{\$30} = 63\%$$

This hefty return is due not only to the profit earned when the price of the stock drops, but also to the limited amount of capital you invested when you originally sold short (the equity deposit equaled only 50 percent of the transaction amount).

## WAYS TO PROFIT BY SELLING SHORT

Investors sell short for one of two reasons: to seek speculative profits when the price of a security is expected to drop, or to protect a profit and defer taxes by hedging their position.

*Speculating with short sales.*   Since short selling is most often used to bet against the market, it is a highly speculative technique that subjects you to a considerable amount of risk. Suppose you find a stock that you believe is about to tumble from its present level of $50 a share to somewhere around $30. To take advantage of this drop, you decide to short sell 300 shares at the prevailing initial margin rate of 50 percent. Now look what happens if the price of the stock does indeed fall to $30 a share:

| | |
|---|---:|
| Short sale initiated: 300 shares sold at $50/share | $15,000 |
| Short sale covered: 300 shares bought back at $30/share | $ 9,000 |
| Net profit | $ 6,000 |
| Equity deposit (.50 × $15,000) | $ 7,500 |

$$\text{Return on invested capital*} = \frac{\$15,000 - \$9,000}{\$7,500} = \frac{\$6,000}{\$7,500} = 80\%$$

*Assume the stock pays no dividends and therefore the short seller has no dividend liability.

With an equity deposit of only $7,500 to meet the 50 percent margin requirement, your return on invested capital is 80 percent.

But see, in the table at the top of the next page, what happens if the market moves against you and, instead of falling to $30, the stock climbs to $60.

| | |
|---|---|
| Short sale initiated: 300 shares sold at $50/share | $15,000 |
| Short sale covered: 300 shares bought back at $60/share | $18,000 |
| Net loss | $ 3,000 |
| Equity deposit (.50 $\times$ $15,000) | $ 7,500 |

$$\text{Return on invested capital} = \frac{\$15,000 - \$18,000}{\$7,500} = \frac{-\$3,000}{\$7,500} = -40\%$$

*Hedging, or shorting-against-the-box.*   Although the name sounds technical, shorting-against-the-box is actually a conservative hedging technique used to protect existing security profits. Like insurance, the purpose of a hedge is to minimize or eliminate exposure to loss. Shorting-against-the-box is a hedging program set up to protect a profit you have already generated in an earlier transaction. This is done by combining a short sale with a profitable long transaction. For example, if you already own 100 shares of stock (the long transaction), you can short an equal number of shares from the same company to protect the profit made in the long transaction. This technique also enables you to defer the taxes on your profit until the next tax year by shorting prior to year-end and using your original stock to cover the short position after year-end.

Here's how the technique works. Suppose that early last year you bought 100 shares of a promising stock at $20 a share and have since watched the price climb to $50. Although you do not want to sell the stock right now, you do not want to lose any of your $3,000 profit either. In essence, you want to hold your position while protecting the profit you have earned up to now. To do this, you sell short 100 shares of the same company, using your own shares as collateral. If the price of the stock remains the same, you'll sell the stock at $50 for a $30-a-share profit. However, if the price goes up to $60, you'll have to deliver your own stock to cover the short position and be content with the original $3,000 profit you earned by buying the stock at $20 and selling it at $50.

If the price drops 10 points instead, you'll make money on your short position but lose it on your long one. You can cover your short purchase in one of two ways. If you purchase new shares, you will still maintain your $3,000 profit, because the 10-point profit on the short sale will be offset by a 10-point loss in stock value. If, instead, you use your own shares to cover your short position, you'll make $1,000 on the short position and only $2,000 on the stock you own. When these two figures are combined, your total $3,000 profit remains the same.

While this short sale transaction is executed with borrowed securities, it is not necessary to put up an equity deposit, since your current stock holdings serve this purpose. Thus, the cost of shorting-against-the-box is reasonably low and involves only the commission and transaction costs involved in initiating and covering the short sale. Your only risk is that if the price of the stock continues to climb, you won't collect any profit as long as the short sale is outstanding.

# 11

# INFORMATION:
# THE KEY
# TO INVESTMENT SUCCESS

———

It's only a bit of an exaggeration to say that there are as many ways to make investment decisions as there are investors. Some people take an intuitive approach: they enjoy a hamburger at McDonalds, buy another pair of Reebok sneakers, or spend a pleasurable day shopping at Sears and decide on the spot to buy stock in the company. Others get a "hot" stock tip from a friend. Still others rely on their broker for all buy and sell decisions.

You certainly might hit it big using any of these approaches, but chances are you won't. Only by becoming well informed about the economy, the market, and specific companies can you hope to succeed in a consistent way. Before buying 500 shares of Reebok, for example, you should know the answers to these questions: How are general economic conditions changing? Is the short-term outlook for the stock market bullish or bearish? Is Reebok making money now and will its profits continue to rise?

The answers to these questions are readily available from a variety of sources. By learning how to tap into these sources and apply them to your particular investment needs, you'll improve your chances of earning the kind of return you're after. Our purpose here is to introduce you to these information sources and to help you feel comfortable using them. While this book is likely to be just the beginning of your investment education, the sources you'll learn about in this chapter will be your constant companions as long as you continue to invest.

## DO THE BENEFITS OF INFORMATION OUTWEIGH THE COSTS?

Although a great deal of investment information is inexpensive or free, you will have to pay for some of it in the form of subscription fees, service fees, and brokerage commissions. Are these charges worth it? One way to answer this question is to tie it to the risk-return behavior of your potential investments. Your intuition alone will not enable you to estimate in any intelligent way how a security's level of risk compares to its expected return. Nor will it help you ferret out factual misrepresentations that put a security in a more favorable light than it deserves. Of course, what you pay has to make economic sense. Spending $100 to increase your potential return by $30 is counterproductive. Your time is also valuable, and its cost should be considered as well. If you take 3 hours away from work, where you could earn $200, to research an investment with a potential $50 return, you're losing sight of a primary economic objective: to earn as much money as you can in as little time as you can. In general, the larger your investment portfolio, the more money and time you can justify spending on information, since whatever you learn can often be used in a number of different ways.

With investment information coming at you from literally thousands of different sources, it is important to be able to put this information in a small number of usable categories. We'll try to do this here starting with the broadest information category: economics and current events. (For additional sources of investor information, see Appendix A, which provides an extensive annotated list.)

## KEEP TABS ON ECONOMIC AND CURRENT EVENTS

You cannot make an intelligent investment decision without understanding what is happening in the world in general and in the economy in particular. You can get this information from the financial news, business periodicals, and special subscription services.

### THE FINANCIAL NEWS

Reading various sources of financial news is an inexpensive way to keep abreast of key financial developments. Here are some major sources:

THE MARKETS AND HOW THEY WORK

- *The Wall Street Journal*—With a circulation of around 2 million, *The Wall Street Journal* is the most popular source of financial news. For many investors, the *Journal*'s main attraction is its daily price quotations on thousands of investment vehicles. In addition, it reports world, national, regional, and corporate news that has the potential to influence securities markets. "Your Money Matters," a personal finance column, which appears on the first page of the second section, is one of the most popular *Journal* features. The *Journal* is published each day of the business week.

- *Barron's*—This weekly is published by Dow Jones, the same company that publishes *The Wall Street Journal. Barron's* focuses on individual investors and offers extensive investment information and advice. Probably the most popular column in *Barron's* is Alan Abelson's "Up and Down Wall Street," which provides a critical and often humorous assessment of major developments affecting the stock market as well as specific industries and companies. Current price quotations and a summary of statistics on a wide range of investment vehicles are also included in each issue.

- *Investor's Daily*—A relatively new financial publication, *Investor's Daily* is similar to *The Wall Street Journal* but contains more detailed price and market data. Like the *Journal,* it is a national business newspaper published every workday.

- *USA Today*—Included in this popular national newspaper are current security price quotations and summary statistics as well as a "Money" section devoted to business and personal financial news. *USA Today* is also published every weekday.

- *Major metropolitan and local newspapers*—Major newspapers such as *The New York Times* and the *Los Angeles Times* provide investors with a wealth of financial information, including price quotations and articles analyzing current economic, industry, and corporate news. Local newspapers also provide a convenient, although limited, source of financial news.

- *Other sources*—The monthly economic letters of the nation's leading banks, including Bank of America (San Francisco), Citibank (New York), and Harris Trust (Chicago), can provide a great deal of useful, although specialized, economic information. Other sources of financial news are the *Commercial and Financial Chronicle,* the *Media General Financial Weekly,* and the *Journal of Commerce.* In addition, your broker has access to breaking news stories that may affect the securities market through subscriptions to such wire services as the Associated Press, United Press International, and Dow Jones.


## BUSINESS PERIODICALS

Some business periodicals present general business and economic articles; others are devoted to the securities markets; and still others focus on specific industries or types of investments. Regardless of the subject matter, most financial periodicals present descriptive information, although some also analyze what this information means. Rarely, however, do they offer specific buy and sell recommendations.

General business and economic articles are found in periodicals such as *Newsweek, Time,* and *U.S. News and World Report.* A number of strictly business and finance-oriented periodicals are also available. These include *Business Week, Fortune,*

*Business Month,* and *Nation's Business.* Other sources of general business and economic articles are government publications such as the *Federal Reserve Bulletin* and the *Survey of Current Business.*

Securities and marketplace articles can be found in a number of financial periodicals, some of which focus on basic information for the general reader. *Forbes,* which is published every two weeks, has the most investment-oriented approach. Each January it publishes an "Annual Report on American Industry," which compares the growth and performance of key industries over the past 5 years. In August of each year *Forbes* also publishes a comparative evaluation of mutual funds. *Fortune,* also a biweekly, describes general business and economic developments, discusses industry and market trends, profiles companies and their management, and reports each spring its rankings—along with summary financial data—of the 500 largest corporations. Both *Changing Times* and *Money* are published monthly and contain a variety of articles concerned with managing personal finances and evaluating specific investments.

Two popular periodicals are aimed at more sophisticated investors. *Financial World,* a semimonthly publication, presents articles on the market and specific industries and companies. Periodically, it also presents statistical data on listed stocks and mutual funds. In addition, it provides an annual reference book to leading stocks. *The Wall Street Transcript* is a similar publication. More technical periodicals available in most public and university libraries include the *Financial Analysts Journal, The Money Manager, The Institutional Investor, Pension and Investment Age, Journal of Portfolio Management,* and *AAII Journal.* Each offers technical information and analysis geared to the professional investor.

## SPECIAL SUBSCRIPTION SERVICES

In addition to the broad range of financial news and business periodicals, special subscription services are available for those who want additional insights into business and economic conditions. These reports usually include business and economic forecasts as well as discussions of new government policies, labor-management issues, taxes, prices, wages, and so on. One of the more popular and useful services is the *Kiplinger Washington Letter,* a weekly publication that costs about $50 a year. Other special subscription services that concentrate on the general economy are McGraw-Hill's *Personal Finance Letter, Babson's Reports,* and the *Wellington Financial Letter.*

## FOLLOW INDUSTRY AND COMPANY TRENDS

After deciding that general world and economic conditions are favorable to investments, you must then find out as much as you can about specific industries and companies. General articles related to the activities of specific industries can be found in such trade publications as *Chemical Week, American Banker, Computer, Public Utilities Fortnightly,* and *Brewers Digest.* These publications are typically available in public and university libraries or through the research department of your broker. You can also learn a great deal through annual reports, subscription services, brokerage firms, and investment letters.

## ANNUAL REPORTS

Annual reports (also known as *stockholders' reports*) are a storehouse of valuable investor information. They include current and recent financial statements as well as a letter to stockholders from the company chairman discussing the past year's performance and the next year's outlook. For more detail, look at the company's *Form 10-K,* a statement that publicly traded firms must file with the SEC. Both the annual report and Form 10-K are published every year by publicly held corporations and are available free of charge.

## SUBSCRIPTION SERVICES

A variety of subscription services furnish information on specific industries and companies. The major services provide both descriptive and analytical information but generally do not make recommendations. Subscribers include corporations, banks, insurance companies, brokerage firms, libraries, and individual investors. You can avoid paying hefty subscription fees by looking at these publications at large public or university libraries or in your stockbroker's office. The three most important subscription services are:

- *Standard & Poor's Corporation*—S&P offers some 25 different financial reports and services, including *Corporation Records,* which describes selected publicly traded securities, and *Stock Reports,* which presents a concise summary of the financial status and prospects of various firms. In addition, the S&P *Trade and Securities Service* provides general business information as well as analyses of specific industries. The *Stock Guide* and *Bond Guide,* published monthly, contain statistics on the major publicly traded stocks and bonds and also rank their investment desirability. Finally, S&P also publishes *Outlook,* a weekly publication that offers investment advice about the market, specific industries, and securities.
- *Moody's Investor Services*—Moody's publishes major reference manuals known as *Moody's Manuals,* which are fairly similar to S&P's *Corporation Records.* Each of the six reference manuals contains a wealth of historical and current financial, organizational, and operational data on all major firms within certain business groups. Frequent updates are available to subscribers. Other Moody's publications are the *Handbook of Common Stocks,* which provides detailed financial information on over 1,000 stocks; *Dividend Record,* which lists the recent dividend announcements of thousands of companies; *Bond Survey,* a weekly publication that assesses market conditions and new offerings; and *Bond Record,* a monthly publication reporting the price and interest rate behavior of thousands of bonds.

- *Value Line Investment Survey*—One of the most popular subscription services for the individual investor, the *Value Line Investment Survey* is published weekly and covers approximately 1,700 stocks and their industries. (This represents about 96 percent of all equities traded in the United States.) For an annual fee of around $495, subscribers receive the "Summary and Index," which shows current ratings for each stock; "Ratings and Reports," which includes a full-page analysis for each of about 130 stocks; and "Selection and Opinion," which contains a detailed analysis of recommended stocks plus valuable background information. *Value Line* rates companies as investment opportunities on the basis of timeliness, safety, and financial strength.

## BROKERAGE FIRMS

Ask your broker for prospectuses of new security issues. A *prospectus* is a legal document that describes in detail all relevant background information on the issuing company. It also details the company's management and financial position and the type and amount of security to be issued.

Your broker can also give you *back-office research reports,* which are published by the brokerage firm and made available to its clients. These reports analyze the securities markets, specific industries, and specific securities and make recommendations for current and future action. Most brokerage houses also publish buy and sell lists of specific securities. These brokerage reports are available at no cost to existing as well as potential customers.

## INVESTMENT LETTERS

You can learn how various investment experts view specific industries and companies by subscribing to their investment letters. Among the most popular are the *Dines Letter,* the *Granville Market Letter,* the *Growth Stock Outlook,* the *Holt Investment Advisory,* the *Professional Tape Reader,* the *Wellington Letter,* and the *Zweig Forecast.* The focus of these letters varies considerably, with some providing specific buy and sell recommendations and others, general assessments of the economy or security markets. Investment letters generally cost between $75 and $300 a year.

---

## KNOW PRICES

Once you've committed your money to an investment, you'll probably want to follow its progress on a day-to-day basis. You can do this by monitoring the security's price quotation. The quotation will not only tell you the security's current price, it will also provide recent price behavior data; that is, you can tell at a glance whether the price has gone up or down or remained the same.

Your broker is the best source for the most up-to-date quotations. Many brokerage houses allow customers to key into computer terminals to obtain quotes or to watch the *ticker*, a lighted screen on which stock transactions made on the floor of the exchange are reported immediately after they occur. Today, sophisticated computers are rapidly displacing the ticker as the major source of up-to-the-minute stock price information. These computers are also available, on a fee basis, to active individual investors who want up-to-the-minute information in their homes or offices.

If you can wait until the close of the market, you will find a full list of price quotations in most major newspapers. As we mentioned earlier, your best source is *The Wall Street Journal*, which contains quotations on stocks, bonds, listed options, commodities and financial futures, mutual funds, and other popular investments.

## STUDY STOCK MARKET AVERAGES AND INDEXES

Swings in stock prices are often related to the behavior of the stock market as a whole. Similarly, market behavior is often tied to the expansion or slowing down of the economy. The only way to measure the perception of various economic swings by investors is to measure overall market activity, through market averages and indexes.

Although the terms *average* and *index* tend to be used interchangeably when discussing market behavior, technically they are different types of measures. *Averages* reflect the arithmetic average of the price behavior of a representative group of stocks at a given point in time; *indexes* measure the current price behavior of a representative group of stocks in relation to a base value set at an earlier point in time. Many investors compare averages (or indexes) at different points in time in order to assess the relative strength or weakness of the market. When these market measures reflect an upward price trend, a bull market is said to exist; in contrast, a downward trend reflects a bear market. Understanding the major market averages and indexes is important because they provide a convenient way of capturing the general mood of the market. Current and recent values of key market measures are quoted daily in the financial news; most local newspapers and many radio and television news programs also provide this information. We'll now take a brief look at the most important of them.

### DOW JONES AVERAGES

There's a vendor hawking newspapers on 43rd Street and Lexington Avenue in New York City. Like every other business person in the city, he knows that the competition is fierce and that he must pull out all the stops to get harried New

Yorkers to buy their afternoon papers from him. When the Dow Jones industrial average ("Dow" for short) is up, he uses it as the meat of his sales pitch, for he knows that New Yorkers, like everyone else, can't resist hearing good news about their money. When the Dow is down, he knows enough to keep his mouth closed. It's no surprise that this vendor sells a lot of newspapers on good market days. And it's also no surprise that news of a climbing Dow sells the papers for him.

The Dow Jones industrial average (DJIA) is the most popular of four stock averages prepared by Dow Jones, publisher of *The Wall Street Journal* and *Barron's*. Investors watch the DJIA because they believe it reflects overall market activity. When the 30 stocks that make up the DJIA go up or down, the overall market generally does the same. The operative word here is *generally*. On any given day, you may find that the activity in the stocks you own has almost nothing in common with the rise or fall of the DJIA. Thus, when you turn to the financial news, it's a good idea to prepare yourself for the unexpected. On a day when the DJIA rises 30 points, your stock may drop 2, or vice versa.

As you can see from the following list, the 30 DJIA stocks are high-quality industrial stocks selected because so many people own them and their market value is so great. Occasionally, a merger, a bankruptcy, or extreme lack of activity causes a particular stock to be dropped from the average. The most recent change involved the dropping of Inco and Owens-Illinois and the addition of Boeing and Coca-Cola. After each change, the average is readjusted so that it continues to behave in a way consistent with the immediate past.

| 30 Stocks in Industrial Average | | |
| --- | --- | --- |
| Allied-Signal | Exxon | Philip Morris |
| Aluminum Co | General Electric | Primerica |
| Amer Express | General Motors | Procter & Gamble |
| Amer T & T | Goodyear | Sears Roebuck |
| Bethlehem Steel | IBM | Texaco |
| Boeing | International Paper | USX Corp |
| Chevron | McDonalds | Union Carbide |
| Coca-Cola | Merck | United Technologies |
| Du Pont | Minnesota M & M | Westinghouse |
| Eastman Kodak | Navistar | Woolworth |

On any given day, the DJIA is only meaningful if you compare it to earlier values. For example, the DJIA for May 15, 1987, was 2272.52, 52.97 points lower than it was the day before. When you interpret this information, it is important to remember that a DJIA point does not equal $1 in the value of an average share. Rather, it represents about 3 cents in share value.

The other three Dow Jones averages deal with transportation, public utilities, and a composite of stocks. The transportation average is based on 20 stocks, including railroads, airlines, freight forwarders, and mixed transportation companies. The public utility average is computed using 15 public utility stocks. The 65-stock composite average is made up of the 30 industrials, the 20 transportations, and the 15 public utilities. All three have the same purpose as the DJIA: to measure the changes in the market over time. Usually, you'll find all four Dow Jones averages side by side in the financial section of your daily paper.

## STANDARD & POOR'S INDEXES

Standard & Poor's Corporation publishes five common stock indexes. As indexes, they relate the current price of a group of stocks to a base, in this case a base established for the 1941–43 period, which has an assigned value of 10. In other words, if an S&P index is currently 100, the average share price of stock in the index has increased by a factor of 10 (100 ÷ 10) since the 1941–43 period. While the Dow Jones averages weight each stock's price equally, the S&P indexes weight each company's share price by the number of shares outstanding to reflect the relative importance of each share in the marketplace. Although the Dow Jones averages are most popular with the general public, many professional investors prefer the S&P indexes, since they are felt to reflect more accurately the price behavior of the overall market.

The five common stock indexes published by Standard & Poor's are the industrials, transportation, utilities, financials, and composite. They reflect the activity of common stock in the following number of firms:

| S&P Common Stock Index | No. of Firms |
| --- | --- |
| Industrials | 400 |
| Transportation | 20 |
| Utilities | 40 |
| Financials | 40 |
| Composite | 500 |

Like the Dow Jones averages, S&P indexes appear in the daily financial news.

Although the Dow Jones averages and S&P's indexes tend to behave in a similar fashion over time, their day-to-day magnitude and even direction (up or down) can differ significantly. However, what appears to be a large difference may actually be relatively small. On May 14, 1987, for example, the DJIA was 2325.49 and the S&P 400 (the industrial index) was 342.46. Although the DJIA declined 52.97 points the following day, the S&P 400 decreased by only 7.89 points. When these changes are viewed in relation to the absolute size of the average or index, the difference in magnitude all but disappears. In this case, the DJIA decreased by 2.28 percent (52.97 ÷ 2325.49), and the S&P 400 decreased by 2.30 percent (7.89 ÷ 342.46).

## EXCHANGE-BASED INDEXES

Three exchange-based indexes are also very popular: the New York Stock Exchange (NYSE) index, the American Stock Exchange (AMEX) index, and the National Association of Securities Dealers Automated Quotation (NASDAQ) index.

The *NYSE* publishes indexes for a composite of stocks as well as for industrials, utilities, transportation, and finance subgroups. The NYSE composite index includes all the approximately 2,300 stocks listed on the "big board." It is calculated in a similar way as the S&P indexes. A base of 50 reflects the value of stocks listed on the NYSE on December 31, 1965. The behavior of the NYSE industrial index is normally quite similar to that of the DJIA and the S&P 400.

The *AMEX index* reflects the price of all shares trading on the exchange relative to a base of 100, which represents share value on August 31, 1973. The AMEX index is calculated in a similar way as the S&P indexes and therefore tends to behave in a similar fashion. Like the NYSE indexes, the AMEX index is often cited in the financial news.

The *NASDAQ indexes*, which reflect over-the-counter market activity, are calculated like the S&P, NYSE, and AMEX indexes and based on a value of 100, which was set on February 5, 1971. The most comprehensive of the NASDAQ indexes is the OTC composite index, which is calculated using more than 3,700 domestic common stocks traded on the NASDAQ system. Other NASDAQ indexes include the industrials, insurance, banks, a national market composite, and the national market industrials—the industrial stocks traded on the NASDAQ National Market System (NMS). Although their degrees of responsiveness may vary, the NASDAQ indexes tend to move in the same direction at the same time as the other major indexes.

## VALUE LINE AVERAGES

Value Line publishes a number of stock averages constructed by equally weighting the price of each stock included in the average and only considering percentage changes in stock prices. This approach is appealing since it eliminates the effects of differing market price and total market value on the relative importance of each stock.

The *Value Line composite average* includes the approximately 1,700 stocks in the *Value Line Investment Survey* that are traded on the NYSE, AMEX, and in the OTC market. A base of 100 reflects the stock average on June 30, 1961. In addition to the composite, Value Line publishes averages for industrials, rails, and utilities. These averages are especially appealing to individual investors because they include stocks that are likely to be held in their portfolios.

## OTHER AVERAGES AND INDEXES

In addition to the major market measures we've described here, a number of others are available. The *Wilshire 5000 Index*, published by Wilshire Associates, Inc., of Santa Monica, California, is reported daily in *The Wall Street Journal*. It represents the total dollar value (in billions of dollars) of 5,000 actively traded stocks, including all those on the NYSE and AMEX as well as active OTC stocks. *Barron's* publishes a 50-stock average, the average price of the 20 most active stocks, and an index of 20 low-priced stocks. *The New York Times* publishes its own average, which is similar to the Dow Jones averages. *Moody's Investors Service* prepares market indicators for a variety of common stock groups.

---

# READ BOND MARKET INDICATORS

If you invest in bonds, it is important to understand the key bond market indicators, which assess the general behavior of the bond markets. Because so few investors trade bonds, relatively few bond market indicators have been developed. The key measures are the Dow Jones bond averages, bond yields, and the New York Stock Exchange bond statistics.

## DOW JONES BOND AVERAGES

Dow Jones publishes utility, industrial, and composite bond averages. Each is a simple mathematical average of closing bond prices rather than yields. The utility bond average is based on the closing prices of 10 utility bonds; the industrial bond average on the closing prices of 10 industrial bonds; and the composite bond average on the closing prices of 10 utility and 10 industrial bonds.

Like bond price quotations, the bond averages are presented in terms of the percentage of face value at which the bond sells. For example, the May 15, 1987, Dow Jones composite bond average of 88.77 indicates that, on average, bonds sold for 88.77 percent of their face or maturity value; that means the average price of a $1,000 bond equaled about $887.70. Dow Jones also publishes a U.S. government bond average, which is calculated the same way. The Dow Jones bond averages are published daily in *The Wall Street Journal* and are summarized on a weekly basis in *Barron's*.

## BOND YIELDS

*Bond yields* capture the behavior of market interest rates and represent a kind of summary measure of the return an investor would receive on a bond if it were held to maturity. Bond yields are reported as an annual rate of return; for example, a bond with a yield of 9.50 percent will provide its owner with a return in the form of periodic interest *and* capital gain or loss that would be equivalent to a 9.50 percent annual rate of earnings on the amount invested, if held to maturity.

Typically, bond yields are quoted for a group of bonds that are similar in type and quality of issuer, bond maturity, and so on. For example, *Barron's* quotes the average yields for the Dow Jones 10 utilities, 10 industrials, and 20 bond composites, as well as for a group of 20 municipal bonds. The yields quoted by *Barron's* for the week ended May 15, 1987, were 9.79 percent for utilities, 9.64 percent for industrials, 9.72 percent for the composite, and 8.21 percent for municipals. Similar bond yield data are also available from S&P, Moody's, and the Federal Reserve. Like stock market averages and indexes, bond yields are especially useful when viewed over time; studying the trend in bond yields can help astute investors time purchases and sales.

## NEW YORK STOCK EXCHANGE BOND STATISTICS

Since the New York Stock Exchange is the dominant organized exchange on which bonds are traded, summary statistics on daily bond-trading activity on the exchange often reflect the behavior of the bond market as a whole. Statistics measure the number of issues traded; the number that advanced, declined, or remained unchanged; the number of new highs and new lows; and total sales volume in dollars. For example, on May 15, 1987, 842 domestic issues were traded: 154 advanced, 539 declined, and 149 remained unchanged. Of the issues traded, 9 achieved new price highs for the year and 103 fell to new lows. Total sales volume was $52,910,000. NYSE bond statistics are published daily in *The Wall Street Journal*, and a weekly summary can be found in *Barron's*.

# **THREE**
## PLAYING IT SAFE—
## STOCKS, BONDS,
## AND MUTUAL FUNDS

# 12

## UNDERSTANDING COMMON STOCKS

———

Few investors were able to resist the raging bull market that began in August 1982 and ran for some five years, to October 1987. In October, we learned that a principle of physics also applies to the stock market: what goes up can come down! The market turned decidedly bearish in October as the Dow Jones industrial average lost roughly 700 points in three trading days; 508 of those points were lost in *one* day, October 19. Nevertheless, most investors would agree the bull market was great while it lasted. Stock prices literally went wild as the market repeatedly reached new heights. Starting from a low of 776.92 on the Dow Jones industrial average, the market soared to 2,700 by August 1987. In 1986 alone, the market rose from 1,546.67 on January 2 to 1,895.95 on December 31—a rise of nearly 350 points, or 22.6 percent. What's more, the performance of specific stocks often surpassed this pace. In 1986, for example, American Can climbed from 60 to 84⅛; Texas Air jumped from 15 to 33¾; Apple Computer rose from 22 to 40½; and Consumers Power more than doubled as it climbed from 7½ to 15⅝. Although we learned it is foolhardy to count on this kind of performance every year, this bull market demonstrated the kind of capital gains profits that can be earned from common stocks.

But capital gains are not the only reason for owning stocks. Many investors are drawn to these securities because of the current income they offer in the form of dividends, especially now that the Tax Reform Act of 1986 has effectively lowered the taxes on dividends and raised the tax on capital gains. Dividends are important to retired people who must live off their accumulated wealth and to those who take a generally conservative approach to investing.

With between 20,000 and 30,000 stocks trading on all the organized stock exchanges and in the over-the-counter market, it is important to understand exactly what common stocks are and how they work. As you read this chapter, keep in mind that not all corporations trade their shares on the securities markets. They may be small, or they may be privately held and neither want nor need outside ownership. The stocks of interest to us here are *publicly traded*—that is, their shares are readily available to the general public and are bought and sold in the open market. Publicly traded firms range from such corporate giants as AT&T and IBM to small regional or local firms, traded either over-the-counter or on one of the regional exchanges. The dimensions of the market for publicly traded stocks are truly staggering. In 1987, for example, the market value of all stocks listed on U.S. exchanges equaled some $2.5 trillion, not including stocks trading on the OTC market.

## COMMON STOCKS SPELL CORPORATE OWNERSHIP

Each share of common stock represents an equal part ownership in a corporation. For example, if a company has 1,000 shares of stock outstanding, each share symbolizes an identical $1/1,000$ ownership position. Each share you own entitles you to an equal share in the corporation's earnings and dividends and a vote at annual meetings to express your view of company management. However, your claim on the company's income is limited. As a *residual owner* of the corporation, you are entitled to dividend income and a prorated share of company earnings only after all the other obligations of the firm have been met. Equally important, common shareholders have no guarantee that they will ever receive a return on their investment.

### VOTING RIGHTS AND PROCEDURES

As a rule, when you own common stock in a company, you have the right to vote on matters that affect general corporate operations. The basic principle of democracy is at work here: since stockholders are owners, they should have at least some input on important issues that affect earnings and dividends. Voting on selected major items takes place at the *annual stockholders' meeting,* where all stockholders are welcome, regardless of the number of shares owned. At this meeting, company executives present and discuss the annual report and future prospects; also, stockholders elect members of the board of directors and vote on other special issues. Each stockholder is entitled to cast one vote for each share of stock held. If you cannot attend, you may vote by *proxy*—a signed form that assigns your voting rights to another party, usually a member of the board of directors, who is then bound to cast your vote in the way you indicated on the proxy form. Although it is nice to know you have the right to vote, as a small stockholder your chances of affecting company policy are slim at best.

## CLASSIFIED COMMON STOCK

For the most part, companies issue just one class of stock and as such, all the stockholders enjoy the same benefits of ownership. Occasionally, however, a company will issue different classes of common stock, each of which entitles the holder to different privileges and benefits. These are known as *classified common stock.* Even though issued by the same company, each class of common stock is different and each has its own value. Classified common stock is customarily used to denote either different voting rights and/or different dividend obligations. For example, a company might issue two forms of common stock: class A stock, which designates nonvoting shares, and class B stock, which carries normal voting rights of one share, one vote. In another case, class A stock may receive no dividends, while class B stock receives a regular dividend flow. A popular variation of this concept, used by some public utilities, is to automatically reinvest the dividend income of class A stock into additional shares of stock and pay out cash dividends to holders of class B stock.

Because of these variations in voting and dividend rights, whenever a company issues more than one class of common stock, it is important to determine the privileges, benefits, and limitations of each class before you buy. For example, Ford Motor Company issues classified common stock: class A stock is owned by the investing public, and class B stock is owned by the Ford family and their trusts or corporations. The two classes of stock share equally in the dividends, but while class A stock entitles shareholders to one vote per share, the voting rights of class B stock are structured to give the Ford family a 40 percent absolute control of the company. Classified stock is used in a slightly different way by General Motors, which in addition to GM common also issues GM-E and GM-H stock. The class E stock was issued when GM purchased Electronic Data Systems, and the class H stock was the result of GM's purchase of Hughes Aircraft. Both classified stock forms have reduced voting rights, and their dividends are linked to the earnings of their respective operating divisions.

## GETTING THE STOCK TO THE PUBLIC

The number of shares issued by a firm depends on the size of the corporation and its financial needs. Common stock has no maturity date and, as a result, remains outstanding indefinitely.

Shares of common stock can be issued in the following ways:

- *Public offering*—The corporation, working with an underwriter, offers the public a certain number of shares of stock at a specified price. The offering may bring the company to the public for the first time, or it may increase the number of shares of outstanding common stock. In either case, the company is attempting to raise money through stock distributions.
- *Rights offerings*—These offerings guarantee that existing stockholders are given first crack at new stock issues and are allowed to purchase new shares in proportion to their current ownership position in the firm. For example, if a stockholder currently owns 1 percent of a firm's stock and the firm issues 10,000 additional shares, the stockholder is given the opportunity, via a rights offering, to purchase 1 percent (or 100 shares) of the new issue.
- *Deferred equity securities*—Warrants enable investors to buy a stipulated number of shares of common stock at a stipulated price within a given time period; convertible securities allow investors to exchange them for a certain number of shares of common stock. Either way, the securities are initially issued in one form and later redeemed or converted into shares of common stock. The net result is the same as with a public offering or a rights offering: the firm ends up with more equity in its capital structure and a greater number of outstanding shares.

## STOCK SPLITS

Companies can also increase the number of shares outstanding by executing a *stock split*. To do this, the company exchanges a specified number of new shares of stock for each outstanding share. For example, in a 2 for 1 stock split, 2 new shares of stock are exchanged for each old share; in a 3 for 2 split, 3 new shares are exchanged for every 2 shares outstanding. Thus, if you owned 200 shares of stock before a 2 for 1 split, you would automatically own 400 shares after the split was complete; in a 3 for 2 split, your share total would increase to 300.

Stock splits are used whenever a firm, believing the price of its stock is too high, wants to enhance the stock's trading appeal by lowering its market price. It is a normal market reaction for the price of a stock to fall in relation to the terms of the split. Using the ratio of the number of old shares to new shares, we can expect a $100 stock to trade at $50 after a 2 for 1 split. Likewise, that same stock would trade at about $67 after a 3 for 2 split. As a result, stockholders may own more shares of stock after a split, but each share is worth less. It's like receiving two $5 bills for a $10: the value of your holdings after a stock split are about the same as they were before.

Most stock splits are executed in order to increase the number of shares outstanding. Sometimes, however, a *reverse stock split* is declared; these splits reduce the number of shares outstanding and increase the share price of the stock by exchanging less than one share of new stock for each outstanding share. For example, in a 1 for 2 split, 1 new share of stock is exchanged for 2 old shares. Reverse stock splits are also used to enhance the trading appeal of the stock. But this time the goal is to boost the price of a stock to a more respectable level.

## TREASURY STOCK: WHEN CORPORATIONS BUY BACK THEIR OWN STOCK

A corporation may decide to reduce the number of shares in the hands of investors. It does this by buying back its own stock. Generally, firms repurchase stock when they believe it is a good buy; for example, when the price of the stock is unusually low. In essence, the company acquires the stock in the open market by becoming an investor like any other individual or institution. The shares it acquires are known as *treasury stock.*

Technically, treasury stocks are shares of stock that have been issued and subsequently repurchased by the issuing firm. They are retained by the corporation for use in mergers and acquisitions, for employee stock option plans, or for payment of stock dividends. In fact, most treasury stock is reissued by the firm in one way or another. From an investor's point of view, unless the stock repurchase plan is substantial, its impact is fairly limited. Stockholders' equity in the firm is increased slightly, and there may be a modest upward effect on market price.

## THE DIFFERENT VALUES OF COMMON STOCK

The worth of a share of common stock can be described in a number of different ways, including par value, book value, liquidation value, market value, and investment value.

### PAR VALUE

A stated value that is placed on stock certificates, par value was intended to represent not the value of the stock but the minimum price at which it could be sold without causing the shareholder to assume any liability for the firm's actions. Today, par value has little or no significance for investors; in fact, many stocks today are issued as no par or low par, but this has no effect whatsoever on their actual trading value. For example, while the par value of a share of National Healthcare is 1 cent, it was issued to the public at a price of $13.50.

### BOOK VALUE

Book value represents the amount of stockholders' equity in a firm. In other words, it indicates the amount of stockholder funds used to finance the firm. It is an accounting measure that is determined by subtracting the firm's liabilities and preferred stock from the amount of assets it holds.

For example, let's assume that a firm has $10 million in assets, owes $5 million in various forms of short- and long-term debt, and has $1 million worth of preferred stock outstanding. The book value of this firm would be $4 million. This amount can be converted to a per share basis—book value per share—if divided by the number of shares outstanding. For example, if this firm has 100,000 shares of common stock outstanding, then its book value per share is $40. As a rule, the market price of a stock is—or should be—greater than its book value.

## LIQUIDATION VALUE

Liquidation value indicates what the firm would bring on the auction block were it to close its doors and cease operations. It reflects the potential value of the firm after its assets are sold and after its liabilities to suppliers, bondholders, preferred stockholders, and other creditors have been met. Obviously, this measure is no more than an estimate of what the firm would be worth under these extraordinary circumstances. Since publicly traded firms rarely are forced to liquidate, this value means little to most investors.

## MARKET VALUE

This is one of the easiest of all values to determine. It is also one of the most important. Market value is simply the prevailing market price of an issue, or the price tag the market as a whole puts on each share of stock. Using this base value, you can obtain the market value of the firm, or what a firm is worth. For example, a firm with 1 million shares outstanding, now trading at $50 a share, is worth $50 million on the market. Market value is much more important to investors than liquidation, par, or book value. It provides information you must have in order to make intelligent buy and sell decisions.

## INVESTMENT VALUE

Investment value is probably the most important measure for investors since it indicates how much they think a stock *should* cost. Determining this value is a fairly complicated process based on expectations of the stock's potential return versus its potential risk. Together, this information enables you to place a maximum price on the stock, which represents the top price you would be willing to pay for it.

## THE PROMISE OF DIVIDEND INCOME

In 1986, corporations paid out some $88 billion in dividends, almost $25 billion more than they had paid 5 years earlier. Dividend income, along with capital gains, are the two basic sources of return to investors. Some investors tend to look down their noses at dividends and view them as an insignificant dimension of investment return. If this is your attitude, it could wind up costing you a great deal of money, since dividend income is now favored under the new tax law.

The preferential treatment of long-term capital gains has been eliminated, and they are now taxed at the same rate as dividends. Thus, dividends have become more valuable, since not only is the amount you can keep after taxes the same as for capital gains, but earning dividends is far less risky. Capital gains still represent the principal vehicle through which really big returns are realized, but the new tax code throws a whole new (and far more favorable) light on dividend income.

## TO PAY OR NOT TO PAY: A DECISION ONLY THE BOARD CAN MAKE

Most companies pay dividends on a fairly regular basis, generally quarterly. The dividend decision is made by the firm's board of directors, which evaluates the firm's financial condition to determine whether or not, and in what amount, dividends should be paid. The board's decision is based on a variety of factors:

- First, the board looks at *corporate earnings.* As you might expect, a healthy profit picture increases the likelihood that dividends will be paid. However, a company does not have to show a profit to pay dividends. That is, since firms can pay dividends from earnings accumulated in previous periods, you may receive dividends even in periods when the firm shows a loss. Annual earnings are usually measured in terms of *earnings per share (EPS),* which translate total corporate profits into profits on a per share basis and provide a convenient measure of the amount of earnings available to stockholders.
- Next, the board looks at the firm's *growth prospects.* It determines how much of the firm's present earnings will be needed to finance expected growth.
- It then examines the firm's *cash position* to make sure there is sufficient liquidity to meet whatever cash dividend is awarded.
- The board also needs assurance that it is meeting all *legal and contractual constraints.* It has to be certain, for example, that no loan agreement limits the amount of dividends the company can pay.
- Finally the board must consider the expected effect its dividend decision will have on the *market price* of the stock. Board members realize that the market generally places a high value on dividends. They also realize that if the company retains earnings, it must show satisfactory growth. The market understands when dividends are not paid only if the company shows promise of an even bigger payoff in the future. Shareholder expectations are also involved in this decision. Since investors interested in high income are attracted to firms that generally pay high dividends, the stock price will drop if a dividend is eliminated or reduced.

## DIVIDEND POLICIES VARY FROM COMPANY TO COMPANY

Taking all of these factors into account, the board of directors decides whether or not to pay dividends and, if so, what amount to pay. In all but a handful of cases, dividends are charged against retained earnings, which represent the amount of past and current corporate earnings not paid out as dividends. Thus, any earnings not paid out as cash dividends are left to accumulate in the firm and are used to finance growth or pay off debt.

Most companies have a stated or implied dividend policy that sets the dividend payment practices the company will follow. The policy is usually established with an eye toward the financing requirements of the firm and the needs of its stockholders. Because these policies can affect the level and consistency of dividend payments, you should know what they are and how they operate. Following are three of the most widely used dividend policies.

*Regular dividends.* The regular dividend approach calls for the payment of a fixed dollar dividend each quarter. It is the most common type of dividend policy. Firms that use it go to almost any length to avoid missing or decreasing a dividend. This attitude forces firms to be absolutely certain before they increase their dividend levels that they can continue to maintain the new level. In general, increases are made only after new earnings levels are proven. For example, a firm that has an annual dividend rate of $2 a share will hold that level until earnings move consistently to a new and higher plateau, which can take several years. Only then will dividends be increased to a higher level of, say, $2.50 a share. The object of this policy is to minimize the uncertainty of the dividend flow and to reinforce the faith stockholders have in the company's strength.

*Extra dividends.* Some firms may declare *extra dividends* if the level of earnings is higher than normal and the firm has a larger than expected pool of funds from which to draw. Extra dividends are usually, but not always, paid in the final quarter of the year and are designated as *extra* in order to avoid giving stockholders the impression that this bonus indicates a new level of regular dividends.

*Fixed payout ratio.* The fixed payout ratio is used by a number of firms, particularly newer ones and those experiencing high growth rates. By definition, a payout ratio describes the percentage of earnings distributed to the owners in the form of cash dividends. For example, if the company had earnings of $2 a share, a payout ratio of 25 percent would result in annual dividends of 50 cents a share (that is, $2 \times .25 = \$.50$).

Little attention is given to the dollar level of dividends. Instead, the thrust of this policy is to keep the ratio of the amount paid out to earnings as constant as possible. As a result, if earnings fluctuate, so do dividends. If the fluctuation is downward, stockholders receive smaller dividends. The market often responds to these unstable dividends by pushing down the common stock price, unless, of course, the company can show that it is using the retained earnings to generate an attractive rate of corporate growth.

## DIVIDENDS CAN TAKE THE FORM OF CASH OR STOCK

More firms pay cash dividends than any other form of dividend. The instant liquidity of these dividends also makes them very popular with investors. If the directors declare a quarterly cash dividend of 50 cents a share, and you own 200 shares, you receive a check for $100.

You can translate these dividends into the rate of current income earned on your investment dollar by using a simple formula to measure dividend yield. Basically, *dividend yield* is a way to measure the dollar amount of dividends you receive in relation to the market price of the stock:

$$\text{dividend yield} = \frac{\text{annual dividends paid per share}}{\text{market price per share of stock}}$$

Thus, if you hold stock in a company that pays an annual dividend of $2 a share and which is now trading at $25, you would be earning a dividend yield of 8 percent.

Occasionally, firms declare *stock dividends,* which are dividends paid in the form of additional shares of stock. For instance, if the board declares a 10 percent stock dividend, each shareholder will receive 1 new share of stock for each 10 shares currently owned. If you own 200 shares of stock, you will receive, at no cost, 20 new shares of stock.

Although this seems to satisfy many investors, in reality stock dividends have no value at all. In effect, they represent the receipt of something already owned. The reason this is so is because the market responds to stock dividends by adjusting share prices downward. Thus, a 10 percent stock dividend will lead to a 10 percent decline in the price of a stock. As a result, if the market value of your shareholdings amounts to $10,000 before a stock dividend, you're likely to have the same amount in your account after the stock dividend takes place. Although you have more shares, each carries a lower market price. There is one nice feature of stock dividends that you should be aware of, however: unlike cash dividends, you don't have to pay taxes on them. As long as you hold onto the additional shares, there's no tax to pay until the stocks are actually sold. Often, companies combine a modest stock dividend with a cash dividend.

Sometimes stock or cash dividends can take unusual forms:

- A *spin-off dividend* is like a stock dividend except that the company pays its stockholders in shares of stock other than its own. Generally, it issues shares in subsidiary companies in which, for one reason or another, the company is reducing, or eliminating, its ownership position.
- *Return-of-capital dividends,* issued by some public utility companies, are cash dividends charged against "original paid-in capital" rather than retained earnings.

Because of this, they are considered different from normal cash dividends. Return-of-capital dividends are highly valued by knowledgeable, income-oriented investors because they are not subject to income tax.

However, one problem with these dividends is that your *investment base* (that is, the amount of money you invested in the stock) has to be lowered for any return-of-capital dividends you receive. Thus, if you originally paid $50 a share for a stock and over time received a total of $5 a share in return-of-capital dividends, the stock would have an adjusted investment base of $45 a share ($50 − $5). This is the amount you compare to the selling price to determine capital gains for tax purposes.

## DIVIDEND REINVESTMENT PLANS

In recent years, a growing number of companies have established *dividend reinvestment plans (DRPs),* which give shareholders the right to reinvest their cash dividends automatically in additional shares of the company's common stock. There are over 1,300 dividend reinvestment plans in existence today—most major corporations have them—and each plan provides investors with a convenient and inexpensive way to accumulate capital. Stocks in most DRPs are acquired free of any brokerage commissions, and some plans even sell stock to their DRP investors at below-market prices. In addition, most plans credit fractional shares to the investor's account.

These plans are easy to join: simply send in a completed authorization form to the company. Once you are in the plan, the number of shares you hold will begin to accumulate with each passing dividend date. The major drawback to these plans is that, even though the dividends are received in the form of additional shares of stock, taxes must be paid as though you had received your dividends in cash. These dividends should not be confused with stock dividends. *Reinvested dividends are taxable in the year they are received as ordinary income,* just as if they had been received in cash.

## SOME IMPORTANT DATES

When the directors declare a dividend, they also indicate several important dates associated with the dividend:

- The *date of record* is the date on which you must be a registered shareholder of the firm to be entitled to receive the dividend. Stockholders who meet this requirement are known as *holders of record.*
- Because of the time needed to make bookkeeping entries when a stock is traded, the stock will sell on what is known as an "ex-dividend" basis (that is, without dividends) for 4 business days prior to the date of record. Thus, the *ex-dividend date* will determine whether or not you are an official shareholder and are therefore eligible to receive the declared dividend. If you sell a stock after the ex-dividend date, you receive the dividend; if you sell before that date, the new shareholder is entitled to it.

- The *payment date* is also set by the board of directors and generally follows the date of record by a few weeks. It is the date on which the company will mail dividend checks to holders of record.

## THE PROS AND CONS OF COMMON STOCK OWNERSHIP

Common stocks are attractive to investors because of the substantial return opportunities they offer in the form of capital gains. These returns are possible because common stocks, as equity securities, are entitled to participate fully in the residual profits of the firm. The market price of a share of stock generally reflects this profit potential, and as corporate profits increase so do stock prices.

Common stocks are also appealing because they are highly liquid and easily transferable. They are easy to buy and sell, and transaction costs are modest. Moreover, price and market information is readily available. The relatively low unit cost of a share of common stock also puts it well within the reach of most individuals. Unlike bonds, which carry minimum denominations of at least $1,000, and some mutual funds, which have fairly hefty minimum investment requirements, many common stocks are priced at less than $50 a share, and any number of shares, no matter how few, can be bought and sold.

Unfortunately, common stock ownership also brings with it considerable risk. Stocks are subject to business and financial risk, purchasing power risk, and market risk, all of which can adversely affect a stock's earnings and dividends, price appreciation, and hence rate of return. Even the best stocks possess elements of risk that are difficult to overcome. Their earnings are at the mercy of many factors, including government regulation, foreign competition, the general state of the economy, and industry trends. Because these factors affect sales and profits, they also affect the price of the stock and, possibly, the amount of dividends paid.

Since the earnings and general performance of stocks are often subject to wide swings, it is extremely difficult to value common stock and consistently select top performers. The selection process is complex because so many elements go into formulating expectations of how the price of the stock should perform in the future. In other words, not only is the future outcome of the company and its stock uncertain, but so is the valuation and selection process itself.

A final disadvantage is the sacrifice in current income. Several types of investments—bonds, for instance—pay higher levels of current income, with much greater certainty. The figure on the next page, which compares the dividend yield of common stocks with the current yield of bonds, shows how the spread in current income has widened over time and reveals the kind of sacrifice common stock investors make. Although the spread has improved since the early 1980s, common stocks still have a long way to go before they catch up with the current income levels available from some other investment vehicles.

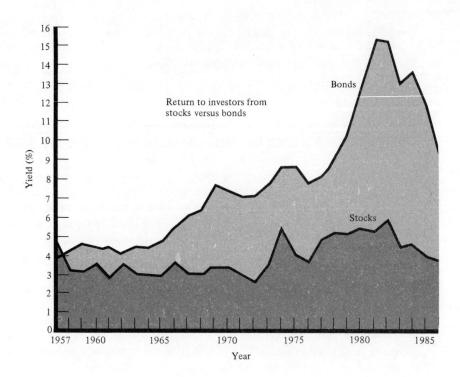

Return to investors from
stocks versus bonds

Bonds

Stocks

Yield (%)

Year

PLAYING IT SAFE—STOCKS, BONDS, AND MUTUAL FUNDS

# 13

## INVESTING IN COMMON STOCKS: BEGINNING THE SELECTION PROCESS

One of the most important facets of investing in common stock is *focus:* With between 20,000 and 30,000 publicly traded common stocks to choose from, you need a way to decide which stocks have the potential to fit into your overall financial plan. You must be able to place these stocks into meaningful categories that will ultimately help you make specific investment choices.

Your focus should then turn to different investment strategies: Should you buy and hold a stock for many years? Should you buy quality issues in the hope of earning high income or capital gains? Should you aggressively trade these issues? Or should you speculate for short-term gain? It is no understatement to say that your choices here can mean the difference between investment success and failure.

Our goal in this chapter is to help you set your focus by first looking at the different categories of common stock and then at the most popular investment strategies. We want to make these basic choices as familiar to you as they are to seasoned investors.

## STOCKS HAVE PERSONALITIES TOO

Common stocks are popular with investors because they offer the opportunity to tailor an investment program to individual needs and preferences. For retired people and others living on accumulated wealth, stocks provide an excellent opportunity to preserve capital and gain current income. For others, common stocks are the basis for long-term wealth-accumulation programs and are used very much like savings accounts. But for many investors, the real appeal of common stocks is their potential for generating attractive returns. To be sure, some investors buy stocks for the dividend income they produce, but as a rule, most investors buy stocks for their capital gains.

The labels the market puts on different types of common stocks tell you a great deal about the stocks themselves. First and foremost, they indicate the stock's fundamental source of return. On a more sophisticated level, they also provide clues to the quality of company earnings, the issue's susceptibility to market and economic risks, and the nature and stability of earnings and dividends. All this information enables you to tell, almost at a glance, whether certain types of stocks have the potential to fit into your investment portfolio. Once you determine this, you can focus your efforts on analyzing and choosing specific stocks. To help guide you through this process, let's take a look at the major stock groups.

### BLUE CHIPS: THE CREAM OF THE COMMON STOCK CROP

With a long and stable record of earnings and dividends, blue chips are unsurpassed in quality. These are the so-called glamor stocks, issued by the strongest of companies, including a number of public utilities as well as such industrial giants as GE, Procter & Gamble, Du Pont, Eastman Kodak, and GM. Some blue chip companies provide consistently high dividend yields, while others are more growth-oriented. Good examples of blue chip growth firms are IBM, Merck, American Express, Marriott, and Pillsbury; some high-yielding blue chips include AT&T, Exxon, Philip Morris, and USX.

In general, investors who are drawn to blue chips are seeking quality stocks that pay respectable dividends and offer some hope of future growth. Many investors buy these stocks to hold onto them. That is, they see these stocks as a way to obtain a steady, dependable return on their investment for a long period of time. Because of their popularity, these stocks are fairly expensive, and their value tends to increase when market conditions are unstable and quality becomes uppermost in investors' minds.

## INCOME STOCKS: THE PROMISE OF STEADY INCOME

Income stocks are appealing because they pay attractive dividend yields. These issues are characterized by a fairly stable stream of earnings and a long and sustained record of paying higher than average dividends. These features make income stocks ideal for those who want a relatively safe and high level of current income from their investment capital. Unlike holders of bonds and preferred stock, holders of income stocks can also expect the amount of dividends they receive to increase over time. It is important to realize, however, that these stocks generally offer only limited growth. Although most of these firms are highly profitable organizations with strong future prospects, their earnings outlook is less growth-oriented than income-oriented.

A number of income stocks are among the giants of American industry, and many are also classified as quality blue chips. The group includes such public utilities as Tucson Electric Power and Houston Industries and such industrial and financial issues as GTE, Union Carbide, American Brands, and Manufacturers Hanover. By their nature, income stocks are more susceptible to interest rate risk than to business or market risk, since their return is usually judged relative to other income-oriented securities, like bonds.

## GROWTH STOCKS: PRICE APPRECIATION IS THE KEY

Shares that have experienced, and are expected to continue experiencing, consistently high rates of growth in earnings are known as growth stocks. These are stocks issued by companies whose sales, earnings, and share of the market are growing at a faster rate than the economy and faster than the average for the industry. While other stocks may grow at a rate of 5 or 6 percent a year, growth stocks will grow at 2 or 3 times that rate. The important feature of this growth is that it is sustained over a long period of time. Boeing, Abbott Labs, Baxter Travenol, Best Products, Digital Equipment, and NCR have all performed in this way. As this list suggests, some growth stocks are blue chips, providing quality growth, while others are more risky.

These companies are generally aggressive and research-minded, plowing back their profits to encourage rapid future growth. As a result, they usually pay little or nothing in dividends. Thus, your potential return is linked to price appreciation in the form of capital gains. Although this expectation is always risky, it does not deter investors who believe that they will see a tremendous rise in the stock price sometime in the future.

## SPECULATIVE STOCKS: HOPE SPRINGS ETERNAL

Stocks that offer little more than the hope that their prices will go up are known as speculative stocks. These stocks lack a lengthy, sustained record of success; their earnings are uncertain and highly unstable; they are subject to wide swings in price; and they usually pay nothing in dividends. Despite these drawbacks, these stocks attract millions of investors, expecially in a bull market, who see them as chances to hit it big. Sometimes it's a new management team taking over a troubled firm, or the introduction of a new product. Other times, it's the possibility that some new information, discovery, or production technique will come along, favorably affect the growth prospects of the firm, and inflate the price of the stock.

The key to success with speculative stocks is identifying the big money winners before the rest of the market catches on. These stocks are used by investors who buy and sell on a fairly short-term basis in the hope of achieving capital gains. If you decide to invest, you should know a great deal about the company and have a stomach strong enough to deal with major drops in stock price. Genentech, Ramada Inns, Lotus Development, America West Airlines, Carter Wallace, and Prime Computers are all examples of speculative issues.

## CYCLICAL STOCKS: A REFLECTION OF THE GENERAL ECONOMY

Cyclical stocks are closely linked to the general level of business activity. That is, their earnings tend to reflect the general state of the economy and move up or down along with the business cycle. Companies tied to business or consumer spending for big-ticket durable items (houses and cars, for example) typically head the list of cyclical stocks. These include the likes of Dow Chemical, Aluminum Company of America, Motorola, Caterpillar, and Ford.

For obvious reasons, these stocks are most appealing when the economy is strong and least appealing when it begins to weaken. To maximize return, most investors trade in and out of these issues as economic conditions change. As you might expect, there's a fair amount of risk associated with the up and down movement of stock prices.

## DEFENSIVE STOCKS: GOING AGAINST THE ECONOMIC TREND

Sometimes it is possible to find stocks whose prices will remain relatively stable, or even increase, when economic activity declines. These securities, known as defensive stocks, tend to be less affected by downswings in the business cycle than the average issue. (For this reason, they are often called *countercyclical.*) The shares of many public utilities, as well as industrial and consumer goods companies that produce food, beverages, drugs, and other staples, are good examples of defensive stocks. Gold mining stocks are perhaps the best known of all defensive stocks because they are fairly resistant to inflation.

Defensive stocks are commonly used as temporary investments while the economy or market is unsettled. When market conditions improve, many investors move their money elsewhere. If you decide to invest, be prepared to trade in and out on a fairly short-term basis as market conditions change. If you're a conservative investor, these stocks probably are *not* for you. Some examples of defensive stocks include Upjohn, Syntex, General Mills, R.J. Reynolds, and Ralston Purina.

## FOREIGN STOCKS: FOR SOME INTRIGUING RETURNS

As strong as the U.S. stock market was in the early to mid-eighties, many foreign markets were doing even better. But there's more; for the return to American stockholders (from foreign stocks) is also affected by the behavior of the dollar in foreign exchange markets. When the value of the dollar drops, the return from a foreign stock goes up, and vice versa, of course. This explains why investing in Japanese stock was so rewarding in 1986–87: not only were Japanese stocks doing great, but relative to the American dollar the Japanese Yen was going way up as well. To American investors, that combination spelled big returns! But the added variable of foreign exchange rates and the complex nature of their returns also mean more risks to investors in foreign stocks. Now you have two things that can go wrong—the stock itself and the value of the dollar. Remember, the dollar doesn't always fall!

Foreign stocks can be purchased directly on foreign stock exchanges, or on American exchanges through *American Depository Receipts (ADRs)*, which eliminate much of the expense and red tape of trading abroad. Basically, an ADR is a negotiable instrument, issued by an American bank, that represents a specific number of shares of stock in a specific foreign company. For example, each Honda ADR represents ownership of 10 shares of Honda stock. While Honda stock is not listed on any American exchange, its ADRs are listed on the New York Stock Exchange, where they trade like shares of American companies. You'll find many different ADRs listed on the NYSE and AMEX and a great many more traded over-the-counter. These include Jaguar, Benguet Corp, British Petroleum, KLM, Sony, and Unilever.

## SMALL COMPANIES: WHEN BIG ISN'T NECESSARILY BEAUTIFUL

Many investors believe that the stocks of small companies hold the greatest opportunity for capital gains, especially in a strong market. With sales generally less than $100 million, these companies are extremely sensitive to growth. Indeed, spurts of growth can dramatically boost earnings per share and stock prices too. Also known as *emerging growth stocks*, these securities can provide very attractive returns to investors. Examples of some recently popular small companies include Quick & Reilly, Alfin Fragrances, Businessland, Tandem Computers, Angen, Lifetime Corp., and Kinder-Care Learning Centers.

However, the risks are great. Many of these firms do not have the solid financial base to weather hard times, and as a result bankruptcy is a real possibility.

Another drawback is limited trading activity. Because these companies have relatively few shares of stock outstanding, you may find that they are difficult to buy and sell.

## INITIAL PUBLIC OFFERINGS: GETTING IN ON THE GROUND FLOOR

Initial public offerings (IPOs) are small, relatively new companies that go public for the first time. Prior to their public offerings, these stocks were privately held. In 1986, 717 companies went public and, in the process, raised a record $22.4 billion in capital.

Like small companies, IPOs are attractive because of their substantial—sometimes phenomenal—capital gains potential. For example, Entertainment Marketing came out in 1985 at an initial price of $2 a share; 6 months later it was trading at $6.50, providing investors with a 222 percent rate of return. Unfortunately, not all IPOs are this successful, and if you choose the wrong one, you may wind up losing all—or nearly all—your investment. For example, when Pizza Transit Authority was first issued in 1985, it sold for $2.75 a share, but by the end of the year it was trading at just $1. Without question, IPOs are extremely risky investments that offer investors the small but real chance of striking it rich. Home Shopping Network, Family Steak Houses, Microsoft, Digitext, Pacific Southwest Airlines, and Enviropact are just a few examples of some well-known IPOs that came out in 1986 and 1987. IPOs are especially popular when the market heats up and speculative stocks start coming into favor (securities markets, like people, are also susceptible to fads).

## COMMON STOCK INVESTMENT STRATEGIES

Investors hold common stocks for three main reasons: (1) as a warehouse of value, (2) as a way to accumulate capital, and/or (3) as a source of income.

Storage of value is important to all investors, since nobody likes to lose money. However, some investors are more concerned about it than others and therefore put safety of principal first in their stock selection process. These investors are quality-conscious and tend to gravitate toward blue chips and other nonspeculative shares. Accumulation of capital is generally an important goal to those with long-term investment horizons. They use the capital gains and dividends that stocks provide to build up their wealth. Some use growth stocks for such purposes; others do it with income shares; still others use a little of both. Finally, for people who use stocks as a source of income, a dependable flow of dividends is essential. High-yield, good quality income shares are usually their preferred investment vehicle.

Whatever your motive for holding stocks, you'll have to follow some investment strategy in order to reach your investment goals. Following are a few of the more popular strategies.

## BUY AND HOLD

This is the most basic and one of the most conservative of all investment strategies; the objective is to place your money in a secure investment outlet (safety of principal is vital) and watch it grow over time. High-quality stocks that offer attractive current income and/or capital gains are selected and held for extended periods—perhaps for as long as 15 or 20 years. This strategy is often used to finance retirement plans, to meet the educational needs of children, or simply to accumulate capital over the long haul. The idea is to let the principle of compound interest work for you.

If you choose this strategy, you invest in a few stocks on a regular basis for extended periods of time. You stick with these securities until you need the money or until there is a dramatic shift in the investment climate. Not only do you regularly add fresh capital to your portfolio (in effect treating it like a savings plan), but you also reinvest annual dividends to purchase additional shares (perhaps through dividend reinvestment plans). This strategy satisfies the needs of many investors who do not want to be bothered with day-to-day portfolio management and who want above all to minimize risk.

## HIGH INCOME

You may want to use common stocks for high levels of current income that tends to increase over time. In this case, you will be most concerned with maintaining your principal and providing a steady flow of income; capital gains will be of secondary importance. High-yielding, high-quality income shares are popular choices. This strategy appeals especially to investors on a fixed or limited income, including retirees.

## QUALITY LONG-TERM GROWTH

This less conservative strategy focuses on long-term capital gains. However, in contrast to the buy-and-hold tactic, you trade in and out of stocks much more aggressively in the hope of a big return. Most of the trading is confined to quality growth stocks with good prospects for considerable price appreciation. Since this approach involves a fair amount of risk, it is a good idea to diversify among various issues. In a bear market, many of these investors retreat to the sidelines by converting their stocks to cash or defensive securities.

## AGGRESSIVE STOCK MANAGEMENT

This investment strategy also involves the aggressive trading of quality issues. But this time the goal is both current income and capital gains. In a bull market, the primary investment vehicles are income, cyclical, and growth stocks, while defensive securities, cash, and short-term debt instruments are better choices in a bear market.

This approach is similar to the quality long-term growth strategy, but it involves considerably more trading, and the investment horizon is generally much shorter. For example, rather than waiting 2 or 3 years for a stock to move, an aggressive stock trader would go after the same investment payoff in 6 months to a year. Timing and rapid turnover are key elements of this strategy. It has obvious and substantial risks and also places real demands on your time and investment skills. But the rewards of success can be substantial.

## SPECULATION AND SHORT-TERM TRADING

This is the least conservative of all investment strategies; getting in and out of the market with substantial capital gains is what this strategy is all about. Although with this strategy you would confine most of your attention to speculative shares, you would also use any type of common stock that offered the opportunity for attractive short-term capital gains. You might find that information about an industry or company is less important than market psychology and the general market tone.

Because the strategy involves so much risk, many transactions end up with little or no profit, or even substantial losses. The hope is, of course, that when a winning stock comes through, the returns will be more than sufficient to offset any previous losses. This investment strategy requires considerable knowledge and time. Perhaps more important, it also demands that you have the psychological and financial fortitude to withstand the shock of financial loss.

# 14

## COMMON STOCK ANALYSIS: LOOKING AT THE PAST

———

Everyone has a friend who tells a similar story: "I don't know why I did it. Maybe it was just dumb luck. But something made me buy 400 shares of this widget company. Boy, was I right! The stock soared 50 points in 2 months and I sold it for three times as much as I paid."

How many winners like this can you expect from dumb luck alone? The number may be slightly higher than your chances of winning the lottery or hitting a slot machine jackpot in Atlantic City, but not much. Most people who take this approach succeed only in making their broker rich.

It probably won't surprise you to learn that the key to making the right stock choices over time is plain, old-fashioned hard work. The form it takes is something called *security analysis*—a method used to evaluate the investment suitability of common stocks. Although we would all like to strike it rich right away, security analysis makes no promise of sudden wealth. Rather, it provides sound principles for formulating a successful long-term investment plan. It may not be glamorous, but it works.

# WHAT IS SECURITY ANALYSIS?

Security analysis consists of gathering information, organizing it into a logical format, and using it to determine the *intrinsic value,* or underlying worth, of a common stock. Given an assessment of risk and a desired rate of return, intrinsic value provides a standard for judging whether a particular stock is undervalued, fairly priced, or overvalued. As with any investment vehicle, it is not the past but the future that counts. The investment must not only promise to be profitable, however—it must be *sufficiently profitable.* Only then will it be a satisfactory investment vehicle; that is, an investment that offers *a level of expected return commensurate with perceived exposure to risk.*

To repeat, security analysis addresses the question of what to buy by determining what a stock *ought* to be worth. Further, it suggests that you consider buying a stock only as long as its prevailing market price does not exceed its computed intrinsic value, which in turn depends on these factors:

- Estimates of the stock's future cash flows (the amount of dividends you can expect to receive over the holding period and the estimated price of the stock at the time of sale)
- The discount rate used to translate these future cash flows into a present value
- The amount of risk you must take to achieve the forecasted level of performance

Traditional security analysis usually takes a "top-down" approach that begins with economic analysis, then moves to industry analysis, and finally to fundamental analysis. *Economic analysis* is concerned with assessing the general state of the economy and its potential effects on security returns; *industry analysis* deals with the outlook for the industry within which a particular company operates; *fundamental analysis* looks in depth at the financial condition of a specific company and the underlying behavior of its common stock.

# STEP 1: EVALUATE THE ECONOMY

On any given day newspapers are filled with information on housing starts, the consumer price index, retail sales, unemployment levels, and more. These measures of economic activity are important because they indicate whether the economy is strong or soft. As you might expect, the overall performance of the economy has a significant effect on the performance and profitability of companies that issue common stock. And as the fortunes of the issuing firms change with economic conditions, so will the prices of their stocks. Indeed, as you can see from the table on the next page, stock prices tend to move up when the economy is strong and retreat when the economy softens.

| Economic Period | Change in Standard & Poor's Stock Index | Change in Economic Activity (Index of Industrial Production) |
|---|---|---|
| Economic recovery: | | |
| March 1961–November 1969 | + 49.8% | +71.8% |
| Recession: | | |
| December 1969–November 1970 | − 7.5 | − 4.0 |
| Economic recovery: | | |
| December 1970–November 1973 | + 13.2 | +30.3 |
| Recession: | | |
| December 1973–March 1975 | − 11.6 | −11.8 |
| Economic recovery: | | |
| April 1975–December 1979 | + 23.6 | +35.4 |
| Recession: January 1980–July 1980 | + 6.5 | − 7.9 |
| Economic recovery: August 1980–July 1981 | + 8.5 | + 9.6 |
| Recession: August 1981–October 1982 | − 8.3 | −12.1 |
| Economic recovery: November 1982–March 1987 | +206.5 | +29.4 |

## AS THE ECONOMY GOES, SO GOES BUSINESS

The behavior of the economy is captured by the *business cycle,* which is an indication of the change in total economic activity over time. Basically, the business cycle moves from periods of economic prosperity to periods of economic weakness, which are known as *recessions* or, if they are severe enough, *depressions.* Starting in a recession, the business cycle will move through economic recovery and expansion to prosperity and then through a period of decline back to a recession. These cycles are repeated over and over again. As measured from peak to peak, each one usually lasts 3 to 6 years, though the severity of the swings can range from mild to severe. Business cycles are important to investors since they set the tone of the economy and the market. These economic cycles are tracked by two widely followed measures:

- The *gross national product* (or GNP, as it is more commonly known) represents the market value of all goods and services produced by a country over the period of a year; issued by the Commerce Department, it is the broadest measure of economic activity and is valuable because it reflects movements in so many areas of the economy. The dollar figures are adjusted to eliminate the effects of inflation on annual growth rates. GNP figures are frequently revised, with each version providing a slightly different picture of economic growth. These revisions can cause wide swings in stock prices.

- The *industrial production index* is a figure issued by the Federal Reserve Board to show changes in the output of factories, mines, and other sources of industrial production. This index is a fairly accurate indicator of economic activity, moving up when the economy is strong and down when it is weak.

In addition to these two overall measures, there are several components of economic activity that provide insight into the current status of the economy and help investors keep track of significant economic developments. These include personal income, retail sales, the consumer price index, the producer price index, levels of employment and unemployment, and housing starts. The index of leading economic indicators is a compilation of many of these statistics.

- *Personal income* is reported monthly by the Commerce Department, and details the various forms of before-tax income received by individuals. Included are such income sources as wages and salaries, interest and dividends, rents, Social Security payments, unemployment compensation, and pensions. Since personal income is a measure of spending power, it often follows that when personal income rises so does consumer spending. The trend in consumer spending is a major part of total GNP.

- *Retail sales* is a figure issued each month by the Commerce Department, estimating total sales at the retail level. This figure includes everything consumers buy, from cars and washing machines to groceries and clothing. If the retail sales figure is strong, companies often respond by increasing production; if it is weak, industrial production may be cut back.

- The *consumer price index* (CPI) is one of the primary tools economists use to measure inflation. The best known consumer price figure shows price changes for a fixed market basket of several hundred goods and services used by urban consumers. The CPI is issued monthly by the Department of Labor.

- The *producer price index* reflects price changes of goods at various stages of production. For example, the index may track the cost to produce a finished piece of furniture from the price of lumber and other raw materials to the price the consumer pays for the furniture in the retail store. Price increases at the various production levels may translate into higher consumer prices—a fact that makes the producer price index a valuable measure of inflationary pressure. This index is issued monthly by the Department of Labor.

- Levels of *employment* and *unemployment,* as issued monthly by the Department of Labor, are broad indicators of economic health. The employment figures indicate the number of people working in payroll jobs. The unemployment figures indicate the percentage of people actively looking for work who are unable to find jobs. Both provide signs of changes in business activity.

- The number of *housing starts* is usually tied to the cost of money in the form of mortgage rates. When housing starts pick up, the economy is generally improving. A slowdown in housing starts follows an increase in interest rates. Housing starts as well as *new building permits,* an even earlier indicator of future construction, are issued each month by the Department of Commerce.

- The *index of leading economic indicators* is a compilation of 12 different statistics into a single number, which is meant to indicate the future direction of the economy. Specifically, it tends to predict or "lead" changes in the GNP. Included are statistics on worker layoffs, new orders placed by manufacturers, changes in the price of raw materials, and restrictions on the money supply. When growth or contraction is extended over a period of months, total economic output generally moves in the same direction soon after. This index is issued monthly by the Commerce Department.

## ECONOMIC FACTORS THAT COUNT

The above measures of economic performance are, of course, influenced by government fiscal and monetary policy. *Fiscal policy* involves taxation, government spending, and debt management, while *monetary policy* involves control of the money supply and interest rates by the Federal Reserve.

Fiscal policy tends to be expansive when it encourages spending. This happens, for example, when the government reduces taxes or increases the size of the national budget. Monetary policy has the same effect when money is readily available and interest rates are relatively low. Other factors influence this economic equation as well, including consumer and business spending and the supply of relatively cheap energy. Of course, these variables can also have a recessionary impact on the economy; for example, an increase in the cost of energy, a tax hike, or a drop in consumer or business spending. These major forces have the potential to affect industrial production, corporate profits, retail sales, personal income, the unemployment rate, inflation, and other key dimensions of the economy. And, as you might expect, they also can cause wide swings in stock prices.

Because of the devastating effects inflation can have on the performance of common stocks, it deserves a discussion of its own. In an inflationary environment, while many companies report higher profits, the quality of their earnings actually declines as profit margins are "squeezed" and the purchasing power of the dollar deteriorates. What's more, the high interest rates that accompany inflation not only contribute to rising costs but also reduce the competitive edge of common stocks. That is, as interest rates rise, bond and preferred stock returns improve, making common stocks less attractive. By the same token, as we saw in the early to mid-1980s, when inflation slows down, the stock market is often one of the major beneficiaries. Certainly, the bull market that began in 1982 was fueled, in large part, by a dramatic drop in the rate of inflation, which brought along with it lower interest rates and higher corporate profits.

## USING ECONOMIC ANALYSIS TO FORMULATE AN INVESTMENT PLAN

Your goal, after reviewing all these factors, is to develop an economic outlook—a view of the way the economy is going. This outlook can help you zero in on specific areas to investigate. If you find, for example, that the economic environment favors major capital expenditures by business, you might want to investigate the investment possibilities of machine tool and other capital goods producers. Similarly, if Washington is about to make major cuts in federal spending, you might want to steer clear of General Dynamics and other defense contractors.

You can also use this general economic information in a slightly different way, this time focusing on how economic conditions will affect specific industries and companies. If, for example, you're interested in apparel companies, you'll want to track the level of discretionary consumer spending, since how well these companies do depends to a great extent on how much money consumers have in their pockets.

Consumer spending is influenced by such economic factors as employment and unemployment, inflation, interest rates, and taxes. In general, consumers tend to spend more when the economy is strong and to tighten their purse strings when the economy slows down. Let's assume for the moment that the economy is on the way up after a prolonged recession. Employment is up, inflation is controlled, interest rates are reasonable, and Congress is putting the finishing touches on a major tax cut. Putting these facts together, you realize that the current environment holds the promise of future economic growth, including significant increases in consumer spending—which can only be good for apparel manufacturers.

Unfortunately, although the economic outlook you develop will help you zero in on specific buys, it often will not help you predict market changes *before* they occur. This is because changes in stock prices normally occur before the various economic indexes pick up the economic trend. Indeed, the current trend in stock prices is frequently used to help predict the course of the economy itself. If this sounds like a no-win situation, remember that the large institutional investors who cause the major movements in stock prices justify their buy and sell decisions by their perception of future economic activity. Your goal is to be able to read the economy along with them, using the movement of stock prices as an important analytic tool.

## STEP 2: SIZE UP THE INDUSTRY

An industry is made up of firms involved in producing similar goods and services—the oil industry, for example, is made up of firms that produce gasoline and other oil-related products. Companies in an industry may be different in size, manner of operation, and specific product lines, but they have similar operating characteristics and are subject to similar socioeconomic forces.

Knowledgeable investors realize that stock prices are influenced, at least in part, by industry conditions. The level of demand in an industry and other industry forces set the tone for individual companies. Clearly, if the outlook for an industry is good, then the prospects are likely to be strong for the companies that make up that industry. Thus, by learning as much as you can about an industry, you will be able to determine the outlook for the industry as a whole and to identify companies within the industry that hold particular promise. This process sets the stage for a more thorough analysis of individual companies and securities.

### WHAT TO LOOK FOR

Analyzing an industry means looking at its makeup, basic characteristics, and the key economic and operating variables that are important to its success and its future outlook. Your goal is to locate specific companies that appear well situated to take advantage of industry conditions.

You can learn a great deal about an industry by seeking answers to these questions:

- What is the nature of industry competition? Do a few companies control the industry or is the field wide open for various size companies?
- To what extent is the industry regulated? What role does the government play in controlling industry activity? How "friendly" are the agencies that regulate and oversee the industry?
- Is organized labor a big factor in the industry? Are union-management relations generally friendly or hostile? Have strikes been called in recent years? When is the next round of contract talks?
- How important are technological developments? How will potential breakthroughs affect productivity and profits?
- What economic forces are especially important to the industry? How is demand for industry goods and services related to key economic variables? What is the outlook for those variables? How important is foreign competition to industry health?
- What are the important financial and operating considerations? Is there an adequate supply of labor, material, and capital? What are the capital spending plans of the industry?

These questions can sometimes be answered in terms of an industry's growth cycle:

- In the first phase, *initial development*, the industry is new and untried, and consequently investment risk is extremely high. Most individual investors know little or nothing about the industry at this stage.
- In the second stage, *rapid expansion*, industry products have hit the market in a big way, and demand often outstrips supply. At this stage, it is easy to see growth possibilities and the investment opportunities that go along with them. This is especially the case since the state of the economy has little to do with the industry's overall performance at this stage; investors do well in almost every economic climate.
- Unfortunately, few industries experience this kind of rapid growth for very long. Most quickly progress to the stage of *mature growth*, which is the stage most influenced by economic developments. Expansion now comes from growth of the economy, a slower source of overall growth than that in stage two. This does not mean these industries are on the downswing. On the contrary, industries that reach this stage are likely to be around for a long time. The food, auto, and heavy equipment industries are all in the mature growth stage.
- In the last stages, *stability* and *decline*, demand for industry products has leveled off and may even be declining, forcing many companies to leave the industry. Before reaching this stage, many companies introduce product changes in an attempt to insure continuing consumer acceptance. If you're after capital gains, stable or declining industries will not interest you. However, they may be attractive to investors seeking dividend income.

## GETTING A HANDLE ON AN INDUSTRY'S OUTLOOK

Many investment publications analyze particular industries. Especially helpful are the *S&P Industry Surveys*, which provide important economic, market, and financial statistics on various industries, as well as relevant commentary. You can also learn a great deal by reading brokerage house reports and analyses in the popular financial press. *Barron's* and *Forbes*, for example, regularly report on industries.

Let's suppose that you're still interested in investing in apparel stocks and that your economic analysis suggests a strong economy for the foreseeable future, including high levels of personal disposable income. To bring your analysis down to an industry level, you have to assess a number of different factors, including product demand in the form of industry sales, labor-management relations (the apparel industry is labor-intensive), and the enormous effect of foreign competition. What you learn will enable you to form judgments about the prospects for industry growth. If you feel good about the future, your next step is to analyze specific companies.

## STEP 3: ZERO IN ON A COMPANY

You can learn a great deal about a company by studying its financial affairs through a process known as *fundamental analysis*. Fundamental analysis rests on the belief that the value of a stock is influenced by the performance of the company that issues the stock. If company prospects look strong, the market price of the stock generally reflects this strength.

Fundamental analysis begins with a historical perspective. In this phase you focus on the financial statements of the firm as the best way to learn the firm's strengths and weaknesses. You also attempt to evaluate the firm's operating efficiency and to determine the effects of emerging trends. The following aspects of a company are especially noteworthy:

- Competitive position
- Composition and trend in sales
- Profit margins and earnings
- Composition and liquidity of resources (asset mix)
- Capital structure (financing mix)

This information helps you formulate expectations about the company's future growth and profitability.

The historical phase of fundamental analysis can be extremely demanding and time-consuming. To shortcut the work, you can gather background material through published sources. Especially helpful are the reports and recommendations of major brokerage houses and the analyses found in the financial press. However, to get the most out of these secondary sources, you must understand the content and implications of the financial statements upon which they're based. Ideally, you should be able to use this information to make your own judgments about the company and its stock.

## USING FINANCIAL STATEMENTS

Financial statements give you a fairly clear picture of the financial condition of a firm. The two principal financial statements are the balance sheet and income statement. These financial statements are prepared on a quarterly basis (these are *abbreviated* statements compiled for each 3-month period of operation) and again at the end of each calendar or *fiscal year* (a 12-month period the company has defined as its operating year, which may or may not end on December 31). Annual financial statements must be verified by independent certified public accountants (CPAs), filed with the U.S. Securities and Exchange Commission, and distributed on a timely basis to all stockholders in the form of annual reports.

*The balance sheet.* The balance sheet is a statement of the company's assets, liabilities, and shareholders' equity. The *assets* represent the resources of the company (the things that belong to the firm), the *liabilities* are its debts, and *shareholders' equity* is the amount of stockholders' capital in the firm. A balance sheet may be thought of as a summary of the firm's assets balanced against its debt and ownership positions *at a single point in time* (on the last day of the calendar or fiscal year, or at the end of the quarter). In order to balance, the total assets must equal the total liabilities and equity.

A typical balance sheet is illustrated in the table on the next page. It shows the comparative 1986–87 figures for Palm Springs Industries, a hypothetical apparel firm we will refer to throughout this chapter and the next. PSI, as our company is known, is a moderate-sized but rapidly growing producer of medium- to high-priced apparel for men and women.

• *Assets* The company's assets are listed in the top half of the balance sheet and are broken into two parts: current and long-term assets. Current assets are made up of cash and other assets that will be converted into cash (or in the case of prepaid expenses, consumed) in 1 year or less. The four most common current assets are: cash and short-term investments, accounts receivable, inventory, and prepaid expenses. The cash account is self-explanatory; accounts receivable represents the amount due the company from customers who purchased goods on credit; inventories are the raw materials used in the production process, work-in-process, and the finished goods ready for shipment to customers; and prepaid expenses represent payments made in advance for such services as utilities and insurance. These assets are the firm's working capital and provide the funds for day-to-day operations. Other than the cash account, these assets represent allocations of corporate funds

## A CORPORATE BALANCE SHEET, PALM SPRINGS INDUSTRIES
## ($ IN THOUSANDS, NOVEMBER 30)

|  | 1987 | 1986 |  |
|---|---|---|---|
| Current assets | $ 7,846 | $ 14,459 | Cash and short-term investments |
|  | 105,400 | 102,889 | Accounts receivable |
|  | 164,356 | 159,238 | Inventories |
|  | 1,778 | 2,111 | Prepaid expenses |
|  | $279,380 | $278,697 | Total current assets |
| Long-term assets | $ 1,366 | $ 1,317 | Land |
|  | 13,873 | 13,889 | Buildings |
|  | 75,717 | 73,199 | Furniture, fixtures, and equipment |
|  | 49,412 | 50,209 | Leasehold improvements |
|  | $140,368 | $138,614 | Gross long-term assets |
|  | (85,203) | (80,865) | Accumulated depreciation |
|  | $ 55,165 | $ 57,749 | Net long-term assets |
|  | $ 4,075 | $ 4,108 | Other assets |
| Total assets | $338,620 | $340,554 |  |
| Current liabilities | $ 2,000 | $ 11,500 | Notes payable |
|  | 4,831 | 1,090 | Current maturities |
|  | 68,849 | 69,696 | Accounts payable and accrued expenses |
|  | 3,806 | 3,119 | Other current liabilities |
|  | 5,460 | 4,550 | Accrued taxes |
|  | $ 84,946 | $ 89,955 | Total current liabilities |
| Long-term debt | $ 53,723 | $ 61,807 | Long-term debt, less current maturities |
| Stockholders' equity | $ 21,787 | $ 21,777 | Common shares, $2.50 par value |
|  | 20,068 | 20,028 | Capital surplus |
|  | 158,096 | 146,987 | Retained earnings |
|  | $199,951 | $188,792 | Stockholders' equity |
| Total liabilities and stockholders' equity | $338,620 | $340,554 |  |

to various resources. For example, Palm Springs Industries had more than $105 million invested in accounts receivable as of November 30, 1987, the last day of their fiscal year.

The long-term assets of PSI are represented mostly by land and facilities, which is typical of most companies. These assets have extended lives of more than 1 year and are resources not intended for sale but for use over and over again in the manufacture, display, warehousing, and transportation of company products. The most common long-term assets are land, buildings, plant and equipment, office furnishings, and leasehold improvements (capital improvements made on property leased by the company). The net amount of long-term assets shown on the balance sheet changes each year because depreciation is charged against these assets. (Depreciation is an accounting entry used to account systematically for the wear and tear on an asset over time.) The *accumulated depreciation* entry reflects the total of past depreciation charged against property still on the books; it is strictly an accounting entry and does *not* represent cash.

• *Liabilities*  The firm's financial structure appears in the lower half of this balance sheet, where the liabilities and stockholders' position are listed. It is divided into three parts: (1) current liabilities, (2) long-term debt, and (3) equity. Current liabilities are the debts owed to lenders (notes payable and current maturities), suppliers (accounts payable), employees (accrued expenses), and the government (accrued taxes). Like their counterparts on the asset side of the balance sheet, they are due and payable within a period of 1 year or less. The current liabilities listed for PSI are typical of those found on most corporate balance sheets.

Long-term debts have maturities that extend beyond 1 year. Note that only the principal amount of current and long-term debt is recorded on the balance sheet; the interest portion appears only on the income statement, as an expense. Long-term liabilities are normally broken into the long-term portion of the debt and that portion due in 1 year or less, which is known as current maturities. Current maturities are like the next 12 monthly payments on a 4-year installment loan. The amount due in the next year would be listed as current maturities while the amount due in years 2 through 4 would be listed as long-term debt.

• *Equity*  In addition to money the company owes, company stockholders also have a limited claim against company assets. This claim is represented by the equity (or net worth) accounts on the balance sheet. Stockholders own a residual position in the firm—that is, their claims come after the claims of all short- and long-term lenders. The major components of stockholders' equity are the common stock account, capital surplus, and retained earnings. The first two represent paid-in capital and are equal to the proceeds realized by the company from the sale of its stock to the investing public. More specifically, the common stock account equals the par or stated value of the stock times the number of shares issued, while capital surplus equals the excess of the net proceeds from the sale of stock above the stock's par value. Retained earnings, in contrast, are an accumulation of prior earnings that have been retained in the company; they are the earnings left after dividends have been paid. Retained earnings are used to pay off debt, acquire facilities, and invest in receivables, inventories, and the like. They do *not* represent cash or a pool of untapped financing, but instead are resources that have been previously allocated to various areas of the firm.

*The income statement.*  The income statement provides a financial summary of the operating results of the firm. Unlike the balance sheet, the income statement covers activities that have occurred over the course of time, or for a given operating period. Typically, this extends no longer than a fiscal or calendar year; Palm Springs Industries' income statement for the years 1986 and 1987 follows. Note that these annual statements cover operations over a 12-month period ending on November

30, which corresponds to the date of the balance sheet. The income statement indicates how successful the firm has been in using the assets listed on the balance sheet; that is, management success is reflected in the profit or loss the company generates during the year.

## A CORPORATE INCOME STATEMENT, PALM SPRINGS INDUSTRIES ($ IN THOUSANDS, YEAR ENDED NOVEMBER 30)

| 1987 | 1986 | |
|---|---|---|
| $614,906 | $575,101 | Net sales |
| $377,322 | $354,424 | Cost of goods sold |
| 195,864 | 184,419 | Selling, administrative, and other operating expenses |
| 5,765 | 5,523 | Interest expense |
| $578,951 | $544,366 | Total costs and expenses |
| $ 35,955 | $ 30,735 | Earnings before taxes |
| $ 17,950 | $ 15,230 | Taxes on earnings |
| $ 18,005 | $ 15,505 | Net earnings (profit) |
| $ 2.09 | $ 1.80 | Earnings per share (in dollars) |
| 8,601 | 8,601 | Number of common shares outstanding (in thousands) |
| $ 6,896 | $ 6,220 | Dividends paid to common stockholders (in thousands of dollars) |

The income statement is simply a summary of the amount of revenues (sales and income) generated over the period, the costs and expenses incurred over the same period, and the company's profits (which, of course, are obtained by subtracting all costs and expenses, including taxes, from revenues). Note that there are four basic types of expenses: *cost of goods sold,* which is often the largest cost item and represents labor, material, and factory overhead expenses; *selling, administrative, and other operating expenses,* which represents salaries, advertising and promotion costs, travel and entertainment, office expenses, utilities and insurance, and other costs of operating the firm; *interest expense,* which reflects the cost of borrowing; and *taxes on earnings,* which is the share of profits that goes to federal, state, and local governments. The net earnings of the firm are the "bottom line" of the income statement. If they are not used to pay common or preferred dividends, they go to retained earnings, where they are used to finance growth or repay debt.

## USING FINANCIAL RATIOS

Ratios lie at the very heart of company analysis; indeed, fundamental analysis as a system of information would be incomplete without this key ingredient. *Ratio analysis* is the study of the relationships among and between various financial statement accounts. Ratios provide a different perspective on the operating results and financial condition of the firm and, as a result, expand the information to be gleaned from the financial statements. Each measure relates one item on the balance sheet (or income statement) to another or, as is more often the case, a balance sheet account to an operating (or income statement) element. In this way, attention is centered not on the absolute size of the financial statement accounts, but on the liquidity, activity, and profitability of the resources, financial structure, and operating results of the firm.

Most importantly, financial ratios enable you to assess the firm's past and present financial condition and operating results. The mechanics are actually quite simple: selected information is obtained from annual financial statements and used to compute a set of ratios, which are then compared to historical or industry standards to evaluate the financial condition and operating results of the company. When historical standards are used, the company's ratios are studied from one year to the next; industry standards, in contrast, involve comparing a particular company's ratios to the average performance of other companies in the same line of business.

While there are many different financial ratios, we are going to confine our attention here to a handful of the most popular and widely used measures. These ratios will enable you to at least get a handle on the general financial condition and operating results of the firm, without having to go into a great deal of detail. All these ratios are widely cited in various types of analytical reports and are used to gain valuable insight into a firm's balance sheet, income statement, and the market performance of its common stock. We will use the 1987 figures from PSI's financial statements to illustrate the calculation and use of these ratios.

*Balance sheet measures.* When you are looking at a company's balance sheet, three things should be of interest to you: what kind of liquidity is the company able to maintain, how well is the firm managing its assets, and what kind of financial structure is being employed. You can learn a lot about a company's liquidity, assets, and financial structure by following four balance sheet ratios: current ratio, total asset turnover, debt-equity ratio, and times interest earned.

• *Current ratio* The current ratio is one of the most commonly cited of all financial ratios. It is used to assess a firm's *liquidity* position, or the ability of the firm to meet its day-to-day operating expenses and satisfy its short-term obligations as they come due. As a measure of liquidity, the current ratio is computed as follows:

$$\text{current ratio} = \frac{\text{current assets}}{\text{current liabilities}}$$

Plugging in the 1987 figures for Palm Springs Industries, we get:

$$\text{current ratio for PSI} = \frac{\$279,380}{\$84,946}$$

$$= \underline{3.29}$$

This figure indicates that PSI had $3.29 in short-term resources to service every dollar of current debt. By most standards, such a current ratio would be considered generous.

• *Total asset turnover*   Total asset turnover indicates how efficiently assets are being used to support sales; it is calculated as follows:

$$\text{total asset turnover} = \frac{\text{sales}}{\text{total assets}}$$

$$\text{for PSI} = \frac{\$614,906}{\$338,620}$$

$$= \underline{1.82}$$

In essence, this turnover figure indicates the kind of return the company is getting from the money it has tied up in its assets. PSI's turnover figure in 1987 was quite respectable as it was able to turn its assets about 1.8 times a year, or put another way, it was able to generate about $1.82 in sales from every dollar invested in assets. Generally, a high (or increasing) total asset turnover figure is viewed as positive because it has a beneficial effect on profitability and return on investment. The principle at work here is much like the return on an investment: earning $100 from a $1,000 investment is far more desirable than earning the same $100 from a $2,000 investment. A high total asset turnover figure suggests that corporate resources are being managed efficiently and that the firm is able to realize a high level of sales—and ultimately, profits—from its asset investments.

• *Debt-equity ratio*   The debt-equity ratio is one of two measures widely used to assess the amount of *leverage* being employed in a firm's financial structure; that is, the amount of debt being used to support the resources and operations of a company. The amount of indebtedness and the ability of the firm to service its debt are major concerns here. The debt-equity ratio is a measure of the relative amount of funds that have been provided by lenders and owners. It is computed as follows:

$$\text{debt-equity ratio} = \frac{\text{long-term debt}}{\text{stockholders' equity}}$$

$$\text{for PSI} = \frac{\$53,723}{\$199,951}$$

$$= \underline{.27}$$

Since the debt-equity ratio measures the amount of financial leverage being used by a company, and since highly leveraged firms (those using large amounts of debt) run an increased risk of bankruptcy, this ratio is particularly helpful in assessing a stock's risk exposure. The 1987 debt-equity ratio for PSI is a *low* 27 percent and discloses that most of the company's capital comes from its owners. Put another way, this figure means there was only 27 cents of debt in the capital structure for every dollar of equity.

• *Times interest earned*   Another financial structure ratio is times interest earned. This so-called coverage ratio measures the ability of the firm to meet its fixed interest payments. It is calculated as follows:

$$\text{times interest earned} = \frac{\text{earnings before interest and taxes}}{\text{interest expense}}$$

$$\text{for PSI} = \frac{\$35,955 + \$5,765}{\$5,765}$$

$$= \underline{7.24}$$

The ability of the company to meet its interest payments (which, with bonds, are fixed contractual obligations) in a timely and orderly fashion is also an important consideration in evaluating risk exposure. In the case of PSI, there is about $7.24 available to cover every dollar of interest expense. Usually, there is little concern until the measure drops to something less than 4 or 5 times earnings.

*Profitability measures: the income statement.* Profitability is a relative measure of success. Each of the various profitability measures relates the returns (profits) of a company to its sales, assets, or equity. There are three widely used profitability measures: net profit margin, return on assets, and return on investment; in one way or another, all three of these ratios are concerned with the operating results of the firm, as captured by the company's income statement.

• *Net profit margin* This is the "bottom line" of operations; it indicates the rate of profit from sales and other revenues. The net profit margin is computed as follows:

$$\text{net profit margin} = \frac{\text{net profit after taxes}}{\text{net sales}}$$

$$\text{for PSI} = \frac{\$18,005}{\$614,906}$$

$$= \underline{2.9\%}$$

The net profit margin presents profits as a percentage of sales, and because it moves with costs, also reveals the type of control management has over the cost structure of the firm. Note that PSI had a net profit margin of 2.9 percent in 1987—that is, the company's return on sales was roughly 3 cents on the dollar. Generally, you like to see a high or increasing net profit margin since that indicates a higher level of profits and therefore an improved return to investors.

• *Return on assets* This profitability measure looks at the amount of resources needed by the firm to support its operations. Return on assets (ROA) reveals management's effectiveness in generating profits from the assets it has available and is perhaps the single most important measure of return. It is computed as follows:

$$\text{ROA} = \frac{\text{net profit after taxes}}{\text{total assets}}$$

$$\text{for PSI} = \frac{\$18,005}{\$338,620}$$

$$= \underline{5.3\%}$$

Because both return on sales (net profit margin) and asset productivity (total asset turnover) are embedded in ROA, it provides a clear picture of a company's managerial effectiveness and the overall profitability of its resource allocation and investment decisions. In the case of PSI, the company earned 5.3 percent on its asset investments in 1987. Other things being equal, the higher this figure, the better.

• *Return on investment* This ratio measures the return to stockholders by relating profits to stockholders' equity:

$$\text{return on investment (ROI)} = \frac{\text{net profit after taxes}}{\text{stockholders' equity}}$$

$$\text{for PSI} = \frac{\$18,005}{\$199,951} = \underline{9.0\%}$$

Essentially, ROI is an extension of ROA and introduces the company's financing decisions into the assessment of profitability; that is, it denotes the extent to which leverage can increase return to stockholders. ROI shows the annual payoff to investors, which in the case of PSI amounts to about 9 cents for every dollar of equity.

*Market measures of common stock performance.* A number of common stock, or so-called market, ratios convert key bits of information about the company to a per share basis and are used to assess the performance of a company for stock valuation purposes. These ratios tell you exactly what portion of total profits, dividends, and equity is allocated to each share of stock. Popular common stock ratios include earnings per share, price/earnings ratio, price/sales ratio, dividends per share, dividend yield, payout ratio, and book value per share.

• *Earnings per share* One of the most important and widely followed measures in the stock market is earnings per share (EPS). Indeed, EPS is a key variable used to value stock and, as such, has a direct and significant impact on the price of a share of common. Basically, earnings per share translates total corporate profits into profits on a per share basis, and provides a convenient measure of the amount of earnings available to stockholders. EPS is found as follows:

$$\text{earnings per share (EPS)} = \frac{\text{net profit after taxes} - \text{preferred dividends}}{\text{no. of common shares outstanding}}$$

$$\text{for PSI} = \frac{\$18,005 - \$0}{8,601} = \underline{\$2.09}$$

Note that preferred dividends are subtracted from profits since they have to be paid before any monies can be made available to common stockholders. The magnitude of earnings per share is considered important because of the positive effects EPS has on the growth prospects of the firm and/or the ability to pay dividends. Earnings per share, in effect, is like a report card that indicates whether or not a company has been doing a good job in generating earnings. Not surprisingly, therefore, the higher a firm's EPS, the better. As a rule, a rising EPS figure contributes to rising stock prices.

• *Price/earnings ratio* This measure is an extension of the earnings per share ratio and is used to determine how the market is pricing the company's common stock. The price/earnings (P/E) ratio is generally viewed as an indication of investor confidence and expectations—the higher the P/E multiple, the more confidence investors are presumed to have in the future prospects of a company and its stock. To compute the P/E ratio, it's necessary to first calculate the stock's EPS. Using the previously computed EPS figure and assuming the stock's current market price is 31½, we can now determine the P/E ratio for Palm Springs Industries as follows:

$$\text{P/E ratio} = \frac{\text{market price of common stock}}{\text{earnings per share}}$$

$$\text{for PSI} = \frac{\$31.50}{\$2.09} = \underline{15.1}$$

In effect, the stock is currently selling at a multiple of about 15 times its 1987 earnings. Price/earnings multiples are widely quoted in the financial press and are, like EPS, an essential part of many stock valuation models.

• *Price/sales ratio* Another way to get a handle on the value of a company's common stock is to compute its price-to-sales ratio (PSR). This measure has attracted a great deal of attention since the early 1980s, mainly because it does a fairly good job of identifying *overpriced* stocks that should be avoided. The basic principle behind this ratio is that the lower the PSR, the less likely the stock will be overpriced. The PSR relates sales per share to the market price of the company's stock:

$$\text{PSR} = \frac{\text{market price of common stock}}{\text{annual sales per share}}$$

To find the annual sales (or revenues) per share, divide the company's annual sales by the number of common shares outstanding:

$$\text{annual sales/share} = \frac{\text{annual sales}}{\text{number of common shares outstanding}}$$

$$\text{for PSI} = \frac{\$614,906}{8,601}$$

$$= \underline{\$71.49}$$

Thus, for each share of common stock, the company is generating $71.49 in sales. Now we can use this figure, along with the latest market price of the stock, to calculate the price-to-sales ratio, as follows:

$$\text{for PSI} = \frac{\$31.50}{\$71.49}$$

$$= \underline{0.44}$$

At the current market price of $31.50, PSI stock is selling at less than half its 1987 sales per share. Under most circumstances, this would be viewed as a fairly low price/sales ratio, making the stock an attractive choice.

• *Dividends per share*   The principle here is the same as for EPS; to translate total (dollar) dividends paid by the company into a per share figure. Dividends per share is measured as follows:

$$\text{dividends per share} = \frac{\text{annual dividends paid}}{\text{number of common shares outstanding}}$$

$$\text{for PSI} = \frac{\$6,896}{8,601}$$

$$= \underline{\$.80}$$

For fiscal 1987, PSI paid out dividends of 80 cents per share—or at a quarterly rate, 20 cents per share. As we saw in Chapter 12, we can relate dividends per share to the market price of the stock to determine its present dividend yield: $0.80/$31.50 = 2.5%.

• *Payout ratio*   Another important dividend measure is the dividend payout ratio; it provides an indication of the amount of earnings paid out to stockholders in the form of dividends. The payout ratio is calculated according to the following equation:

$$\text{payout ratio} = \frac{\text{dividends per share}}{\text{earnings per share}}$$

$$\text{for PSI} = \frac{\$.80}{\$2.09}$$

$$= \underline{.38}$$

For PSI in 1987, dividends accounted for about 38 percent of earnings. This is fairly typical; most companies that pay dividends tend to pay out somewhere between 40 and 60 percent of earnings.

• *Book value per share*   The last common stock ratio is book value per share, a measure that deals with stockholders' equity. Actually, book value is simply another word for equity (or net worth); it represents the difference between total assets and total liabilities. Book value per share is computed as follows:

$$\text{book value per share} = \frac{\text{stockholders' equity}}{\text{number of common shares outstanding}}$$

$$\text{for PSI} = \frac{\$199,951}{8,601}$$

$$= \underline{\$23.25}$$

A stock should sell for *more* than its book value (note that PSI does). Otherwise, it could be an indication that something is seriously wrong with the outlook and profitability of the company.

*Interpreting financial ratios.* Many large brokerage houses and a variety of financial services publish reports that compute all these financial ratios for you. Although these reports will simplify your life a great deal, you still must be able to evaluate what you read. This evaluation involves comparing company and industry ratios to see how the company stacks up against the industry as a whole.

To see how this is done, let's look one more time at Palm Springs Industries and specifically at the following table, which summarizes historical and industry figures for the ratios we've discussed in this chapter.

## COMPARATIVE HISTORICAL AND INDUSTRY RATIOS

| | HISTORICAL FIGURES FOR PALM SPRINGS INDUSTRIES | | 1987 Industry Averages for the Apparel Industry |
|---|---|---|---|
| | 1986 | 1987 | |
| BALANCE SHEET MEASURES | | | |
| Current ratio | 3.10 | 3.29 | 2.87 |
| Total asset turnover | 1.69 | 1.82 | 1.42 |
| Debt-equity ratio | .33 | .27 | .49 |
| Times interest earned | 6.56 | 7.24 | 4.70 |
| PROFITABILITY MEASURES | | | |
| Net profit margin | 2.7% | 2.9% | 2.1% |
| Return on assets | 4.6% | 5.3% | 3.9% |
| Return on investment | 8.2% | 9.0% | 7.9% |
| COMMON STOCK MEASURES | | | |
| Earnings per share | $ 1.80 | $ 2.09 | $ 1.45 |
| Price/earnings ratio | 16.20 | 15.10 | 14.00 |
| Price/sales ratio | 0.43 | 0.44 | 0.68 |
| Dividends per share | $ 0.70 | $ 0.80 | $ 0.40 |
| Dividend yield | 2.4% | 2.5% | 1.9% |
| Payout ratio | 39.0% | 38.0% | 28.0% |
| Book value per share | $21.95 | $23.25 | $16.00 |

Here's what our analysis shows:

- We can see a modest improvement in an already strong liquidity position, as the current ratio remains well above the industry standard.
- Total asset turnover is up from last year and continues well above average.
- The leverage position of PSI seems well controlled; the company tends to use a lot less debt in its financial structure than the average firm in the apparel industry. The payoff for this judicious use of debt comes in the form of a coverage ratio that is well above average.
- The profitability picture for PSI is equally attractive; the net profit margin, return on assets, and return on investment are all improving and remain well above the industry norm.

- In summary, our analysis suggests that Palm Springs Industries is a fairly well-managed and highly profitable business. The results of this show up in common stock ratios that are consistently equal or superior to industry figures.

Thus far, the fundamental analysis of PSI has provided insight into the financial condition and operating results of the company. Certainly, the company has done well in the past and appears to be well managed today. Our major concern at this point is whether or not PSI will continue to be an industry leader and provide above-average returns to investors. Thus, our next step is to *use the historical information to get a handle on what the future holds.*

# 15

## COMMON STOCK ANALYSIS: LOOKING TOWARD THE FUTURE

———

How much would you be willing to pay for a share of stock? Investors have been wrestling with that question for as long as common stocks have been traded. The answer, of course, depends on the kind of return you expect and the amount of risk you are willing to take. This chapter looks at the question of a stock's worth in considerable detail as we continue our discussion of the stock valuation process. Our attention here is directed toward the *future* so we can get an idea of the *expected* return from a stock. This final step should enable you to complete the valuation process and arrive at a judgment concerning the attractiveness of a particular stock.

You need a standard of performance to judge the investment merits of a stock. A stock's intrinsic value furnishes this standard. Intrinsic value represents the price you would be willing to pay for a stock given its expected dividends and price behavior and considering the minimum rate of return you want. By comparing the stock's current market price to its intrinsic value, you can tell whether, and to what extent, the stock is under- or overvalued.

At any given point, the price of a stock depends on investor expectations about the future behavior of the security. If the outlook for the company is good, the price of the company's stock will probably rise. If conditions deteriorate, the price of the stock can be expected to drop. As this discussion suggests, the single most important issue in the stock valuation process is the future.

While security analysts and money managers might take the steps we are about to describe to estimate the future performance of a stock and ultimately establish its value, it is highly unlikely that you will go through this process yourself. You'll probably rely instead on such published secondary sources as *Value Line* or brokerage house reports to obtain the forecast figures. Even so, you should understand the mechanics of stock valuation so that you can intelligently evaluate what these published materials have to say about such critical issues as future operations, profits, dividends, and capital gains. In this case, as in all other areas of investing, familiarity breeds success.

## PREDICTING FUTURE RETURN

Until now, we have examined the historical performance of the company and its stock. It should be clear, however, that when it comes to making money in the stock market, it is not the past that matters but the future. Even though past performance provides no guarantees about future return, it can give you a good idea of company strengths and weaknesses. It can tell you how company products or services have done in the marketplace, how company management tends to respond in difficult situations, how the company's fiscal health shapes up, and much more. Nevertheless, you still have to project key financial variables into the future. Your main focus now is on using this historical information to determine the most probable future outlook for the company, with particular emphasis on the outlook for dividends and capital gains. Once you have an idea of what the future dividends and capital gains should be, you can use that information to determine the intrinsic value of the stock. Thus, *before you can determine what a stock is worth, you have to forecast the stock's future return performance.* This process begins by forecasting company sales and profits.

### FORECASTING SALES AND PROFITS

As you might expect, we're especially interested in the outlook for sales. One way to forecast future sales is to assume that the company will continue to perform as it has in the past, and simply extend the historical trend. For example, if sales have been growing at a rate of 8 percent a year, we can assume that they will continue to grow at this rate. Of course, if there is some evidence that economic, industry, or corporate trends will speed up or slow down the rate of growth, the forecast must be adjusted. More often than not, this "naive" approach will be just about as effective as other, more complex techniques for projecting future sales, however.

Your sales estimate should cover a period of roughly 1 to 3 years. Extending it any further introduces too many uncertainties and increases the likelihood that the forecast will be off the mark.

Given a sales forecast, you can shift your attention to the company's net profit margin, which tells you the return on sales you can expect from the company. Once more, you can come up with a "naive" estimate based on the average profit margin that has prevailed for the last several years. If necessary, this figure should also be adjusted to account for any unusual economic, industry, or company developments.

Don't make these sales and net profit projections in a vacuum, however. It's worth your time and effort to review a number of publications for information that can help you make your forecast. Look especially at brokerage house reports on the company and the industry, at *Value Line* and other advisory services, and at such financial publications as *Forbes, Business Week, Barron's,* and *The Wall Street Journal.*

In the last chapter, you became acquainted with a company called Palm Springs Industries. Let's return now to that familiar company and use the latest (1987) PSI figures to show how you can project the needed information into the future. Our initial comments will center on coming up with next year's (1988) figures, then we'll repeat the process for 1989 and 1990.

Recall from the income statement in Chapter 14 that PSI had net sales of approximately $615 million in 1987. Now, while sales have been growing by roughly 9 percent for the past 5 years, let's say you decide to use a 9½ percent growth rate for 1988, due in large part to the healthy economic environment expected to prevail. Using a 1-year time frame, you can estimate next year's sales as follows:

$$\text{estimated sales} = \text{latest sales} \times (1 + \text{expected growth rate})$$
$$\text{1988 sales for PSI} = \text{1987 sales} \times (1 + .095)$$
$$= \$615 \text{ million} \times 1.095$$
$$= \underline{\$673.4 \text{ million}}$$

So now you have a sales forecast for 1988. This is vital information in the forecasting process, since you can combine your estimate of future sales with an expected net profit margin to arrive at an estimate of future earnings:

$$\begin{matrix} \text{future after-tax} \\ \text{earnings in year } t \end{matrix} = \begin{matrix} \text{estimated sales} \\ \text{for year } t \end{matrix} \times \begin{matrix} \text{net profit margin} \\ \text{expected in year } t \end{matrix}$$

Year *t* in the formula simply indicates a given calendar or fiscal year, sometime in the future; in our illustration, it is 1988. Back to our example, you already have an estimate of future sales, so all you need now is a handle on the kind of net profit rate the company will be able to maintain in the future. Unless you have some information to the contrary, probably the best (and easiest) thing to do is simply assume *no change* in the firm's net profit margin—in other words, use last year's net profit margin. Thus, using a 3 percent net profit margin (which is about what PSI had last year), you can find 1988 earnings as follows:

$$\text{future after-tax earnings in 1988} = \$673.4 \text{ million} \times .03$$
$$= \underline{\$20.2 \text{ million}}$$

In essence, you've forecast that PSI will have profits next year of $20.2 million on projected sales of $673.4 million. Given your 1988 forecasts, you would use this same process to estimate sales and earnings for the second and third years in your forecast period.

## FORECASTING PAYOUT AND PRICE/EARNINGS RATIOS

At this point, you have an idea of what the future earnings of PSI will be—assuming, of course, that your expectations are correct. You are now ready to evaluate the effects of this performance on returns to common stockholders. Before you can do this, however, you need three additional pieces of information:

- An estimate of future dividend payout ratios
- The number of common shares that will be outstanding over the forecast period
- A future price/earnings (P/E) ratio

The first two items are fairly easy to obtain. Unless you have evidence to the contrary, you can continue to project the recent experience of the company into the future. Payout ratios are usually fairly stable, so there is little risk in using a recent average figure. As we saw in the preceding chapter, PSI had a dividend payout ratio of 38 percent last year, and it has fallen within the 38 to 40 percent range over the past 5 years (1983–87). Therefore a payout ratio of, say, 40 percent would probably be appropriate for this firm. (Of course, if the company follows a fixed dividend policy, you can use the latest dividend rate [dollar amount] in your forecast.) It is also generally safe to assume that the number of common shares outstanding will remain the same during the forecast period. PSI had 8.6 million shares of stock outstanding in 1987, so use that number.

The only thorny issue is the future P/E ratio. This is an important figure, since it has considerable bearing on the future price of the stock. The P/E ratio is a function of several variables:

- The growth rate in earnings
- The general state of the market
- The amount of debt the company is carrying
- The level of dividends

As a rule, higher P/E ratios can be expected when the growth in earnings is strong, the market outlook is optimistic, and corporate debt is low (because the smaller the debt, the smaller the financial risk). In addition, because growth in earning tends to be more valuable than dividends, especially in companies with high rates of return on equity, most companies with high P/E ratios have low dividend payouts.

A useful starting point in evaluating the P/E ratio is to consider the average *market multiple.* This measure, which is the average P/E ratio of stocks in the marketplace, helps you analyze the general state of the market and the level of optimism imbedded in stock prices. Other things being equal, the higher the market multiple, the more optimistic the market. The following table lists year-end price/earning multiples for the last 25 years and shows that market multiples move over a fairly wide range.

### AVERAGE MARKET P/E MULTIPLES 1961–86: AVERAGE YEAR-END MULTIPLES DERIVED FROM THE S&P INDEX OF 500 STOCKS

| Year | Market Multiple (Avg. S&P P/E Ratio) | Year | Market Multiple (Avg. S&P P/E Ratio) |
|------|------|------|------|
| 61 | 22.4 | 74 | 7.3 |
| 62 | 17.2 | 75 | 11.7 |
| 63 | 18.7 | 76 | 11.0 |
| 64 | 18.6 | 77 | 8.8 |
| 65 | 17.8 | 78 | 8.3 |
| 66 | 14.8 | 79 | 7.4 |
| 67 | 17.7 | 80 | 9.1 |
| 68 | 18.1 | 81 | 8.1 |
| 69 | 15.1 | 82 | 10.2 |
| 70 | 16.7 | 83 | 12.4 |
| 71 | 18.3 | 84 | 10.0 |
| 72 | 19.1 | 85 | 13.7 |
| 73 | 12.2 | 86 | 16.3 |

*Source:* Standard & Poor's *Statistical Service Security Price Index Record.*

With the market multiple as a benchmark, you can then evaluate a stock's P/E performance relative to the market. That is, a *relative P/E multiple* can be found by dividing a stock's P/E by the market multiple. For example, if a stock currently has a P/E ratio of 25 while the market multiple is 15, the stock's relative P/E is 25/15, or 1.67 times the market. By looking at the relative P/E for a stock over a period of years, you can quickly get a feel for how aggressively the stock has been priced in the market and what the usual relative P/E for the stock is.

This information will help you forecast what the stock's P/E is likely to be over the next several years. For example, if you believe the market multiple will increase as the market becomes more bullish, you might also expect the company's P/E to increase as both dividends and the rate of growth in earnings move up along with the market itself. Let's say that for PSI you decide to use a P/E multiple of 15.5 times earnings for 1988, up slightly from the 1987 ratio of 15.1. As we'll see below, this forecast P/E ratio can be combined with projected EPS to find the future market price of the stock.

## FORECASTING EPS, DIVIDENDS, AND STOCK PRICES

You're now ready to complete the forecasting process. At this point, you want to get a handle on the kind of returns you can expect from the stock—namely, the dividends you will receive and the price of the stock at the end of the first year. The only missing piece of information is projected earnings per share (EPS). Fortunately, that's fairly easy to find. Armed with an earnings estimate and a projection of the number of shares of common stock outstanding, you can forecast EPS as follows:

$$\text{estimated EPS in year } t = \frac{\text{future after-tax earnings in year } t}{\text{number of shares of common stock outstanding in year } t}$$

Since you've already forecast 1988 after-tax earnings for PSI at $20.2 million, and you expect the number of common shares outstanding to remain at 8.6 million, PSI's earnings per share for 1988 should amount to:

$$\text{estimated EPS in 1988} = \frac{\$20.2 \text{ million}}{\$8.6 \text{ million}}$$

$$= \underline{\$2.35}$$

Now that you have an idea of what earnings per share should be next year, it's easy to estimate dividends per share:

$$\frac{\text{estimated dividends}}{\text{per share in year } t} = \frac{\text{estimated EPS}}{\text{in year } t} \times \frac{\text{estimated}}{\text{payout ratio}}$$

Using your forecast EPS figure of $2.35 along with the payout ratio that you estimated at 40 percent,

$$\text{estimated dividends per share in 1988} = \$2.35 \times .40$$

$$= \underline{\$0.95}$$

Thus, if everything works out as planned, PSI should pay about 95 cents a share in dividends, up from the 80 cents a share it paid stockholders in 1987. Of course, if PSI has been following a fixed dividend policy, your dividend forecast should reflect that. For example, if for years PSI has been paying the same 80 cents a share in annual dividends and is expected to continue doing so for the foreseeable future, then simply assume that dividends will remain at that level (of 80¢ a share).

And now the final step—finding the future price of the stock:

$$\frac{\text{estimated share price}}{\text{in year } t} = \frac{\text{estimated EPS}}{\text{in year } t} \times \frac{\text{estimated}}{\text{P/E ratio}}$$

$$\text{estimated share price in 1988} = \$2.35 \times 15.5$$

$$= \underline{\$36.40}$$

So $36.40 is what you think you'll be able to sell the stock for by year-end 1988. Obviously, if you can buy it today at its most recent price of $31.50, you stand to earn a capital gain of around $5 a share ($36.40 − $31.50 = $4.90). Thus, if all your expectations—about growth in sales, profit margins, etc.—hold up in 1988, you should earn 95 cents a share in dividends *and* generate a capital gains of nearly $5 a share by investing in Palm Springs Industries.

Actually, you are interested in the price of the stock at the end of your anticipated *investment horizon*—the period of time over which you expect to hold the stock. Thus, if you had a 1-year horizon, the $36.40 figure would be appropriate. However, if you had a 3-year holding period, you would have to extend the EPS figure for 2 more years and repeat the calculations with the new data.

Once again, the steps in the forecast process are:

1. Estimate future sales
2. Estimate a future net profit margin
3. Derive future after-tax earnings
4. Estimate a future dividend payout ratio (or fixed dividend rate)
5. Estimate the future number of common shares outstanding
6. Estimate a future price/earnings (P/E) ratio
7. Derive a future EPS figure
8. Derive future dividends per share
9. Derive a future share price
10. Repeat the process for each year in the forecast period

## A 3-YEAR FORECAST FOR PSI

So far you've come up with a 1-year (1988) forecast for PSI. Let's say, however, that based on various economic, industry, and market factors, you feel it might make sense to invest in PSI for a 3-year period, through 1990. You decide on a 3-year investment horizon because you're convinced from earlier studies of economic and industry factors that the economy as a whole and the market for apparel stocks in particular should start running out of steam sometime near the end of 1990.

The table on the next page, which includes selected financial data on PSI over an 8-year period (ending with the latest 1987 fiscal year), provides the basis for much of the 3-year forecast.

As you can see, with the exception of 1981 and 1982, which were off years for PSI, the company has performed at a fairly stable pace and been able to maintain a respectable rate of growth. Your economic analysis suggests that things are beginning to pick up. And based on earlier studies, you feel the industry and company are well situated to take advantage of the upswing. Therefore, you conclude that the rate of growth in sales should pick up in 1988 to about 9.5 percent. Then, once a modest amount of pent-up demand is worked off, the rate of growth in sales should drop to about 9 percent in 1989 and stay there through 1990.

Since various published industry and company reports suggest a comfortable improvement in earnings, you decide to use a profit margin of 3.0 percent in 1988, followed by an even better 3.2 percent margin in 1989. However, because of some

# SELECTED FINANCIAL DATA, PALM SPRINGS INDUSTRIES (FOR FISCAL YEARS ENDING NOVEMBER 30)

| | 1980 | 1981 | 1982 | 1983 | 1984 | 1985 | 1986 | 1987 |
|---|---|---|---|---|---|---|---|---|
| Total assets (millions) | $262.8 | $254.2 | $220.9 | $240.7 | $274.3 | $318.2 | $340.5 | $338.6 |
| Debt-equity ratio | 31% | 37% | 31% | 29% | 30% | 33% | 33% | 27% |
| Total asset turnover (times) | 1.75× | 1.68× | 1.83× | 1.83× | 1.77× | 1.67× | 1.69 | 1.82 |
| Net sales (millions) | $461.5 | $428.5 | $404.2 | $441.6 | $486.8 | $532.7 | $575.1 | $614.9 |
| Annual rate of growth in sales* | — | −7.2% | −5.7% | 9.3% | 10.2% | 9.4% | 8.2% | 6.8% |
| Net profit margin | 2.6% | 0.6% | 1.1% | 2.0% | 3.6% | 3.0% | 2.7% | 2.9% |
| Payout ratio | 36.0% | 83.0% | 97.0% | 38.0% | 40.0% | 40.0% | 39.0% | 38.0% |
| Price earnings ratio (times) | 14.5× | 6.2× | 8.3× | 12.8× | 9.5× | 13.6× | 16.2× | 15.1× |
| Number of common shares outstanding (millions) | 7.0 | 7.0 | 7.1 | 7.1 | 8.5 | 8.6 | 8.6 | 8.6 |

*Annual rate of growth in sales = change in sales from one year to the next divided by the level of sales in the base (or earliest) year; for 1983, the annual rate of growth in sales equaled 9.3% = (1983 sales − 1982 sales)/1982 sales = ($441.6 − $404.2)/$404.2 = .093.

PLAYING IT SAFE—STOCKS, BONDS, AND MUTUAL FUNDS

anticipated capacity problems in 1990, you drop the profit margin to 3.0 percent in that year. Your assessment also indicates that the company has no need to issue additional shares of common stock during your investment period and that the dividend payout ratio will hold at about 40 percent of earnings, as it has for most of the recent past, with the notable exceptions of 1981 and 1982. Finally, based primarily on the outlook for a strong market, coupled with the expectations of improved growth in revenues and earnings, you project a P/E ratio that will rise from its present 15.1 to 17 times earnings by 1990.

The following table includes the essential elements of the financial forecast for 1988, 1989, and 1990. In it you can see the sequence used to arrive at the forecast figures for 1988. What you have to do at this point is use the new information to come up with projected figures for 1989 and 1990. As you can see in the table, the only thing that changes is the input information (like rate of growth in sales, net profit margin, and P/E ratio); the forecasting procedures followed are just like the ones used to arrive at the 1988 figures.

## SUMMARY FORECAST STATISTICS, PALM SPRINGS INDUSTRIES

|  | Average for the Last 5 Years (1983–87) | Latest Actual Figures (fiscal 1987) | FORECAST FIGURES | | |
|---|---|---|---|---|---|
|  |  |  | 1988 | 1989 | 1990 |
| Annual rate of growth in sales | 8.8% | 6.8% | 9.5% | 9.0% | 9.0% |
| Net sales (millions) | $530.2 | $614.9 | $673.4 | $734.0 | $800.0 |
| × Net profit margin | 2.8% | 2.9% | 3.0% | 3.2% | 3.0% |
| = Net after-tax earnings (millions) | $ 14.8 | $ 18.0 | $ 20.2 | $ 23.5 | $ 24.0 |
| ÷ Common shares outstanding (millions) | 8.3 | 8.6 | 8.6 | 8.6 | 8.6 |
| = Earnings per share (EPS) | $ 1.79 | $ 2.09 | $ 2.35 | $ 2.73 | $ 2.80 |
| × Payout ratio | 39.0% | 38.0% | 40.0% | 40.0% | 40.0% |
| = Dividends per share | $ 0.70 | $ 0.80 | $ 0.95 | $ 1.10 | $ 1.12 |
| Earnings per share (EPS) | $ 1.79 | $ 2.09 | $ 2.35 | $ 2.73 | $ 2.80 |
| × P/E ratio | 13.45 | 15.10 | 15.50 | 16.00 | 17.00 |
| = Share price at year-end | $ 24.07 | $ 31.50 | $ 36.40 | $ 43.70 | $ 47.60 |

The bottom line of these forecasts is the dividend and capital gains returns you can expect from each share of Palm Springs Industries stock. Based on your assumptions about net sales, profit margins, earnings per share, and so forth, dividends should go up by about 30 cents a share over the next 3 years and the price of the stock should climb by more than 50 percent from its latest price of $31.50 to $47.60 a share. You now have the needed figures on expected shareholder return and are in a position to establish an intrinsic value for Palm Springs Industries stock.

# FIND REQUIRED RATE OF RETURN

Basically, our analysis of Palm Springs Industries up to now has focused on just one thing: defining what the future cash flow of the investment is likely to be. This is summarized in the preceding table, where the forecast cash flow stream for PSI is shown in terms of the amount of the expected cash flow (from dividends and the future price of the stock), as well as the timing of these receipts. The only element missing is the required rate of return, which tells you how much return you must have to compensate for the investment risk. As is always the case, the more risk you take, the higher the return you should expect to earn. The required rate of return is a part of the valuation process; it is the rate that is used to discount the future cash flows of an investment. In essence, the required rate of return is used along with expected cash flows to derive the intrinsic value of an investment.

## A POPULAR STOCK VALUATION MODEL

Some stock valuation models, such as the so-called Graham and Dodd model, emphasize appropriate price/earnings multiples as the key element. Others are based on culling out the bad investments from the good and then using the principles of portfolio diversification as a basis for selecting stock. Still others use such variables as dividend yield, book value per share, abnormally low P/E ratios, and so on as key elements in the decision-making process. Our discussion will center on a model that is not only popular with many investors, but is also theoretically sound. It is derived from a procedure known as the *dividend valuation model.*

Basically, the dividend valuation model assumes that the value of a share of stock is equal to the present value of all its future dividends. In its purest form, the dividend valuation model uses an infinite holding period and assumes that dividends grow at a constant (fixed) rate forever. Although the essential features of the model have considerable theoretical merit, there are some obvious problems in applying it in practice—notably, the herculean task of forecasting dividends to perpetuity. The valuation model we employ here is based on the present value of future dividends and other cash flows, but is relatively easy to use, primarily because it has a *finite* holding period that seldom exceeds 2 to 3 years.

There are four main elements to this model: (1) the stock's present market price, (2) its future price, (3) the level of future dividends, and (4) the required return on the investment. The model gains much of its strength from the fact that it considers both risk and return in a convenient format and recognizes the time value of money.

If you intend to invest for only a short period of time—1 year or less—then holding period return should be used to assess the value of a stock. If the investment period is longer, then approximate yield is more appropriate. In *both* cases, value is determined by the expected cash flows of the stock (dividends and future price) over a defined investment period. Our first example will use holding period return.

*Expected rate of return using HPR.*    Holding period return (HPR), which was first introduced in Chapter 4, is useful whenever the holding period is 1 year or less. It is computed as follows:

$$HPR = \frac{\text{future dividend receipts} + \text{expected future price of the stock} - \text{current purchase price of the stock}}{\text{current purchase price of the stock}}$$

Holding period return provides a measure of the yield that will be realized *if* the actual performance of the stock lives up to its expectations. The holding period return for Palm Springs Industries, assuming that the stock can be purchased at its current market price of $31.50 and sold 1 year later at a price of $36.40, is as follows:

$$HPR = \frac{\$.95 + \$36.40 - \$31.50}{\$31.50}$$

$$= \frac{\$.95 + \$4.90}{\$31.50}$$

$$= \underline{18.6\%}$$

Note that although we do not use capital gains specifically in the valuation model, it is embedded in the formula as the difference between the future selling price of the stock and its current purchase price.

As it turns out, PSI should provide an expected rate of return in the first year of around 18.6 percent. That expected yield is, in effect, our standard of performance. To decide whether that is acceptable or not, it is necessary to formulate a *required (or desired) rate of return.* Again, the amount of return you should earn is related to the level of risk you are taking in order to generate that return. The higher the amount of perceived risk, the greater the return potential the investment should offer.

If your assessment of the historical performance of the company shows wide swings in sales and earnings, you can conclude that the stock is subject to a high degree of intrinsic risk. As a rule, the higher the intrinsic risk, the greater the return the stock should offer. The risk may come from the economy as a whole, the industry, or the company itself. It can also be related to the market, which you can tell by checking the stock's beta. Beta, as you may recall from Chapter 5, is a measure of how a stock responds to market forces; beta for the market equals 1. Generally, high betas—for example, a beta of 1.3—suggest the stock has high market risk. Although beta is difficult to compute, it is widely available from brokerage houses and a variety of investor subscription services, like *Value Line.*

A valuable reference point in arriving at a measure of risk is the rate of return available on less risky but competitive investment vehicles. For example, you can use the rate of return on Treasury bonds or high-grade corporate issues as a benchmark for defining your desired rate of return. That is, starting with yields on long-term, low-risk bonds, you can adjust the rate of return you would expect from an investment according to the level of intrinsic and market risks to which the stock is exposed.

To see how these elements make up the desired rate of return, consider the case of Palm Springs Industries once more. Assume it is now early 1988 and rates on high-grade corporate bonds are hovering around 9 percent. Since our analysis so far indicates that the apparel industry, and Palm Springs Industries in particular, are subject to a substantial amount of intrinsic risk, we must adjust these figures upward—probably by around 3 points. In addition, by looking up the company in *Value Line,* we see that PSI has a beta of 1.35, so we can conclude that the stock carries a good deal of market risk that should translate into an even higher rate of return.

Starting with the base rate for high-grade corporate bonds, we can make the necessary adjustments for intrinsic and market risks to arrive at an appropriate rate of return. From our example above, we saw that high-grade corporate bonds were yielding 9 percent and that the perceived intrinsic risk of PSI was sufficient to warrant another 3 percent return; finally, we can tack on another 3 percent for the higher-than-average market risk, as reflected in the stock's beta of 1.35. Adding these all together, we find that a stock as risky as PSI should provide a minimum (desired) rate of return of 15 percent (the total of 9% + 3% + 3%).

Using this desired rate of return as a benchmark, it is clear that the holding period return of 18.6 percent, which we computed previously, is sufficient compensation for the risk involved, and therefore PSI should be considered a worthwhile investment candidate. In short, it is an attractive stock prospect because it offers a rate of return that's comfortably above our minimum desired rate of return.

*Expected rate of return using approximate yield.*   Whenever you invest for longer than a year, holding period return becomes an inappropriate measure since it fails to consider the time value of money and gives an overall, rather than an annual, rate of return. For example, using the forecast data for a 3-year investment period, the HPR for PSI would be a whopping 61.2 percent. That is, you would receive total dividends over the 3-year period of $3.17 ($0.95 + $1.10 + $1.12), and the price of the stock would go from $31.50 to $47.60, for a capital gain of $16.10 a share, which plugged into the HPR formula would give you:

$$\text{HPR} = \frac{\$3.17 + \$47.60 - \$31.50}{\$31.50}$$
$$= \underline{61.2\%}$$

Unfortunately, this number greatly overstates the investment return. Even if you divide this number by 3 for the 3 years in the holding period, you'll still get a figure (20.4 percent) that's way too high. To overcome these problems, you must use *approximate yield* as your return measure.

The approximate yield measure enables you to find a present-value-based rate of return from long-term transactions, or the fully compounded annual rate of return. This measure of return, first introduced in Chapter 4, is determined as follows:

$$\text{approximate yield} = \frac{\text{average annual dividend} + \dfrac{\begin{array}{l}\text{expected future} \\ \text{price of the stock}\end{array} - \begin{array}{l}\text{current purchase} \\ \text{price of the stock}\end{array}}{\text{number of years in investment horizon}}}{\dfrac{\text{future price of the stock} + \text{purchase price of the stock}}{2}}$$

$$\text{for PSI} = \frac{\$1.06 + \dfrac{\$47.60 - \$31.50}{3}}{\dfrac{\$47.60 + \$31.50}{2}}$$

$$= \frac{\$1.06 + \$5.37}{\$39.55}$$

$$= \underline{16.3\%}$$

We see that PSI will yield a return of around 16.3 percent (well below the figures obtained using HPR), assuming that the stock can be bought at $31.50, held for 3 years, and then sold for $47.60 a share. Note that in this version of the stock valuation model it is the average annual dividend that is used, rather than the specific dividend. For PSI, dividends will average $1.06 a share over each of the next 3 years: ($0.95 + $1.10 + $1.12)/3 = $1.06.

When compared to the 15 percent rate of return you need, the 16.3 percent yield this investment offers is still an attractive return.

## MAKING THE INVESTMENT DECISION

Security analysis begins with economic and industry evaluations and ends in the determination of a stock's value, according to one of the valuation models we examined here. Whether you deal in holding period return or approximate yield measures, the end result is a standard of performance that you can use to determine the investment merits of a stock.

When HPR or yield is used as the standard, as in the model we've used, it is compared to a desired rate of return to determine whether the investment is a good one. As long as the HPR or approximate yield is equal to or greater than the desired rate of return, the stock should be considered a good investment choice: it promises to meet or exceed the minimum rate of return you need in view of the risk. It is important to keep in mind that a stock is acceptable even if its yield simply equals the rate of return you want. As long as it meets this minimum standard, it is a worthwhile investment choice.

A final word of caution: Although valuation models play an important part in the investment process, there is absolutely no assurance that the actual outcome will be even remotely similar to your forecast. The stock is still subject to economic, industry, company, and market risks that can negate all the assumptions you've made about the future. Security analysis and stock valuation models are used not to guarantee success, but rather to help you better understand the return and risk dimensions of potential stock transactions.

# 16

## TECHNICAL ANALYSIS: LET THE MARKET BE YOUR GUIDE

On the surface, the logic is infallible. Choose a stock with the right fundamentals and then just sit back and watch the stock price climb. Unfortunately, you may be waiting a long time or, worse yet, digging yourself out of a hole after the price falls.

How could this happen? How could you let yourself get into this position? Often disaster strikes in the form of an uncooperative market—one that can play havoc with even the best stocks.

### MARKET INFLUENCE ON STOCK PRICES

Without a doubt, the market plays a major role in determining the price behavior of common stocks. But some analysts go even further: They believe that the market is the *single most important factor* in determining stock price. They argue that security analysis is largely useless, because it is the market that determines the price behavior of stocks, not the worth of individual companies. Although most analysts believe that this view is extreme, few would dispute that understanding the stock market can help you time your investment decisions better.

*Technical analysis*—the study of the various forces at work in the marketplace—dates back to the 1800s, when industry and company analysis did not exist. Because companies were not required to issue financial reports, about the only thing investors could study was the market itself. Some analysts, known as chartists, used detailed charts to monitor what major market operators were doing. These charts focused on stock price movements and the formations these movements created. Chartists were convinced that these formations would help them determine when to buy and sell. Modern-day chartists believe the same thing, arguing that such market factors as trading volume and price movements often reveal the market's future direction before it is evident in financial statistics.

If the behavior of stock prices were completely independent of the market, technical analysis would indeed be useless. But we have ample evidence to suggest that this is not the case. In fact, stock prices tend to move with the market. Studies of stock betas have shown that, as a rule, anywhere from 20 to 50 percent of the price behavior of a stock can be traced to market forces. When the market is bullish, most stock prices will rise; when it is bearish, most issues will fall. This is because stock prices react to various supply and demand forces at work in the market. It is the demand for securities and the supply of funds that determines a bull or a bear market. As long as a given supply and demand relationship holds, the market will remain stable. However, when the balance begins to shift, prices can be expected to change as the market itself changes. More than anything, technical analysis is aimed at monitoring the pulse of the supply and demand forces in the market and detecting any shifts in this relationship.

## DIFFERENT APPROACHES TO TECHNICAL ANALYSIS

Technical analysis focuses on those forces in the marketplace that affect the price movement of stocks. Investment services, major brokerage houses, and such popular financial media as *Barron's* provide this kind of technical information at little or no cost. Of the many approaches to technical analysis, particularly noteworthy are the Dow theory, trading action, and bellwether stocks.

### THE DOW THEORY

One of the oldest approaches, this theory holds that the price trend in the overall market can be used to call turns of the market. Named after Charles H. Dow, a founder of Dow Jones, the Dow theory is supposed to signal the end of both bull and bear markets. It is important to keep in mind that the Dow theory approach does not predict when a reversal will occur. Rather, it verifies after the fact what has already taken place.

The Dow theory concentrates on the long-term trend in market behavior (known as the primary trend) and largely ignores day-to-day fluctuations or secondary movements. The Dow Jones industrial and transportation averages are used to assess the position of the market. Once a primary trend in the Dow Jones industrial average has been established, the market tends to move in that direction until the trend is canceled out by both the industrial and transportation averages. When movements in the industrial average are followed by movements in the transportation average, a crucial point known as *confirmation* has been reached. When confirmation occurs, the market has changed from bull to bear, or vice versa, and a new primary trend is established. The key elements of the Dow theory are captured in the illustration below. Observe that the bull market comes to an end at the point of confirmation.

The major drawback of this theory is that it is an after-the-fact measure with no predictive power. Thus it gives you no way of knowing whether an existing primary trend has a long way to go or is just about to end.

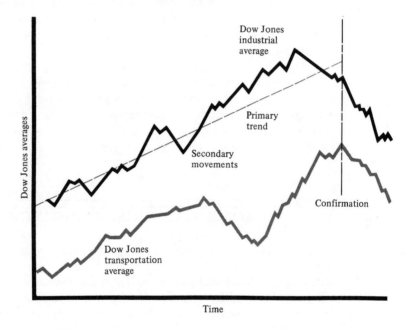

## TRADING ACTION

This approach to technical analysis concentrates on the trading characteristics of the market. Daily trading activity over long periods of time (sometimes extending back a quarter century or more) is examined in detail to identify trends that occur with a high degree of frequency. The results of this statistical analysis are a series of trading rules, some of which are a bit odd. For example, did you know that Monday is the worst day to sell stocks, and Friday the best, or that, if January is a good month for the market, chances are that the rest of the year will be good as well? Other trading rules predict that if the party in power wins the presidential election, the market will also do well over the year, and that it is best to buy air conditioning stocks in October and sell the following March (this buy and sell strategy was found to be significantly more profitable over the long haul than buy and hold). One of the most unusual, but highly successful, market adages holds that if a team from the original NFL wins the Super Bowl, the market is in for a good year. Incredibly, this rule has proven accurate in 19 of 20 Super Bowls. Clearly, the trading action approach is based on the simple assumption that the market moves in cycles that have a tendency to repeat themselves. As a result, the contention is that what has happened in the past (on Mondays or Fridays or in January) will probably happen again in the future.

## BELLWETHER STOCKS

The idea behind the bellwether approach is that a few major stocks in the market reflect the current state of the market with a high degree of accuracy. When the market moves up, these stocks move up. When it moves down, these stocks do the same. Bellwether stocks include General Motors, IBM, Du Pont, AT&T, Exxon, and Merrill Lynch.

Supposedly, if you follow one or more of these stocks, you'll be able to determine shifts in market behavior. Advocates contend that, in a bull market, when a bellwether stock fails to hit a new yearly high for 3 or 4 months, a market top is at hand. In a bear market, when the stock fails to hit a new low during a similar time period, a market bottom is coming. Although the bellwether approach draws a great deal of criticism, it seems to have some value as a market predictor.

## SOME TECHNICAL INDICATORS

If assessing the market is a worthwhile activity, it follows that some sort of tool or measure is needed to do it. One approach involves the use of various market statistics known as technical indicators. Technical indicators are used to assess the current state of the market as well as the possibility of change in market direction. While technical analysts and seasoned investors use a number of technical indicators to form complex ratios and measures, most individual investors use them in a far less structured way. We will take the less formal approach as we focus on a few of the most popular measures.

### MARKET VOLUME

Market volume is an obvious indicator of investor interest, for it reflects the eagerness of investors to buy and sell. By tracking the volume of the market as a whole you may be able to learn a great deal about underlying market strengths and weaknesses. The market is considered strong when volume goes up in a rising market or drops during market declines. In contrast, the market is considered weak when volume rises during a decline or drops off during a rally. In a strong market, the DJIA may climb 18 points on volume of over 250 million shares. In a weak market, the same 18-point rise is supported by a volume of only 100 million shares. Market volume information is published daily in the financial press.

## BREADTH OF THE MARKET

Each trading day, some stocks go up in price and others go down; in market terminology, some stocks *advance* and others *decline.* The breadth-of-the-market indicator focuses on these advances and declines to determine market strength and underlying investor sentiment.

Specifically, the market is considered strong as long as the number of advancing stocks exceeds the number of decliners. A reversal indicates market weakness. Degrees of strength are measured by the spread between the number of advances and declines: as the number of declines approaches the number of advances, market strength is deteriorating. Information on the number of advancing and declining stocks is published daily in the financial press.

## SHORT INTEREST

When investors sell a stock short, they sell borrowed stock in anticipation of a market decline. (Chapter 10 contains a complete explanation of short selling.) The number of stocks sold short in the market at any given point is known as the *short interest*; the more stocks that are sold short, the higher the short interest. Since all short sales must eventually be *covered* (the borrowed shares must be returned), a short sale, in effect, assures future demand for the stock. Thus, when the level of short interest is relatively high by historical standards, the situation is considered pessimistic for the current market but optimistic for the future. Short sellers are betting that current stock prices will drop. But they are also guaranteeing that the additional demand they create when they buy shares back to cover their short position will push prices up. Since most short sellers are sophisticated investors, the level of short interest is considered an important barometer of market sentiment. (Keep in mind, however, that their trading record is far from perfect.) The amount of short interest on the New York Stock Exchange and the American Stock Exchange is published twice a month in *Barron's.*

## ODD-LOT TRADING

Cynics suggest that the best way to make money in the market is to watch what the small investor does and do just the opposite. This view reflects the unfortunate fact that many small investors have no idea of how to time buy and sell decisions. A case in point: small investors usually do not come into the market in force until after a bull market has nearly run its course, and they do not get out until late in a bear market.

This view forms the basis for the *theory of contrary opinion*, which uses odd-lot trading as an indicator of current market activity and future market trends. (Recall from Chapter 7 that an odd lot involves transactions of less than 100 shares of stock.) Because many individual investors deal in transactions of less than 100 shares, the combined sentiments of these investors are thought to be reflected in the odd-lot figures. When there is little or no difference in the spread between the volume of odd-lot purchases and sales, it is safe to conclude that the market will probably continue along its current line (either up or down). But a shifting balance of odd-lot purchases and sales may signal that a bull or bear market is about to end. For example, when the amount of odd-lot purchases starts to exceed odd-lot sales by an ever-widening margin, it suggests that speculation by small investors is beginning to heat up—a sign that the final stages of a bull market may be at hand. (That is, according to the theory of contrary opinion, it must be late in the bull market if small investors are finally starting to enter the market in a big way.) Similarly, if the small guy starts selling out, it must be a sign that the bear market has about run its course, and the bull can't be far behind.

# CHARTING

Charting is perhaps the best known activity of the technical analyst. Technicians—analysts who believe that the forces of supply and demand establish stock prices—often use sophisticated charts to plot the behavior of everything from the Dow Jones industrial average to the share price movements of listed and OTC stocks. In addition, just about every type of technical indicator from advance-decline ratios to short interest is charted in one form or another.

Charts are popular because they provide a visual summary of activity over time, and, perhaps more importantly, because they may contain valuable information about developing trends and future market or stock behavior. Chartists believe price patterns evolve into *chart formations* that provide signals about the future course of the market or a stock. Because they believe that history repeats itself, they study the historical behavior of stocks or the market and devise trading rules based on these observations.

## TYPES OF CHARTS

The two most popular types of charts are bar charts and point-and-figure charts.

*Bar charts.* The simplest and probably most widely used chart type is the *bar chart*, in which market or share prices are plotted on the vertical axis and time on the horizontal axis. This type of chart derives its name from the fact that prices are recorded as vertical bars that depict high, low, and closing prices, as shown in the illustration below. Note, for example, that on 12/31, the stock reached a high of 31, a low of 27, and closed at 27½. Because bar charts contain a time element, technicians frequently use them to plot a variety of other important facts, including stock or market volume.

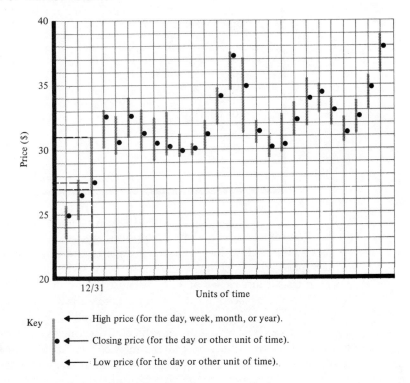

*Point-and-figure charts.* These charts have only one use: to keep track of emerging price patterns. They have three special characteristics:

- Because they have no time dimension, they cannot be used to plot technical measures.
- They record only significant price changes. That is, prices have to move by a certain minimum amount—usually a point or two—before a new price level is recognized.
- Price reversals show up only after a predetermined change in direction occurs.

In the example on the next page, note that an X on the chart indicates an increase in price, an O a decrease. This chart uses a 2-point box, which means that the stock must move by a minimum of 2 points before any changes are recorded. If the stock is highly active, the chart could cover a span of months; if it is inactive, it may represent a period of a year or more. Chartists generally use 1-point boxes

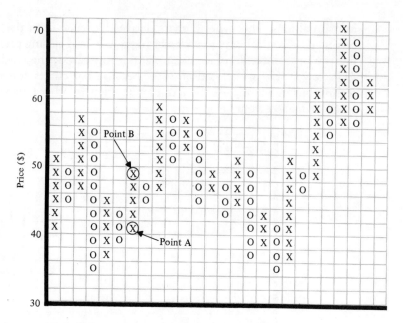

to chart low-priced stocks, 2- to 3-point boxes to chart moderately priced stocks, and 3- to 5-point boxes to chart high-priced stocks.

Let's take a close look at our example to see how a point-and-figure chart works. Suppose the stock has been hovering for some time at point A, the $40–41 mark, but that it just closed at 42⅛. Because the minimum 2-point movement has been made, an X is placed in the box immediately above point A. The chartist would remain with this new box as long as the price moved (up or down) within the 2-point range of 42 to 43⅞. Thus, although the chartist follows *daily* closing prices, a new entry is made on the chart only after the price has moved into a new 2-point box. We can see that from point A, the price moved up over time to nearly $50 a share. At that point, indicated by point B on the chart, a reversal set in. That is, the price of the stock began to drift downward and in time moved out of the 48–50 box. This reversal prompts the chartist to change columns and symbols, moving one column to the right and recording the new price level with an O in the 46–48 box. The chartist will continue to use the Os as long as the stock continues to move downward.

## CHART FORMATIONS

The information charts supposedly contain about the future course of the market or a stock is revealed in chart formations. That is, by reflecting the forces of supply and demand, charts indicate through their formations that certain types of market behavior are imminent. If you know how to interpret charts (which, by the way, is no easy task), you can see formations building and recognize buy and sell signals. Some popular formations have rather exotic-sounding names:

| | |
|---|---|
| Head and shoulders | Broadening top |
| Double top | Dormant bottom |
| Triple bottom | Ascending triangle |
| Diamond | Exhaustion gap |
| Falling wedge | Island reversal |
| Pennant | Trend channel |
| Scallop and saucer | Complex top |

The figure on the next page shows some popular formations. The patterns form *support levels* and *resistance lines* which, when combined with the basic formations, yield buy and sell signals. Panel A is an example of a buy signal; the price being charted has broken out above a *resistance line* after a particular pattern has been formed. In contrast, Panel B shows a price break in the opposite direction, below a *support level*; this breakthrough is a clear signal to sell. Chartists believe that a sell signal means that everything is in place for a major drop in the market or in the price of a particular security, and that a buy signal indicates an impending market or stock boom. Unfortunately, chart formations rarely appear as neatly and cleanly as they do in our illustration—a fact that can make them extremely difficult to identify and interpret, even by the experts.

## THE VALUE OF THIS INFORMATION

Investors have a wide range of choices with respect to technical analysis. They can use the charts and complex ratios of the technical analysts or follow a more informal approach and use technical analysis just to get a general sense of the market. Presumably, in the latter case, it's not market behavior per se that is important as much as the implications such market behavior can have on the price performance of a particular common stock. For example, you might use technical analysis in conjunction with fundamental analysis to determine whether or not it is the proper time to add a particular investment candidate to your portfolio. Some investors and professional money managers, in fact, look at the technical side of a stock *before* doing any fundamental analysis. Then, if they find the stock to be technically sound, they'll spend the time to look at its fundamentals; if not, they'll look for another stock. For these investors, the concerns of technical analysis are still the same: do the technical factors indicate that this might be a good time to buy the stock?

Most investors rely on published sources to obtain necessary technical insights. Many find it helpful to use several different approaches. For example, you might follow a favorite stock, such as McDonald's, or Boeing, and at the same time keep track of information on market volume and breadth of the market. This information is readily available to every investor, and is a low-cost way of keeping track of the market.

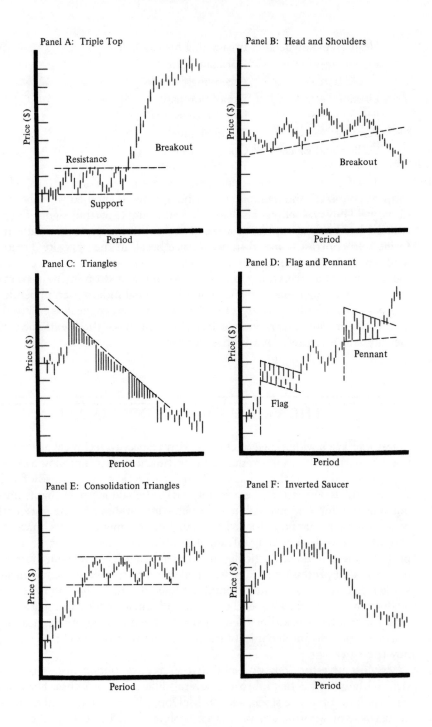

Panel A: Triple Top

Panel B: Head and Shoulders

Panel C: Triangles

Panel D: Flag and Pennant

Panel E: Consolidation Triangles

Panel F: Inverted Saucer

Unlike other types of technical measures, charting is seldom done on an informal basis; you either chart because you believe in its value, or you don't chart at all. A chart by itself tells you little more than where the market or a stock has been. But to a chartist, these price patterns hold the promise of predicting future price activity.

The value of charts lies in knowing how to read them and how to respond to the signals they supposedly give off about the future. There is a long-standing debate on Wall Street (some would call it a feud) regarding the merits of charting. While charts are scoffed at by a large number of investors, others swear by them, especially if they've proven helpful in the past.

# 17

## A PRIMER ON BONDS

Bonds are publicly traded long-term debt securities that are issued in convenient denominations by a variety of borrowing organizations, including the U.S. Treasury, various agencies of the U.S. government, state and municipal governments, corporations, and nonprofit institutions. They are often referred to as *fixed income securities,* because the debt service obligations of the issues are fixed. That is, the issuing organization agrees to pay a fixed amount of interest periodically and to repay a fixed amount of principal at maturity.

For many years, bonds were viewed as rather dull investment vehicles that produced current income and little else. This is no longer true. Today, bonds are viewed by institutional and individual investors as highly competitive investment vehicles that offer the potential for attractive returns in the form of both current income and capital gains. Indeed, bonds are now as well suited for aggressive investors who actively trade in and out of various issues as they are for conservative investors who want to preserve their capital and earn steady income.

# WHY INVEST IN BONDS?

Like any other type of investment, bonds can provide investors with two kinds of income: current income and capital gains. While the current income is fairly certain (it comes from the interest payments paid over the life of the issue), the capital gains are not, since they depend entirely on the movement of interest rates.

Bonds are versatile investments that can be used in at least three different ways:

- If your goal is to preserve and accumulate capital over a long period of time, you may decide to commit all or a major portion of your investment funds to high-quality bonds. This type of investment approach is extremely conservative and extremely safe. True, you have to contend with occasional swings in bond prices, but if you're in the investment for the long haul (and don't need to sell your bonds on short notice), such price savings shouldn't bother you.
- Even if you're a less conservative investor after high current income, bonds are still appealing, especially since the Tax Reform Act of 1986 (which sharply reduced taxes on interest income) has effectively increased the after-tax returns of bonds and other income-oriented securities.
- If you're an aggressive investor after substantial capital gains, bonds can be an excellent trading vehicle when interest rates are volatile, which they have been since the 1970s. The wider and more frequent the swings in interest rates, the greater the opportunity to trade in and out of various issues to achieve capital gains.

# WHAT YOU SHOULD KNOW ABOUT BONDS

A bond is a negotiable, long-term debt instrument that carries certain obligations on the part of the issuer. Unlike the holders of common stock, bondholders have no ownership or equity position in the firm or organization that issues the bond. Bondholders are only lending money to the issuer.

### BOND INTEREST AND PRINCIPAL: WHAT YOU SEE IS WHAT YOU GET

Bond issues are viewed as fixed income securities because, in the absence of any trading, your return is limited to fixed interest and principal payments. In essence, bonds involve a fixed claim on the issuer's income (as defined by the size of the periodic interest payments) and a fixed claim on the assets of the issuer (equal to the repayment of principal).

As a rule, bonds pay interest every 6 months. There are a few exceptions, however: some issues pay interest every month while others pay once a year. The *coupon* defines the annual interest income that will be paid by the issuer to the bondholder. For instance, a $1,000 bond with an 8 percent coupon will pay $80 in interest annually, generally in the form of two $40 semiannual payments. The principal amount of a bond, also known as an issue's *par value,* specifies the amount of capital that must be repaid at maturity. For example, there is $1,000 of principal in a $1,000 bond.

To attract investors to the bond market, issues are broken down into standard principal amounts, known as *denominations.* Although most bonds are issued in denominations of $1,000 to $5,000, some issues carry 6- or 7-figure denominations; these are purchased mainly by institutional investors.

Bonds regularly trade in the open market at prices that differ from their principal, or par, values. This occurs whenever an issue's coupon differs from the prevailing market rate of interest. The price of the issue will change inversely with interest rates until its yield is compatible with the prevailing market yield. This relationship explains why a 7 percent, $1,000 bond will carry a market price of only $825 in a 9 percent market; the drop in price is necessary to raise the yield on this bond from 7 to 9 percent. Issues with market values lower than par are known as *discount bonds* and carry coupons that are less than those on new issues. In contrast, issues with market values in excess of par are called *premium bonds* and have coupons greater than those currently being offered on new issues.

## INTEREST RATES MOVE THE MARKET

A basic trading rule in the bond market is that interest rates and bond prices move in opposite directions. When interest rates rise, bond prices fall; and when interest rates drop, bond prices move up. So it is possible to buy bonds at one price and, if interest rate conditions are right, to sell them some time later at a higher price. Of course, it is also possible to lose money if interest rates move against you.

The behavior of interest rates is, in fact, the single most important force in the bond market, determining not only the amount of current income you will receive but also your possible capital gains (or losses). It is not surprising, therefore, that interest rates are so closely followed by market participants and that bond market performance is generally seen as a function of interest rate changes.

The figure on the next page tracks bond interest rates over the 25-year period from 1961 to 1986. It shows that from a state of relative stability, interest rates exploded in 1965, and over the course of the next 15 years the rates paid on high-grade bonds almost tripled. More specifically, interest rates rose from the 4 to 5 percent range in the early 1960s to over 16 percent in 1982. Between 1982 and 1986, however, rates dropped sharply back to the single-digit range once again. Thus, after a sustained 15-year bear market for bonds, the market abruptly reversed course, bringing with it one of the strongest bull markets on record. (The bond market is considered bearish when interest rates are high or rising and bullish when rates are low or falling.) Although by historical standards, interest rates were still a bit high in 1987, they were at levels that had not been seen since the early 1970s.

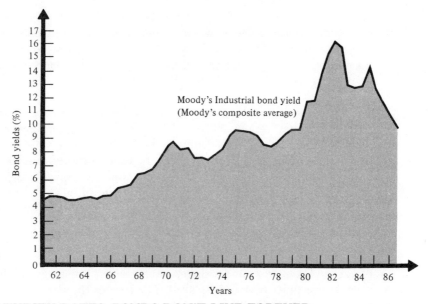

Bond yields (%)

Moody's Industrial bond yield
(Moody's composite average)

Years

## MATURITY DATES: BONDS DON'T LIVE FOREVER

Unlike common stock, all debt securities have limited lives and expire on a given date, which is known as the issue's *maturity date.* Although a bond carries a series of specific interest payment dates, the principal is repaid only once: on or before maturity. Because the maturity date is fixed and never changes, it not only defines the lives of new issues, but also tells you the amount of time remaining on older, outstanding bonds. This time span is known as the bond's *term to maturity.* For example, a new issue may come out as a 25-year bond and, five years later, have twenty years remaining to maturity.

Two types of bonds are distinguished on the basis of maturity: *Term bonds* have a single, fairly lengthy term to maturity and are the most common type of issue. *Serial bonds,* in contrast, have a series of maturity dates, perhaps as many as 15 or 20, within a single issue. For example, a 20-year term bond issued in 1986 would have a maturity date of 2006. If that same bond were issued in serial form, it might have 20 annual maturity dates extending from 1987 through 2006. At each of these annual maturity dates, a certain portion of the issue would come due and be paid off.

## CALL FEATURE: BONDS CAN BE RETIRED
## BEFORE THEIR TIME

Every bond is issued with a *call feature,* which specifies whether or not the issuer will be allowed to retire the bond prematurely. There are three types of call provisions:

- A bond can be *freely callable,* which means that the issuer can retire the bond at any time.

- It can be *noncallable,* in which case the issuer is prohibited from calling the bond prior to maturity.
- It can carry a *deferred call feature,* which stipulates that the obligation cannot be called until a certain period of time has passed, generally 5 to 10 years.

When interest rates are dropping, the bond issuer may use the call feature to retire bonds that were financed earlier at relatively high interest rates. This feature gives bond issuers the opportunity to lower the amount of interest they must pay to maintain their debt. Thus, when market interest rates undergo a sharp decline, as they did between 1982 and 1986, bond issuers (especially corporate issuers) will retire their high-yielding bonds (by calling them in) and replace them with lower yielding obligations. For the investor, this results in a much lower rate of return than originally expected.

*Call premiums.* In a half-hearted attempt to compensate investors who find their bonds called out from under them, a *call premium* is paid along with the issue's par value at the time the bond is called. The sum of the par value and call premium represents the issue's *call price* and this is what the issuer must pay to retire the bond prematurely. As a general rule, call premiums equal about 1 year's interest at the earliest date of call, and gradually become smaller as the issue nears maturity. Thus, the initial call price of a 9 percent $1,000 bond would be $1,090, with $90 representing the call premium.

*Refunding provisions.* In place of a call feature, some bonds contain a specific refunding provision that prohibits the premature retirement of an issue from the proceeds of a lower coupon refunding bond. The distinction is important, since these *nonrefunding,* or *deferred refunding,* issues can still be prematurely retired for any reason other than refunding. For example, you may have a high-yield nonrefundable issue called out from under you if the issuer has enough cash to retire the bond without having to go back into the bond market for refunding.

## SINKING FUND: A REPAYMENT PROVISION

A *sinking fund* provision specifies how a bond will be paid off over time. In essence, it indicates how much of the bond's principal will be retired each year. Sinking fund requirements generally begin 1 to 5 years after the date of issue and continue every year after that until all, or most, of the issue is paid off. Any amount not repaid by maturity (this might equal 10 to 25 percent of the issue) is then retired with a single balloon payment. Like the call provision, the sinking fund feature also carries a call premium, although it is generally nominal, amounting to perhaps 1 percent or less of the principal being retired. The sinking fund provision applies only to term bonds, since serial issues already have a predetermined method of repayment. However, not all term bonds have it, so check before you invest.

# SOME OTHER BOND FEATURES

What differentiates one bond from another? One factor is *collateral*—what the issuer will use to make good on a bond if it can't meet its obligation to pay. Bonds differ from one another in the type and amount of collateral standing behind them.

## SENIORS AND JUNIORS

*Senior bonds* hold the smallest risk because they're backed by a legal claim on some specific property the issuer owns. If you own mortgage bonds—a particular type of senior bond—the collateral is real estate. If you buy an *equipment trust certificate* (yet another senior bond form) from a railroad or airline, your bond is backed by the equipment the company owns.

On the other hand, when you buy a *junior bond,* all you get is a promise that the issuer will regularly pay you interest and principal. Because junior bonds are *unsecured,* if the promise falls through, there's no collateral to back it up. A *debenture* is a form of unsecured (junior) bond. In effect, it is nothing more than the issuer's unsecured IOU. This does not mean that the bond is worthless or that it is high risk. On the contrary, a major portion of the debt market is made up of debenture bonds, and all but a small fraction are high quality investments. Some companies issue a type of junior debenture bond called a *subordinated debenture.* These bonds have a claim on income that is secondary to other debenture bonds.

In the final analysis, you should only purchase a bond if you feel the issuer can repay the debt. If you buy a bond just because it is secured (a mortgage bond, for example,) you may be asking for trouble if the issuer is financially unstable. Similarly, if you pass up a bond just because it is an unsecured debenture, you may lose the opportunity to invest in a high-quality bond that has almost no chance of default. Always keep in mind that it is the ability of the issuer to repay the bond that matters, not the amount of collateral backing up the debt.

## REGISTERED AND BEARER BONDS

Regardless of the collateral standing behind a bond, a bond may be registered or issued in bearer form. When you buy a *registered bond,* your name is formally registered with the bond issuer, who keeps a running account of ownership and automatically pays interest to all owners of record. When you buy a *bearer bond,* the issuer keeps no record of ownership; you receive interest by "clipping coupons" attached to the bond and sending them in for payment. You are considered the owner of the bond by virtue of the fact that it is in your physical possession. *If you happen to own a bearer bond, be very careful with it since if it is lost or stolen, it can NOT be replaced.* If you lose a bearer bond, you lose everything: you don't get your money back and you don't earn any interest.

Although bearer bonds have been the most popular type of bond issue, they are destined to become a thing of the past. Since bearer bonds give the government no record of ownership, a significant number of investors never report the interest income received from them. To discourage tax cheating, effective July 1983, Congress mandated that all bonds be issued in registered form.

# 18

## THE MARKET FOR BONDS

What kind of bonds can you invest in? How can you tell if a bond is too risky—or too conservative—for your investment taste? How do market interest rates affect bond returns? This chapter will help you answer these and other important question. It will help you tell one type of bond from another and understand bond ratings and interest rate behavior. A clear understanding of this information is vital to becoming a successful bond investor.

## MAJOR TYPES OF BONDS

No matter what your investment temperament or objective, there are issues available in today's bond market to meet your needs. As a matter of convenience, the bond market is usually divided into five segments according to the type of issuer: Treasury, agency, municipal, corporate, and institutional. As you can see from the following figures, the market for these issues has exploded since 1950, with the most rapid growth occurring in recent years. Between 1980 and 1985, the value of these bonds more than doubled.

| Type of Issuer* | YEAR-END AMOUNTS OUTSTANDING (IN BILLIONS) | | | | |
|---|---|---|---|---|---|
| | 1950 | 1960 | 1970 | 1980 | 1985 |
| U.S. Treasury | $138.7 | $149.5 | $159.8 | $ 427.0 | $1,023.6 |
| U.S. agencies | 1.1 | 8.8 | 17.6 | 276.1 | 447.3 |
| States and municipalities | 24.0 | 66.5 | 144.4 | 322.3 | 734.9 |
| Corporations | 93.8 | 105.4 | 181.0 | 421.7 | 752.3 |
| Total | $257.6 | $330.2 | $502.8 | $1,447.1 | $2,958.1 |

*Data unavailable for institutional issues.

Source: Federal Reserve Bulletin, U.S. Treasury Bulletin, and Survey of Current Business.

Before we take a look at specific issues, it is important to mention two things about the bond market itself. First, most bonds are traded over-the-counter. Listed bonds—issues traded on the major stock exchanges—represent only a small portion of total outstanding debt obligations. Second, the bond market has far more price stability than the stock market. Although interest rates—and therefore bond prices—have been volatile in recent years, when bond price activity is measured on a daily basis, it is remarkably stable.

## TREASURY BONDS: THE GIANT OF THE MARKET

With more than $1 trillion outstanding, U.S. Treasury bonds (also known as *Treasuries* and *governments*) are the dominant force in the bond market. The U.S. Treasury issues bonds, notes, and other types of debt securities, including Treasury bills, to finance federal spending and debt maintenance. Treasury *notes* mature in 10 years or less, while Treasury *bonds* have maturities of 25 years or more. Both bonds and notes come in denominations of $1,000 to $10,000 and are issued in registered form. Interest income is subject to normal federal income tax but is exempt from state and local taxes. All Treasury obligations are backed by the full faith and credit of the U.S. government—a fact that makes them an extremely safe and popular investment vehicle. They are also highly liquid; they can be converted to cash at any time by selling them in a highly active secondary market.

Government bonds are either noncallable or issued with lengthy deferred call features. Deferment features that expire 5 years before final maturity are common with Treasuries. The bond listing will tell you whether a bond has a deferred call feature. For example, an 8 percent Treasury bond listed with an expiration of 2005–10 has a maturity date of 2010 and a deferred call feature that extends through 2005.

A unique feature of Treasuries is the unusual capital gains opportunity some of the bonds offer. That is, a number of older government bonds can be used, at par, to pay federal estate taxes. In other words, it is possible to purchase a Treasury issue at a discount and use it at par to pay estate taxes. The initial (purchase) transaction has to take place prior to death and the provision is beneficial only to the heirs (and only to the extent that there is a federal estate tax liability). These bonds have been nicknamed *flower bonds*. Although the Treasury no longer issues new flower bonds, there still are a half-dozen such issues available in the market, most of which carry 2¾ to 4½ percent coupons and have maturities as far out as 1999. The relatively low interest rate offered by these bonds provides investors with assurance that the bonds will appreciate by the time of death.

## AGENCY BONDS: ANOTHER WAY TO BUY ISSUES OF THE U.S. GOVERNMENT

Agency bonds are issued by federal agencies and other political subdivisions of the U.S. government. In 1985, there were more than $447 billion in agency bonds outstanding. These bonds, which are not direct obligations of the Treasury, generally provide higher yields than Treasuries, enabling you to increase your return with

| Type of Issue | Minimum Denomination | Initial Maturity | TAX STATUS* | | |
|---|---|---|---|---|---|
| | | | Fed. | State | Local |
| Federal Farm Credit Bank | $ 1,000 | 13 mos.–15 yrs. | T | E | E |
| Federal Intermediate Credit Banks | 5,000 | 9 mos.–4 yrs. | T | E | E |
| Federal Home Loan Bank | 10,000 | 1–20 yrs. | T | E | E |
| Federal Land Banks | 1,000 | 1–10 yrs. | T | E | E |
| Farmers Home Administration | 25,000 | 1–25 yrs. | T | T | T |
| Federal Housing Administration | 50,000 | 1–40 yrs. | T | T | T |
| Federal Home Loan Mortgage Corp. ("Freddie Macs")** | 25,000 | 18–30 yrs. | T | T | T |
| Federal National Mortgage Association ("Fannie Maes")** | 25,000 | 1–30 yrs. | T | T | T |
| Government National Mortgage Association (GNMA, "Ginnie Maes")** | 25,000 | 1–25 yrs. | T | T | T |
| Student Loan Marketing Association | 10,000 | 3–10 yrs. | T | E | E |
| Tennessee Valley Authority (TVA) | 1,000 | 3–25 yrs. | T | E | E |
| U.S. Postal Service | 10,000 | 25 yrs. | T | E | E |
| Federal Financing Bank | 1,000 | 1–20 yrs. | T | E | E |

*T = taxable; E = tax-exempt.

**Mortgage-backed securities; interest is paid monthly on these securities.

little or no difference in risk. This combination of high interest rates and safety has made agency bonds a rapidly growing segment of the U.S. bond market.

There are two types of agency issues: government-sponsored issues and federal agency issues. Included among the more than two dozen federal agencies are the Farmers Home Administration, the Government National Mortgage Association (GNMA, often referred to as Ginnie Mae), and the Tennessee Valley Authority (TVA). Government-sponsored issuers include the Federal Home Loan Banks, the Federal Intermediate Credit Banks, the Federal Land Banks, and the Federal Home Loan Mortgage Corporation. As a rule, the generic term *agency* is used for both government-sponsored and federal agency obligations.

The list on the previous page describes some of the more popular agency bonds. Although these issues are not the direct obligation of the U.S. government, a number actually carry government guarantees and therefore effectively represent the full faith and credit of the U.S. government. Moreover, some pay interest monthly, and many are exempt from state and local taxes.

Since 1986, all new agency and Treasury securities have been issued in *book entry* form. This means that no certificate of ownership is issued when you buy the bonds. Rather, the government sends you a transaction confirmation and enters your name in a computerized log book where it remains as long as you own the bond. Many experts believe that in the not-too-distant future, all security transactions will be handled in this way.

## MUNICIPAL BONDS: THE APPEAL OF TAX-FREE INCOME

Municipal bonds—or *munis*, as they are often called—are issued by states, counties, cities, and other political subdivisions like school, water, and sewer districts. In 1985, the value of outstanding municipal issues amounted to nearly $735 billion. Municipals are generally issued as serial obligations, which means that the issue is broken into a series of smaller bonds, each with its own maturity date and coupon. They are customarily issued in $5,000 denominations.

*General obligation vs. revenue bonds.*    Municipal bonds are brought to the market as either general obligation or revenue bonds. *General obligation bonds* are backed by the full faith and credit, and taxing power, of the issuer. *Revenue bonds*, in contrast, are serviced from the income generated by specific projects, such as toll roads and mass transit systems. Although general obligation bonds dominated the municipal market prior to the mid-1970s, the vast majority of municipals issued today are revenue bonds. These bonds account for between 65 and 70 percent of all new issues.

The distinction between general obligation and revenue bonds could mean a big difference to you as an investor, for the issuers of revenue bonds are obligated to pay principal and interest only if a sufficient level of revenue is generated. If the funds aren't there, issuers do not have to make payment on the bonds. On the other hand, the issuers of general obligation bonds are required to pay bondholders on schedule, whether or not tax revenues are as high as they expected.

*Municipal bond guarantees.* Many municipal bonds are issued with municipal bond guarantees, which provide the bondholder with third-party assurance that principal and interest payments will be made on time. The third party, in essence, provides an additional source of collateral in the form of nonrevocable insurance placed on the bond at the date of issue.

Several states and four private organizations provide municipal bond guarantees. The four private insurers are the Municipal Bond Insurance Association (MBIA), the American Municipal Bond Assurance Corporation (AMBAC), Bond Investors Guaranty Insurance Company (BIG), and the Financial Guaranty Investment Corporation (FGIC). All four insure any general obligation or revenue bond as long as it carries an S&P rating of triple-B or better. (These ratings are described later in the chapter.) Municipal bond insurance improves bond ratings, bringing many up to triple-A. It also improves liquidity, since these bonds are generally more actively traded in the secondary markets than uninsured bonds.

*Most munis are tax-free.* The main attraction of municipal securities is the exemption of their interest income from federal income taxes. In most cases, they are also exempt from state and local taxes in the state in which they are issued. For example, if you live in California and buy a California issue, you do not have to pay any state tax on the bond's interest income. However, if you live in Connecticut and buy the same California issue, the interest income will be subject to Connecticut state tax.

The following table shows you how the various states treat municipal bond interest at tax time. As you can see, only seven states do not levy taxes on the interest you collect from municipal bonds issued by other states.

### HOW THE STATES TAX INTEREST INCOME FROM MUNICIPAL BONDS

| State | Interest on Own Bonds | Interest on Bonds Issued by Other States |
| --- | --- | --- |
| Alabama | Exempt | Taxable |
| Alaska | No Income Tax* | No Income Tax* |
| Arizona | Exempt | Taxable |
| Arkansas | Exempt | Taxable |
| California | Exempt | Taxable |
| Colorado | Exempt (exceptions) | Taxable |
| Connecticut | Exempt | Taxable |
| Delaware | Exempt | Taxable |
| D.C. | Exempt | Exempt |
| Florida | No Income Tax* | No Income Tax* |
| Georgia | Exempt | Taxable |
| Hawaii | Exempt | Taxable |
| Idaho | Exempt | Taxable |
| Illinois | Taxable (limited exceptions) | Taxable |
| Indiana | Exempt | Exempt |
| Iowa | Taxable (limited exceptions) | Taxable |

*"No Income Tax" means the state does not have an income tax.

(Continued)

| State | Interest on Own Bonds | Interest on Bonds Issued by Other States |
|---|---|---|
| Kansas | Specified Issues Exempt | Taxable |
| Kentucky | Exempt | Taxable |
| Louisiana | Exempt | Taxable |
| Maine | Exempt | Taxable |
| Maryland | Exempt | Taxable |
| Massachusetts | Exempt | Taxable |
| Michigan | Exempt | Taxable |
| Minnesota | Exempt | Taxable |
| Mississippi | Exempt | Taxable |
| Missouri | Exempt | Taxable |
| Montana | Exempt | Taxable |
| Nebraska | Exempt | Exempt |
| Nevada | No Income Tax* | No Income Tax* |
| New Hampshire | Exempt | Taxable |
| New Jersey | Exempt | Taxable |
| New Mexico | Exempt | Exempt |
| New York | Exempt | Taxable |
| North Carolina | Exempt | Taxable |
| North Dakota | Exempt | Taxable |
| Ohio | Exempt | Taxable |
| Oklahoma | Specified Issues Exempt | Taxable |
| Oregon | Exempt | Taxable |
| Pennsylvania | Exempt | Taxable |
| Rhode Island | Exempt | Taxable |
| South Carolina | Exempt | Taxable |
| South Dakota | No Income Tax* | No Income Tax* |
| Tennessee | Exempt | Taxable |
| Texas | No Income Tax* | No Income Tax* |
| Utah | Exempt | Exempt |
| Vermont | Exempt | Exempt |
| Virginia | Exempt | Taxable |
| Washington | No Income Tax* | No Income Tax* |
| West Virginia | Exempt | Taxable |
| Wisconsin | Taxable | Taxable |
| Wyoming | No Income Tax* | No Income Tax* |

*"No Income Tax" means the state does not have an income tax.

This favorable tax treatment does not extend to capital gains, however. Any capital gains you earn when you sell a municipal bond are subject to the usual federal, state, and local income tax.

The table on the next page shows the yields you would have to receive on taxable bonds to equal the yields on tax-free municipals. It demonstrates how the yield attractiveness of munis varies with an investor's income level. That is, the higher your tax bracket, the more attractive a municipal bond becomes. For example, for someone in the 15 percent tax bracket, a 5 percent tax-free yield equals a 5.88 percent return on a fully taxable issue. The same yield translates to a 7.46

## TAXABLE EQUIVALENT YIELDS FOR VARIOUS TAX-EXEMPT RETURNS

| Joint Returns ($000) | Individual Returns ($000) | Tax Bracket | 5% | 6% | 7% | 8% | 9% | 10% | 12% | 14% |
|---|---|---|---|---|---|---|---|---|---|---|
| $ 0 –$ 29.8 | $ 0 –$ 17.8 | 15% | 5.88 | 7.06 | 8.24 | 9.41 | 10.59 | 11.76 | 14.12 | 16.47 |
| $29.8–$ 71.9 | $17.8–$ 43.2 | 28 | 6.94 | 8.33 | 9.72 | 11.11 | 12.50 | 13.89 | 16.67 | 19.44 |
| $71.9–$171.1** | $43.2–$100.5** | 33 | 7.46 | 8.96 | 10.45 | 11.94 | 13.43 | 14.92 | 17.91 | 20.90 |

The top portion of the header reads: TAXABLE INCOME* (spanning Joint Returns and Individual Returns) and TAX-FREE YIELD (spanning the 5%–14% columns).

*Tax rates effective January 1, 1988.

**Income over these amounts may be taxed at the 28% rate.

percent return for an investor in the 33 percent bracket. Since municipal bond yields are substantially lower than the yields available on fully taxable issues, you're relying on the bond's tax-free status to raise the yield. Generally, you must be in either the 28 or 33 percent tax bracket before municipal bonds beat the yields you receive on fully taxable issues.

You can use the following formula to determine the return a fully taxable bond would have to provide in order to match the after-tax return of a municipal:

$$\text{fully taxable equivalent yield} = \frac{\text{yield of municipal bond}}{1 - \text{tax rate}}$$

For example, if a municipal offers a yield of 6.5 percent and you are in the 33 percent tax bracket, you should invest in taxable bonds only if they yield 9.7 percent or more (6.5%/.67 = 9.7%); if you can't find such bonds, then you'll be better off with the lower yielding municipal issue.

Clearly, taxes are an important variable in deciding whether or not to buy municipal bonds; they may or may not be right for you, depending on what tax bracket you're in. It should come as no surprise, therefore, that the reduced tax rates of the 1986 Tax Reform Act had the effect of generally reducing the appeal of tax-exempt securities. With lower tax rates, investors have less incentive to hold municipal bonds.

*Taxable munis.* The 1986 tax law also changed the tax-exempt status of some municipal bonds. Specifically, if bonds are used to finance what are considered "nonessential" projects, their interest income is not tax-exempt. This tax law change created a whole new breed of municipal bonds. Known as taxable munis, these issues are expected to account for between 20 and 25 percent of the municipal bond market within a relatively short time. As the name implies, the interest income on these bonds is fully taxable by the federal government. (It is not clear how the states will handle these bonds, although it is likely that some will continue to consider all their munis exempt from state tax while others, following the lead of the IRS, will subject some of their own munis to state taxes.) Although the after-tax yields of these bonds may not measure up to those of tax-free municipals, they do offer considerably higher yields than Treasury bonds. In addition, taxable municipals are usually noncallable—a fact that allows you to lock in high yields for a number of years.

## CORPORATE BONDS: THE PRIVATE SECTOR GETS A PIECE OF THE ACTION

The major nongovernmental issuers of bonds are corporations. In 1985, the total value of outstanding corporate bonds was more than $750 billion. The market for *corporates,* as these bonds are called, is divided into several segments:

- *Industrial* bonds, which include the most diverse bond issues
- *Public utility* bonds, which are the dominant group in terms of volume of new issues
- Rail and other *transportation* bonds
- *Financial* bonds, issued by banks, finance companies, and other financial organizations

You'll find the widest range of issues in the corporate bond market, including first mortgage bonds, convertible bonds, debentures, subordinated debentures, income bonds, and collateral trust bonds (which are backed by financial assets that can be sold to pay off the bonds in case of default). Corporate issues are popular among investors because of their relatively attractive yields.

Corporate bonds usually come in $1,000 denominations and are issued on a term basis, with a single maturity date. Maturities usually range from 25 to 40 years, and nearly all corporates carry deferred call provisions that prohibit prepayment for the first 5 to 10 years. Interest is paid semiannually, and sinking funds are popular.

While most corporates fit this general description, the *equipment trust certificate* does not. These bonds are issued by railroads, airlines, and other transportation companies. The proceeds from these certificates are used to purchase such equipment as freight cars and airplanes, which in turn serve as the collateral for the issues. Unlike most corporates, equipment trust certificates are issued in serial form and carry uniform annual installments throughout the bond's life. These bonds normally have maturities ranging from 1 year to a maximum of 17 years. What makes these bonds especially attractive is their relatively high yields. In spite of a nearly perfect payment record that dates back to predepression days, these bonds offer yields that are well above average.

## INSTITUTIONAL BONDS: BONDS THAT TUG AT THE HEART

By far the smallest segment of the bond market, institutional bonds are marketed by a variety of private, nonprofit institutions, including schools, hospitals, and churches. These bonds are sometimes called *heart bonds* because of their emotional appeal. Indeed, some people equate investing in institutional bonds with giving to charity.

Even though these obligations have a virtually spotless default record, they regularly provide returns that are 1 to 1½ percentage points above the yields on comparable corporate bonds. Issuers are forced to offer these high rates because almost no secondary market exists for these bonds. You can overcome this problem by purchasing bonds with specific, desired maturities—a move that reduces or eliminates the need to trade these bonds later on. This is relatively easy to do, since institutional bonds are issued on a serial basis, with relatively short maximum maturities that seldom exceed 15 to 18 years. Institutional bonds are usually issued in $1,000 denominations.

## SPECIALTY ISSUES

Wall Street has never been shy about bringing out new products if it sees a market for them. This has certainly been the case in the fixed income securities market, which in recent years has seen a growth in new investment vehicles.

### ZERO COUPON BONDS

A large number of investors have flocked to a specialty issue known as the zero coupon bond (zeros, for short). As the name implies, zero coupon bonds have no coupons; rather, the securities are sold at a deep discount from their par values and then increase in value over time at a compound rate of return so that, at maturity, they are worth much more than their initial cost. Other things being equal, the cheaper the bond, the greater the return (for example, whereas a 10 percent bond might cost $239, an issue with a 15 percent yield will cost only $123). Because they don't have coupons, these bonds do not pay interest semiannually and, in fact, they pay nothing to the investor until the issue matures. As strange as it might seem, this is the main attraction of zero coupon bonds; that is, since there are no interest payments, investors do not have to worry about reinvesting coupon income twice a year. Instead, the full compounded rate of return on a zero coupon bond is virtually guaranteed at the stated rate that existed when the issue was purchased.

In early 1987, high-grade zero coupon bonds with 20-year maturities were available at yields of around 9 percent. Thus for just $175 you could buy a bond that will be worth nearly 6 times that amount, or $1,000, when it matures in 20 years. The difference between what you put in and what you get back—in this case $825—is your income.

But there are also some serious disadvantages to zeros. One is that, if rates move up over time, you won't be able to participate in the higher return, since you'll have no coupon income to reinvest. In addition, zero coupon bonds are subject to tremendous price volatility. Thus, if market rates do climb, you'll experience high capital losses as the prices of zero coupons plunge. Of course, if interest rates drop way down, the way they did in 1984–86, you'll reap the rewards of enormous capital gains if you hold long-term zeros. Indeed, these issues are unsurpassed in capital gains potential. Finally, the IRS has ruled that zero coupon bondholders must report interest on an accrual basis, even though no interest is actually received. For this reason, most fully taxable zero coupon bonds should either be used in tax-sheltered investments, like individual retirement accounts (IRAs), or be held by minor children (14 or older) who are likely to be taxed at the lowest rate, if at all.

Zeros are issued by corporations, municipalities, federal agencies, and the U.S. Treasury. In addition, many of the major brokerage houses package U.S. Treasury securities as zeros and sell them to investors in the form of investment trusts, marketed under such names as TIGRS, CATS, and LIONS.

## MORTGAGE-BACKED SECURITIES

These bonds give bondholders an undivided interest in a pool of insured residential and commercial mortgages. Secured by the mortgages, these bonds work in the following way: When a homeowner makes a monthly mortgage payment, that payment is, in effect, "passed through" to the bondholder to pay off the mortgage-backed bond. Thus, each mortgage payment the homeowner makes ultimately pays interest and principal to the mortgage-backed bondholder.

Mortage-backed securities, which were first issued by such federal agencies as the Government National Mortgage Association (GNMA) and the Federal National Mortgage Association (FNMA), are now issued by a number of other federal agencies as well as private corporate issuers. Each issuer puts together a pool containing several hundred million dollars worth of mortgages and then issues securities in the amount of the mortgage pool.

Bondholders usually receive monthly payments from the issuer, which are made up of both principal and interest. Since the principal represents return of capital, it is nontaxable. Interest income, however, is subject to ordinary federal, state, and local income taxes. Mortgage-backed securities are usually issued in denominations of at least $25,000 and have maturities of 20 to 25 years. In reality, the average life span of these bonds is about 12 years since so many of the pooled mortgages are paid off early.

Mortgage-backed securities are self-liquidating, since part of the monthly cash flow you receive is the principal you originally invested. Thus, since the principal is paid back in little chunks over the life of the bond, you receive no big principal payment when the bond matures—a situation that is extremely disconcerting to many investors. A number of mutual funds specializing in mortgage-backed securities have solved this problem by automatically reinvesting the principal you would receive each month and sending you interest payments alone. This enables you to preserve your capital, and at the same time receive high competitive yields.

Investors also face the problem of loan prepayment. In a regular mortgage-backed security, as pooled mortgages are paid off early, all bondholders receive a pro rata share of the prepayments. The net effect of this prepayment is to sharply reduce the life of the bond. *Collateralized mortgage obligations* (CMOs) were created to deal with this problem. CMOs divide investors into classes, depending on whether they want a short-, intermediate-, or long-term investment. Then, as mortgages in the pool are prepaid, that principal is channeled to those in the short-term group first. Only when all the investors in this group have been fully repaid do those in the intermediate group start receiving prepayments, and so on.

## JUNK BONDS

Junk bonds, or *high-yield bonds* as they are also called, are speculative issues that have received low ratings from Moody's or Standard & Poor's. These bonds have enjoyed enormous popularity lately because of their extremely high returns. In 1987, for example, 12 to 14 percent yields were not uncommon. Unfortunately, these dazzling returns bring an equal measure of risk.

Many junk bonds are issued by troubled companies plagued by such problems as corporate mismanagement and fierce foreign and domestic competition. Navistar, Eastern Airlines, and Public Service Company of New Hampshire all issued junk bonds in 1986. Young, rapidly growing companies also use junk bonds to finance mergers and acquisitions. For example, junk bonds were prominent in Ted Turner's unsuccessful takeover attempt of CBS in 1986. The financing of mergers and acquisitions has accounted for most of the rapid growth in the junk bond market. Even though the growth firms backing these bonds are not in trouble themselves, these debt issues have low ratings since they carry with them a high risk of default. This risk makes diversification critical. If you have the disposition to invest in junk bonds, be sure to invest in several instead of just one.

## AND MORE SPECIALTY ISSUES

You should also know about three other specialty issues:

- *Variable rate notes,* which were first issued in this country in 1974, are probably the oldest type of specialty issue. These notes have two unique features: (1) After the first 6 to 18 months of an issue's life, the coupon rate "floats" as it is adjusted upward or downward according to prevailing Treasury bill or Treasury note rates. This adjustment, which takes place every 6 to 12 months, keeps the return a specified amount above these benchmark rates. (2) Every year, these notes are redeemable at par and at the holder's option. Thus, variable rate notes represent long-term commitments on the part of borrowers (they're usually issued with 15- to 25-year maturities), yet they provide all the advantages (especially price stability) of short-term obligations. The nice thing about variable rate notes is that when market rates go up, so do the returns on these issues. Unfortunately, just the opposite occurs when market rates fall.

- *Put bonds* give you the right to redeem the bonds before they mature. Usually, this can be done 3 to 5 years after the date of issue and then every 1 to 5 years after that. In return for the right to periodically "put the bond" for redemption, you receive a lower yield. Unlike a variable rate note, the coupons on put bonds are fixed for the life of the issue.
- *Extendable notes* are short-term securities, typically with 1- to 5-year maturities, which can be redeemed or renewed for the same period at a new interest rate. For example, an issue might come out as a series of 3-year renewable notes, over a period of 15 years. Every 3 years, the notes are extendable for another 3 years at a yield comparable to the market interest rates that prevail at the time. Thus, the return on these securities changes every 3 to 5 years as market rates move over time.

# BOND RATINGS

Bond ratings are assigned to bond issues on the basis of extensive, professionally conducted financial analyses that designate investment quality and risk. These ratings, issued by such rating agencies as Moody's and Standard & Poor's, are used in the municipal, corporate, and institutional bond markets. Bond ratings are an indication of the issuer's ability to service the debt (that is, make principal and interest payments) in a prompt and timely fashion. A high rating means that the firm should have little difficulty servicing its debt. Thus, higher ratings mean higher quality issues. Bond ratings relieve investors of the drudgery of evaluating the investment quality of individual bond issues.

## HOW RATINGS WORK

Every time a new issue comes to the market, it is analyzed by a staff of professional bond analysts to determine investment quality and risk of default. The financial records of the issuing organization are thoroughly examined and its future prospects assessed. Although the specifics of the credit analysis conducted by the ratings agencies change with each issue, several major characteristics of the issuing organization enter into most bond ratings:

- Its *earning power,* including the stability of earnings
- Its *liquidity* and how it is managed
- Its relative *debt burden*
- Its *coverage ratios,* which indicate how well the organization can service both existing debt and the new bond being proposed

The result of this analysis is a bond rating, assigned at the time of issue, that indicates the ability of the issuing organization to service its debt on schedule.

The following table lists the ratings assigned to bonds by the two major services. In addition to these standard rating categories, Moody's uses numerical modifiers, (1, 2, or 3) on bonds rated double-A to B, while Standard & Poor's uses plus (+) and minus (−) signs on the same rating classes to show relative standing within a major rating category. For example, an A+ (or A1) means a strong, high A rating, but an A− (or A3) indicates that the issue is on the low end of the scale. Except for slight variations in designations (Aaa vs. AAA), the meaning and interpretation of these ratings is basically the same. In most cases, Moody's and S&P assign identical ratings. Occasionally, however, an issue carries two different ratings, known as *split ratings,* which shades the quality of an issue in one way or another. For example, when an issue is rated Aa by Moody's and A by S& P, it is not considered as strong as an issue that receives a double-A rating from both Moody's and S&P.

## BOND RATINGS

| Moody's | S&P | Definition |
|---------|-----|------------|
| Aaa | AAA | *Best quality investment bonds.* The highest rating assigned, denoting extremely strong capacity to pay principal and interest. Often called "gilt edge" securities. |
| Aa | AA | *High-grade investment bonds.* High quality by all standards, but rated lower primarily because the margins of protection are not quite as strong. |
| A | A | *Upper medium-grade investment bonds.* Many favorable investment attributes, but elements may be present which suggest susceptibility to adverse economic changes. |
| Baa | BBB | *Medium-grade investment bonds.* Adequate capacity to pay principal and interest but possibly lacking certain protective elements against adverse economic conditions. |
| Ba | BB | *Speculative issues.* Only moderate protection of principal and interest in varied economic times. |
| B | B | *Speculative issues.* Generally lacking desirable characteristics of investment bonds. Assurance of principal and interest may be small. |
| Caa | CCC | *Default.* Poor-quality issues that may be in default or in danger of default. |
| Ca | CC | *Default.* Highly speculative issues, often in default or possessing other market shortcomings. |
| C | | *Default.* These issues may be regarded as extremely poor in investment quality. |
| | C | *Default.* Rating given to income bonds on which no interest is paid. |
| | D | *Default.* Issues actually in default, with principal or interest in arrears. |

*Source:* Moody's *Bond Record* and Standard & Poor's *Bond Guide.*

Older, outstanding issues are regularly reviewed to insure that the ratings assigned to them are still valid. Most issues carry a single rating to maturity, but occasionally ratings are revised during the life of the bond.

Finally, although it may appear that the firm is receiving the rating, it is actually the issue that is being rated. As a result, a firm can have different ratings assigned to its issues: the senior securities, for example, might carry one rating and the junior issues another, lower rating.

## WHAT RATINGS MEAN

Most bond investors pay careful attention to agency ratings since they can affect not only the yield but the price behavior of a bond as well. Specifically, the higher the rating a bond receives, the lower the yield. While you might be able to get 9 percent on an A-rated issue, for example, you'll probably get no more than 8½ to 8¾ percent on a comparable triple-A issue. What's more, *investment-grade securities*— securities that receive one of the top four ratings—are more sensitive to interest rate changes and tend to exhibit more uniform price behavior than lower rated (specula-tive-grade) issues.

A word of caution is in order: Bond ratings are intended as a measure of an issue's default risk alone and have absolutely nothing to do with the issue's market risk. Thus, when interest rates rise, *even the highest quality issues will lose value*, subjecting you to what could be a major capital loss.

---

## HOW MARKET INTEREST RATES AFFECT BOND PRICES

As we have noted, the behavior of interest rates has a significant impact on bond yields and prices. Interest rates are important to conservative investors since one of their major objectives is to lock in high yields. Aggressive investors are also inter-ested in interest rates because their programs are built on the capital gains oppor-tunities that accompany major swings in rates.

### WHY INTEREST RATES MOVE

Although the subject of interest rates is complex, we do know that certain forces influence the general behavior of market rates.

Perhaps no variable has a greater effect on interest rates than *inflation*. Changes in the inflation rate, or even expectations about the future course of inflation, have had a direct and pronounced effect on market interest rates and have been a leading cause of their wide swings. The figure on the next page demonstrates how strong the link is between interest rates and inflation. You can see that as inflation drifted upward during the late 1970s and early 1980s, so did interest rates. When inflation dropped off around 1982, interest rates took a similar plunge.

Interest rates are also influenced by the following factors:

- Changes in the money supply
- Size of the federal deficit

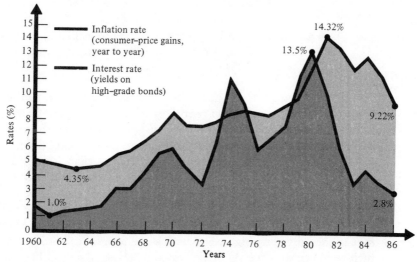

Source: *U.S. News & World Report*, March 31, 1986.

- Demand for money
- Level of economic activity
- Discount rate set by the Federal Reserve

An increase in any of these factors puts upward pressure on interest rates.

## YIELD SPREADS

Just as there is no single bond market, but several market sectors, so too there is no single interest rate applicable to all segments of the market. Rather, each segment has its own, somewhat unique, level of interest rates. Although the various rates tend to drift in the same direction and to follow the same general pattern of behavior, it is not uncommon for interest rate differentials—known as *yield spreads*—to exist in the various market sectors. The following list summarizes some of the more important things you should know about market yields and yield spreads.

- Municipal bonds have the lowest market rates because of their tax-exempt status. As a rule, their market yields are about three-quarters to 85 percent of those on corporate bonds. In the taxable sector, Treasuries have the lowest yields (and the least risk), followed by agency bonds, corporates, and institutional obligations.
- Issues that carry agency ratings generally display the same behavior: the lower the agency rating, the higher the yield.
- A direct relationship generally exists between the coupon an issue carries and its yield: discount (low-coupon) bonds have the lowest yield, while premium (high-coupon) bonds have the highest.
- In the corporate sector, industrial bonds generally provide the lowest yields, followed by utilities and rails.
- In the municipal sector, revenues yield more than general obligations.
- Bonds that are freely callable provide higher returns, at least at date of issue, than deferred call obligations. Noncallable bonds have an even lower yield.

- As a rule, bonds with long maturities tend to yield more than short-term issues. There are exceptions, however. In 1980–81, for example, short-term yields exceeded the yields on long-term bonds.

This information will help you find the highest yielding bonds in each market segment. If, for example, you're interested in receiving the highest possible return on your municipal bond investment, you should consider revenue bonds instead of general obligations. Similarly, if you're a corporate bond investor after high yields, you'll probably get a higher return from utilities than from industrials.

You should pay close attention to interest rates and yield spreads, and try to stay abreast not only of the current state of the market, but also the future direction of market rates. If you're a conservative (income-oriented) bond investor, and think, for example, that rates have just about peaked out, that should be a clue to try to lock in the prevailing high yields with some form of call protection. You might buy high-yield bonds—like A- or Baa-rated utilities—that still have lengthy call deferments. In contrast, if you're an aggressive bond trader who thinks rates have peaked (and are about to drop), that should be a signal to buy bonds that offer maximum price appreciation potential—like low-coupon bonds that still have a long time to go before they mature. Clearly, in either case, *the future direction of interest rates is important!*

But how do you formulate such expectations? Unless you have considerable training in economics, you will have to rely on various published sources. Fortunately, there is a wealth of such information available. Your broker is an excellent source, as are investor services like Moody's or Standard & Poor's; finally, there are widely circulated business and financial publications—like *The Wall Street Journal, Forbes, Business Week,* and *Fortune*—that regularly address the current state and future direction of market interest rates. Make no mistake, it's not an easy task. In fact, it's next to impossible to consistently predict the future direction of interest rates with a high degree of precision. But by taking the time to read some of the publications and reports regularly and carefully, you can readily keep track of the behavior of interest rates and at least get a handle on what is likely to occur in the near future.

PLAYING IT SAFE—STOCKS, BONDS, AND MUTUAL FUNDS

# 19

## INVESTING IN BONDS: SHOULD YOU OR SHOULDN'T YOU?

Success in the bond market can come only if you understand how interest rates affect bond yields. This information will help you choose the bond that will do what you want it to do and the investment strategy that is likely to get you where you want to be.

### PULLS AND TUGS ON BOND PRICES

The price of a bond is a function of the movement of market interest rates and the bond's coupon and maturity. As the figure on the next page shows, there is an inverse relationship between bond prices and market interest rates: when interest rates drop, bond prices rise, and vice versa.

The figure also shows the trading characteristics of premium and discount bonds. *Premium bonds* sell for more than par value, which occurs whenever market interest rates drop below the coupon rate on the bond. *Discount* bonds sell for less

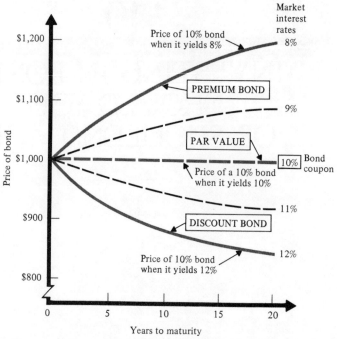

**Price of bond** (y-axis) · **Years to maturity** (x-axis)

Market interest rates — 8%

Price of 10% bond when it yields 8%

PREMIUM BOND

9%

PAR VALUE

10% Bond coupon

Price of a 10% bond when it yields 10%

11%

DISCOUNT BOND

Price of 10% bond when it yields 12%

12%

$1,200 · $1,100 · $1,000 · $900 · $800

0 · 5 · 10 · 15 · 20

than par, which occurs when market rates are greater than the issue's coupon rate. Thus, the 10 percent bond in our illustration traded as a premium bond when market rates fell to 8 percent, and as a discount bond when rates rose to 12 percent.

The extent to which bond prices move depends not only on the direction and magnitude of change in interest rates, but also on the coupon and maturity of the bond. That is, bonds with lower coupons and/or longer maturities will respond more vigorously to changes in market rates and therefore undergo greater price swings. In the preceding illustration, you can see that for any given change in interest rates—from 10 percent to 8 percent, for example—the largest price change occurs when the bond has the greatest number of years to maturity.

You, as an investor, can take advantage of this relationship. Just remember: when interest rates drop, look for bonds with low coupons and long maturities. This sets you up for maximum capital gains if the market goes your way. Do the opposite when interest rates rise. Invest in securities with high coupons and short maturities in order to minimize price variations and preserve your capital; for example, put your money into T-bills or money funds.

## USE BOND YIELD TO DETERMINE BOND VALUE

The question is the same for any investment vehicle: how do you put a price tag on your investment? In the case of fixed income securities, how do you determine what various bonds are actually worth? You can answer this question by calculating yield.

Yield is the single most important bond market measure and is used in a variety of ways. It tracks the behavior of the market in general as well as the return of individual issues. Basically, there are three different types of yield: current yield, promised yield, and realized yield.

## CURRENT YIELD

Current yield is the simplest of all return measures and has the most limited application. It indicates the amount of current (annual coupon) income a bond provides relative to its prevailing market price:

$$\text{current yield} = \frac{\text{annual interest income}}{\text{current market price of the bond}}$$

For example, an 8 percent bond would pay $80 a year in interest for every $1,000 of principal. However, if the bond were currently priced at $800, its current yield would be 10 percent ($80/$800 = .10). This information is especially important to investors seeking high levels of current income.

## PROMISED YIELD

Promised yield, the most important and widely used bond valuation measure, evaluates both interest income and price appreciation, and considers total cash flow received over the life of an issue. Also known as *yield to maturity,* it indicates the fully compounded rate of return available to you, assuming you hold the bond to maturity. Promised yield provides valuable insight into an issue's investment merit and is used to determine the competitive attractiveness of alternative vehicles. Other things being equal, the higher the promised yield of an issue, the more attractive it is.

Although there are several ways to compute promised yield, the simplest is to adapt a procedure first introduced in Chapter 4, known as the approximate yield method:

$$\text{promised yield} = \frac{\text{annual interest income} + \dfrac{\$1,000 - \text{current market price}}{\text{years remaining till maturity}}}{\dfrac{\$1,000 + \text{current market price}}{2}}$$

Consider the following hypothetical situation. Assume that a 7½ percent bond, with a par value of $1,000, has 18 years remaining to maturity and is currently priced at $825. Using this information, we see that the promised yield of this bond is:

$$\text{promised yield} = \frac{\$75 + \dfrac{\$1,000 - \$825}{18}}{\dfrac{\$1,000 + \$825}{2}}$$

$$= \frac{\$75 + \$9.72}{\$912.50}$$

$$= \underline{9.28\%}$$

This same approximate yield formula can be used to find the promised yield to maturity of a zero coupon bond. The only variation is that the coupon income portion of the equation can be ignored since it will, of course, equal zero.

A word of warning: the calculated yield-to-maturity figure is only the return "promised" if the issuer meets all interest and principal obligations on time and the investor reinvests all coupon income—from the date of receipt to maturity—at an average rate equal to or greater than the computed promised yield. In essence, the promised yield figure tells you the minimum required reinvestment rate you must earn on each of the interim coupon receipts to realize a return equal to, or greater than, the promised yield.

In the example we just gave, you would have to reinvest each of the coupons you receive over the next 18 years at a rate of about 9¼ percent. If you fail to do this, the realized yield (that is, the amount that you *actually earn* on the bond) will be less than 9.28 percent. In the worst possible situation, when no attempt is made to reinvest any of the coupon income, the realized yield over the 18-year investment period will be only 6 percent. Thus, unless you own a zero coupon bond, keep in mind that *a significant portion of a bond's total return over time comes from the reinvestment of coupons.*

## REALIZED YIELD

Rather than buying a bond and holding it to maturity, as the promised yield formula presumes you will do, you may decide to trade in and out of the bond long before it matures. The success of this investment strategy is measured by the bond's realized yield.

If you hold the bond for less than a year, you can calculate your return by using the holding period return measure described in Chapter 4. However, when the holding period extends much beyond a year, you should turn to the following realized yield formula to compare the yield you can expect from various investments:

$$\text{realized yield} = \frac{\text{annual interest income} + \dfrac{\text{expected future selling price} - \text{current market price}}{\text{years in holding period}}}{\dfrac{\text{expected future selling price} + \text{current market price}}{2}}$$

This measure is simply a variation of promised yield—note that only two variables are changed: expected future selling price is used in place of par value ($1,000), and length of holding period is used in place of term to maturity. This formula also requires the expected future price of the bond. You can compute this important piece of information by estimating what market interest rates will be when the bond is sold. This is the toughest part of coming up with a reliable future price for the bond, but it has to be done. As a bond trader, you have to estimate what's going to happen to interest rates, since the behavior of market rates determines, to a large extent, whether bond prices will go up or down. Obviously, therefore, the future behavior of interest rates will play a major role in defining the kind of yield you realize.

To illustrate, let's consider our 7½ percent, 18-year bond once more. Assume this time that you anticipate holding the bond for only 3 years and that you estimate interest changes will move the bond's price from its present level of $825 to $950. This change in price is based on the assumption that interest rates will fall from 9¼ to 8 percent in 3 years. Thus, assuming you buy the bond today at a market price of $825 and sell it 3 years later—after interest rates have declined to about 8 percent—at a price of $950, the expected realized yield of this bond would be:

$$\text{realized yield} = \frac{\$75 + \dfrac{\$950 - \$825}{3}}{\dfrac{\$950 + \$825}{2}}$$

$$= \underline{13.15\%}$$

The better than 13 percent return this investment offers may lull you into believing that it is the amount you will actually receive. Keep in mind, however, that this is a measure of expected yield only. It is subject to variation if things do not work out as you anticipated, particularly with regard to the market yield (and therefore, bond price) expected to prevail at the end of the holding period.


## VALUING A BOND

Depending on your objectives, you can determine the value of a bond by either its promised yield or its expected realized yield. If you are a conservative, income-oriented investor, you will employ promised yield, because coupon income over extended periods of time is your principal objective, and promised yield provides a viable measure of return under those conditions. If you are a more aggressive bond trader, on the other hand, you will use expected realized yield, because the capital gains you can earn by buying and selling bonds over relatively short holding periods is your chief concern, and expected realized yield is more important to you than the promised yield that exists at the time the bond is purchased. In either case, promised or realized yields provide *measures of return* that can be used to determine the relative attractiveness of fixed income securities.

In using these measures, you should evaluate them in light of the amount of *risk* involved in the investment. Bonds are no different than stocks in this way: the amount of expected return should be sufficient to cover your exposure to risk. The greater the amount of perceived risk, the greater the amount of return the bond should generate. If the bond meets this criterion, it can then be compared to other potential investment outlets; if you find it difficult to do better elsewhere (in a risk-return sense), then you should give the bond serious consideration as an investment outlet.

# DEVELOP AN INVESTMENT STRATEGY

As we said at the beginning of this material on bonds, fixed income investors tend to fall into three general categories: (1) conservative, quality-conscious, income-oriented investors who want the maximum amount of current income they can get, (2) bond traders who are after maximum capital gains, often within a short period of time, and (3) investors who want both high current income and capital gains over fairly long holding periods.

You'll need a well-thought-out strategy to achieve any one of these investment goals. Although many extremely complicated strategies are used by professional money managers, most individual investors rely on three basic approaches to bond investments: the buy-and-hold strategy, bond trading based on forecasts of interest rate behavior, and bond swaps.

## THE BUY-AND-HOLD TECHNIQUE

The most important part of this strategy is to find a bond with the quality, coupon, maturity, and call feature you want and then hold it for an extended period—often to maturity. This strategy involves little trading. Rather, it is a highly conservative approach that amounts to little more than clipping coupons and collecting income.

If you feel comfortable with this basic approach but want to increase your return somewhat, you may trade a bond you intended to hold to maturity if there's an opportunity for substantial capital gains. The key ingredient of any buy-and-hold strategy is choosing an investment vehicle that has attractive features, yield, and maturity.

## TRADING ON FORECASTS OF INTEREST RATE BEHAVIOR

This highly risky approach to bond investing relies on forecasting future interest rates—an imperfect art, at best. Its goal is to earn attractive capital gains when interest rates are expected to decline, and to preserve capital when interest rates are expected to rise. Most of the trading is done with high-grade investment securities, since a high degree of interest sensitivity is required to capture the maximum amount of price behavior.

Once interest rate expectations are set, the rest of the strategy is almost automatic. For example, if you anticipate a drop in interest rates, you should buy long-maturity and low-coupon (discount) issues, which earn the highest capital gains in the shortest period of time. Long-term zero coupon bonds are ideal for this purpose. Since these interest rate swings are usually short-lived, your goal is to earn as much as possible as quickly as possible. You may decide to use margin trading—borrowed funds—to magnify your returns.

When rates level off and begin to move up, shift your money out of long, discounted bonds and into high-yielding issues with short maturities. In effect, completely reverse your position. Your goal during this period is to protect your money from capital loss while at the same time obtaining a high yield. Such high-yield, short-term obligations as Treasury bills, certificates of deposit, money funds, and variable rate notes are ideal for these periods.

## BOND SWAPS

In a bond swap, you liquidate your holding in one bond and simultaneously buy another bond in its place. You may decide to do this to increase current yield or yield to maturity, to take advantage of shifts in interest rates, to improve the quality of your portfolio, or to minimize your tax liability. Although bond swaps go by a variety of colorful names, such as *profit take-out, substitution swap,* and *tax swap,* they all have the same purpose: to improve bond portfolio performance. Most bond swaps are fairly simple transactions, including the two we will review here.

In a *yield pickup swap,* you switch out of a low-coupon bond into a comparable higher coupon issue in order to realize an automatic and instantaneous pickup of current yield and yield to maturity. This would occur, for example, if you sold a 20-year, A-rated, 6½ percent bond, yielding 8 percent, and replaced it with a 20-year, A-rated, 7 percent bond, yielding 8½ percent. The swap enables you to improve your current yield—the coupon income increases from $65 a year to $70 a year—and your yield to maturity, which rises from 8 to 8½ percent. The mechanics of this swap are fairly simple, and you can handle it on your own or ask your broker to help you do it (your broker will be eager to find swap candidates for you). Before you proceed, however, be sure that commission and transaction costs don't eat up all your profit.

The objective of a *tax swap* is to eliminate, or substantially reduce, the tax liability that accompanies large capital gains. You can do this by simply selling an issue that has undergone a capital loss and replacing it with a comparable obligation. For example, assume that you had $10,000 worth of corporate bonds that you sold (in the current year) for $15,000, resulting in a capital gain of $5,000. You can eliminate the tax liability that accompanies this capital gain by selling securities (*any security,* not just another bond) that have capital losses of $5,000. As you will see, a bond swap is a simple yet highly effective way of legitimately reducing your tax liability and, therefore, increasing the return on your investment.

Let's assume you hold a 20-year, 4¾ percent municipal bond, which, strictly by coincidence, has dropped in value by $5,000. This bond provides the tax shield you need if you can find a viable swap candidate. Suppose you find a comparable 20-year, 5 percent municipal issue currently trading at about the same price as the issue being sold. Again, your broker should have no trouble coming up with viable swap candidates. By selling the 4¾s and simultaneously buying the 5s, you will not only increase your tax-free current yield (from 4¾ to 5), you'll also eliminate your capital gains tax liability.

Keep in mind that identical issues cannot be used in these transactions, since the IRS would consider this a *wash sale* and disallow the loss. Thus, you could not sell an 8 percent, 20-year bond and then turn around and replace it with the *same* 8 percent, 20-year issue. Also be sure that both the capital gain and the capital loss occur in the same calendar year.

This technique is extremely popular with knowledgeable investors, particularly at year-end when it is clear how much of a tax loss is needed to offset the year's capital gains. It is an extremely effective way to lower your taxes, and the only reason it is not more widely used is that most individual investors simply do not know about it or don't know enough to execute the swap. This is unfortunate, since tax swaps are a very safe procedure that offers almost instantaneous returns.

## SHOULD YOU DO IT?

You can invest in bonds for the same reasons you invest in stocks. If you're after a high, competitive return on your investment and want to avoid as much risk as possible, bonds might be the perfect vehicle. If you're more aggressive and seek capital gains instead, falling interest rates may provide the perfect opportunity for active trading. Bonds also offer a unique opportunity for tax savings. By investing in municipals, Treasuries, and agency issues, you'll come away with at least part of your income tax-free. (Remember, municipals are exempt from federal and some state taxes, while Treasuries and many agency bonds are free from state tax.)

On the other hand, there are also some disadvantages to investing in bonds. One of the biggest is the relatively large denominations of the issues. Another is that the coupons are usually fixed for the life of the issue and therefore cannot move up over time in response to higher levels of inflation: 5 percent coupons may have looked good in the early 1960s, but they are not very competitive today. In fact, inflation is probably the biggest worry for bond investors. Not only does it erode the purchasing power of the principal portion of a bond, but it also has a strong influence on the behavior of interest rates. And as we noted earlier, violent swings in interest rates will lead to violent swings in bond prices, all of which can cause substantial capital losses. A final disadvantage of bonds is the often inactive secondary market, which tends to limit the amount of aggressive bond trading and speculation that can take place.

# 20

# CONVERTIBLE SECURITIES: A HYBRID INVESTMENT VEHICLE

If you're looking for an investment that offers the current income of a bond along with the capital gains potential of a common stock, then you should look into convertible securities. These securities are initially issued as bonds (or preferred stock) but in time can be converted into—that is, cashed in for—shares of the issuing firm's common stock. In essence, *convertibles* are fixed income securities that possess the features and performance characteristics of both bonds and stocks. Even so, these hybrid investment vehicles are valued in the marketplace more as a stock than a bond, mainly because their ultimate worth is tied to the performance of the underlying common stock.

Indeed, most investors buy convertibles not because of the attractive yields they offer, but because of the potential price performance that stems from their connection to the stock. It is always a good idea to determine whether a company has convertibles outstanding whenever you're considering a common stock investment, for there may well be circumstances in which the convertible will be a better investment than the common stock.

# BASIC FEATURES OF CONVERTIBLES

Convertible securities are popular with individual investors because of the equity kicker they provide. That is, the market price of these issues tends to behave much like that of the common stock into which they can be converted. Convertibles are usually viewed as a form of deferred equity because they are intended to be converted eventually into shares of common stock. Not surprisingly, because of their link to common stock, whenever the stock market is strong, convertibles tend to be strong; when the market softens, so do convertibles.

Convertible securities can take the form of bonds or preferred stock. Both are linked to the equity position of the firm and are therefore usually considered interchangeable for investment purposes. Despite certain differences—convertible preferreds pay quarterly dividends while convertible bonds pay semiannual interest—both are evaluated similarly. Therefore, although our discussion will focus on convertible bonds, the information applies equally well to convertible preferreds.

Convertible bonds are usually issued as debentures (long-term, unsecured corporate debt), but carry the provision that, within a stipulated time period, the bond can be converted into a certain number of shares of the issuing company's common stock. Generally, the conversion involves little or no cash. Investors merely trade in their convertible bond for a predetermined number of shares of common stock.

An example of a convertible bond offering appears on the next page. This obligation was originally issued as a 6 percent subordinated debenture bond exchangeable into common stock at any time prior to the bond's maturity. Specifically, each $1,000 bond can be converted into 18.56 shares of Pep Boys stock at $53.88 a share ($1,000/$53.88 = 18.56 shares). Thus, *regardless of what happens to the market price of the stock,* the convertible bond investor can redeem each $1,000 bond for 18.56 shares of stock. If at the time of conversion, the stock is trading at $100 a share, investors can convert each $1,000 bond into $1,856 worth of stock (18.56 shares × $100 a share = $1,856).

*Forced conversion.* Although the bondholder has the right to convert the bond at any time, the issuing firm usually initiates conversion by calling the bonds—a practice known as *forced conversion.* Because of this feature, it is not a good idea to buy a convertible unless you would be completely comfortable owning its underlying stock. Convertibles are issued as freely callable bonds to give the corporation the flexibility to force conversion and retire the debt.

To force conversion, the corporation would simply notify the convertible bondholders that the bonds were being called for retirement. The bondholders would then have two options: to convert the bond into common stock, or to redeem the bond for cash at the stipulated call price. (Convertible call provisions contain very little call premium.) As long as the market value of the stock exceeds the call price of the convertible, you'll make the most by converting the bonds to stock. After the conversion is complete, the bonds no longer exist; instead, there is additional common stock in their place.

Source: *The Wall Street Journal;* courtesy Goldman, Sachs & Company.

*The conversion privilege.* The key element of any convertible is its *conversion privilege,* which stipulates the various conditions under which the bond can be converted. The most important piece of information you'll find in the conversion privilege is the conversion price, or conversion ratio. These terms are used interchangeably and specify the number of shares into which the bond can be converted. *Conversion ratio* specifies the number of common shares into which the bond can be converted; *conversion price* indicates the stated value per share at which the common stock will be delivered to the investor in exchange for the bond. For example, a $1,000 convertible bond might stipulate a conversion ratio of 20, meaning that the bond could be converted into 20 shares of common stock. This same privilege could also be stated in terms of a conversion price—for example, that the $1,000 bond could be used to acquire stock at a price of $50 a share. In the Pep Boys convertible offering we looked at earlier, both the conversion price ($53.88) and the conversion ratio (18.56) are used to describe the conversion feature.

Here are some additional facts you should know about the conversion ratio:

- The conversion ratio is generally fixed over the conversion period, although some convertibles are issued with variable ratios (prices). In these cases, the conversion ratio decreases—while the conversion price increases—over the life of the conversion period to reflect the supposedly higher value of the equity. Thus, it's a good idea to find out if the common stock exchange value varies over the life of the bond.

- The conversion ratio is adjusted for stock splits and significant stock dividends to maintain the conversion rights of investors. As a result, if a firm declares a 2-for-1 stock split, the conversion ratio of any of its outstanding convertible issues will also double.

- When the conversion ratio includes a fraction, such as 33⅓ shares of common, the conversion privilege will specify how any fractional shares are to be handled: usually, you can either put up the additional funds necessary to purchase another full share of stock at the conversion price, or you can receive the cash equivalent of the fractional share (at the conversion price).

- While the conversion ratio of a convertible debenture generally involves large multiples of common stock—15, 20, or 30 shares are common—the conversion ratio of a convertible preferred is generally very small, often less than 1 share of common and seldom exceeding more than 2 or 3 shares. For example, the table on the next page lists the conversion ratios for some actively traded convertible bonds and convertible preferreds. Also provided for each convertible is the amount of convertible outstanding and its S&P rating.

- The conversion privilege tells you exactly when the debenture can be converted. Generally, you'll have to wait between 6 months and 2 years after the date of issue before you have the right to convert the security. Once this waiting period is over, you can convert the issue at any time. In most cases, the conversion period lasts until the bond matures, although some companies restrict this period to a limited number of years in order to maintain greater control over their capital structure. In this case, if the issue has not been converted by the end of its conversion period, it becomes a straight debt issue with no further conversion privileges.

## SOURCES OF VALUE

Because convertibles are fixed income securities linked to the equity position of the firm, they normally derive their value from both the stock and bond dimensions of the issue. This explains why it is so important to analyze the common stock that underlies the issue, and to formulate interest rate expectations whenever you are considering a convertible as an investment outlet.

## FEATURES OF SOME ACTIVELY TRADED CONVERTIBLE SECURITIES

| Issue | S&P Rating | Amount Outstanding (Millions) | Conversion Ratio |
|---|---|---|---|
| **CONVERTIBLE BONDS** | | | |
| Armstrong Rubber 7¾ (2011) | BBB | $ 50.0 | 20.0 |
| Caterpillar Tractor 5½ (2000) | BBB+ | 126.0 | 19.8 |
| Crane 8¾ (2005) | BB+ | 75.0 | 23.2 |
| Cray Research 6⅛ (2011) | BBB | 100.0 | 11.9 |
| Great Western Fin. 8½ (2010) | BBB+ | 150.0 | 30.1 |
| Humana 8½ (2009) | A− | 200.0 | 26.4 |
| IBM 7⅞ (2004) | AAA | 1,285.0 | 6.5 |
| Kaiser Cement 9 (2005) | BB | 30.0 | 30.5 |
| Union Carbide 10 (2006) | BBB | 150.0 | 45.5 |
| Wendy's International 7¼ (2010) | BBB+ | 55.0 | 45.9 |
| **CONVERTIBLE PREFERREDS*** | | | |
| American Hoist $1.95 pfd. | C | 1.10 | 1.70 |
| Atlantic Richfield $2.80 pfd. | AA | 1.83 | 2.40 |
| Baxter Travenol Labs $3.50 pfd. | BBB− | 10.84 | 2.98 |
| ITT $5.00 pfd. | BBB | 0.99 | 1.45 |
| Ingersoll-Rand $2.35 prd. | BBB+ | 1.84 | 0.60 |
| Johnson Controls $4.25 pfd. | A | 1.50 | 0.98 |
| Paine Webber $2.25 pfd. | BB+ | 3.45 | 0.89 |
| Piedmont Aviation $3.25 pfd. | BBB+ | 2.40 | 1.00 |
| Potlatch Corp. $3.75 pfd. | BBB | 1.00 | 0.94 |
| Weyerhaeuser $2.80 pfd. | A | 3.98 | 1.21 |

*The amount outstanding for preferreds is measured in millions of shares.

*Source:* S&P's *Bond Guide* and *Stock Guide*, November 1986.

## LINK TO COMMON STOCK

Convertible securities trade much like common stock—in effect, they derive their value from the common stock—whenever the market price of the stock is equal to or greater than the stated conversion price. This means that whenever a convertible trades at or above its par value ($1,000), its price behavior closely matches that of the underlying stock: if the stock goes up (or down) in price, the convertible will too.

When convertibles behave like common stock, then the conversion ratio defines the convertible's rate of price change. For example, if a convertible carries a conversion ratio of 20, then for every point the common stock goes up (or down) in price, the price of the convertible will move in the same direction by 20 times that amount.

## LINK TO BONDS

When the price of the common stock is depressed well below the stated conversion price, the convertible loses its ties to the underlying common stock and begins to trade like a bond. When this happens, prevailing bond yields determine how the issue will trade—a fact that turns investor concern toward interest rates. When interest rates drop, convertibles go up in price; when the rates rise, the price falls.

However, because most convertibles tend to carry relatively low agency ratings (they tend to be used by the riskier, more speculative firms), convertibles are generally not highly sensitive to interest rate changes. This makes it difficult to come up with more than a rough estimate of what the prevailing yield of the convertible should be. For example, if an issue is rated Baa by Moody's and if the market rate for this quality is 9 percent, the convertible should be priced to yield around 9 percent, plus or minus a half percentage point or so.

The bond feature establishes a *price floor* for the convertible, which tends to parallel interest rates and exists independently of the depressed behavior of the common stock. Thus, no matter how low the stock price falls, the price of the convertible will not drop below the price for which it would sell if it were an ordinary bond.

There is a point at which the convertible will completely sever its ties to the underlying stock and start trading strictly as a bond. When this occurs, it doesn't make any difference how low the price of the stock falls, the convertible, behaving like any other bond, will move up or down in price in concert with the behavior of market interest rates.

Given the way convertibles are tied to both stock prices and interest rates, it is not surprising that the market of 1985–86 was so good to convertible bondholders. These investors were able to enjoy the best of both worlds: not only did stock prices jump way up, but bond interest rates dropped way down. Thus, both the stock values of convertibles and their bond price floors were going up together, providing investors with improved returns *and* reduced exposure to risk.

## EVALUATING THE INVESTMENT MERITS OF CONVERTIBLES

The worth of a convertible security is defined in large part by its conversion feature. Two critical parts of this feature, conversion value and investment value, influence the convertible's price behavior and holding period return.

### LOOK AT CONVERSION VALUE

In essence, conversion value tells you what a convertible issue would trade for if it were priced to sell on the basis of its stock value. Conversion value is easy to find:

$$\text{conversion value} = \frac{\text{conversion ratio on}}{\text{the convertible issue} } \times \frac{\text{current market price}}{\text{of the stock}}$$

For example, a convertible with a conversion ratio of 20 would have a conversion value of $1,200 if the firm's stock traded at a current market price of $60 a share (20 × $60 = $1,200).

Convertible issues, however, seldom trade precisely at their conversion value. Rather, they invariably trade at a *conversion premium*. The average premium is about 20 percent, but it can be as much as 30 percent or more. Conversion premiums exist because of the income edge convertibles have over their underlying stock. The absolute size of an issue's premium is simply the difference between the convertible's market price and its conversion value. For example, if a convertible trades at $1,400 and its conversion value is $1,200, its conversion premium is $200 ($1,400 − $1,200 = $200). In relation to the price at which the convertible should be trading, this difference amounts to a conversion premium of 16.7 percent (the dollar amount of the conversion premium divided by the issue's conversion value, or $200/$1,200).

What you, as an investor, have to do is determine whether the premium on a convertible is justified. As long as the issue has a promising price potential, investors are usually willing to pay a conversion premium because of the added current income a convertible provides relative to the underlying common stock. An investor can recover the conversion premium from the added income the convertible provides or by subsequently selling the issue at a premium equal to, or greater than, the price paid at the time of purchase.

Unfortunately, conversion premiums generally diminish as the price of the issue increases. Therefore, if a convertible is bought for its potential price appreciation, all or a major part of its price premium will disappear as the convertible appreciates and moves closer to its true conversion value. Because of this, high conversion premiums can become extremely costly. As a general rule, for convertibles selling near or above their call prices, you should think twice about paying a premium larger than half a year's interest.

## AND DON'T IGNORE INVESTMENT VALUE

Investment value is the price at which the bond would trade if it were nonconvertible and priced at or near the prevailing market yield of a comparable straight debt issue. Investment value defines the price floor of a convertible security and, as such, helps you assess the amount of risk exposure involved. For example, if nonconvertible bonds are trading at a yield of 9 percent, and if a particular 20-year convertible carries a 6 percent coupon, its investment value will be $725. This value represents the price the issue should be trading at *as a bond* and indicates how far the convertible will have to fall before it hits its price floor and begins trading as a straight debt instrument. Other things being equal, the greater the distance between the current market price of a convertible and its investment value, the farther the issue can fall in price before it hits its bond floor, and as a result, the greater the downside risk.

# AN OVERVIEW OF PRICE AND INVESTMENT BEHAVIOR

The typical price behavior of a convertible issue is shown in the following illustration. In the top panel are the three market elements of a convertible bond: the bond (investment) value, or price floor; the stock (conversion) value; and the actual market price of the convertible. The figure reveals the customary relationship among these three important elements. Note especially that the conversion premium tends to lessen as the price of the stock increases. This presentation is somewhat simplified, showing a steady price floor (which unrealistically assumes no variation in interest rates) and a steady upswing in stock value.

   The lower panel shows these conditions in a more realistic way, although for simplicity it ignores the conversion premium. The figure illustrates how the market value of a convertible approximates the price behavior of the underlying stock as long as the stock value is greater than the bond value. When the stock value drops below the bond value floor, as it does in the middle of the graph, the market value of the convertible becomes linked to the bond value of the obligation. It continues to move as a debt security until the price of the underlying stock picks up and approaches, or equals, the price floor.

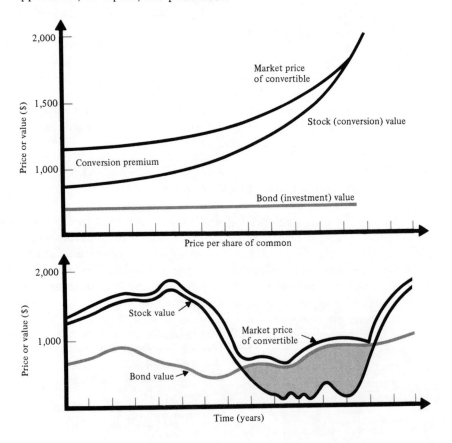

# DECIDING ON AN INVESTMENT STRATEGY

Convertible securities offer some unusual, though highly rewarding, investment opportunities. Some investors buy them because of the value of the underlying stock, while others buy them because of the attractive yields they offer as fixed income securities.

## BUYING CONVERTIBLES AS DEFERRED EQUITY INVESTMENTS

The usual reason for buying a convertible is because of its attractive equity attributes. You may be able to generate a better return by investing in a firm's convertibles than by investing directly in its common stock; also, relative to stocks, convertibles offer a chance to improve current income. Convertibles can be profitably used as alternative equity investments whenever it is felt that the underlying stock offers desired capital gains opportunities. In order to achieve maximum price appreciation under such circumstances, you would want assurance that the convertible is trading in concert with its stock value and that it does not have an inordinate amount of conversion premium. If these necessary conditions do in fact exist, your attention should logically center on the potential market behavior of the underlying stock. To assess such behavior, it is necessary to evaluate current and expected conversion value.

For example, assume a 7 percent convertible bond carries a conversion ratio of 25 and is presently trading in the market at $900. In addition, assume the stock (which pays no dividends) is currently trading at $32 and the convertible is trading at a conversion premium of $100, or 12.5 percent. Assume also that you expect the price of the stock to rise to $60 a share within the next 2 years. A conversion ratio of 25 would then yield a future *conversion value* of $1,500 (i.e., 25 × $60). If an expected conversion premium of, say, 6 to 7 percent (or about $100) is added, it follows that the market price of the convertible should rise to about $1,600 by the end of the 2-year investment period. This expected future price of the convertible, along with its annual coupon payment and current market price, could then be used in the approximate yield equation, identical to the one used with straight bonds, to determine the issue's expected realized yield. For example,

$$\text{expected realized yield} = \frac{\$70 + \dfrac{\$1,600 - \$900}{2}}{\dfrac{\$1,600 + \$900}{2}}$$

$$= \frac{\$70 + \$350}{\$1,250}$$

$$= \underline{33.6\%}$$

Although this 33.6 percent rate of return may indeed appear attractive, you should be sure of several points before committing capital to this security—in particular, that the convertible is, in fact, superior to a direct investment in the issuer's common stock (at least from a risk-return trade-off point of view), and that there is no better rate of return (with commensurate risk exposure) available from some other investment vehicle. To the extent that these conditions are met, investing in a convertible may be a suitable course of action, especially if: (1) the price of the underlying common stock is under strong upward pressure; (2) bond interest rates are falling off sharply; and (3) there is little or no conversion premium in the price of the convertible. The first attribute means conversion value should move up, leading to appreciation in the price of the convertible; the second that the bond value (price floor) should also move up and thereby reduce exposure to risk; and the third feature means you should be able to capture all or most of the price appreciation of the underlying common stock, rather than lose a chunk of it to the inevitable drop in conversion premium. Unfortunately, seldom do all three of these conditions exist at once.

## BUYING CONVERTIBLES AS HIGH-YIELD FIXED INCOME INVESTMENTS

When buying convertibles for the attractive fixed income returns they offer, the key element is the issue's bond dimension. Many convertible securities provide current yields and yields to maturity that are safe and highly competitive with straight debt obligations. You must be sure to make certain, however, that the high yields are not a function of low (speculative) ratings. Normally, you will seek discount issues, particularly those trading close to their bond price floor. Issues trading at a premium price will certainly involve a yield give-up, perhaps a substantial one. Convertibles are ideal for locking in high rates of return. They are not widely used for speculating on interest rates, because even investment-grade convertibles often lack the needed interest sensitivity (due to the equity kicker of the issue). Yet if you use convertibles to seek high, safe yields, the equity kicker can provide an added source of return if the underlying stock does indeed take off.

## THE SCORE CARD ON CONVERTIBLES

How do the advantages of convertibles stack up against the disadvantages?

*Advantages*

- The major advantage of convertibles is that they reduce the downside risk, via the issue's bond value or price floor, and at the same time provide potential for price appreciation commensurate with the firm's common stock. This two-sided feature is impossible to match with straight common stock or straight bonds.

- The current income from bond interest payments normally exceeds the dividend income you would receive if you invested in the underlying stock. For example, a $1,000 convertible with an 8 percent coupon would yield $80 a year. If the convertible carried a conversion ratio of 20 and if each share of stock paid $2.50 in dividends, an investment in 20 shares of stock would provide only $50 in dividend income a year. Thus, it is possible with convertibles to reap the advantages of common stock—in the form of potential upward price appreciation—while generating improved current income in the form of interest payments.

### Disadvantages

- Because of the conversion premium, a convertible will almost always trade at a price above its true value, although this will not happen as much when the market price of the stock moves way up and exceeds the conversion price by a wide margin. This conversion premium dilutes the price appreciation potential of a convertible, and as a result you can usually realize greater capital gains by investing directly in the common stock.
- You can almost certainly find better current and promised yields from straight debt obligations than from convertibles.

*The score.*   So if improved returns are normally available from a direct investment in either straight debt or straight equity, why buy a convertible? The answer for most investors is that convertibles provide attractive risk-return trade-offs. In particular, they offer some risk protection and at the same time considerable, although by no means maximum, upward price potential. Thus, although the return may not be the highest in absolute terms, neither is the risk.

# 21

## PREFERRED STOCK: A HYBRID OF A DIFFERENT SORT

It looks like a stock but really isn't; on the other hand, its price behaves very much like a bond's but it isn't that either. What is it? A preferred stock. In the last chapter, we looked at convertibles—bonds that behave like stocks. Now we'll look at preferreds—stocks that behave like bonds.

A preferred stock carries a stipulated dividend that is paid quarterly and is stated either in dollar terms or as a percentage of the stock's par (or stated) value. Like convertible securities, preferreds hold a senior position to common stocks. That is, preferred dividends must be paid before any payment can be made to common stockholders. Although preferreds are actually a form of equity ownership, they are considered to be a type of fixed income security because their level of current income is fixed. In effect, they—like convertibles—represent a form of hybrid security, having the characteristics of both equity and debt.

Preferreds are like common stock to the extent that they too pay dividends, which may be suspended when corporate earnings fall below a certain level. And they are issued without stated maturity dates. But they are like bonds in providing investors with a prior claim on income and assets. Most importantly, because preferreds usually trade on the basis of the yield they offer, they are viewed in the marketplace as fixed income obligations and, as a result, are considered competitive with bonds. Indeed, most investors buy or trade preferreds because of their dividends or dividend yield.

There are about 1,000 preferred stocks listed on the organized exchanges and traded over-the-counter. Most are issued by public utilities, although an increasing number are issued by industrial and financial firms. The following table shows a representative sample of some actively traded preferred stocks, with their ratings, annual dividends, market prices, and dividend yields. Note that preferreds are available in a wide range of quality ratings—from investment-grade issues to highly speculative stock—and that, as you might expect, the higher yields generally are associated with lower ratings.

## A SAMPLE OF SOME HIGH-YIELDING PREFERRED STOCK (NOV. '86)*

| S&P Rating | Issuer | Annual Dividends | Market Price | Dividend Yield |
|---|---|---|---|---|
| AA | AT&T | $ 3.64 | 49¾ | 7.3% |
| AA− | Capitol Holdings | 6.99 | 104¾ | 6.7 |
| A+ | Chase Manhattan Bank | 6.75 | 93 | 7.3 |
| BBB− | Cincinnati Gas | 4.75 | 53¼ | 8.9 |
| CCC | Control Data | 4.50 | 53½ | 8.4 |
| AA | Du Pont | 3.50 | 48½ | 7.2 |
| AA+ | GM | 3.75 | 53 | 7.1 |
| B | Gulf States Utilities | 3.85 | 27⅝ | 13.9 |
| A | Illinois Power | 3.78 | 42½ | 8.9 |
| BBB | Occidental Petroleum | 14.00 | 115½ | 12.1 |
| BB+ | Philadelphia Electric | 1.41 | 12⅝ | 11.2 |
| A− | R J Reynolds | 11.50 | 124 | 9.3 |
| A+ | Republic Bank (NY) | 2.12 | 26 | 8.2 |
| A | Utah Power & Light | 2.36 | 26½ | 8.9 |

*All of these issues are straight (nonconvertible) preferred stocks traded on the NYSE.

## BASIC FEATURES OF PREFERREDS

Various features of preferred stocks not only distinguish them from other types of securities but also help distinguish them from one another. For example, preferred stocks may be issued as convertible or nonconvertible, although the majority fall into the nonconvertible category. Convertible preferreds can be exchanged for the issuing company's common stock. Because they are, for all intents and purposes, very much like convertible bonds, we will not discuss them here. Look back at Chapter 20 for a thorough discussion of convertible securities. Here we will concentrate on nonconvertible issues.

## PREFERRED STOCKHOLDERS HAVE SPECIAL RIGHTS

When a company issues preferred stock, it guarantees certain rights and privileges to the investors, including:

- *A minimum fixed level of quarterly dividends that take priority over common stock dividends.* The only condition of these payments is that the firm generate a sufficient amount of cash flow to meet the preferred dividend requirement. Although the firm is not *legally* bound to honor this dividend obligation, it cannot suspend dividends on preferred stocks and pay them on common stock, since this would violate the preferreds' prior claim on income.

  Most preferred stocks are issued with dividend rates that remain fixed for the life of the issue. However, in the early 1980s, some preferreds began to appear with floating dividend rates, known as *adjustable (or floating) rate preferreds.* The dividends on these issues are adjusted quarterly in line with yields on specific Treasury issues. In most cases, minimum and maximum dividend rates are established as a safeguard for both the firm and the investor.

- *Voting rights.* Although preferred stockholders hold an ownership position in the firm, they normally have no voting rights. If, however, the company is doing so poorly that it is forced to suspend one or more quarterly dividends, preferred shareholders are often given the right to elect a certain number of corporate directors to represent their views.

- *A prior claim on assets in the event of liquidation.* If a company is forced to liquidate, preferred claims, limited to the par or stated value of the stock, must be satisfied before any of the claims of common stockholders are met. This does not *guarantee* that you will receive the full par value of the preferred, since the claims of senior securities, like bonds, must be met first. When a company has more than one issue of preferred stock outstanding, it sometimes issues *preference (or prior preferred) stock.* Essentially, these stocks have seniority over other preferred stock in dividends and claims on assets in the event of liquidation. Because of this preferential treatment, preference stock should be viewed as "senior preferred."

## CUMULATIVE PROVISIONS: THE FOCUS IS ON DIVIDENDS

Most preferred stocks are issued on a *cumulative basis.* This means that any preferred dividends that have been passed must be made up in full before dividends can be restored to common stockholders. Thus, as long as the dividends on preferred stocks remain *in arrears* (a term that tells you there are preferred dividend obligations that have not been met), a corporation will not be able to make dividend payments on common shares.

Assume, for example, that a firm normally pays a $1 quarterly dividend on its preferred stock but has missed 3 quarterly payments. In this case, the firm has preferred dividends in arrears of $3 a share, which it is obligated to meet. It could fulfill this obligation immediately, by paying all the arrears in the next quarterly payment, or gradually, over several quarters. It could, for instance, add $1 a share to the next quarterly dividend payment and $2 to the one following that. Only at this point could the firm resume paying common stock dividends.

Some preferred stocks carry a *noncumulative provision*, freeing the issuing company from any obligation to make up passed dividends. In this case, when a preferred stock dividend is suspended, the firm still cannot pay dividends on common stock, but it can resume paying common stock dividends by simply meeting the next quarterly preferred dividend payment. As you might expect, because of this provision, cumulative preferred stock is valued more highly than noncumulative stock—a fact that translates into a higher price, and a lower yield, for the cumulative issues.

## PARTICIPATING PREFERREDS . . . AND MORE DIVIDENDS

Occasionally, a preferred is issued on a *participating* basis, which means that the preferred stockholder can enjoy additional dividends if payments to common stockholders exceed a certain amount. This type of security not only specifies the annual dividend rate on preferred stock, but also sets the maximum dividend common stockholders can receive each year. Once the maximum is met, any additional dividends to common stockholders must be shared, according to a predetermined ratio, with preferred stockholders.

For example, assume the maximum common stock dividend is $2 a share and the participation provision calls for a 50–50 split of excess dividends. Under these conditions, if the firm wants to pay another $1 a share to common stockholders, it must also pay an equal amount ($1 a share) to participating preferred stockholders. Unless this provision is amended, the company must continue paying participating dividends to preferred stockholders as long as the amount of dividends to common shareholders exceeds the maximum of $2 a share. The tendency for common stock dividends to increase over time makes the participating provision extremely appealing and tends to increase the value of participating preferred issues. Unfortunately, if you go out into the marketplace looking for these issues, you'll probably have a hard time finding them; most preferred stocks do not carry participating provisions.

## CALL FEATURE MEANS POSSIBLE EARLY RETIREMENT

Beginning in the early 1970s, it became increasingly popular to issue preferred stocks with call features. Today a large number of preferreds carry this provision, which gives the firm the right to call the preferred for retirement. Usually, preferreds are issued on a deferred call basis, which means that they cannot be called for a certain number of years after the date of issue. After the deferral period, which often extends for 5 to 7 years, the preferreds become freely callable. These issues are then susceptible to call if the market rate for preferreds declines dramatically, which explains why the yields on freely callable preferreds should be higher than those on noncallable issues. As with bonds, the call price of a preferred is made up of the par value of the issue and a call premium that generally amounts to approximately 1 year's dividends.

## SINKING FUND PROVISIONS

Another preferred stock feature that has become popular in the last 10 years or so is the *sinking fund provision,* which specifies how an issue will be amortized, or paid off, over time. Sinking fund preferreds actually have implied maturity dates and are used by firms to reduce the cost of financing. (Sinking fund issues generally have lower yields than nonsinking fund preferreds.) For example, a typical sinking fund preferred might require the firm to retire half the issue over a 10-year period by retiring 5 percent of the issue each year. Unfortunately, you have no control over which shares are called for sinking fund purposes.

---

# ARE PREFERREDS A GOOD INVESTMENT VEHICLE?

For many years, the preferred stock market was dominated by institutional and corporate investors. While these investors are still important to the market today, things began to change dramatically in the early 1970s, when preferred stocks became increasingly popular with individual investors. The issuers of preferreds enhanced this popularity by reducing the par values on new issues to the $10 to $25 range and by pushing annual dividend levels to new heights. These moves put fixed income investment vehicles with reasonable unit prices and attractive yields well within the reach of individual investors.

## DIVIDEND YIELDS ARE THE KEY TO VALUE

With the exception of convertible preferreds, the value of high-grade preferred stocks is determined by the dividend yield they provide investors. More specifically, the value (or market price) of a preferred stock is closely related to prevailing market interest rates. Thus, as the general level of interest rates moves up, yields rise and preferred stock prices decline. When, on the other hand, interest rates drop, yields drop as well and prices rise. Like a bond, a preferred stock's price behavior is inversely related to market interest rates.

Moreover, its price is directly linked to the issue's level of income—that is, the higher the dividend payout, the higher the market price of the issue. The price of a preferred stock can be defined in this way:

$$\text{price} = \frac{\text{annual dividend income}}{\text{prevailing market yield}}$$

This equation is simply a variation of the dividend yield formula; it is used to price preferred stocks and to compute the future price of a preferred, given an estimate of expected market interest rates. For example, a $2.50 preferred stock (a stock that pays a dividend of $2.50 a year) would be priced at $20.83 if the prevailing market yield were 12 percent:

$$\text{price} = \frac{\$2.50}{.12} = \underline{\$20.83}$$

Note that higher stock prices are obtained by increasing the dividend level and/or decreasing market yield.

In addition to yield, the value of a preferred stock is a function of the issue's quality—that is, the lower the quality of a preferred, the higher its yield. This behavior is compatible with the risk-return trade-offs that usually exist in the marketplace. Fortunately, Moody's and Standard & Poor's rate the quality of preferred stocks, much as they rate the quality of bonds.

Finally, the value of preferreds is also affected by such issue characteristics as call features and sinking fund provisions. For example, because they can be called at any time, freely callable preferreds normally provide higher yields than noncallable issues. Quality and issue features, however, have only a slight effect on price behavior over time, and certainly do not compare in importance to the movement of market yields.

## WHAT ARE THE RISKS?

Since preferreds are a form of equity ownership, they are exposed to many of the same business risks as common stock while lacking many of the legal protections available with bonds. Though they don't share in profits like common stock, they are sensitive, for example, to changes in annual operating costs and to increases or decreases in corporate earnings.

Because of their nature as fixed income securities, they are also subject to interest rate risk. This risk is generally viewed as the most important risk faced by preferred stockholders, since investment-quality preferreds are fairly sensitive to interest rate changes.

## PUTTING A VALUE ON PREFERREDS

How do you evaluate the investment suitability of a preferred? The best way is to compare its return opportunities to the opportunities available from other investments. Let's look now at some of the return measures that are important in this evaluation.

## EVALUATE THE DIVIDEND YIELD

Dividend yield is the key to determining the price and return behavior of most preferred stocks. It is computed using the following formula:

$$\text{dividend yield} = \frac{\text{annual dividend income}}{\text{preferred stock price}}$$

Dividend yield is a reflection of an issue's current income and is the basis upon which comparable preferred investment opportunities are evaluated. For example, suppose a $2 preferred stock is trading at $20 a share. It would have a dividend yield of:

$$\text{dividend yield} = \frac{\$2}{\$20} = \underline{10\%}$$

The 10 percent figure represents the "promised" yield of this particular issue. In practice, you must compute, or have available, a current dividend yield measure for each preferred you are considering and then make an investment decision by assessing the differences between them.

If you're a long-term investor, promised dividend yield is a critical factor in your investment decisions. If you're a short-term trader, you will generally center your attention on anticipated price behavior and the expected return from buying and selling an issue over a short period of time; thus, the expected future price of a preferred will be important to you. Future price is found by first forecasting future market interest rates. To illustrate, suppose a preferred stock pays $3 in dividends and its yield is expected to decline to 6 percent within the next 2 years. If this market rate prevails, then 2 years from now the issue will have a market price of $50 (annual dividend ÷ yield = $3 ÷ .06 = $50). This forecast price, along with the current market price and level of annual dividends, can now be used to compute the expected realized yield from the transaction. For example, if the stock were currently priced at $28 a share, the expected realized yield of this issue (over the 2-year investment period) would be a very attractive 35.9 percent.

$$\text{expected realized yield} = \frac{\text{annual dividend} + \dfrac{\text{expected future selling price} - \text{current market price}}{\text{years in holding period}}}{\dfrac{\text{expected future selling price} + \text{current market price}}{2}}$$

$$= \frac{\$3 + \dfrac{\$50 - \$28}{2}}{\dfrac{\$50 + \$28}{2}}$$

$$= \frac{\$3 + \$11}{\$39}$$

$$= \underline{35.9\%}$$

This is the same approximate yield measure we introduced with common stocks and bonds. As with these other securities, it is used to judge the relative attractiveness of preferred stock. Other things being equal, the higher the expected realized yield figure, the more appealing the investment.

## LOOK ALSO AT BOOK VALUE

The book value (or *net asset value*) of a preferred stock is a measure of the amount of debt-free assets supporting each share of preferred stock. Book value is found by subtracting the total liabilities of the firm from its total assets and dividing the difference by the number of preferred shares outstanding. It reflects the quality of an issue with regard to the preferred's *claim on assets.* Obviously, a preferred with a book value of $150 a share enjoys generous asset support, and more than adequately secures a par value of, say, $25 a share. Book value is most relevant when it is used relative to an issue's par or stated value; other things being equal, *the quality of an issue improves as the margin by which book value exceeds par or stated value increases.*

## UNDERSTAND FIXED CHARGE COVERAGE

This measure focuses on the firm's ability to service its preferred stock and live up to the preferred's preferential claim on income. This makes it an important ingredient in determining the quality of a preferred issue. Fixed charge coverage is computed in the following way:

$$\text{fixed charge coverage} = \frac{\text{earnings before interest and taxes}}{\text{interest expense} + \dfrac{\text{preferred dividends}}{.66}}$$

The preferred dividends are adjusted by a factor of .66, which is equivalent to multiplying dividends by 1.5, to take into account a maximum corporate tax rate of 34 percent and to place preferred dividends on the same base as interest paid on bonds. (Recall that bond interest is tax-deductible while preferred dividends are not.) In general, the higher the fixed charge coverage ratio, the greater the margin of safety. A coverage ratio of 1.0, for example, means the company is generating just enough earnings to meet its preferred dividend payment, which is certainly not a very healthy situation. A ratio of 0.5, on the other hand, would suggest the potential for some real problems, while a coverage of 5.0 would indicate that the preferred dividends are fairly secure, at least for the time being.

## PAY ATTENTION TO AGENCY RATINGS

Both Standard & Poor's and Moody's rate the investment quality of preferred stocks. These agencies evaluate and assign ratings largely on the basis of their judgment regarding the relative safety of dividends. S&P uses what is in effect the same rating system it developed for bonds, while Moody's uses a slightly different system. The following figure shows Moody's system and indicates why the various ratings are assigned. Most preferreds tend to fall into the medium-grade categories (a and baa), although any agency rating is possible. Generally, higher agency ratings reduce the market yield of an issue and increase its interest sensitivity. These ratings not only eliminate much of the need for fundamental analysis, they also reveal the yield and potential price behavior of an issue.

| Rating Symbol | Definition |
| --- | --- |
| aaa | Indicates a *top quality* issue that provides good asset protection and the least risk of dividend impairment. |
| aa | A *high-grade* issue with reasonable assurance that earnings will be relatively well protected in the near future. |
| a | *Upper medium grade.* Somewhat greater risk than *aa* and *aaa*, but dividends are still considered adequately protected. |
| baa | *Lower medium grade.* Earnings protection adequate at present but may be questionable in the future. |
| ba | A *speculative* issue, its future earnings may be moderate and not well safeguarded. Uncertainty of position is common for this class. |
| b | Generally lacking in desirable investment quality, this class may have little assurance of future dividends. |
| caa-c | Likely to be already in arrears on dividend payments. These categories are reserved for securities that offer little or no likelihood of eventual payment. |

*Preferred stock ratings should not be compared with bond ratings as they are not equivalent; preferreds occupy a position junior to the bonds.

*Source:* Moody's Investors Service.

## DECIDING ON AN INVESTMENT STRATEGY

There are several investment strategies you can follow with preferred stock. As you will see, each meets a different investment objective and each offers a different level of return and exposure to risk.

### USING PREFERREDS TO OBTAIN ATTRACTIVE YIELDS

This strategy is perhaps the most popular use of preferred stocks and is ideally suited for serious long-term investors. In this case, the objective is high current income which can be achieved by seeking out preferreds that offer attractive yields. And as an added attraction, since preferreds don't have maturity dates, you can lock in the high yields for as long as you want. The use of preferreds got a big boost when Congress sharply reduced tax rates in 1986, since investors gain more from income-oriented securities, like preferred stocks, when tax rates are lower. In essence, by eliminating the preferential treatment on capital gains while cutting the tax rates on dividend income, the 1986 tax law provides an incentive for investors to buy good quality preferred stocks that pay high dividends. Certainty of income and safety are obviously important to this strategy, since yields are attractive only if dividends are paid.

Some investors buy only the highest quality preferreds. Others may sacrifice quality in return for higher yields when the economy is strong and use higher quality issues only during periods of economic distress. It is important to keep in mind that whenever you leave one of the top four agency ratings, you are buying a speculative issue that holds a great deal of risk. This risk is especially great with preferreds, since their dividends lack legal enforcement.

As a preferred-stock investor, you should recognize that no matter what the quality of the issue you choose, investing in preferreds usually involves a yield sacrifice relative to what you could obtain from comparably rated corporate bonds. For as you can see in the following figure, preferreds usually generate somewhat *lower* yields than bonds, even though they are less secure and may be subject to a bit more risk. This is because when a corporation invests in the preferred stock of another corporation, 80 percent of the preferred dividends are exempt from federal income tax. Thus, if IBM holds some AT&T preferred stock, 80 percent of the dividends received by IBM would be tax-free. It might sound peculiar, but that's the law. The net result is that these corporate investors treat preferreds almost like tax-exempt securities and, therefore, drive down their yields.

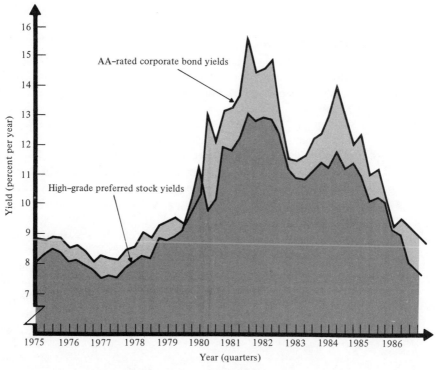

Source: Data from Standard & Poor's *Trade and Securities Statistics*, 1986.

## TRADING ON INTEREST RATE SWINGS

Rather than assuming a relatively safe buy-and-hold position, you can adopt an aggressive short-term investment posture by trading on movements in interest rates. If market interest rates are expected to decline substantially, attractive capital gains are possible. Keep in mind however, that, along with the potential for high return, this approach brings equally high risk.

Trading on interest rates with preferred stock is much like trading with bonds. The same principles apply in both cases:

- Choose only high-quality preferreds (and bonds) because of their sensitivity to interest rate changes.
- Magnify short-term holding period return by trading on margin. In this case, preferreds are more restrictive than bonds. While you can achieve extremely high leverage by margining a bond, your leverage opportunities are limited with preferreds since they are subject to the same (less generous) margin requirements as common stocks.

You'll have an easier time choosing preferreds than bonds since neither maturity nor the size of the annual preferred dividend (which is comparable to the bond's coupon) has an effect on price volatility; that is, a $2 preferred will appreciate just as much, on a percentage basis, as an $8 preferred for a given change in market yields.

## SPECULATING ON TURNAROUNDS

This strategy involves finding preferred stocks whose dividends have gone into arrears and whose rating has tumbled to one of the speculative categories. The price of the issue will be depressed to reflect the issuer's problems. The difficult part of this strategy is to uncover a speculative issue whose fortunes, for one reason or another, are about to undergo a substantial turnaround. This requires a good deal of fundamental analysis of the corporate issuer, and the ability to predict a turnaround before it is widely recognized in the market. This highly risky tactic is similar in many respects to investing in speculative common stock. In essence, you are banking that the firm will once again be able to service its preferred dividend obligations.

Unfortunately, although the rewards can be substantial, they are somewhat limited. For example, even if the turnaround candidate is expected to recover to a single-a rating, its capital gains potential is limited by the price level of other a-rated preferreds. This situation is depicted in the illustration on the next page. As you can see, while the preferred's price performance is somewhat limited, it still amounts to a holding period return of 100 percent or more. In view of the substantial risk you are taking, these returns are certainly not out of line.

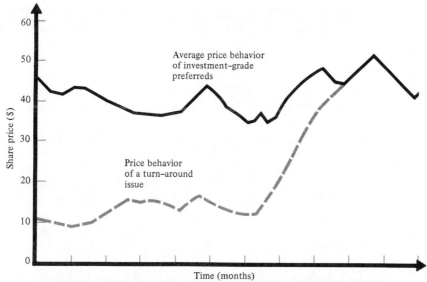

USING CONVERTIBLE AND PARTICIPATING PREFERREDS

If you follow this strategy, you use certain preferred stock features to go after speculative opportunities and the chance to earn attractive returns. By investing in convertible preferreds, for instance, you are pinning your investment hopes to the underlying common stock. If it appreciates in value, so will the market price of the convertible preferred. Because of this equity tie, it is critical to examine the fundamentals of the common stock before you invest. In essence, your goal is to find an equity situation that holds considerable promise of capital gains, and then instead of buying the common stock, buy the convertible preferred.

Participating preferreds are fairly rare, but the use of such issues can sometimes prove rewarding as long as the issuing firm is enjoying prosperity and is likely to be in a position to declare participating dividends to preferred stockholders. If you believe strongly that the likelihood of a declared participating dividend is fairly high, the purchase of that preferred may be appropriate. Of course, you would want to make sure that the market has not already discounted such a possibility; this can be done by seeing whether the issue is trading at a yield well below comparable preferreds (which would happen if the price of the preferred were forced up by the likelihood of a participating dividend). Assuming this is not the case, a participating dividend very likely would lead to an increase in the price of the stock. For example, consider a $4 preferred stock that is priced to yield 6 percent; this issue would be trading at about $67. If the firm declared a participating dividend of, say, $1 per share, the price of the stock should jump to about $83, as long as it continues to yield 6 percent. The catch, of course, is to identify a participating preferred before it begins to participate, and to have some assurance that the firm will continue to pay this level of participating dividend for the foreseeable future.

# THE SCORE CARD ON PREFERRED STOCK

*Advantages*

- Most investors buy preferred stocks for current dividend income, which in most cases is highly predictable, even though the dividends lack legal backing and can be suspended.
- Despite a few well-publicized incidents (such as the suspending of preferred dividends by Consolidated Edison in 1974), high-grade preferred stocks have an excellent record of meeting dividend payments on time.
- A low unit cost ($10 to $25 a share) also makes these issues especially attractive to small investors who cannot afford to buy any other type of fixed income security.

*Disadvantages*

- Preferred stock yield is susceptible to inflation and high interest rates. (Like many financial assets, it has not proven to be a satisfactory long-term hedge against inflation.)
- Most preferreds also lack the potential for extremely large capital gains. Although it is possible to enjoy fairly attractive capital gains from preferred stocks when interest rates decline dramatically, these amounts generally do not match the price performance of common stocks.
- According to many market observers, perhaps the biggest disadvantage of preferred stocks is the yield you sacrifice relative to bonds. In essence, there is almost nothing a preferred has to offer that you can't get from a comparably rated corporate bond and at less risk and more return than you can earn from a preferred.

# 22

## THE REWARDING WORLD
## OF MUTUAL FUNDS

———

In many ways, mutual funds take the work out of investing. When you buy shares of a mutual fund, you acquire the expertise of a team of professional money managers who buy and sell various types of securities for you. If you're happy with the results, you can simply sit back and watch your money grow. If you're not, you can pull your money out and try another fund that you believe makes better investment sense.

## THE MUTUAL FUND PHENOMENON

This indirect route to the market has drawn millions of investors in recent years. Between 1980 and 1986, the number of mutual fund shareholders more than tripled, from 12 million to nearly 45 million. And to keep up with the demand, the number of mutual funds grew over the same period from some 564 to over 1,800. Indeed, there are more mutual funds today than there are stocks listed on the New York Stock Exchange. There are so many, in fact, that by the end of 1986, mutual fund assets totaled nearly three-quarters of a trillion dollars.

Part of the reason for this phenomenal growth is the perception that mutual funds are an investment for everyone. Investors come from all walks of life and all income levels. CEOs of major corporations may own shares in the same mutual fund as workers in the company mailroom. And people with years of investment experience may be aligned with those who have never invested before.

These investors came in droves during the early 1980s because of two key factors: the introduction of individual retirement accounts (IRAs), which created a strong demand for mutual fund products; and a dramatically improved investment environment that led to record-breaking performances in both stocks and bonds. These factors came together to make mutual funds a driving force in the securities markets and a major financial institution in our economy.

## THE APPEAL OF MUTUAL FUNDS

Even if you're a seasoned investor, there are times when investment decisions are nothing short of nerve-racking. Choosing what to buy and when to buy it, and, perhaps hardest of all, timing a sale are decisions that do not come easy to most of us. Even if you have no trouble making these decisions, you may not have the time or commitment to manage your own portfolio. You may want—or need—a professional to do it for you.

When you turn your money over to a mutual fund, you place it in the hands of a professional money manager. In essence, a mutual fund is a company that combines the capital of many people with similar financial goals, and invests this money in a diversified portfolio of securities. By pooling your money with that of other investors, you can buy securities you would never be able to buy on your own. Recently, for example, one major fund held over 1½ million shares of National Semiconductor and a million shares of Pier 1, Inc. This fund also diversified its portfolio holdings among different industry groups, including electronics companies, integrated domestic energy companies, energy service companies, and many more.

Each mutual fund investor is, in essence, a part owner of a diversified portfolio. Unless you are among the super-rich, this kind of diversification is far more than you could ever hope to achieve on your own. Why is this type of diversification important? As we have stressed throughout this book, by diversifying into many different investments, you are less likely to take a serious loss if the market drops. The beauty of mutual funds is that you can achieve this diversification through a single investment decision. The table on the next page illustrates how the notion of diversification applies to the equity holdings of 60 of the country's largest mutual funds. The table also shows how money managers shift their investment focus over time as the market outlook for different industry groups changes. In 1985, for

## DIVERSIFICATION OF MUTUAL FUND PORTFOLIOS
Percent of Total Common Stock by Industry

|  | 1985 | 1986 |
|---|---|---|
| Agricultural equipment | 0.59% | 0.36% |
| Aircraft manufacturing and aerospace | 2.09 | 1.57 |
| Air transport | 1.37 | 1.70 |
| Auto and accessories (excl. tires) | 3.94 | 4.33 |
| Building materials and equipment | 1.59 | 1.82 |
| Chemicals | 4.74 | 5.14 |
| Communications (TV, radio, motion pictures, telephone) | 6.23 | 6.17 |
| Computer services | 1.18 | 0.80 |
| Conglomerates | 2.07 | 2.13 |
| Containers | 0.48 | 0.47 |
| Drugs and cosmetics | 5.13 | 6.24 |
| Electric equipment and electronics (excl. TV & radio) | 9.03 | 6.98 |
| Financial (incl. banks and insurance) | 14.08 | 17.14 |
| Foods and beverages | 2.84 | 2.86 |
| Hospital supplies and services | 1.28 | 1.35 |
| Leisure time | 2.68 | 2.64 |
| Machinery | 1.66 | 1.19 |
| Metals and mining | 3.37 | 2.82 |
| Office equipment | 6.37 | 4.68 |
| Oil | 5.34 | 4.64 |
| Paper | 2.40 | 3.36 |
| Printing and publishing | 1.44 | 1.41 |
| Public utilities (incl. natural gas) | 5.90 | 6.74 |
| Railroads and railroad equipment | 1.71 | 0.88 |
| Retail trade | 5.99 | 6.11 |
| Rubber (incl. tires) | 0.49 | 0.71 |
| Steel | 0.69 | 0.29 |
| Textiles | 0.59 | 0.65 |
| Tobacco | 1.17 | 1.41 |
| Miscellaneous | 3.56 | 3.41 |
| Total | 100.0 | 100.0 |

*Note:* Composite industry investments drawn from the portfolios of 60 of the largest investment companies as of the end of the calendar year 1986 whose total net assets represented 53.3% of total net assets of all reporting equity companies.
*Source: 1987 Mutual Fund Fact Book.*

example, these funds had roughly 14 percent of their holdings in banks and insurance companies. A year later, this percentage had risen to over 17 percent.

Although diversification is clearly the number-one reason people invest in mutual funds, other fund features draw investors as well. These include:

- *Full-time professional management* Few individual investors can compete with the talent and experience of mutual fund money managers. Not only do these experts take day-to-day investment decisions off your shoulders, they also handle the arduous recordkeeping chores.

- *Convenience* Mutual funds are relatively easy to acquire; they handle all the paperwork, and their prices are widely quoted.

- *Modest capital requirements* In most cases, you can open a mutual fund account with relatively little money. Sometimes there is no minimum investment requirement at all. And once you're a fund investor, you can usually purchase additional shares in small amounts, even fractional shares.

- *Investor services* As you will see later in this chapter, such mutual fund services as automatic reinvestment of dividends, withdrawal plans, and exchange privileges are strong draws to many investors who want to invest with the same ease as they bank. In many ways, today's mutual funds are truly a one-stop investment service.

## . . . AND THEIR DRAWBACKS

Although these factors are certainly appealing, mutual funds are by no means perfect. On the contrary, like every other investment vehicle they have some serious drawbacks. Ironically, the number-one drawback is performance. Despite the expertise of professional money managers, average fund performance over the long haul is, at best, just about equal to what you would expect from the market as a whole. There are some notable exceptions, of course, but most funds just keep up with the market.

Look at the figure on the next page, which graphs the investment performance of 18 groups of mutual funds over a 3½-year period. When compared to the S&P 500 and the Dow Jones industrial average, only *one* type of fund outperformed the market, and many fell far short of the mark. The lesson is clear: consistently beating the market is no easy task—not even for professional money managers.

Even though a handful of funds have given investors above-average, and even spectacular, rates of return, most mutual funds do not meet this level of performance. This is not to say that the long-term returns from mutual funds are substandard, or that they fail to equal what you could achieve by putting your money in a risk-free savings account. Quite the contrary: the long-term returns from mutual funds have been substantial; but most of this can be traced to strong market conditions and to the reinvestment of dividends and capital gains.

Another serious drawback is lack of liquidity. Although funds are easy to buy, they are not as easy to sell. More often than not, you'll have to sell your shares back to the fund on your own. At best, your broker will be unenthusiastic about helping since there are usually no commissions on mutual fund sales.

Substantial up-front costs may also discourage you from investing. Many funds carry sizable commission charges (known as *load charges*) as well as an annual management fee. You can expect the fund to collect this management fee regardless of whether it has made or lost money for you. In bad years as well as good, this fee is deducted right off the top.

You'll get a better feeling for the attractions and drawbacks of mutual

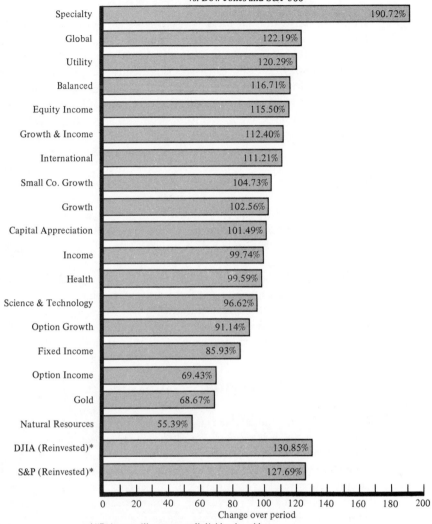

**The Performance of 18 Groups of Funds
From June 30, 1982, to Jan. 31, 1986
vs. Dow Jones and S&P 500**

| Fund Group | Change over period |
|---|---|
| Specialty | 190.72% |
| Global | 122.19% |
| Utility | 120.29% |
| Balanced | 116.71% |
| Equity Income | 115.50% |
| Growth & Income | 112.40% |
| International | 111.21% |
| Small Co. Growth | 104.73% |
| Growth | 102.56% |
| Capital Appreciation | 101.49% |
| Income | 99.74% |
| Health | 99.59% |
| Science & Technology | 96.62% |
| Option Growth | 91.14% |
| Fixed Income | 85.93% |
| Option Income | 69.43% |
| Gold | 68.67% |
| Natural Resources | 55.39% |
| DJIA (Reinvested)* | 130.85% |
| S&P (Reinvested)* | 127.69% |

Change over period

*"Reinvested": assumes all dividends paid are
reinvested in additional shares of stock.

funds as you look more closely at fund characteristics. As you will see, there are major differences in organization, investor fees, and methods of buying and selling funds.

## SOME ESSENTIALS ABOUT MUTUAL FUNDS

Before you invest, take the time to understand these basic facts about mutual funds.

## OPEN-END FUNDS

When the term mutual fund is used, it usually refers to an open-end investment company. In this type of operation, investors actually buy their shares from, and sell them back to, the mutual fund itself. When you buy shares in an open-end fund, the fund issues new shares of stock and fills the purchase order with these new shares. The fund is considered open-ended because there is no limit on the number of shares the fund can issue. All open-end mutual funds stand behind their shares and buy them back when investors decide to sell. Thus, there is never any trading between individuals.

Both buy and sell transactions are carried out at prices based on the current value of all the securities held in the fund's portfolio. This is known as the fund's *net asset value (NAV)*. It is calculated at least once a day and represents the value of a share of stock in a particular mutual fund. NAV is found by taking the total market value of all securities held by the fund, less any liabilities, and dividing this amount by the number of fund shares outstanding. For example, if on a given day the market value of all the securities held by the XYZ mutual fund equals some $10 million, and if XYZ on that particular day has 500,000 shares outstanding, the fund's net asset value per share would amount to $20 ($10,000,000/500,000 = $20). This figure is then used to determine the price at which the fund shares are bought and sold.

Mutual funds are the dominant type of investment company and account for well over 95 percent of the assets under management. Many of these funds have investment portfolios that amount to a billion dollars or more.

## CLOSED-END INVESTMENT COMPANIES

While the term *mutual fund* is supposed to refer only to open-end funds, as a practical matter, it is regularly used to refer to closed-end investment companies as well. Closed-end investment companies operate with a fixed number of shares outstanding and do *not* regularly issue new shares of stock. In effect, they have a capital structure like that of an ordinary corporation, except that the corporation's business happens to be investing in marketable securities. There are around 100 publicly traded closed-end funds, whose shares, at the end of 1986, had a combined market value of more than $16 billion. Closed-end company shares are actively traded in the secondary market, just like any other common stock. Most are traded on the New York Stock Exchange, several are on the American Exchange, and a few are traded in the OTC market.

The share prices of closed-end companies are determined not only by their net asset value but by general supply and demand conditions in the stock market. As a result, closed-end companies generally trade at a discount or premium to NAV. For example, if a fund has a net asset value of $10 per share and is trading at $9, it is selling at a discount of $1; it would be selling at a premium of $1 if it were quoted at a price of $11. Share price discounts and premiums can at times become quite large—for example, it's not unusual for such spreads to amount to as much as 25 to 30 percent of net asset value.

## BUYING AND SELLING FUND SHARES

Buying and selling shares of closed-end investment companies is no different from buying a share of common stock. The transactions are executed on listed exchanges or in the OTC market through brokers or dealers who handle the orders in the normal way. They are subject to usual transaction costs, and because they are treated like any other listed or OTC stock, the shares of closed-end funds can even be margined or sold short.

The situation is considerably different, however, with open-end funds. There are several ways of acquiring these shares, depending on whether the fund is load or no-load.

You can buy a *load* fund from a broker or through salespeople employed by the mutual fund. Most brokerage firms are authorized to sell shares in a variety of load funds, and this is the easiest and most convenient way of buying funds if you have an established brokerage account. When the fund is not sold through broker-age houses, you must deal directly with the fund's commissioned salespeople—individuals who are employed by the mutual fund for the sole purpose of selling its shares. If you want to buy shares in a *no-load* fund, you are strictly on your own. You must write or call the mutual fund directly to obtain information. You will then receive an order form from the fund and instructions on how to buy shares; no salesperson will ever call on you. To complete the transaction, you simply mail your check, along with the completed order form, to the mutual fund or its designated agent. Appendix B provides the names, addresses, telephone numbers, and pur-chase requirements for many major load and no-load funds.

Selling shares in a fund is also a do-it-yourself affair, whether the fund is load or no-load. Because commissions are not usually levied on fund sales, brokers and salespeople have little motivation to execute a sell order. Normally, to redeem shares you must directly notify the mutual fund by mail of your intention to sell. The fund then buys the shares back and mails you a check. If you're with a fund that offers conversion privileges (explained later), you can get out of a fund by simply phoning an order to switch your money to another fund. With funds that offer check-writing privileges, it is possible to redeem shares simply by writing a check on the fund large enough to clean out the balance of the account. It is as simple as writing a check on a checking account and is obviously much easier and quicker than having to notify the fund directly.

## INVESTMENT TRUSTS

An investment trust (or *unit investment trust,* as it is also known) represents little more than an interest in an unmanaged pool of investments. In essence, a portfolio of securities is simply held in safekeeping for investors under conditions set down in a trust agreement. The portfolios usually consist of corporate, government, or municipal bonds, with tax-free municipal bonds and mortgage-backed securities being the most popular investment vehicles. There is *no trading* in the portfolios; as a result, the returns, or yields, are fixed and usually predictable. A trust manager simply puts together a stated portfolio. After the securities are deposited with a trustee, no new securities are added and, with rare exceptions, none are sold unless they mature or are called by the issuer.

Various sponsoring brokerage houses put these diversified pools of securities together and then sell units of the pool to investors (each *unit* is like a share in a mutual fund). For example, a brokerage house might put together a diversified pool of corporate bonds that amount to, say, $10 million. The sponsoring firm would then sell units in this pool to the investing public at a price of $1,000 per unit (a common price for these issues). The sponsoring organization does little more than routine recordkeeping, servicing the investments by clipping coupons and distributing the income (often on a monthly basis) to the holders of the trust units.

Unit trusts are attractive to investors who want a diversified portfolio of generally high-yielding securities and monthly (rather than semiannual) income. These trusts eventually expire when the securities in the portfolio mature. If you decide to sell your trust units before this expiration date, the sponsor will usually buy them back at a price equal (or close) to the prevailing net asset value, less a sales commission.

*REITs—A special type of investment trust.* In the world of investments, *REIT* stands for *real estate investment trust.* Basically, a REIT is a type of closed-end investment company that invests in mortgages and various types of real estate. A REIT is like a mutual fund in that it sells shares of stock to the investing public and uses the proceeds, along with borrowed funds, to invest in a portfolio of real estate investments. In essence, it's a way to participate in the real estate market, since, as an investor, you own part of the real estate portfolio held by the real estate investment trust.

There are three basic types of REITs: those that invest in properties, such as shopping centers, hotels, apartments, and office buildings (the so-called *property,* or *equity,* REITs); *mortgage* REITs—those that invest in mortgages; and *hybrid* REITs, which invest in both properties and mortgages. REITs must abide by the Real Estate Investment Trust Act of 1960, which established requirements for forming a REIT, as well as rules and procedures for making investments and distributing income. Since they are required to pay out nearly all of their earnings to their shareholders, REITs do quite a bit of borrowing to obtain funds for investment. As with mutual funds, REITs themselves do not pay tax on the income they earn; rather, the income is passed to shareholders and then it is taxed as ordinary investment income.

Although the poor performance of REITs during the 1973–75 recession caused them to fall into disfavor among investors, subsequent restructuring of their portfolios has rekindled interest in them. Indeed, REITs have staged a real comeback in the past several years, due in no small part to the attractive rates of return they are providing investors. For example, in 1986, annual rates of return of 10 to 20 percent were not uncommon, and some trusts yielded 30 percent or more. REITs also got a big boost from the Tax Reform Act of 1986, which greatly reduced the appeal of other types of real estate investment vehicles, such as limited partnerships. Nevertheless, while REITs may yield appealing returns, they can also be fairly risky.

A number of insurance companies, mortgage bankers, commercial banks, and real estate investment companies have formed REITs, many of which are traded on major securities exchanges. In 1987, there were over 150 such investment companies. Some of the better known and more actively traded REITs include Pennsylvania REIT, First Union Realty, Federal Realty, Health Care Properties, Lomas and Nettleton Mortgage Investors, ICM Property, and Mortgage Growth Investors. Your stockbroker should be able to give you advice about REITs and help you select those that will be consistent with your investment objectives.

## LOAD AND NO-LOAD FUNDS

The question of whether a fund is load or no-load will only concern you if you invest in an open-end fund. The *load* charge is the commission you must pay when buying shares in an open-end fund. Since closed-end funds are bought and sold on the listed exchanges and in the OTC market, they are subject to the same commission costs as any other common stock.

A *load fund* charges a commission when shares are bought; a *no-load fund* levies no sales charges. Load charges can be fairly substantial, often ranging from 7 to 8.5 percent of the purchase price of the shares. Most funds, however, offer quantity discounts, which usually start with single investments of 1,000 shares or more. Rather than levy the maximum load charge of 8½ percent of the purchase price, a growing number of funds are opting to charge commissions of only 1 to 3 percent. These are the so-called *low-load funds.*

In 1987, perhaps two-thirds of all mutual funds were of the no-load type. The reason for this is twofold: (1) a large number of money market funds exist, just about all of which are no-loads, and (2) instead of paying load charges, most investors would rather have every dollar working for them to achieve the highest possible rate of return. Any money spent on sales commissions is money diverted from this goal. Justifying a sales commission becomes even more difficult when you realize that the performance of load funds is really no better than the performance of no-load funds.

Unfortunately, true no-load funds may become extinct in the very near future as more and more no-loads are becoming *12(b)-1 funds.* These funds do not directly charge commissions at the time of purchase (so they can technically call themselves no-loads) but assess what are known as 12(b)-1 charges. Under this plan, which was first created by the SEC in 1980, the mutual fund can deduct as much as 1¼ percent of the average net assets it manages each year to cover such costs as commissions, advertising, and general marketing expenses. And the law permits the fund to charge these fees whether or not it actually spends any money.

Occasionally, a no-load fund will have a small *back-end load,* which amounts to a 1 to 2 percent commission on the sale of shares. Some funds have even gone so far as to charge *contingent deferred sales loads,* which are sales charges of between 4 and 5 percent levied on investors who decide to sell their fund shares within 2 to 3 years of the purchase date. Fortunately, only a handful of funds have adopted these charges, which are, in effect, a poorly disguised fee structure. Not surprisingly, these organizations are *not* among the top performing funds.

## OTHER FEES AND COSTS

Regardless of whether a fund is load or no-load, or whether it is open-end or closed, you'll have to pay a *management fee* to the professional managers who administer the fund's portfolio. Fees generally equal .50 to 1.75 percent of the average dollar amount of assets under management. These expense ratios bear watching, since high expenses take their toll on fund performance and on the net asset value of your shares.

Unlike load charges, which are one-time costs, management fees (and 12(b)-1 charges, if assessed) are levied *annually* and are paid *regardless of the performance of the portfolio.* In addition, there are the administrative costs of operating the fund; these are fairly modest and represent the normal cost of doing business (commissions paid when the fund buys and sells securities are part of these costs).

A final cost is the taxes paid on security transactions. In order to avoid double taxation, nearly all mutual funds operate as *regulated investment companies.* This means that all (or nearly all) of the dividend and interest income is passed on to the investor, as are any capital gains realized when securities are sold. The mutual fund thus pays no taxes, but instead passes the tax liability on to its shareholders. This holds true regardless of whether such distributions are reinvested in the company (in the form of additional mutual fund shares) or paid out in cash. Mutual funds annually provide each stockholder with a convenient summary report on the amount of dividends and capital gains received, and the amount of taxable income earned (and to be reported) by the fund shareholder.

## A FUND FOR EVERY PURPOSE

In recent years, the mutual fund industry has made huge profits by developing mutual funds for nearly every investment purpose imaginable. Fund objectives are supposed to be clearly stated in the fund *prospectus,* which you should request—and read—before investing any money. The prospectus also describes the operation of the fund and all its fees. A note of caution is in order, however, since the prospectuses provided by many mutual funds today are not as detailed as they once were. In fact, since many are little more than warmed-over sales pitches, you have to read between the lines to be sure you're getting exactly what you expect. If you want more detailed or factual information, you'll have to look to an awkwardly named document known as a *Statement of Additional Information.* But funds do *not* have to send them out, so you probably will have to ask for one.

We'll take a close look at the major types of mutual funds here to give you an idea of the range of investment possibilities open to you. These include growth funds, performance funds, income funds, growth and income funds, bond funds, money funds, and some speciality funds, including sector funds and international funds.

## GROWTH FUNDS

The objective of a growth fund is simple: capital appreciation. Long-term growth and capital gains are the primary goals of these funds. As a result, they invest principally in common stocks that have above-average growth potential but offer little (if anything) in the form of dividends and current income. Because of the uncertain nature of their investment income, growth funds involve a fair amount of risk. They are usually viewed as long-term investment vehicles most suitable for the more aggressive investor who wants to build capital and has little interest in current income. Some of the growth funds that have been "popular" (another word for performance leaders) in recent years include Twentieth Century Growth, Evergreen Fund, Strong Opportunity, Fidelity Magellan, Oppenheimer Fund, and NEL Growth Fund.

## PERFORMANCE FUNDS

These are the so-called go-go funds that were popular during the 1960s and are once again favored by aggressive investors. Also known as *maximum capital gains* or *aggressive growth* funds, they are highly speculative funds that seek large profits from capital gains; in many respects, they are an extension of the growth fund concept. Most are fairly small, and their portfolios consist mainly of high-flying common stocks. Performance funds often buy stocks of small, unseasoned companies; stocks with relatively high price/earnings multiples; and common stocks whose prices are highly volatile. Many of these funds use leverage in their portfolios (that is, they buy stocks on margin); they also use options very aggressively, various hedging techniques, and short selling. All this is designed, of course, to yield big returns. But performance funds are also highly speculative and are among the most volatile of all the types of funds. When the markets are good, performance funds do well; when the markets are bad, these funds often experience substantial losses.

Some performance funds that have been top performers in recent years include Constellation Growth, Fidelity Special Situations, Weingarten Equity, the Quest for Value fund, Hartwell Growth, and the ABT Emerging Growth fund.

## INCOME FUNDS

The primary investment objective of an income fund is current income in the form of interest and dividends. Securities are not chosen for their capital gains potential and if any are earned it is strictly coincidental (though, at times, the capital gains on income funds can be substantial). The portfolios of these funds are heavily invested in various combinations of high-yielding common stocks, different types of bonds, and attractive preferred stocks. These investment vehicles are bought for the income they generate and for their safety. To insure that a fund's investment principal remains intact, money managers usually choose bonds and preferred stocks with investment-grade ratings.

If you want high current income, which you can receive monthly or quarterly, or are simply attracted to a high rate of return, an income fund may be an appealing choice. Because of their investment objectives, they are usually considered fairly conservative investments with only a small amount of risk, though some so-called high-yield or high-income funds involve much more risk, since they're big buyers of junk bonds (which they use to drive up their yield). Some income funds popular among investors include Dreyfus Special Income Fund, Vanguard Qualified Dividend-I, Kemper High Yield, Fidelity High Income, and the Liberty Fund.

## GROWTH AND INCOME FUNDS

The objective of growth and income funds is both long-term growth and income. To accomplish this, money managers invest in both high-grade growth stocks for capital gains and conservative fixed income securities, like bonds and preferred stock, for current income. Between 25 and 40 percent of a fund's portfolio is usually invested in fixed income securities and the remaining amount in stocks.

This combination usually involves only a small amount of risk—a fact that makes it attractive to fairly conservative investors who want a reasonably good, but safe, return. Not surprisingly, because growth and income funds are a hybrid, combining objectives of both growth and income funds, they achieve neither the level of capital gains nor the current income of single-purpose funds. Growth and income funds are similar in many ways to *balanced funds,* which attempt to maintain a balanced portfolio of stocks, bonds, and preferreds to generate an attractive level of income and capital gains. Popular growth and income funds include Fidelity Growth and Income, Century Shares Trust, Eaton Vance Total Return, United Continental Income, Strong Total Return, and Sigma Investment Shares.

## BOND FUNDS

As the name implies, these funds invest exclusively in various kinds and grades of bonds—from Treasury and agency bonds to corporates and municipals. Income is the primary investment objective, although capital gains are not ignored. Two important advantages to buying shares in bond funds rather than investing directly in bonds are that bond funds are generally more liquid, and they offer diversification. Although bond funds are usually considered a fairly conservative investment, they are not risk-free. Since the prices of the bonds held in fund portfolios fluctuate with changing interest rates, you can lose money on your investment if interest rates undergo a sharp increase.

PLAYING IT SAFE—STOCKS, BONDS, AND MUTUAL FUNDS

For many years, bond funds held little appeal to investors. This changed in the mid-1970s when fund managers began adopting a more aggressive investment stance. Today, although most funds are still basically conservative, a growing number are extremely aggressive, investing in junk bonds and other highly speculative vehicles. Changes in the federal tax law also contributed to the growth of bond funds. Since April 1976, investors have been able to purchase municipal bond funds that offer tax-free income. (Of course, only interest, not capital gains, is tax-exempt.) These funds have been especially attractive to high-income investors who need to shelter large chunks of income from taxation.

Recently, a growing number of bond funds have been organized to invest in government-backed mortgage securities such as GNMA pass-through securities and collateralized mortgage obligations (CMOs). These funds have been extremely attractive, not only because of their high rates of return and built-in diversification, but also because they offer an affordable means of entering the mortgage-backed securities market. They also offer reinvestment of principal each month—an option that helps preserve your capital. Some popular bond funds include the Vanguard Fixed Income-High Yield Fund, National Securities Bond Fund, Bull & Bear High Yield, Value Line U.S. Government Securities, Venture Income Plus, and the Paine Webber GNMA Fund.

## MONEY MARKET FUNDS

Since the first money market fund was set up in November 1972 (with only $100,000 in total assets), the growth in these funds has been nothing short of phenomenal. Today, about 35 percent of all mutual fund assets are held in money market accounts. The reason for this success is easy to understand: they offer investors of modest means access to the high-yielding money market, where many instruments require minimum investments of $100,000 or more. Although the growth in mutual fund assets leveled off a bit after the introduction of bank money market deposit accounts in 1982, these funds still remain a major force in the mutual fund industry and show no sign of fading away. Indeed, by late 1987, money fund assets amounted to some $250 billion.

Actually, there are several different kinds of money market mutual funds:

- *General purpose money funds* invest in any and all types of money market investment vehicles—from Treasury bills to corporate commercial paper and bank certificates of deposit. They invest their money wherever they can find attractive short-term returns. The vast majority of money funds are of this type.
- *Tax-exempt money funds* limit their investments to tax-exempt municipal securities with very short (30- to 90-day) maturities. Since their income is free from federal taxation, they appeal predominantly to investors in high tax brackets.
- *Government securities money funds* were established as a way to meet investor concerns about safety. These funds effectively eliminate any risk of default by confining their investment to Treasury bills and other short-term securities of the U.S. government or its agencies (like the Federal National Mortgage Association).

Money market funds require minimum investments of $1,000 to $10,000. Because of the nature of the investments, these funds are highly liquid and virtually immune to capital loss. However, the return they offer is by no means guaranteed. You should expect a high rate of return when interest rates are high and a modest one when they are low. Many investors consider money funds to be viable alternatives to savings accounts. They are seen as a convenient, safe, and profitable way to accumulate capital and temporarily store idle cash. Checkwriting privileges give these accounts added convenience; you have immediate access to your money whenever you want it. Popular general purpose money funds include the Sears Liquid Assets Fund and the CMA Money Fund. Tax-exempt funds include the Calvert Tax-Free Reserve Fund and the Municipal Cash Reserve Management Fund. Government securities funds include the Dreyfus Money Market Investments-Governments Fund and the Shearson Government & Agencies Fund. All money funds are no-load.

## SPECIALTY FUNDS

Specialty funds thrive on the unorthodox by seeking attractive—sometimes spectacular—rates of return from unusual investment vehicles. Here are just a few of their investment approaches:

- *Tax-management funds* try to minimize taxes by committing funds to tax-preferenced investments.
- *Index funds* simply strive to match the return from the stock market as a whole, as measured by the S&P 500 stock index or some other stock market index.
- *Yield-enhanced (or hedge) funds* hedge their portfolios with futures and options.
- *Socially conscious funds* invest only in those companies that meet the moral and ethical standards they set.
- *Sector funds* invest only within a single industry or sector of the economy.
- *International funds* focus primarily on foreign securities.

Before investing in any of these funds, remember to weigh the potential for gain against what is at times an equal potential for loss. Investing in these funds can become especially risky if you lack the knowledge to understand fund operations or simply cannot spend the time to carefully monitor fund progress.

Although specialty funds make up about 15 to 20 percent of the total number of mutual funds, their assets are relatively small. The GIT Special Growth Fund, the Lexington Gold Fund, and the Eaton Vance Tax Managed Fund are among the popular no-load specialty funds. Popular load funds include the John Hancock Special Equity Fund and the United New Concepts Fund.

Sector and international funds—two of the most popular kinds of specialty funds—deserve a closer look.

*Sector funds.* Imagine a mutual fund that just buys companies located along the Washington, D.C. Beltway; another that specializes in small regional bank stocks;

and a third that puts all its money in companies likely to be gobbled up in corporate takeovers. Too specialized, you think. Not for Wall Street. These mutual funds—called sector funds—are among the newest and hottest funds around.

As the name tells you, sector funds zero in on a narrow part, or sector, of the market. Money managers carefully target their investment holdings in one or more related industries and look for capital gains. For example, if you buy stock in a health care sector fund, you'll wind up with holdings in drug companies, hospital management firms, medical suppliers, and biotech concerns. Not just any companies in these industries, though: only those seen as good candidates for rapid growth. Glamor industries such as computers, telecommunications, leisure and entertainment, and financial services are popular sector fund choices.

Like any growth fund, sector funds are risky. Some money managers even think they're bad business. In their view, sector funds violate the basic principle of mutual funds: diversify, and *never* put all your eggs in one basket, even if the basket looks like solid gold, because appearances can deceive. Supporters don't deny the risk, but they don't scoff at the potential for enormous profit either. If you're smart (or lucky) enough to put your money into a winning fund—a fund that can sniff out a market trend before anyone else—you can do incredibly well. Some lucky investors parlayed a mere $1,000 into more than $28,000 between 1981 and 1986. On the flip side, those who chose the worst fund during this period saw their $1,000 investment shrink to a paltry $124.

In 1986, Fidelity had 36 sector funds (including Fidelity Select Health Care Fund and Fidelity Select Financial Services Fund); Financial Programs had nine; and Vanguard had five (the Vanguard Special Portfolio-Service Economy Fund was one). With total assets of $1.6 billion, sector funds are a small but significant part of the equity mutual fund business. And they show no sign of losing their popularity.

*International funds.*    Another top-performing fund category in the mid-1980s was the international fund—a type of mutual fund that does all, or most, of its investing in foreign securities. These funds are designed for people who would like to invest in foreign securities but don't have the experience or knowledge to do so.

The objective of these funds is substantial capital gains. Fund managers attempt to capitalize on changing global market conditions and to position themselves to benefit from evaluation of the dollar. By their very nature, these strategies are extremely risky and should be approached with a great deal of caution. At the very least, you'll need a working knowledge of such international economic issues as balance of trade and currency devaluation in order to monitor fund progress.

International funds fall into two basic categories: *global funds,* which invest mostly in foreign securities but also in some U.S. companies and U.S.-based multinational firms; and *overseas funds,* which invest exclusively outside the United States, sometimes confining their investments to specific geographic regions like Japan or Australia. Some popular international funds: the Transatlantic Fund, Merrill Lynch Pacific, Prudential-Bache Global, Fidelity Overseas, and Paine Webber Atlas.

# INVESTOR SERVICES

Many people are drawn to funds because of their attractive returns; but there are other reasons to invest as well, including the savings and reinvestment plans they offer, their regular income programs, conversion and checkwriting privileges, and retirement programs. These are all examples of mutual fund services, which many investors consider valuable. In fact, some investors buy funds primarily to receive one or more of these services.

## SAVINGS PLANS

In a savings plan, you agree, either formally or informally, to add a certain amount of money to your account on a regular (monthly or quarterly) basis. For example, you might agree to add $250 every quarter. The money is then used to buy additional shares in the fund. *Voluntary savings plans* are excellent devices for regularly adding to an investment program. In contrast, *contractual savings plans* that involve substantial front-end loads should be avoided. If you get hooked into one of these plans, you'll find yourself paying for the plan's commissions before you start getting full credit for your investments.

For example, if you agree to invest $1,000 a year for each of the next 15 years, the total size of this contractual accumulation plan would be $15,000. If the fund charges an 8.5 percent sales commission (not surprisingly, most funds that offer front-end contractual plans charge the maximum commission), the total commission over the life of this contract would be $1,275 (that is, .085 $\times$ $15,000). This commission is deducted from the first several payments, whether you stick with the plan for 15 years or not. These arrangements can be extremely costly since if you drop out you sacrifice some or all of the prepaid commissions. In addition, you'll find that the number of shares you actually own is considerably *less* than what you could have bought through regular purchases. While the SEC requires a full refund of prepaid commissions if you cancel the plan within 45 days, it requires a refund of only 85 percent of prepaid loads if you cancel within 18 months of enrollment, and no refund at all if you cancel after that. These contractual arrangements have been under considerable fire for some time, and are prohibited in some states, including California, Illinois, Ohio, and Wisconsin.

## AUTOMATIC REINVESTMENT PLANS

Through this service, dividend and/or capital gains income is used to buy additional shares in the fund. Rather than taking this money in the form of cash, you can reinvest the proceeds in additional shares of the fund. Keep in mind, however, that even though you reinvest your dividends and capital gains, the IRS treats them as cash receipts and taxes them in the year in which they are paid. Most funds deal in fractional shares, and these purchases are often commission-free.

Automatic reinvestment plans enable you to keep all your capital working for you, earning fully compounded rates of return. By plowing back the profits you receive in the form of dividends and capital gains distributions, you can generate substantially more earnings than would be possible without this reinvestment option. The following graph shows the long-term impact of one such plan, using actual performance figures for the Twentieth Century Growth Investors Fund. In the illustration, we assume the investor starts with $10,000 and, except for the reinvestment of dividends and capital gains, adds no new capital over time. Even so, note that the initial investment of $10,000 grew to more than $380,000 over a 27-year period (which, by the way, amounts to a compounded rate of return of 14.4 percent). Of course, not all periods will match this performance, nor will all mutual funds be able to perform as well, even in strong markets. But the point is that as long as care is taken in selecting an appropriate fund, attractive benefits can be derived from the systematic accumulation of capital offered by savings and automatic reinvestment plans. Clearly, you should consider very seriously the idea of incorporating one or both of these plans into your mutual fund investment program.

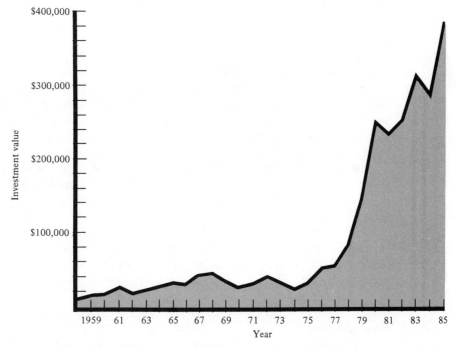

Source: Twentieth Century Investors.

## WITHDRAWAL PLANS

Many funds offer you the opportunity to receive payments at regular intervals through withdrawal plans. If you enroll in a withdrawal plan, you'll automatically receive a predetermined amount of money every month or quarter. In most cases, you'll have to keep a minimum balance of $5,000 or more in order to participate in the plan. The size of the minimum payment is normally $50 or more per period, but there is no limit on the maximum amount you can withdraw. These monthly or quarterly withdrawals usually come from dividends or capital gains, although they can also be taken from principal if there's not enough money in your account from these two sources to cover them.

There are several popular types of systematic withdrawal plans. The most common plan allows you to specify the fixed dollar amount you want to withdraw each period. For example, you might choose to receive $200 a month, every month, regardless of the source of payment. Another popular arrangement specifies a fixed number of shares to be liquidated each period; this method results in an uneven level of income, since the price of the fund's shares will vary in the marketplace. Still another arrangement is to pay out a fixed percentage of the net asset growth; as long as the stated percentage value is less than 100 percent, this plan can produce a periodic, although uncertain, payout of income, and still allow for some reinvestment and growth in the account as long as the fund is profitable.

## CONVERSION PRIVILEGES

At times, you may find it necessary or desirable to switch out of one fund and into another. The switch may come after you reevaluate your investment objectives, after you decide to take a more aggressive role in the management of your account, or after you analyze the changing investment climate and realize that one type of fund is more advantageous than another. Conversion (or exchange) privileges were devised to make this type of exchange possible.

Investment companies that offer a number of different mutual funds usually allow you to move money from one fund to another through a single phone call. Most companies charge very little or nothing at all for these shifts, although funds that offer free exchange privileges often place a limit on the number of times you can switch each year. Of course, you must confine your switches to the same family of funds. For example, you can switch from a Dreyfus growth fund to a Dreyfus money or income fund or to any other fund managed by Dreyfus. The alternatives open to you in some fund families may seem almost limitless. Fidelity, for example, one of the largest investment companies, offers over 70 different funds ranging from the most conservative to the most speculative.

Despite the many advantages in switching, there is one major drawback that may discourage you from changing the status quo. For tax purposes, the exchange of shares from one fund to another is regarded as a sale transaction, followed by a subsequent purchase of a new security. As a result, if any capital gains exist at the time of the exchange, you are liable for the taxes on that profit even though the holdings were not truly liquidated.

## CHECKWRITING PRIVILEGES

This service is now available from virtually every money fund and a handful of other funds. Exactly as the name implies, you are given a supply of checks that you can use to draw against the money you have invested in the mutual fund. These checks are like any other except that they usually have to be written in minimum amounts, often $500 or more. A major benefit of this privilege is that the checks, once written, continue to draw income until they actually clear. For example, if you write a $1,000 check against the funds in your money market account and the check takes a week to clear, you receive the full daily interest on that $1,000 for each of the 7 days the check is in "float."

## RETIREMENT PROGRAMS

As a result of government legislation, self-employed individuals are permitted to divert a portion of their pretax income into self-directed retirement plans. Moreover, wage earners can put up to $2,000 a year into Individual Retirement Accounts (IRAs). Even after the Tax Reform Act of 1986, every employed person can still invest in an IRA, although only certain individuals can deduct the capital contributions from their income tax. (All earnings from IRA investments, however, are *tax-deferred.*)

Today, nearly all mutual funds provide a special service that enables individuals to quickly and easily set up tax-deferred retirement programs as either IRA or Keogh accounts. The funds set up the plans and handle all the administrative details in such a way that the shareholder can take full advantage of available tax savings. There is usually a small fee for this service (of perhaps $25 to $50 a year).

# 23

## INVESTING IN MUTUAL FUNDS

Suppose you are confronted with the following situation: You have money to invest and are trying to select the right stock in which to put it. You want to pick an issue with acceptable risk, but also one that will generate an attractive rate of return. The problem is, you have to make the selection from a list of over 1,800 securities and you don't know where to begin.

Sound like a mission impossible? Well, this is exactly what you're up against in trying to select a mutual fund. With a range of choices that's nothing short of enormous, the task ahead of you is not easy. But if you approach the selection process in a systematic way and patiently whittle down the alternatives, you're likely to make an investment choice that promises the kind of return you're after.

# WHY INVEST?

The answer to this question is the same as it is for any investment. Regardless of the kind of income a mutual fund provides, investors tend to use mutual funds for one of three reasons: (1) to build investment capital, (2) to speculate by using aggressive funds and short-term trading, and (3) to store money for the long and short term.

## TO BUILD CAPITAL

This is probably the most common reason for investing in mutual funds. Basically, it involves using mutual funds over the long haul as a way to accumulate investment capital toward some personal financial goal—to educate your children, to build a vacation home, for retirement, or whatever.

Depending upon your personality, a modest amount of risk may be acceptable, but usually preservation of capital and capital stability are considered important. Moreover, the source of return is far less important than the amount; investors are therefore just as likely to use income or balanced funds for capital accumulation purposes as they are to use growth funds. The whole idea is to form a "partnership" with the mutual fund in building up as big a capital pool as possible: you provide the capital by systematically investing and reinvesting in the fund, and the fund provides the return by doing its best to invest the resources wisely.

## TO SPECULATE

This is not a very common use of mutual funds, because most mutual funds are long term in nature and simply not suitable as aggressive trading vehicles. But some funds do cater to speculators, and some investors find that mutual funds are indeed attractive outlets for speculation and short-term trading. One way to do this is to trade in and out of funds as the general investment climate changes. For example, you might use a performance fund when the market is strong, and switch to a money fund when it begins to soften. Or you might employ funds more aggressively by using them as short-term trading vehicles. For example, you can use sector funds to take advantage of unusual profit opportunities in specific industries or selected international funds when the international economy becomes unsettled. Load charges can be avoided (or reduced) by dealing in families of funds offering low-cost conversion privileges and/or by dealing only in no-load funds.

You might choose to invest in funds for the long run, but still seek extraordinarily high rates of return by investing in aggressive mutual funds. There are a number of funds that follow very aggressive trading strategies and that may well appeal to you if you're willing to accept the substantial risk exposure. These are usually the fairly specialized smaller funds; sophisticated hedge funds, leverage funds, option funds, global funds, performance funds, and sector funds are examples. In this case, you are simply applying the basic mutual fund concept to your investment needs by letting professional money managers handle your accounts in a way you would like to see them handled: aggressively.

## TO STORE VALUE

You can also use mutual funds as a storehouse of value. The idea here is to find a place where your investment capital can be fairly secure and relatively free from deterioration, yet still generate a relatively attractive rate of return. Income and bond funds are the logical choices for such purposes, and so are money market funds (which are rapidly becoming the most popular way of meeting this investment objective). You could be after capital preservation and income over the long haul, or you might seek storage of value only for the short term, as a way to "sit it out" until a more attractive opportunity comes along. For example, you might use money funds to store your money while the market is weak or until you find better outlets.

## HOW TO CHOOSE A MUTUAL FUND

In many respects, selecting a mutual fund is no different from selecting any other kind of investment vehicle. You begin by clarifying your own objectives, learning what the different funds offer, and finally whittling down the choices.

### CLARIFY YOUR OBJECTIVES

Selecting the right investment outlet means finding the funds that are most suitable to *your* total investment needs. In other words, why do you want to invest in mutual funds, and what are you looking for in a fund? Obviously, an attractive rate of return would be desirable; but there is also the matter of a tolerable amount of risk exposure. Face it: some investors are more willing to take risks than others, and this is an important ingredient in the selection process. More than likely, when you look at your own risk temperament in relation to the various types of mutual funds, you will discover that certain types of funds are more appealing to you than others. For instance, performance or sector funds will probably *not* be particularly attractive to those of you who wish to avoid high exposure to risk.

Another important factor in the selection process is the intended use of the mutual fund. That is, do you want to invest in mutual funds to accumulate wealth, to speculate for high rates of return, or to store value? Finally, there is the matter of the services provided by the fund. If there are services you are particularly interested in, you should look for them in the funds you select. All these variables are important in defining why you use funds and are vital ingredients in the selection process. Having assessed what you are looking for in a fund, you can look at what the funds have to offer.

## LEARN WHAT THE DIFFERENT FUNDS HAVE TO OFFER

The ideal mutual fund would achieve maximum capital growth when security prices rise, provide complete protection against capital loss when prices decline, and achieve high levels of current income at all times. Unfortunately, this fund does not exist. Instead, just as you have your own set of investment needs, each fund has (1) its own investment objective, (2) its own manner of operation, and (3) its own range of services. These three parameters will be useful to you as you assess the different investment alternatives. But where can you find this information? The place to begin is in the fund prospectus (or Statement of Additional Information), which details the fund's investment objectives, portfolio composition, management, and past performance. In addition, publications such as *The Wall Street Journal, Barron's, Financial World,* and *Forbes* provide informative analyses of mutual funds. Several of these sources provide a wealth of operating and performance information in a convenient and easy-to-read format. For instance, *Forbes* rates hundreds of mutual funds each year and *Barron's* publishes an extensive mutual fund performance report every quarter. You should also look at such financial publications as *Money* and *Changing Times,* which periodically list the top-performing funds. If you're willing to spend more money, you can subscribe to such specialized mutual fund assessment services as *Investment Companies,* an annual publication (with quarterly updates) of Weisenberger Services, Inc. This publication provides extensive information on each of over 600 funds, including historical statistics and reviews of past performance, investment policy summaries, portfolio analyses, and a summary of fund services. (The Appendixes provide detailed lists of mutual fund services and publications.)

## WHITTLE DOWN THE ALTERNATIVES

At this point, selecting a fund becomes a process of elimination as you weigh your needs against the types of funds available. You can eliminate a great many funds simply because their investment objectives are different from your own. Some may be too risky; others too conservative. Thus, rather than trying to evaluate 1,800 different funds, you can narrow the list down to two or three *types* of funds that are most compatible with your investment goals. Other factors will help you narrow your choices even more. For example, to avoid commission fees, you may prefer to deal only with no-load funds. Or you may want a fund that is part of a large fund family or one that offers low-cost conversion privileges.

The final, but by no means least important, issue to consider is the fund's past performance. Find out how the fund has performed over time; the type of return it has generated in good markets as well as bad; the level of dividend and capital gains distributions; and its investment stability. These facts will point you to some of the more successful mutual funds—those that are both compatible with your investment objectives and provide the best payoffs.

This investment process gives considerable weight to past performance, mainly because it tells you a great deal about the investment skills of the fund managers. Now as a rule, the past is given little or no attention in the investment decision—after all, it's the future that matters. While the *future performance* of a mutual fund is still the variable that holds the key to success, a good deal of time is spent on past investment results in order to get a handle on how successful the fund's investment managers have been. In essence, the success of a mutual fund rests in large part on the investment skills of the fund managers. Thus, when investing in a mutual fund, look for consistently good performance, in up as well as down markets, over *extended* periods of time (5 years or more); most important, check to see if the same key people are still running the fund. Although past success is certainly no guarantee of future performance, a strong team of money managers can have a significant bearing on the level of fund returns.

## HOW TO MEASURE PERFORMANCE

By analyzing how a fund has performed—by examining the dividend level, capital gains, and capital growth it has achieved—you can evaluate the fund's investment behavior and appraise its performance in relation to other funds and investment vehicles. Here we will look at different sources and measures of mutual fund return and—because it is so important—at risk as well.

### SOURCES OF RETURN

An open-end fund has three potential sources of return: (1) dividend income, (2) capital gains distribution, and (3) change in the price (or net asset value) of the fund. Depending on the type of fund, one source may be more important than another; for example, we would normally expect income funds to have much higher dividend income than capital gains distributions.

Mutual funds publish periodic reports summarizing their investment performance. One such report is *The Summary of Income and Capital Changes,* an example of which is shown on the next page. This summary statement, usually found in the fund's prospectus, gives a brief overview of the fund's investment activity, including income and expense ratios and portfolio turnover rates. The top part of the report, which includes information on investment income and expenses, capital changes, and NAV, is especially interesting since it reveals the amount of dividend income and capital gains distributed to shareholders, along with the change in the fund's net asset value.

# PER SHARE INCOME AND CAPITAL CHANGES
For a share outstanding throughout the year

|  |  | 1986 | 1985 | 1984 |
|---|---|---|---|---|
|  | **INCOME AND EXPENSES** |  |  |  |
|  | 1. Investment income | $.76 | $.88 | $.67 |
|  | 2. Less expenses | .16 | .22 | .17 |
|  | 3. Net investment income | .60 | .66 | .50 |
| Dividend income → | 4. Dividends from net investment income | (.55) | (.64) | (.50) |
|  | **CAPITAL CHANGES** |  |  |  |
|  | 5. Net realized and unrealized gains (or losses) on security transactions | 6.37 | (1.74) | 3.79 |
| Capital gains distribution → | 6. Distributions from realized gains | (1.75) | (.84) | (1.02) |
| Change in NAV → | 7. Net increase (decrease) in NAV | 4.67* | (2.56) | 2.77 |
|  | 8. NAV at beginning of year | 24.47 | 27.03 | 24.26 |
|  | 9. NAV at end of year | $29.14 | $24.47 | $27.03 |
|  | 10. Ratio of operating expenses to average net assets | 1.04% | .85% | 1.34% |
|  | 11. Ratio of net investment income to average net assets | 1.47% | 2.56% | 2.39% |
|  | 12. Portfolio turnover rate** | 85% | 144% | 74% |
|  | 13. Shares outstanding at end of year (000s omitted) | 10,568 | 6,268 | 4,029 |

*Net increase (decrease) in NAV, line 7 = line 3 − line 4 + line 5 − line 6.

**Portfolio turnover rate relates the number of shares bought and sold by the fund to the total number of shares held in the fund's portfolio; a high turnover rate (for example, in excess of 100 percent) would mean the fund has been doing a lot of trading.

The dividend income received by shareholders is derived from the dividend and interest income earned by the security holdings of the mutual fund. It is paid out of the *net investment income* left after all operating expenses have been met. The fund accumulates all the current income it has received for the quarter (or the year) and then pays it out on a prorated basis. If a fund earned, say, $1 million in dividends and interest in a given quarter, and if that fund had 1 million shares outstanding, each share would receive a quarterly dividend payment of $1. Capital gains distributions work in much the same way, except that these payments are derived from the capital gains earned by the fund. For example, suppose a fund bought some stock a year ago for $50 and sold it in the current quarter for $75 a share. Clearly, the fund has achieved capital gains of $25 a share. If it held 50,000 shares of this stock, it would realize a total capital gain of $1,250,000 ($25 × 50,000 = $1,250,000). Given that the fund has 1 million shares outstanding, each share would be entitled to $1.25 in the form of a capital gains distribution. Note that this capital gains distribution applies only to *realized* capital gains—that is, to security holdings that were actually sold and capital gains actually earned.

Unrealized capital gains (or paper profits) make up the third and final element of fund return. When the fund's holdings go up or down in price, the net asset value of the fund moves accordingly. Suppose you buy into a fund at $10 per share, and some time later it is worth $12.50; the difference of $2.50 a share is the unrealized capital gains contained in the fund's security holdings. It represents the profit shareholders would receive if the fund were to sell its holdings.

The return on closed-end investment companies is derived from the same three sources and from a fourth source as well: changes in price discounts or premiums. Because closed-end companies are traded like any common stock, they seldom trade exactly at their net asset value. Instead, they tend to trade below (at a discount) or above (at a premium) their NAV. As these discounts or premiums change over time, the return to shareholders also changes because changes in discount or premium affect the market price of the fund. Thus, for closed-end funds, the third element of return (change in share price) is defined not only by changes in the net asset value of the fund's holdings, but also by changes in price discount or premium.

## MEASURES OF RETURN

A simple but effective way of measuring mutual fund performance is to describe return in terms of the three major sources noted above: dividends earned, capital gains distributions received, and change in price. These payoffs can be converted to a convenient yield figure by using the standard holding period return formula. You can see how this is done by using the 1986 figures from the previous table. This hypothetical no-load fund paid 55 cents a share in dividends, another $1.75 in capital gains distributions, and had a price at the beginning of the year of $24.47, which climbed to $29.14 by the end of the year. Here is a summary of the fund's investment performance:

| | |
|---|---:|
| Price (NAV) at the *beginning* of the year | $24.47 |
| Price (NAV) at the *end* of the year | 29.14 |
| Net increase | $ 4.67 |
| Return for the year: | |
| Dividends received | $ .55 |
| Capital gains distributions | 1.75 |
| Net increase in price (NAV) | 4.67 |
| Total return | $ 6.97 |
| Holding period return (total return/beginning price) | 28.5% |

The measure is simple to calculate and follows the standard HPR format; it not only captures all the important elements of mutual fund return, but also provides a handy indication of yield. With a total dollar return of $6.97 and a beginning investment of $24.47 (the initial share price of the fund), the annual rate of return was 28.5 percent.

But what happens if dividends and capital gains distributions are reinvested into the fund? In this case, instead of cash, you receive additional shares of stock. You can still use holding period return to measure return, but you must keep track of the number of shares acquired through reinvestment. To illustrate, let's continue with our example and assume that you initially bought 200 shares in the mutual fund. Assume also that you were able to acquire shares through the fund's reinvestment program at an average price of $26.50 a share; thus, the $460 in dividends and capital gains distributions [($.55 + $1.75) × 200] provided you with another 17.36 shares in the fund ($460/$26.50). Under these circumstances, holding period return would relate the market value of the stock holdings at the beginning of the period to holdings at the end:

$$\text{holding period return} = \frac{\left(\begin{array}{c}\text{number of shares} \times \\ \text{ending price}\end{array}\right) - \left(\begin{array}{c}\text{number of shares} \times \\ \text{initial price}\end{array}\right)}{(\text{number of shares} \times \text{initial price})}$$

Thus, the holding period return would be:

$$\text{holding period return} = \frac{(217.36 \times \$29.14) - (200 \times \$24.47)}{(200 \times \$24.47)}$$

$$= \frac{(\$6333.87) - (\$4894.00)}{(\$4894.00)}$$

$$= \underline{29.4\%}$$

This holding period yield, like the preceding one, can now be used to compare the performance of this fund to that of other funds and other investment vehicles.

Rather than using 1-year holding periods, it is sometimes necessary to assess the performance of mutual funds over extended periods of time. Under such circumstances, the standard approximate yield measure can be used to determine the fund's effective annual compound rate of return. This can be done by following established approximate yield procedures except for one slight modification: that is, capital gains distributions should be added to dividends received to find total average annual income. Returning to our example once more, assume that this time we want to find the annual rate of return over the 3-year period 1984 through 1986. In this case, the mutual fund had *average* annual dividends of 56 cents a share [(.55 + 64 + .50)/3], *average* annual capital gains distributions of $1.20 a share [(1.75 + .84 + 1.02)/3], and total *average* annual income of $1.76 a share (1.20 + .56). Given that the beginning price of the fund in 1984 was $24.26 and its ending price in 1986 was $29.14, we can find the fund's approximate yield in the following way:

$$\text{approximate yield} = \frac{\text{total average annual income} + \dfrac{\begin{array}{c}\text{ending} \\ \text{share price}\end{array} - \begin{array}{c}\text{beginning} \\ \text{share price}\end{array}}{\text{number of years held}}}{\dfrac{\begin{array}{c}\text{ending} \\ \text{share price}\end{array} + \begin{array}{c}\text{beginning} \\ \text{share price}\end{array}}{2}}$$

$$= \frac{\$1.76 + \dfrac{\$29.14 - \$24.26}{3}}{\dfrac{\$29.14 + \$24.26}{2}}$$

$$= \underline{12.7\%}$$

This mutual fund provided its investors with an annual compound rate of return of approximately 12.7 percent over this 3-year period. This information can help you compare the performance of one fund to other funds as well as to other investment vehicles.

## THE MATTER OF RISK

Because most mutual funds are so diversified, they protect you fairly well from the financial risk associated with buying individual securities. However, this diversification does not protect you from a considerable amount of *market risk*. On the contrary, because mutual fund portfolios are so well diversified, they often reflect the behavior of the marketplace itself. Thus, if the market is drifting downward, most funds—especially stock funds—will also drift downward. In general, only such defensive (or countercyclical) funds as gold funds will resist this trend.

Thus, before you invest, it is important to be aware of the general market's effect on the performance of specific mutual funds. If you think the market is headed down over the short run, you may want to hold off investing in performance or growth funds, since they'll probably perform poorly. Instead, consider investing in a money market fund until the market trend reverses itself. Once this happens, you can make a more permanent investment commitment.

Another important risk consideration revolves around the management practices of the fund itself. If the fund's portfolio is managed conservatively, the risk of loss in capital is likely to be much less than if it is managed aggressively. Obviously, the more speculative the investment goals of the fund, the greater the risk of instability in the net asset value. On the other hand, a conservatively managed portfolio does not necessarily eliminate all price volatility, since the securities in the portfolio are still subject to inflation, interest rate swings, and general market risks. However, these risks become less and less important as the investment objectives and portfolio management practices of the fund become increasingly conservative.

# FOUR
## TAKING CHANCES—
## TAX SHELTERS, OPTIONS,
## COMMODITIES, AND
## FINANCIAL FUTURES

# 24

## TAX-SHELTERED INVESTMENTS

――――――

It is often said that the necessities of life include food, clothing, and shelter. Shelter is important because it protects us from the elements—rain, wind, snow, and extreme heat or cold. It's not stretching the point too far to say that investors need shelter as well—not from the elements, but from the IRS. Without adequate protection, you'll keep only a small portion of the money you earn on your investments. That means it's essential to consider the tax consequences of every investment you make or are thinking of making.

What you're after are vehicles that provide the maximum after-tax return for a given risk. If, for example, you're in the 33 percent federal tax bracket, you will keep more money after your taxes are paid if you invest in a nontaxable municipal bond yielding 8 percent than if you choose a fully taxable corporate bond yielding 9 percent. Our aim in this chapter is to introduce you to various methods of legally reducing your tax liability, including investment vehicles that can provide the highest possible after-tax returns for a given level of risk.

# TAX AVOIDANCE AND TAX DEFERRAL
## ARE WORTHY GOALS

If you're like all the rest of us, your tax strategy year after year is to walk away with as much after-tax income as you possibly can. You can do this by avoiding taxable income altogether—by investing, for example, in municipal instead of corporate bonds—or by deferring the income to another period when it will be taxed at a lower rate. These tax strategies are completely legal and should not be confused with *tax evasion* tactics, such as omitting income or overstating deductions, which are illegal.

Specifically, *tax avoidance* is concerned with reducing or eliminating taxes in ways that are consistent with the intent of Congress. These ways range from buying tax-free municipals to claiming child-care credits. *Tax deferral*, on the other hand, focuses on methods of delaying taxes, including such long-term strategies as putting money away in pension and retirement plans, IRAs, and annuities. Tax deferral can also be used on a short-term basis, depending on your particular situation, to defer taxes from one year to the next. This strategy can be especially attractive if you know that your taxable income next year will be lower than it is this year. This may occur after the birth of a baby—if you plan to take an extended period of time off to care for the child—or if you are changing careers and expect to take a substantial pay cut until you get established. You might also want to defer income to take advantage of scheduled reductions in tax rates. For example, many people deferred income from 1987 to 1988 for this reason.

# TAX-FAVORED INCOME

If an investment offers a return that is not taxable, is taxed at a rate less than that of other similar investments, defers the payment of tax to a later period, or trades current income for unrealized capital gains, it gives you *tax-favored income*. Tax favors have been written into the tax law to encourage certain activities.

## INCOME EXCLUDED FROM TAXATION

Some items are simply excluded from taxation, either totally or partially. These include interest earned on municipal, Treasury, and government agency bonds and certain proceeds from the sale of a personal residence. Because of their tax benefits, these income sources are particularly attractive.

*Municipal bond interest.* All interest received from municipal bonds is free from federal income tax; in fact, it does not even need to be reported on your tax return.

However, any gains or losses resulting from the sale of municipal bonds are included as capital gains or losses. In addition, if you borrow money to purchase municipal bonds and pay interest on it, the interest is not tax-deductible. (See Chapter 18 for a complete discussion of the tax benefits of municipal bonds.)

*Treasury and government agency issues.* Although you pay federal income taxes on the interest you earn from these securities, you pay no state or local taxes. Since in some parts of the country, these combined tax rates can be as high as 20 percent, this exclusion can save you a great deal, especially if you are in a high tax bracket.

*Sale of a personal residence.* You'll earn capital gains if you sell your personal residence for more than you paid for it (including the cost of improvements). However, provisions in the tax law soften the tax consequences of the sale and actually make an investment in a home an excellent tax shelter. First, if a gain exists from the sale of your home, it can be deferred from taxation if you purchase another home at a price equal to or greater than the price of the home you sold—as long as you buy the other home within 24 months. Second—and this is the really important tax implication—you have a one-time opportunity to exclude $125,000 from your gross income on the sale of a personal residence. On a joint return, both spouses must be 55 or older and meet certain other conditions to be eligible for the exclusion. This offers a major tax benefit to most people and certainly enhances the investment appeal of the personal residence.

## STRATEGIES THAT DEFER TAX LIABILITIES TO THE NEXT YEAR

Investors often purchase securities and enjoy sizable gains within a relatively short period of time. For example, suppose you bought 100 shares of NCR common stock in mid-1985; by year-end 1986 your investment would have increased in value by 50 percent, since the price of this stock rose from $30 a share to around $45. If you now believed the stock was fully valued in the market and decided to sell it and invest the $4,500 elsewhere, you would be taxed on a capital gain of $1,500 ($4,500 sale price — $3,000 cost). If you were in the 28 percent tax bracket, you would owe $420 in taxes on the sale at the end of the year. Suppose you wanted to defer the taxes on this transaction to the following year while locking in your gain; you could use three different strategies: a short sale against the box, a put hedge, or a deep-in-the-money call option.

*Short sale against the box.* By shorting-against-the-box—that is, short selling a number of shares equal to what you already own—you lock in an existing profit, thus eliminating any risk of a price decline. Although you also give up any future increases in price, you are comfortable with your profit since you believe that the current price is relatively high. For example, to lock in and defer the $1,500 capital gain on the NCR transaction you would, prior to year-end, sell short 100 shares of NCR. You would then have two positions—one long and one short—both involving an equal number of NCR shares. After year-end you would use the 100 shares held long to close out the short position, thereby realizing the $1,500 capital gain.

*Put hedge.*   A put hedge also defers taxes on your profits from one year to the next. But unlike short selling against the box, it allows you to cash in on additional price appreciation. Essentially, a put hedge involves buying a put option on shares you currently own. If the price of the stock falls, your losses on the shares are offset by a profit on the put option. For example, suppose that when NCR was trading at $45 you purchased a 6-month put option, with a striking price of $45, for $150. You have then locked in a price of $45, because if the price falls, say to $40 a share, your $500 loss on the stock is offset exactly by a $500 profit on the option. However, you are still out the cost of the option—$150. If the stock closed at $40, your after-tax position would be:

| | | | |
|---|---|---|---|
| 1. | Initial cost of 100 shares | | $3,000 |
| 2. | Profit on 100 shares [(100) × ($40 assumed price − $30 original purchase price)] | | 1,000 |
| 3. | Profit on the put option | $ 500 | |
| 4. | Cost of the put option | 150 | |
| 5. | Taxable gain on put option [(3) − (4)] | 350 | |
| 6. | Total tax on transaction | | |
| | Profit on stock (2) | $1,000 | |
| | + Taxable gain on put (5) | 350 | |
| | Total gain | $1,350 | |
| | × Tax rate | × .28 | |
| | Total tax | | 378 |
| 7. | After-tax position [(1) + (2) + (5) − (6)] | | $3,972 |

If you had simply held the stock and sold it at around $43.50 a share, your final after-tax position would be about the same. But the put hedge gives you the advantage of locking in this position regardless of how low the price might fall (which simply holding the stock does not) while also participating in the price appreciation of the stock.

*Deep-in-the-money call option.*   A third tax deferral strategy involves deep-in-the-money call options. Although selling these options is similar to buying a put hedge, there are important differences. In this case, you give up any potential future price increases while you lock in a price defined by the amount you receive from the sale of the call option. To illustrate, suppose call options on NCR with a $40 striking price and 6-month maturity were traded at $600 ($6 per share) when NCR was selling for $45. If 6 months later NCR closed at $40, your after-tax position would be:

1. Initial cost of 100 shares     $3,000

2. Profit on 100 shares [(100) × ($40 − $30)]     1,000

3. Profit on the sale of the option (since it closed at the striking price, profit is the total amount received)     600

4. Total tax on transaction

   | | |
   |---|---:|
   | Profit on stock (2) | $1,000 |
   | + Profit on option (3) | 600 |
   | Total gain | $1,600 |
   | × Tax rate | × .28 |
   | Total tax | 448 |

5. After-tax position [(1) + (2) + (3) − (4)]     **$4,152**

Although you're better off now than you were when you bought the put hedge, you won't earn any more money if the price of the stock climbs. In effect, when you sell the call option, you are agreeing to deliver your shares at the option's striking price. So even if the price of NCR increases, say to $50 or beyond, you'll have to sell your shares at $40. Furthermore, your downside protection extends only to the amount you receive for the option—in this case $6 a share. If NCR's price dropped to $35 you would lose $4 a share before taxes [$45 − ($35 + $6)].

*One last look.* As you can see, deferring tax liabilities to the next year is a potentially rewarding activity. You can simplify your choice of strategy by considering how each strategy performs under different expectations of future price behavior, as summarized in the following table.

| Strategy | Price Will Vary by a Small Amount Above or Below Current Price | Price Will Vary by a Large Amount Above or Below Current Price | Future Price Will Be Higher Than Current Price | Future Price Will Be Lower Than Current Price |
|---|:---:|:---:|:---:|:---:|
| Do nothing—hold into next tax year | 2 | 4 | 1 | 4 |
| Short sale against the box | 3+ | 2+ | 4 | 1 |
| Put hedge | 3+ | 1 | 2 | 2+ |
| Sell deep-in-the-money call option | 1 | 2+ | 3 | 2+ |

Note: 1, best ranking; 4, worst ranking.

To complete the analysis you would have to consider commission costs, something we have omitted. Although these can be somewhat high in absolute dollars, they are usually a minor part of the total dollars involved if the potential savings are as large as the ones we have considered here. However, if the savings are relatively small, say under $200, then commissions may be disproportionately large in relation to the amount you save in taxes. Clearly, you need to work out the specific figures for each situation.

## STRATEGIES THAT TRADE CURRENT INCOME FOR CAPITAL GAINS

While ordinary income is taxed in the year it is received, capital gains are not taxed until they are actually realized. In other words, unrealized capital gains are not taxed. For example, if you receive $100 in cash dividends from a stock this year and are in the 28 percent tax bracket, you are left with $72 of after-tax income. On the other hand, if the stock price rises by $100 this year, you owe no taxes on this amount until you sell the stock. Therefore, if the market price of a stock is stable or increasing and your objective is a tax-deferred buildup of funds, you should consider using this capital gains strategy. From a strict tax viewpoint, investments that provide a tax-deferred buildup of value through unrealized capital gains may be more attractive than those that provide annual taxable income. Two main ways of trading current income for capital gains are described below.

*Choose growth instead of income stocks.* This is a simple yet basic way to earn income from capital gains. Companies that pay out a low percentage of earnings as dividends usually reinvest the retained earnings to take advantage of opportunities. If you select a company that pays dividends that amount to a 10 percent current return on your investment, your after-tax return will be 7.2 percent, assuming you are in the 28 percent tax bracket. If, on the other hand, you choose a company that pays no dividends but is expected to experience 10 percent annual growth in its share price from reinvestment of earnings, your after-tax rate of return will also be 7.2 percent [$(1.0 - 0.28) \times .10$]. This time, however, the taxes on this return are not due until the stock is sold and the gain is actually realized. Clearly, this tax deferral feature is appealing as long as the stock price continues to climb.

*Consider deep discount bonds.* Purchasing a bond that is selling at a price far below its par value also offers the possibility for capital gains. To illustrate, suppose you have the choice of buying an ABC bond, which has a coupon rate of 5 percent and is selling for $700 in the market, or an XYZ bond with a coupon of 10 percent selling at par. Which would you prefer if both mature to their $1,000 par values at the end of 10 years? With the ABC bond, you will earn interest income of $50 a year taxed as ordinary income. At the end of 10 years, you will also have a $300 capital gain, which will also be taxed as ordinary income. With the XYZ bond, all of your return—that is, the $100 you receive each year—is ordinary income. From a strict tax perspective, the ABC bond is clearly the better of the two, since the portion of the return represented by the capital gain is not taxed until you actually receive it at maturity. Remember, though, that the higher coupon bond gives you a higher return earlier, which adds to its attractiveness.

Before choosing between the two bonds, you should analyze the rate of return you'll get from each, assuming that you invest the same amount of money in each bond. For example, with an investment of $7,000 you can purchase 10 ABC bonds that yield $500 in total annual interest. For the same amount of money, you can purchase 7 XYZ bonds that yield $700 a year. If you are in the 28 percent tax bracket, the after-tax advantage of the XYZ bonds is $144 (0.72 × $200) a year. But the ABC bonds will be worth $10,000 at maturity compared to the $7,000 value of the XYZ bonds. On an after-tax basis, the additional $3,000 is worth $2,160 [$3,000 − (.28)($3,000)].

The choice boils down to whether you prefer $144 of additional income each year for the next 10 years or an additional $2,160 at the end of 10 years. By using the future value techniques developed in Chapter 4, you'll see that you'll need about a 9 percent rate of return to accumulate approximately $2,160 at the end of 10 years. That is, if you can invest $144 a year for 10 years at an after-tax rate higher than 9 percent, the XYZ bond is your best bet. If you believe your after-tax reinvestment rate will be lower, you should select the ABC bond instead.

## TAX SWAPS: A STRATEGY THAT REDUCES OR ELIMINATES A TAX LIABILITY

Although the strategies we have focused on so far have the potential to reduce your tax liability, they do not eliminate taxes by any stretch of the imagination. There is another strategy, however, that has the potential to do exactly that if you use it correctly. This procedure, discussed in Chapter 19, is known as a tax swap and is extremely popular at year-end with knowledgeable stock and bond investors.

Basically, a tax swap is nothing more than the replacement of one security with another for the purpose of partially or fully offsetting a capital gain that has been realized in another part of your portfolio. Of course, since you are trying to offset a gain, the security that you sell in a tax swap must be a poor performer that has lost money for you so far. Thus, tax swapping involves selling one security that has experienced a capital loss and replacing it with a similar security. In this case, your stock or bond position is essentially unchanged although your tax liability has been reduced—and often eliminated.

Tax swapping works like this. Suppose that during the current year you realized a $1,100 capital gain on the sale of bonds. Assume also that in your portfolio you hold 100 shares of common stock of an oil company, Unocal Corp., purchased 20 months earlier for $38 a share and currently selling for $28 a share. While you want to include an oil stock in your portfolio, the choice of stock makes little difference to you. You would be as happy with 100 shares of another multinational oil as you are with Unocal. To realize the $10 a share capital loss on Unocal without changing the composition of your portfolio, you sell the 100 shares of Unocal and buy 100 shares of Occidental Petroleum, which is also selling at $28 a share. The result is a realized capital loss of $1,000 [$100 × ($28 − $38)], which can be used to offset all but $100 of the $1,100 capital gain you earned on the bonds. Clearly, the tax swap is an effective way of almost eliminating your tax liability without altering the composition of your portfolio.

Common stock swaps such as this are an important part of year-end tax planning. However, bond swaps are even more popular because it is usually fairly easy to find a substitute bond for the one you already hold. Most full-service brokerage houses publish a list of recommended year-end swaps for both stocks and bonds. You might be wondering why it wouldn't make more sense just to sell the security for tax purposes and then immediately buy it back. Unfortunately, this is called a *wash sale* and is disallowed under the tax law. A sold security cannot be repurchased within 30 days without losing the tax deduction.

# DEFERRED ANNUITIES AND SINGLE-PREMIUM LIFE INSURANCE

As we noted in the discussion of tax-favored income, one of the goals of a good tax strategy is to defer taxable income for extended periods of time. Although this strategy may not reduce your total taxes, you'll find that it can still help you substantially, since investment earnings not taxed when earned are therefore available for reinvestment during the period of deferment. You'll find the additional earnings that result from investing pretax rather than after-tax dollars over long periods of time can be large. One of the best mechanisms for achieving this tax deferrment is a tax-deferred annuity. This may be worth more to you than any other single tax strategy. A similar product that is rapidly growing in popularity is single-premium life insurance.

## ANNUITIES: AN OVERVIEW

An annuity is a series of payments guaranteed for a number of years or over a lifetime. Many types of annuities are issued by hundreds of insurance companies. The two main types of annuities are classified by their purchase provisions:

- A *single-premium annuity* is a contract purchased with a single lump sum payment. You pay a certain amount and receive a series of future payments that begins immediately or at some future date.
- An *installment annuity*, on the other hand, is acquired by making payments over time. At a specified future date, the installment payments plus interest earned on them are used to purchase an annuity contract.

The person to whom the future payments are directed is called the *annuitant.*

An *immediate annuity* is a contract under which payments to the annuitant begin as soon as it is purchased. The amount of the payment is based on statistical analyses performed by the insurance company and depends on the annuitant's age and sex—the payment is a function of how long the insurance company expects the person to live. A *deferred annuity* is one in which the payments to the annuitant begin at some future date. The date is specified in the contract or at the annuitant's option. The amount the annuitant will periodically receive depends on his or her contributions, the interest earned by these contributions until the annuity payments commence, the annuitant's sex, and the annuitant's age when payments begin.

The period of time between the beginning of payments to the insurance company and the beginning of repayment to the annuitant is the *accumulation period.* All interest earned on the accumulated payments during this period is tax deferred: it stays in the account and, because it is not paid out to the purchaser, no tax liability is created. The period of time over which payments are made to the annuitant is the *distribution period.* Earnings on the annuity during the accumulation and distribution period become taxable to the annuitant when received.

## CHARACTERISTICS OF DEFERRED ANNUITIES

The rapid growth in popularity of deferred annuities stems from the competitive interest rates paid on these contracts. Although they fluctuate with interest rates in general and are *not* guaranteed, many of the new contracts have a "bailout" provision that allows an annuity holder to withdraw the contract value—principal and all earned interest—if the company fails to pay a minimum return. In the following discussion, the contract offered and heavily promoted by a major life insurance company, summarized in the table on the next page, is used as an example. It is typical of the contracts currently being written.

*Current interest rate.*    An annuity contract's current interest rate is the yearly return the insurance company is paying now on accumulated deposits. The current interest rate fluctuates with market rates over time and is not guaranteed by the insurance company. Our sample policy offers a guaranteed 1-year rate of 8.3 percent.

*Minimum guaranteed interest rate.*    The deferred annuity purchase contract will specify a minimum guaranteed interest rate on contributions. The insurance company will guarantee this rate over the full accumulation period. The minimum rate is usually substantially less than the current interest rate. The sample policy guarantees a rate of 5.5 percent, but notice that its bailout provision is tied to a minimum current rate of 7.3 percent. Study the prospectus or contract and remember that *the minimum rate is all you are guaranteed.* Very often, the promotional literature emphasizes the high current interest rate.

*Special tax features.*    Interest earned on your contributions to either a single-premium or installment deferred annuity is not subject to income tax until it is actually paid to you by the insurance company. Suppose that you invest $10,000

# TYPICAL FEATURES OF A DEFERRED ANNUITY CONTRACT

| Feature | Covered in This Contract |
|---|---|
| 1. Minimum contribution | The minimum single premium required is $2,000 in tax-qualified contracts such as IRAs and tax-sheltered annuities, and $4,000 otherwise. Single premiums in excess of $500,000 require prior company approval. |
| 2. Withdrawal privileges | Funds can be withdrawn anytime; before payments begin, up to 10% of the annuity contract value can be withdrawn once a year without charges. Withdrawals in excess of this amount will incur a surrender charge of 7% of annuity value in the first year, reducing by 1% each year thereafter, with no surrender charges after the seventh year. In no instance will the investor receive less than 100% of the original single premium, less any prior withdrawals. |
| 3. Guaranteed rates | 8.3% in the first year, 5.5% thereafter. |
| 4. Bailout provision | Yes, wherever the declared rate is one percentage point less than the initial rate (7.3% in this example). |
| 5. Sales charge | None. |
| 6. Payment options | Withdrawal of all or part in a lump sum, or select how, when, and where payments are to be made. |
| 7. Income tax implications | Any withdrawal of income within the first 10 years is assessed a 10% penalty unless the investor is over age 59½; penalty is also waived for death or disability. |
| | Any withdrawal of income is taxed at the investor's tax rate in the year of withdrawal. |
| | The contract can (a tax consultant should provide an expert opinion) be rolled over to another annuity if the registration stays the same. |

*Source:* Compilation of features of a deferred annuity offered by a major life insurance company in early 1987.

in an 8.3 percent single-premium deferred annuity. During the first year the contract is in effect, the account earns $830 in interest. If none of this interest is withdrawn, no income tax is due. If you are in the 28 percent tax bracket, your first year's tax savings are $232. The tax deferral privilege permits the accumulation of substantial sums at compound interest that can help to provide a comfortable retirement income. Note that the Tax Reform Act of 1986 makes this tax-favored treatment available only on annuity contracts held by individuals or trusts or other entities such as a decedent's estate, a qualified employer plan, a qualified annuity plan, or an IRA. In all other cases, the income on the annuity is taxed when earned.

Certain employees of institutions such as schools, universities, governments, and not-for-profit organizations may qualify for a *tax-sheltered annuity* under what are known as 403(b) plans. A special provision in the income tax laws allows these employees to make a *tax-free contribution* from current income to purchase a deferred annuity. The interest on these contributions is tax-deferred as well. For example, Professor Hector Gomez teaches history at Crown University in Maine. His pretax salary is $2,500 per month. Professor Gomez can contribute approximately $435 per month to a tax-sheltered annuity program. (Note: The maximum amount he can contribute is limited and can be determined by a formula.) This $435 is excluded from current income taxation; as a result, his taxes are based on only $2,065 per month. He does not have to pay any income tax on his contributions or his interest earnings until he actually receives annuity payments in future years. If Professor Gomez's income tax bracket is lower when he retires, he will pay a lower income tax on his deferred income. The tax-sheltered annuity is attractive because it can save income taxes today as well as provide a higher level of retirement income later.

*Investment payout.* The investment return, or payout, provided by an annuity contract is realized when the distribution period begins. You can choose a straight annuity, which is a series of payments for the rest of your life, or a variety of other payout options. Some contracts specify payments for both annuitant and spouse for the rest of both their lives. Some specify rapid payout of accumulated payments with interest over a short period of time. The amount you receive depends on the amount accumulated in the account and the payout plan chosen. It is important to choose the program that provides the highest return for the desired payout plan. Such a plan will probably have a relatively high interest rate and a relatively low (or no) sales charge. The contract illustrated in the previous table allows the annuitant to select how, when, and where payments are made.

*Withdrawal provisions and penalties.* Most annuity contracts specify conditions under which accumulated contributions and interest can be withdrawn by the purchaser. Read these provisions carefully; some insurers impose heavy penalties for premature withdrawal of funds. (The sample contract provides comparatively liberal withdrawal provisions.) Equally important, the Tax Reform Act of 1986 levies an additional income tax of 10 percent on early distributions from both deferred and tax-sheltered annuities.

*Sales charge.* Many annuities are sold by salespersons who receive a commission of up to 10 percent of the first year's premium. This commission charge is paid by the purchaser. No-load annuities, on the other hand, require no such payment; the insurance company pays the salesperson directly, as is the case with our example. However, even if you buy a no-load annuity, you may have to pay additional charges, such as management fees, yearly maintenance fees, and one-time "setup charges." Because these fees can quickly mount up, it is critical that you analyze the actual return on investment after all commissions, fees, and charges are deducted.

## FIXED VS. VARIABLE ANNUITIES

The annuity payout during the distribution period can be fixed or variable. Most contracts are written as *fixed annuities.* This means that once a payment schedule is selected, the amount of monthly income does not change. The advantage of a fixed annuity is that the dollar amount of monthly income is guaranteed to the annuitant regardless of how poorly or how well the insurer's investments perform. A major disadvantage, however, is that in periods of inflation the purchasing power of the dollar erodes. For example, with a 5 percent annual inflation rate, $1 is reduced in purchasing power to 78 cents in just 5 years.

To overcome this disadvantage, the *variable annuity* was developed. This plan adjusts the monthly income according to the actual investment returns (and sometimes changes in mortality statistics) experienced by the insurer. With this plan, annuitants face a different risk. They cannot be certain how well the insurer's investments—which may consist of common stocks, bonds, or money market funds—will do. Annuitants take a chance that they will receive an even lower monthly income in absolute dollars than a fixed dollar contract would provide. Most people who participate in variable annuity plans anticipate that they will at least be able to keep up with the cost of living. Unfortunately, variable annuity values and inflation as measured by the consumer price index, or CPI, do not always perform the same. During the 1970s and early 1980s, a period of significant inflation, a number of variable annuities earned rates of return well below the CPI. This shows that a real risk of reduced benefits from variable annuities does exist. Indeed, as a result of the dip in common stock values, the payments made under many variable annuity plans during the 1970s fell below the amount paid by corresponding fixed dollar plans.

Although most premiums paid into variable annuities are invested in common stocks, annuitants are sometimes allowed to have their monies exclusively placed in common stocks throughout the accumulation period as well as during the distribution period. In some cases, annuitants may prefer to have their premiums build up in a variable plan and then switch to a fixed dollar plan at retirement. In this manner they participate in the growth of the economy over their working careers but guard against short-term recessions that may occur during their retirement.

## INVESTMENT SUITABILITY

The principal positive feature of deferred annuities is that they allow you to accumulate tax-deferred earnings in order to create a source of future income. The tax-deferred feature allows interest to accumulate more quickly than would be the case if it were taxed. For those who qualify for the tax-sheltered annuity, current income tax on premium payments can be deferred as well. Annuities are also considered a low-risk investment.

On the negative side, deferred annuities offer no inflation protection. In spite of their fluctuating interest rate during the accumulation period, most annuities do not keep ahead of the rate of inflation. The second negative feature of annuities is their relatively high administrative and sales commission charges. Insurance companies have high overheads that must be met from annuity proceeds. In addition, sales commissions, whether paid by the purchaser or the insurance company, are generous and tend to lower the purchaser's return. In general, then, although annuities can play an important role in an investment portfolio, they should not be the only vehicle held. Other vehicles providing higher returns (and probably carrying higher risk) are available.

*Buying annuities.* Licensed insurance salespersons and many stockbrokers sell annuities. Prior to investing, you should obtain a prospectus and any other available literature on a number of different plans. Compare these materials carefully, and choose the annuity that meets your investment objectives and offers the highest actual return on investment after all commissions, fees, and charges are deducted.

*Deferred annuity vs. nonannuity income.* To illustrate the benefits of deferring income tax on the accumulated interest in an annuity, assume you purchase a $10,000 single-premium deferred annuity (SPDA) paying interest at an annual rate of 8.3 percent. As shown in the following table, if the interest on the contract is allowed to accumulate, the investment will be worth $14,899 at the end of 5 years, $22,197 at the end of 10 years, and $109,359 at the end of 30 years. In this case, the interest compounds without taxes.

## COMPARISON OF TWO $10,000 INVESTMENTS—A DEFERRED ANNUITY AND A NONANNUITY*

| End of Year | ANNUITY Earnings | ANNUITY Year-End Value | | | NONANNUITY Earnings | Taxes | NONANNUITY Year-End Value | | | |
|---|---|---|---|---|---|---|---|---|---|---|
| 1 | $ 830 | $10,000 + $ 830 = | $ 10,830 | | $ 830 | $232 | $10,000 + $ 830 − $232 = | $10,598 | | |
| 2 | 899 | 10,830 + 899 = | 11,729 | | 880 | 246 | 10,598 + 880 − 246 = | 11,232 | | |
| 3 | 974 | 11,729 + 974 = | 12,703 | | 932 | 261 | 11,232 + 932 − 261 = | 11,903 | | |
| 4 | 1,054 | 12,703 + 1,054 = | 13,757 | | 988 | 277 | 11,903 + 988 − 277 = | 12,614 | | |
| 5 | 1,142 | 13,757 + 1,142 = | 14,899 | | 1,047 | 293 | 12,614 + 1,047 − 293 = | 13,368 | | |
| 10 | — | — + — = | 22,197 | | — | — | — + — − — = | 17,868 | | |
| 20 | — | — + — = | 49,268 | | — | — | — + — − — = | 31,926 | | |
| 30 | — | — + — = | 109,359 | | — | — | — + — − — = | 57,046 | | |

*Assumptions: (1) Each investment earns 8.3 percent a year and (2) the investor is in the 28 percent tax bracket.

If the $10,000 had been placed in a taxable investment at 8.3 percent interest, the accumulated amount would have been substantially less. If you were in the 28 percent bracket, you would have accumulated only $13,368 at the end of 5 years, $17,868 at the end of 10 years, and $57,046 at the end of 30 years. The tax savings, coupled with more interest to compound, allows an additional capital buildup of more than $50,000 over 30 years. Of course, you must pay the taxes on the interest from the annuity once the payout begins. But even so, you have gained considerably through the tax deferral feature; and the benefits are even greater for someone in the graduated phaseout range paying 33 percent taxes.

## DEFERRED ANNUITIES AND RETIREMENT PLANS

Many investors tie the purchase of deferred annuities to their overall retirement plans. Recall from the discussion in Chapter 3 that Keogh plans and Individual Retirement Accounts (IRAs) are partial substitutes for deferred annuities and therefore should be evaluated with them. If you are not fully using your allowable IRA exclusion each year, you may prefer adding to it rather than purchasing a tax-deferred annuity; far greater benefit will result from deducting the full allowable IRA payment from your taxable income. Unless you're in one of the qualified professional fields we mentioned earlier, you cannot deduct the annuity's purchase price—you can only defer earned income.

While both IRA and deferred annuity withdrawals prior to age 59½ are subject to a 10 percent additional tax, income withdrawn from a deferred annuity will also be taxed in the year it is withdrawn. Moreover, any annuity withdrawal is first viewed for tax purposes as income; once all income is withdrawn, subsequent withdrawals are treated as a return of principal, so any partial withdrawal will most likely be fully taxable.

## SINGLE-PREMIUM LIFE INSURANCE (SPLI): A POPULAR ALTERNATIVE

Since 1982, tax legislation, including the Tax Reform Act of 1986, has reduced the tax shelter appeal of single-premium deferred annuities (SPDAs). Currently, a 10 percent federal tax penalty is charged on withdrawals made prior to age 59½, regardless of how long the annuity has been held. In addition, most insurers charge withdrawal penalties—typically on withdrawals of 10 percent or more made during the first 7 to 10 years. Clearly these restrictions limit the tax-shelter appeal of SPDAs.

Consequently, single-premium life insurance (SPLI) policies have become a popular alternative investment vehicle. In addition to offering all the features of SPDAs, these policies provide a mechanism for making tax-sheltered withdrawals prior to age 59½. Typically the policyholder pays a large premium, often $15,000 or more, to purchase a whole life policy providing a stated death benefit and earning a competitive interest rate on the cash value buildup. As with any whole life policy, the policyholder can cancel the policy and withdraw its cash value at any time. In such a case, taxes would be due on any gains above the amount originally invested. The most attractive feature of SPLI policies is the opportunity to make tax-free cash withdrawals at any time by means of a policy loan. These loans typically have a low contractual interest rate, most commonly in the range of 6 to 9 percent. Because they are tax-free, they are less costly than the taxable penalized withdrawals from SPDAs. Note that if the funds used to purchase an SPLI policy are obtained through borrowing, the interest paid on them is not deductible; nor is the interest paid on any loans for which the policy is used as collateral.

Single-premium life insurance comes in two different forms:

- *Single-premium whole life* offers you no investment choices. In 1987, most insurance companies offered guaranteed rates of 4 percent. Any return above that varies depending upon investment return. In the same year, returns of 8 to 9 percent before commissions were common.

- *Single-premium variable life* gives you the choice of investing in stocks, bonds, and money market portfolios and the option of switching from one to the other. Your return moves up and down with investment performance.

Currently (late 1987) insurance companies are offering attractive interest (earnings) rates on SPLI policies. Frequently these rates are guaranteed if you hold the policy for 7 to 10 years and are significantly reduced if you hold the policy for shorter periods. Alternatively, some insurers levy a cancellation penalty that declines with the passage of time.

Critics of SPLI point out that although the tax-shelter features of these policies are attractive, the rate of return on investment is frequently below the return on tax-exempt municipals, and their value as life insurance is not as great as that available from term insurance. In spite of these negative features, single-premium life insurance is believed by many to represent one of the remaining attractive vehicles for tax shelter. Until the IRS acts on SPLI policies (which seems likely to happen), they appear to offer an attractive vehicle for achieving a tax-deferred buildup of value while obtaining life insurance protection and the opportunity to make tax-free withdrawals using policy loans.

# 25

# OPTIONS:
# THE POWER OF LEVERAGE
# SWEETENS THE POT

---

When you buy shares of common or preferred stock, you become the registered owner of the securities and are entitled to all the rights and privileges of ownership. Similarly, if you buy bonds or convertibles, you are also entitled to the benefits of ownership. But *options* are another matter altogether, for when you buy them, you acquire nothing more than the right to subsequently buy or sell other securities at specified prices for specified periods of time.

Starting in the 1970s, huge numbers of investors discovered a new investment vehicle—put and call options on common stock. By the early 1980s, this interest spilled over to other kinds of financial assets and was a major factor behind the development of interest rate, currency, index, and futures options. Not surprisingly, much of the popularity of the options market stems from leverage: investors quickly discovered that options enabled them to buy a lot of price action with a limited amount of capital and, at the same time, nearly always enjoy limited exposure to risk.

# WHAT ARE PUTS AND CALLS?

Puts and calls are negotiable instruments issued in bearer form that allow the holder to buy or sell a specified amount of a specified security at a specified price during a specified time period. A single stock option always involves 100 shares of stock. One *put* enables the holder to *sell* 100 shares of the underlying securities; one *call* gives the holder the right to *buy* 100 shares of the securities. Puts and calls possess value to the extent that they allow you to participate in the price behavior of the underlying financial asset. As with any option, there is no interest or dividend income, no voting rights, and no privileges of ownership.

Most puts and calls are traded on listed exchanges and, on a much smaller scale, in the over-the-counter market. They provide attractive leverage opportunities because they carry relatively low prices—at least relative to the market price of the underlying financial assets. To illustrate, consider a call on a common stock that gives you the right to buy 100 shares of a $50 stock at a price of, say, $45 a share. The stock would be priced at $50, but the call would trade at an effective price of only $5 a share (or the difference between the market price of the common stock and the price specified on the call). The actual market price of your $5 call would be $500: ($5 × 100 shares = $500). In a similar fashion, if the price of the underlying stock rose by $10 a share, the value of the call would go up 100 times that amount, or $1,000.

## INVESTORS CREATE THESE INSTRUMENTS

Puts and calls are a unique type of security since they are not issued by the corporations that issue the underlying stocks and bonds. Instead, puts and calls *are created by investors.* The system works like this: Suppose Sam Jones wants to sell to Bob Smith the right to buy 100 shares of common stock. Sam will *write* a call—the individual or institution writing the option is known as the *option maker* or *writer.* The maker who writes (and sells) an option is entitled to receive the price paid for the put or call (less modest commissions and other transaction costs). The person or institution buying the call, Bob in this case, is known as the *option buyer* or *holder.* The buyer is the only one who has the right to exercise the option.

After the transaction between the option writer (Sam) and the buyer (Bob) is completed, the put or call becomes a full-fledged financial asset and trades in the open market much like any other security. Puts and calls are written and purchased through security brokers and dealers, and they are actively traded in the secondary market. The writer stands behind the option at all times, regardless of how many times the security has been traded or who the current owners are, for it is the *writer* who must buy or deliver the stock or other financial asset according to the terms of the option.

Investors buy calls when they think the price of the underlying stock is going to rise; they buy puts if they think the price of the underlying stock will fall. Put and call option writers, of course, are betting just the opposite. They write calls if they don't believe the price of the stock is going to move up, and they write puts in the belief that the price of the stock is not about to fall. For their efforts, the option writers get to pocket a big chunk of the commissions paid by the buyers at the time of the transaction.

Actually, the motives for writing options are far more complex than this; some of the principal reasons are explained later in the chapter. For now, suffice it to say that writing (selling) options can be extremely profitable, since, more often than not, options expire unexercised. But when they do hit, they usually hit big. As a result, investors are lured to the buy side of these securities by the profits they offer as well as their low-cost speculative nature. In essence, buyers of puts and calls are willing to invest their capital in return for the right to participate in the future price performance of the underlying security at a low unit cost and with limited exposure to risk.

## HOW PUTS AND CALLS WORK

We'll take the buyer's point of view to see how puts and calls work and how they derive their value, focusing on what interests investors the most—the profit-making potential of these securities.

*Calls.* Using stock options as the basis for our discussion, consider a stock currently priced at $50 a share. Assume you can buy a call on the stock for $500, which enables you to purchase 100 shares of the stock at a fixed price of $50 each. A rise in the price of the underlying security—the common stock—is what you hope for. If the price of the stock moves up to, say, $75 a share by the expiration date on the call, you earn $25 ($75 − $50) on each of the 100 shares of stock in the call and walk away with approximately $2,500—all from an investment of only $500. Your profit is based on the fact that you can buy 100 shares of the stock—from the option writer—at a price of $50 each and immediately turn around and sell them in the market for $75 a share.

Although you could have made the same profit by investing directly in the common stock, your rate of return would have been much lower. If you bought the stock, your total investment would be $5,000 (100 shares × $50 a share)—10 times more than the option price. It is this considerable difference in profit potential between common stocks and calls that attracts investors and speculators to calls whenever the price outlook for the underlying financial asset is strong.

*Puts.* Let's assume this time that you could pay $500 for a put to sell 100 shares of the stock at $50 each. In this case, you hope that the price of the stock drops. If you are correct and the price drops to, say, $25 a share, you will earn $25 for each of the 100 shares covered by the put. You could do this by going into the market and buying 100 shares of the stock at a price of $25 a share and immediately turning around and selling them to the writer of the put at the agreed-upon price of $50 a share.

Fortunately, put and call investors do not have to exercise these options and make simultaneous buy and sell transactions in order to collect their profit, since options have a value of their own and, as such, can be traded in the secondary market. The value of puts and calls is directly linked to the market price of the underlying financial asset. That is, the value of calls increases as the market price of the underlying security rises, while the value of puts increases as the price of the security declines. Thus, you can get your money out of options by simply selling them in the open market, just as you would any other security.

## WHERE OPTIONS ARE TRADED

Before April 26, 1973, when the Chicago Board Options Exchange (CBOE) was created, options trading was a fairly small, largely unorganized activity that was strictly over-the-counter and almost completely the private domain of a handful of sophisticated traders. Investors who wished to purchase puts and calls dealt with these options dealers via their own brokers, and the dealers would find individuals or institutions willing to write the options. When buyers wished to exercise an option, they did so with the option writer and no one else. Although this system largely prohibited trading in the secondary market, there were virtually no limits on what could be written, as long as the buyer was willing to pay the price. Put and call options were written on listed stocks as well as on stocks trading over-the-counter and for as little as thirty days or as long as a year. Over-the-counter options, known today as *conventional options,* were hard hit by the creation of the CBOE and other options exchanges. Although the conventional market still exists today, its operations—and importance—have been greatly reduced.

The creation of the CBOE marked the first time in American capital market history that stock options were traded on listed exchanges. It marked the birth of so-called *listed options,* a term used to denote put and call options traded on organized exchanges as opposed to conventional options traded in the over-the-counter market.

The first listed options traded on the CBOE included calls on just 16 stocks. Within a relatively short time, however, a large and very active market for listed options developed. Today, both put and call options are traded on five exchanges: the Chicago Board Options Exchange, the largest options exchange; the American Stock Exchange; the New York Stock Exchange; the Philadelphia Exchange; and the Pacific Stock Exchange. There are now over 400 stock options traded on these exchanges, most of which are on such NYSE stocks as Delta Airlines, Exxon, CBS, Motorola, and Sears. Options on several dozen OTC stocks are also traded, including Apple Computer, Intel, Liz Claiborne, and MCI.

The listed options exchanges have not only provided a convenient market for the trading of puts and calls, they have also standardized expiration dates and options prices. The exchanges created a clearinghouse that eliminated direct ties between buyers and writers of options and reduced the cost of executing put and call transactions. They also developed an active secondary market offering investors readily available price information. As a result, it is now as easy to trade a listed option as a listed stock.

The advent of the listed options exchanges had a quick and dramatic impact on the trading volume of puts and calls. As the following figure shows, the level of activity in listed stock options grew rapidly between 1973 and 1985. It took only eight short years for the annual volume of contracts traded to surpass the 100 million mark. By 1985, the volume rose to nearly 120 million contracts involving almost 12 billion shares of stock. (As noted earlier, each option contract covers 100 shares of the underlying common stock.) This figure equaled 43 percent of all the shares traded on the NYSE in 1985. As a rule, calls are far more popular than puts: about 70 percent of the contract volume is in calls, and the balance is in puts.

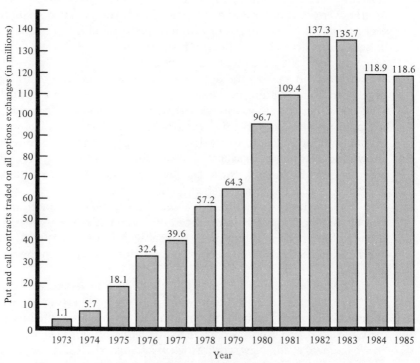

*Source:* Data compiled by the Chicago Board Options Exchange.

## GETTING A GRIP ON STOCK OPTIONS

There is so much money to be made with stock options that you may be tempted to jump into this investment before you've learned the basics. Don't do it. Stock options are far too complicated for casual investing. In order to use these investments correctly and avoid serious—and potentially expensive—mistakes, you've got to fully understand what you're doing.

Stock options—or *equity options* as they are also called—are the most popular type of option, accounting for over half of all option market activity. Except for the underlying financial asset, stock options have the same provisions as other kinds of puts and calls. In particular, there are three major provisions you should be aware of: (1) the price at which the stock can be bought or sold (the striking price), (2) the amount of time remaining until expiration (the expiration date), and (3) the purchase price of the option itself (the premium).

## STRIKING PRICE

The striking price represents the price contract between the buyer of the option and the writer. For a call, the striking price specifies the price at which each of the 100 shares of stock can be bought; for a put, it represents the price at which the option holder may sell the stock to the writer. The striking price is also known as the *exercise price*. With conventional options (those that trade over-the-counter), there are no constraints on what the striking price must be, although it is usually specified at or near the market price of the stock at the time the option is written. With listed options, however, the striking prices are standardized: Stocks selling for less than $25 carry striking prices that are set in $2½ increments ($7.50, $10, $12.50, $15, etc.). The increment jumps to $5 for stocks selling between $25 and $200 a share, and to $10 for stocks that trade at prices in excess of $200 a share. The striking price of both conventional and listed options is adjusted for substantial stock dividends and stock splits.

## EXPIRATION DATE

The expiration date specifies the life of the option much the same way as the maturity date indicates the life of a bond. The expiration date, in effect, specifies the length of the contract between the holder and the writer of the option. Thus, if you hold a 6-month call on Sears, that option gives you the right to buy 100 shares of Sears common stock at a striking price of, say, $40 a share at any time over the next 6 months. No matter what happens to the market price of the stock, you can use your call option to buy 100 shares of Sears at $40 a share for the next 6 months. If the price moves up, you stand to make money; if it goes down, you'll be out the cost of the option.

Expiration dates for options in the conventional market can fall on any working day of the month. Expiration dates are standardized in the listed options market. The exchanges have created three expiration cycles for all listed options, and assigned each issue to one of the cycles. The first cycle is January, April, July, and October; the second is February, May, August, and November; and the third is March, June, September, and December. Prices are quoted for only three of the four maturities, with the expiration dates rolling over every 3 months. For example, the January, April, and July expiration dates are quoted until the January options expire. Then the April, July, and October dates are used. (Recently the exchanges started also listing the two nearest interim months in each cycle; thus in the January cycle for instance, trading can now occur in November and December options, as well as January, April, and July.) Options can be bought, sold, or written for any of the expiration dates currently outstanding. Since no transaction can take place in the fourth (unlisted) expiration date of a cycle, 9 months is the longest option on the listed exchanges. No matter what the month of expiration, the actual day of expiration is always the same: the Saturday following the third Friday of each expiration month. Thus, for all practical purposes, all listed options expire the third Friday of the month of expiration.

## PREMIUM

The purchase price of an option is known as the premium. It represents the cost of the option and the price the buyer must pay to the writer (or seller) in order to acquire it. The size of the option premium is obviously important to buyers, writers, and sellers. One factor that affects the size of option premiums is the current market price of the underlying stock: the greater the difference between the price of the stock and the striking price on the option, the greater the value of the put or call. Another factor is the length of time until the expiration date of the option; the longer the time until expiration, the greater the size of the premium. Still another is the volatility of the underlying security, which can enhance or detract from the speculative appeal of the option. Other, less important, variables include the dividend yield of the underlying stock, the trading volume of the option, and the exchange on which the option is listed.

---

# MEASURING THE VALUE OF PUTS AND CALLS

While the quoted market price (premium) of a put or call is affected by such factors as time to expiration, stock volatility, market interest rates, and supply and demand, by far the most important variable is the market price behavior of the underlying common stock. This variable moves the price of the option and determines, to a large extent, the profit potential of an option: when the underlying stock moves up in price, calls do well; when the price of the stock drops, puts do well. This relationship explains why stock selection is so important to success. So before you buy or write an option, spend some time researching the stock that underlies the option in order to get a handle on its future price behavior—and that of the option.

## RELATION TO PRICE OF SECURITY

The typical price behavior of a stock option is illustrated in the figure on the next page. The diagram on the left depicts a call, the one on the right a put. The assumption behind the call diagram is that you pay $500 for a call that carries an

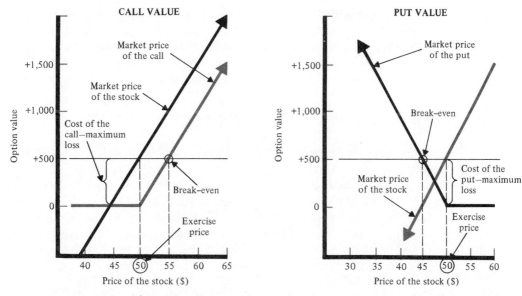

CALL VALUE

PUT VALUE

exercise price of $50. The diagram shows what happens to the value of the option when the price of the stock increases. Observe that the call does not gain in value until the price of the stock advances past the stated exercise price of $50. Also, since it costs $500 to buy the call, the stock has to move another 5 points—from $50 to $55—just to recover the premium and break even. Once the premium is recouped by the purchaser, the profit from the call is limited only by increases in the stock price over the remaining life of the contract.

The put diagram assumes you can buy a put for $500 and obtain the right to sell the underlying stock at $50 a share. The diagram shows what happens when the price of the stock falls. In this case, the market price of the stock and the value of the put move in opposite directions. Again, the value of the put remains constant until the market price of the stock drops to the exercise price ($50) on the put. Then, as the price of the stock continues to fall, the value of the option increases accordingly. Note once again that, since the put costs $500, you do not start making money until the price of the stock drops below the break-even point of $45 a share. At this point, the profit from the put is defined by the extent to which the price of the underlying stock continues to fall over the remaining life of the option.

## FORMULAS FOR MEASURING VALUE

As we have seen, the value of a put or call ultimately depends on the striking price stated on the option and the prevailing market price of the underlying common stock. More specifically, the value of a call is determined by the following formula:

$$\text{value of a call} = \left( \begin{array}{c} \text{market price of} \\ \text{underlying} \\ \text{common stock} \end{array} - \begin{array}{c} \text{striking price} \\ \text{on} \\ \text{the call} \end{array} \right) \times 100$$

In other words, the value of a call is nothing more than the difference between the market price of the stock and the striking price on the call. For example, a call carrying a striking price of $50 on a stock presently trading at $60 has a value of $1,000 [($60 − $50) × 100 = $10 × 100 = $1,000]. To find the value of a put, reverse the order of the equation so that you have:

$$\text{value of a put} = \left(\begin{array}{ccc}\text{striking price} & & \text{market price of} \\ \text{on the} & - & \text{underlying} \\ \text{put} & & \text{common stock}\end{array}\right) \times 100$$

Thus, if the striking price is $30 and the market price of the stock is $25, the value of the put is $500 [($30 − $25) × 100 = 5 × 100 = $500].

The put and call values determined by these formulas indicate what these options should be valued at—not their actual prices. These securities almost always trade at prices higher than their true value, especially if they still have a long time to run. This difference is known as the *investment premium* and indicates the amount of *water*, or excess value, embedded in the quoted price of the put or call. The investment premium can be found in the following way:

$$\text{investment premium} = \frac{\text{option premium} - \text{value of the option}}{\text{value of the option}}$$

For example, if a put has a value of $2,000 and carries a price (option premium) of $2,200, the investment premium is 10 percent [($2,200 − $2,000)/$2,000 = $200/$2,000 = .10]. Many of the same factors that affect option premium also affect investment premium: that is, investment premiums tend to increase for longer options and for options on highly volatile stock. Unless you can recover this premium when you sell the option, it is a *sunk cost*; that is, it is lost for good.

## IN-THE-MONEY AND OUT-OF-THE-MONEY OPTIONS

When written, options do not necessarily have to carry striking prices at the prevailing market price of the underlying common stock. And as options subsequently trade on the listed exchanges, the price of the option will move in response to moves in the price of the underlying common stock. When a call has a striking price that is less than the market price of the underlying common stock, it has a positive value and is known as an *in-the-money* option. A major portion of the option premium is then based on (or derived from) the true value of the call. When the striking price exceeds the market price of the stock, the call has no real value and is known as an *out-of-the-money* option. Its price is then made up solely of investment premium. A put option is in-the-money when its striking price is greater than the market price of the stock; it is out-of-the-money when the market price of the stock exceeds the striking price. These terms are much more than convenient, exotic names given to options, for as you will see next, they characterize the investment behavior of options and affect both return and risk.

# TRADING STRATEGIES

There are three basic strategies for trading in stock options: (1) trading for speculation, (2) hedging, and (3) option writing and spreading.

## TRADING FOR SPECULATION

This is the simplest and most straightforward use of puts and calls. Basically, it's the same strategy you use when you buy stock (buy low and sell high) and, in fact, it represents an alternative to investing in stock. For example, if you feel the market price of a stock is going to move up, you can earn capital gains by buying a call on the stock. In contrast, if you feel the stock is about to drop in price, you can convert the price decline into a profit by buying a put. The reason for buying options rather than stock is that options are often likely to yield a greater return because of the leverage they offer.

For example, suppose you find a stock you expect to move up in price over the next 6 months and you want to capitalize on the gain. You can do this in two ways: you can buy the common stock itself or a call on the stock. To find out which is better, you begin working with the numbers to determine the relative return on each investment.

Assume the price of the stock is now $49 and you anticipate that within 6 months it will climb to about $65. If your expectations about the stock are correct, its 16-point rise will provide you with a 33 percent holding period return [($65 − $49)/$49 = $16/$49 = .33]. If, on the other hand, you decide to buy a call on the stock, you can do considerably better. The table at the top of the next page shows how much you would earn if you bought calls with $40 and $50 striking prices. Clearly, either call option represents a superior investment to buying the stock. For example, according to the table, you can buy the $50 call for $400 and sell it some 6 months later for $1,500, earning a profit of $1,100 on the deal. Although the dollar amount of profit may be a bit more with the stock, the size of the required investment ($4,900) is also a lot more.

Observe that the $40 call is in-the-money (less than the market price of the stock) and the $50 call is out-of-the-money (more than the price of the stock). The difference in returns generated by these calls is rather typical. Investors are usually able to generate better rates of return with out-of-the-money options and also enjoy less exposure to loss, because they cost less than in-the-money options. Of course, the major drawback of out-of-the-money options is that their price is made up wholly of investment premium—a sunk cost which will be lost if the stock does not move in price.

To see how you can speculate in puts, consider the following situation: Assume that the price of your stock is now $51, but this time you anticipate a drop in price to about $35 within the next 6 months. If that occurs, then you could short sell the

## SPECULATING WITH CALL OPTIONS

| | 100 Shares of Underlying Common Stock | 6-MONTH CALL OPTIONS ON THE STOCK | |
|---|---|---|---|
| | | $40 Striking Price | $50 Striking Price |
| **TODAY** | | | |
| Market value of stock (at $49/sh.) | $4,900 | | |
| Market price of calls* | | $1,100 | $ 400 |
| **6 MONTHS LATER** | | | |
| Expected value of stock (at $65/sh.) | $6,500 | | |
| Expected price of calls* | | $2,500 | $1,500 |
| Profit | $1,600 | $1,400 | $1,100 |
| Holding period return | 33% | 127% | 275% |

*The price of the calls was computed according to the call valuation formula and includes some investment premium in the purchase price of the calls, but *none* in the expected sales price.

stock and make a profit of $16 per share (see Chapter 10 for a discussion of short selling). Alternatively, an out-of-the-money put (with a striking price of $50) can be purchased for, say, $300. Again, if the price of the underlying stock does indeed drop, you will make money with the put. The profit and rate of return on the put are summarized below, along with the comparative returns from short selling the stock:

| | Buy 1 Put | Short Sell 100 Shares of Stock |
|---|---|---|
| Purchase price (today) | $ 300 | |
| Selling price (6 months later) | 1,500 | |
| Short sell (today) | | $5,100 |
| Cover (6 months later) | | 3,500 |
| Profit | $1,200 | $1,600 |
| Holding period return | 400% | 63%* |

*Assumes the short sale was made with a required margin deposit of 50 percent.

As you can see, the stock option once more is the superior investment vehicle—by a wide margin. Of course, not all option investments end up nearly as well as the ones in our examples, for success in this strategy rests on picking the right underlying common stock. Security analysis and proper stock selection are critical dimensions of this technique. Trading options is a highly risky investment strategy, but it may be well suited for speculative investors.

## HEDGING

A hedge is nothing more than a combination of two or more securities that are put into a single investment position for the purpose of reducing risk. This strategy might involve, for example, buying stock and simultaneously buying a put on that stock or buying stock and then writing a call. There are many types of hedges, some very sophisticated, some very simple; but they all are used as a way to earn or protect a profit, or limit potential loss.

For example, an options hedge may be appropriate if you have generated a profit from an earlier common stock investment and want to protect that profit, or if you are about to invest in a common stock and want to protect your capital by limiting your potential loss. If you hold a stock that has gone up in price, a put would provide the type of downside protection you need. A call, on the other hand, protects short sellers. Thus, option hedging always involves two transactions: the initial common stock position (long or short) and the simultaneous or subsequent purchase of the option.

Let's examine a simple options hedge to see how a put can be used to limit capital loss or protect profit. Say you want to buy 100 shares of stock even though you are a bit apprehensive about the stock's future outlook. To protect your position, you also buy a put on the stock, which fully covers the 100 shares you own. Preferably, the put is a low-priced option with a striking price at or near the current market price of the stock: suppose you purchase the common at $25 and pay $150 for a put with a $25 striking price. Now, no matter what happens to the price of the stock (over the life of the put), you can lose no more than $150, or the price of the put. At the same time, the gains are almost unlimited. If the stock does not move, you will be out the cost of the put. If it drops in price, then whatever you lose on the stock you will make up with the put. However, if the price of the stock goes up (as hoped), the put becomes useless, and you'll rake in the capital gains from the stock. The essentials of this option hedge are shown in the table on the next page. Note that the $150 paid for the put is lost no matter what happens to the price of the stock; in effect, it is the price paid for the hedge. Moreover, this hedge is good only for as long as you hold the put. When this put expires, you must replace it with another one to protect your position.

You can also enter into an options hedge after you've made a profit on the stock. You might do this because of investment uncertainty or for tax purposes—if, for example, you want to carry over a profit to the next taxable year. For example, if you buy 100 shares of stock at $35 and it moves to $75, you have a $40 a share profit to protect. You can do this by buying a 3-month put with a $75 striking price at a cost of, say, $250. Now, regardless of what happens to the price of the stock over the life of the put, you are guaranteed a minimum profit of $3,750 (the $4,000 profit you've made in the stock so far less the $250 cost of the put). This is shown in the table on page 313. Notice that if the price of the stock falls, the worst that can happen is that you walk away with a profit of $3,750. On the flip side, there is no limit to how much you can earn. As long as the stock rises, your profit will rise too.

## LIMITING CAPITAL LOSS WITH A PUT HEDGE

|  |  |  | Stock | Put |
|---|---|---|---|---|
| **TODAY** |  |  |  |  |
| Purchase price of the stock |  |  | $25 |  |
| Purchase price of the put (purchased simultaneously, with a striking price of $25) |  |  |  | $ 150 |
| **SOME TIME LATER** |  |  |  |  |
| A. Price of common goes *up* to: |  |  | $50 |  |
|    Value of put |  |  |  | $ 0 |
|    Profit: |  |  |  |  |
|      100 shares of stock ($50 − $25) |  | $2,500 |  |  |
|      Less: Cost of put |  | − 150 |  |  |
|       | Profit: | $2,350 |  |  |
| B. Price of common goes *down* to: |  |  | $10 |  |
|    Value of put (see put valuation formula) |  |  |  | $1,500 |
|    Profit: |  |  |  |  |
|      100 shares of stock (loss) |  | −$1,500 |  |  |
|      Value of put (profit) |  | + 1,500 |  |  |
|      Less: Cost of put |  | − 150 |  |  |
|       | Loss: | $ 150 |  |  |

While we've focused our discussion on put hedges, it should be clear that call hedges can also be used to limit a loss or protect a profit on a short sale. Essentially, when you sell a stock short, you can purchase a call to protect you against a rise in the stock price—with the same basic results outlined above.

## OPTION WRITING AND SPREADING

The advent of listed options has led to many intriguing options trading strategies. In spite of the appeal of these exotic techniques, there is one important point that all the experts agree on: *such specialized trading strategies should be left to experienced investors who fully understand their subtleties.* Our goal at this point is not to master these specialized strategies, but to learn in general terms what they are and how they operate. There are two main types of specialized options strategies: (1) writing options, and (2) spreading options.

*Option writing.*    Generally, investors write (that is, sell) options because they expect the price of the underlying stock to move in their favor: that is, not to rise as much as the buyer of a call expects or to fall as much as the buyer of a put hopes. More often than not, the option writer is correct—option writers make money far more often than buyers. These favorable odds explain, in part, the underlying

# PROTECTING PROFITS WITH A PUT HEDGE

|  | | Stock | 3-month Put with a $75 Striking Price |
|---|---|---|---|
| Purchase price of the stock (some time ago) | | $35 | |
| **TODAY** | | | |
| Market price of the stock | | $75 | |
| Market price of the put | | | $ 250 |
| **3 MONTHS LATER** | | | |
| A. Price of common keeps going *up* to: | | $100 | |
| Value of put | | | $ 0 |
| Profit: | | | |
| 100 shares of stock ($100 − $35) | $ 6,500 | | |
| Less: Cost of put | − 250 | | |
| Profit: | $ 6,250 | | |
| B. Price of common goes *down* to: | | $50 | |
| Value of put (see put valuation formula) | | | $2,500 |
| Profit: | | | |
| 100 shares of stock ($50 − $35) | $ 1,500 | | |
| Value of put (profit) | 2,500 | | |
| Less: Cost of put | − 250 | | |
| Profit: | $ 3,750 | | |

economic motivation for writing put and call options. Options writing represents an investment transaction to the writers, since they receive the option premium (less normal transaction costs) in exchange for agreeing to live up to the terms of the option.

You can write options in one of two ways. One is to write *naked options,* which involves writing options on stock you do not own. In this case, you write the put or call, collect the option premium, and hope the price of the underlying stock does not move against you. If successful, naked writing can be highly profitable because of the very modest amount of capital required. Keep in mind also that the amount of return to the writer is always limited to the amount of option premium received. Yet there is really no limit to the loss, which is the catch. The reason is that sooner or later, you have to cover your position. In the options market, this is almost always done by offsetting one options transaction with another rather than dealing in the underlying security. Thus, when you sell an option, that position is closed out by buying the option back. If you write a call and the price of the stock goes down (that is, falls below its striking price), you don't have to do a thing since the call buyer will not exercise a worthless option. In contrast, if the price of the stock goes up, the call will be worth something (perhaps a lot of money) and you'll have to buy it back to cover your position. As a result, you may end up having to pay a lot more to buy the option back than you received for it to begin with. And the more the stock rises in price, the bigger your potential loss becomes.

You can partially offset this risk by writing *covered options*; that is, writing options against stocks you already own or, in the case of a short sale, have a position in. For example, you might write a call against stock you own or a put against stock you have sold short. In this way, you can use the long or short position to meet the terms of the option. This strategy represents a fairly conservative way to generate attractive rates of return. The object is to write a slightly out-of-the-money option, pocket the option premium, and hope that the price of the underlying stock will move up or down to—but not in excess of—the option striking price. In effect, you are adding the option premium to the other usual sources of return that accompany stock ownership or short sales (dividends and capital gains), while at the same time reducing your risk.

There is a hitch to this, however. If the stock exceeds the striking price by a large enough margin to cover the option premium, be prepared for an option call. That is, if you write a call, be prepared to buy back the call, at a loss to you, or surrender your stock to the option holder. For example, say that in December you own 300 shares of a stock priced at $28 a share. You write calls with April expiration dates and striking prices of $35 a share and collect a premium of $400 on each of the three calls you write. If the stock climbs above 35, say to 38, by April, the stock will probably be called, leaving you in the comfortable position of collecting $35 a share plus $1,200 in option premiums. One of the dangers of this strategy is that you won't partake in any windfall if the stock continues to rise. If, for example, your $28-a-share stock climbs to $60 by April on news of a takeover bid, you'll have to be content with collecting $35 a share plus the option premiums—unless you buy back the options, which now cost more than you originally paid. The logic is clear: if the stock is now at 45 and climbing, investors are willing to pay a great deal more for the option of buying the stock at 35—10 points less than it is now—than they were when the stock was at 28, with no way of knowing it would rise.

If the stock moves against you during the option period, the covered call will reduce at least part of your loss. For example, if instead of moving up, your $28 stock drops to $22, your real loss is $200 for each 100 shares you own rather than $600, since the $400 you received when you wrote the call will cushion the blow.

On the whole, covered calls are an extremely conservative investment that guarantees you a healthy profit if the stock moves in your favor and, at the same time, protects you from loss if the stock moves against you. A word of caution: do not write covered calls unless you are prepared to sell your stock.

*Options spreads.* In an options spread, you combine two or more options with different striking prices and/or expiration dates into a single transaction. The spread is the difference between them. Spreads account for a substantial amount of the trading activity on the listed options exchanges. They go by a variety of exotic names, such as *bull spreads, bear spreads, money spreads, calendar spreads,* and *butterfly spreads.* Each is constructed to meet a certain type of investment goal. For example, bull spreads are used with call options when prices are moving up as a way to capture the benefits of a rising market. Others are used to profit from a falling market, and still others to try to make money when the price of the underlying stock goes up *or* down! Whatever the objective, most spreads are written to take advantage of differences in prevailing option premiums. The payoff from spreading is usually substantial, but so is the risk. In fact, some spreads that seem to involve almost no risk may end up with devastating results if the market (and the spread between option premiums) moves against you.

One variation of this theme involves *option straddles*, the simultaneous purchase of a put and a call on the same underlying common stock. Unlike spreads, straddles often involve the same striking price and expiration date. Here the object is to earn a profit from a modest increase or decrease in the price of the underlying stock. Otherwise, the principles of straddles are much like those of spreads: to build an investment position with combinations of options that will enable you to capture the benefits of certain types of stock price behavior. But keep in mind that if the price of the underlying stock and/or the option premiums do not behave in the anticipated manner, you lose. Spreads and straddles are extremely tricky and should not be used by novice investors.

## THE SCORE CARD ON PUTS AND CALLS

Leverage is the primary reason for the popularity of puts and calls. For a limited investment, you can earn what is at times a spectacular return. While you're doing this, your risk is relatively small. If, for example, the stock moves against your option position, you can only lose the purchase price of the option.

However, when you write a call, be prepared to lose the stock if the underlying stock rises above the call price. Although you'll collect the call premium and sell the stock at the strike price, you will not be able to collect the profit on any further rise in the price of the stock. Similarly when you write a put and the stock drops below the striking price, the stock will be *put to you;* that is, you'll have to come up with enough cash to buy the stock, even if you don't want to own it. The option premium, which you keep as long as you do not trade the option, will help offset the cost.

Despite their cost and their tie to an underlying stock, options do not give you any ownership rights. That is, you'll collect no dividend income and have no voting rights. Moreover, if you're going to make money on the option, you have a limited time in which to do it.

On the whole, puts and calls are extremely complicated investments that require a great deal of specialized knowledge and considerable time. If you lack either, don't invest.

# A COUPLE OF OTHER STOCK OPTIONS YOU SHOULD KNOW ABOUT

In addition to puts and calls, there are two other types of options you should be aware of. One is a right; the other is a warrant. Both are linked primarily to the common stock of the issuing company. Rights have short market lives and generally hold little investment appeal. Warrants, in contrast, have very long lives and offer investors a chance to generate some very attractive rates of return.

## KNOW YOUR RIGHTS

A *right* is a special type of option that usually exists for no more than several weeks. Rights are associated with new common stock issues. That is, rights originate when corporations want to raise money by issuing additional shares of common. In effect, they are the vehicle through which the company will issue the new shares of common stock. From your perspective as a stockholder, a right enables you to buy shares of the new issue at a specified price, over a specified (but fairly short) period of time. Although not specifically designed for speculation or for trading, *rights do have value* and, as a result, should never be lightly discarded. Instead, unwanted rights should always be sold in the open market.

Let's say a firm has 1 million shares of common stock outstanding and that it has decided to issue another 250,000 shares. This might well be done through a *rights offering* whereby the firm, rather than directly issuing the new shares of common, would issue stock rights to all the current stockholders instead. These rights could then be used by their holders to purchase the new issue of stock. This procedure would be followed when existing stockholders are given the right to maintain their proportionate share of ownership in a firm, a privilege known as a *preemptive right.* Since each stockholder receives, without charge by the issuing firm, one right for each share of stock currently owned, it would take, in our example, four rights to buy one new share of common (i.e., 1 million outstanding shares ÷ 250,000 new shares).

Because most stock rights allow their holders to purchase only a fractional share of the new common stock, two or more rights are usually needed to buy a single new share. The price of the new stock is spelled out in the right. This is known as the *exercise* (or *subscription*) *price,* and it is always set below the prevailing market price of the stock. For each new share of common stock you purchase, you are expected to redeem a specified number of rights and pay the stipulated subscription price in cash. Rights not used by their expiration date lose all value and simply cease to exist. Unfortunately, many investors allow their rights to expire, thus losing money they are entitled to.

Stock rights are quoted in the financial press just like common stock; they are listed just below the common and are identified with the initials *rt* after the name of the company. If you want to see what your rights are worth, just look up their quotes. If you want to exercise your rights (that is, you want to buy more stock in the company), just follow the instructions that come with the rights. If, however, you do not want to exercise your rights, then don't let them just expire. Rather, sell them in the secondary market through your broker. When the sale is complete, you'll receive a check (or your account will be credited) for the market value of these rights, less the brokerage commissions, of course.

## A PRIMER ON WARRANTS

A *warrant* is an option that enables you to buy a stipulated number of shares of common stock, at a stipulated price, within a stipulated time period. (Occasionally, warrants are issued on preferred stock or even bonds, but common stock is the leading redemption vehicle.) Warrants come into existence as "sweeteners" to bond issues. That is, as a way to make bonds more attractive, the issuing company will sometimes attach warrants to their bonds, thereby giving the issue an "equity kicker." Buyers of these bonds get a debt issue on the one hand and a warrant on the other.

With maturities that regularly extend to 5, 10, or even 20 years, warrants have the longest life span of all options. (Occasionally, they have no maturity date at all.) They give you the opportunity to participate indirectly in the market behavior of the common stock and generate some capital gains. Warrants have no voting rights, pay no dividends, and have no claim on the assets of the company. The only thing they offer you as an investor is *the opportunity to generate some capital gains.*

A single warrant usually enables you to buy one full share of stock, although some involve more than one share per warrant and a few deal in fractional shares. The life of a warrant is specified by its *expiration date,* and the stock purchase price stipulated on the warrant is known as the *exercise price.*

Warrants are issued by all types of corporations, ranging from the blue chips to speculative growth firms. Since warrants are considered a type of equity issue, they can be margined at the same rate as common stock. They are purchased through brokers and are subject to commission and transaction costs similar to those for common stock.

*How warrants work.* Three aspects of warrants that are particularly important include: (1) the issue's exercise price; (2) the value of a warrant; and (3) the amount of investment premium.

• *Exercise price* The exercise price is the price you must pay to buy a share of the underlying common stock. It is the share price paid to the firm when the warrant is "exercised." Although the exercise price usually remains fixed for the issue's full life, some warrants increase or decrease in value as the expiration date draws near. In addition, the exercise price is automatically adjusted for stock splits and major stock dividends. The table on the next page illustrates the features of some actively traded warrants.

| Issuer | Market Where Traded | Exercise Price | Expiration Date |
|---|---|---|---|
| Atlas Corp. | American | $31.25 | None |
| Charter Co. | New York | 10.00 | 9-1-88 |
| Golden Nugget | New York | 18.00 | 7-1-88 |
| International Banknote | American | 7.00 | 7-31-88 |
| McDermott International | New York | 25.00 | 4-1-90 |
| Pan Am | New York | 8.00 | 5-1-93 |
| American General | New York | 24.25 | 1-5-89 |
| Collins Food International | American | 12.11 | 12-15-88 |
| Digicon Inc. | American | 16.50 | 6-15-88 |
| First Central Financial | American | 3.50 | 4-15-90 |
| Geothermal Resources Int'l. | American | 13.50 | 11-15-91 |
| Keystone Camera Products | American | 7.50 | 5-7-91 |
| Federal Nat'l Mortgage | OTC | 44.25 | 2-25-91 |
| Eli Lilly | New York | 75.98 | 3-31-91 |
| Southwest Airlines | OTC | 35.00 | 6-25-90 |

All these warrants enable the holder to purchase *one* share of stock at the stated exercise price.

• **Value** Warrants have value whenever the market price of the underlying common stock exceeds the exercise price of the warrant. This value is determined in the following way:

$$\text{value of a warrant} = \left( \begin{array}{c} \text{prevailing market price} \\ \text{of the common stock} \end{array} - \text{exercise price} \right) \times \begin{array}{c} \text{number of shares of stock} \\ \text{that can be acquired with 1 warrant} \end{array}$$

For example, consider a warrant that carries an exercise price of $40 per share and enables the holder to purchase one share of stock per warrant. If the common stock has a current market price of $50 a share, then the warrants would be valued at $10 each:

$$\text{value of a warrant} = (\$50 - \$40) \times 1 = (\$10) \times 1 = \$10$$

Obviously, the greater the spread in the market and exercise prices, the greater the market value of a warrant. In addition, as long as the market price of the stock exceeds the exercise price, the value of a warrant will be directly linked to the price behavior of the common stock.

• **Premium** Our formula indicates what the value of warrants *should be*, but they are seldom priced exactly that way in the marketplace. Instead, the market price of a warrant invariably exceeds its computed value. This happens when warrants with negative values trade at prices greater than zero. It also occurs when warrants with positive values trade at even higher market prices; for example, when a $10 warrant trades at $15. This discrepancy is known as *premium*, and it exists because warrants possess speculative value. As a rule, the premium on a warrant is directly related to the amount of time left before the option expires and to the volatility of the underlying common stock. That is, the greater the amount of time before the expiration date and the more volatile the stock, the greater the size of the premium.

On the other hand, the relative amount of premium tends to diminish as the price of a warrant goes up.

*Basic investment attributes of a warrant.* Warrants are used chiefly as alternatives to common stock investments. Assume that you're considering buying some stock in a company that you believe will perform strongly in the foreseeable future. Although you have enough money to buy the company's stock, you consider buying the warrants instead. Your main reason is this: Because warrants are much cheaper, they have much greater price volatility and the potential for generating substantially higher rates of return than a direct investment in the underlying common stock.

Say the price of the common is now $50 a share and the warrant, which carries a one-to-one redemption provision (that is, one warrant gives you the right to buy one share of stock), has a $40 exercise price. Here is what happens when the price of the stock increases by $10:

|  | Common Stock | Warrant |
|---|---|---|
| Issue price *before* increase | $50 | $10 |
| Increase in price of common | $10 | — |
| Issue price *after* increase | $60 | $20 |
| Increase in market value | $10 | $10 |
| Holding period return (increase in value/beginning issue price) | 20% | 100% |

As you can see, the two issues move parallel to one another, even though the warrant carries a lower unit cost. As a result, the warrants provide a rate of return that is five times greater than the return you can get on the common.

There are two trading strategies that are popular with warrants. First, as the preceding example illustrates, warrants can be used to increase the return on your investment capital. This is a fairly aggressive approach that involves a good deal of risk, but the payoff is a much higher rate of return. Which would you rather have: 20 percent or 100 percent? If you choose the latter, just remember there's a price to pay in the form of a much higher exposure to loss—indeed, if the price of the underlying stock moves against you, it's possible to lose just about everything with the warrant. A $10 drop in the price of a $50 stock translates into a 20 percent loss; but a $10 drop in a $10 warrant spells total loss!

Alternatively, you can take a more conservative approach by using the low unit cost of warrants to reduce the amount of invested capital and thereby limit your losses. In essence, your goal here is to buy only enough warrants to realize the same amount of capital gains as you can get from the common stock. In our example above, you can earn $1,000 in profits in two ways: buy 100 shares of the stock or buy 100 warrants. If the underlying stock goes up by $10 a share, you'll earn $1,000 in profits in either case! However, whereas the stocks will cost you $5,000, the warrants can be had for only $1,000. Clearly, in the case of the warrants, if the price of the stock goes up, you'll benefit just as much as the stockholder. But if the price of the stock *drops,* the most you can lose is $1,000; the common stockholder, in contrast, can lose a lot more, depending upon the extent of the drop in the price of the stock. Look what happens to the stockholder's investment if the price of his 100 shares of stock drops by $25 a share: a $2,500 loss for him compared to a $1,000 loss for the warrants.

Regardless of how you use warrants, security selection is a critical dimension in the investment process, since the price behavior of the underlying stock is the key factor in determining the price behavior of the warrant. Because of this relationship, you need to satisfy yourself that the common stock does indeed have the kind of price potential you're looking for. In addition, in order to obtain maximum price behavior, it is also important that the market price of the common be equal to or greater than the exercise price of the warrant. (And remember, other things being equal, *low-priced* warrants give you bigger bang for your money than high-priced ones!) Once you carefully assess the price potential of the common and the potential price behavior of the warrant, the question of stocks versus warrants boils down to one of comparative return, risk exposure, and investor preference.

# 26

## STOCK INDEX
## AND OTHER OPTIONS

———

For years, activity in puts and calls was confined almost exclusively to common stock. But all this changed in the early 1980s when trading began in other kinds of options, including stock indexes, debt securities (interest rate options), and foreign currencies. Although the underlying financial assets may vary, the basic features and behavioral characteristics of all these options are basically the same.

## INDEX OPTIONS

A stock index option is nothing more than a put or call option written on a specific stock market index, such as the S&P 500. Since there are no stocks or other financial assets backing these options, the value of the option is always expressed in terms of cash. Specifically, the cash value of an index option equals 100 times the published market index that underlies the option. For example, if the S&P 500 is at 238, the cash value of an S&P 500 index option is: $100 × 238 = $23,800. As the underlying index moves up or down, so does the option's cash value.

Even though index options have been around only since 1983, they have become immensely popular with both individual and institutional investors. In fact, the volume of trading in index options comes close to matching the trading in stock options. In 1985, for example, 110 million index options were traded, as compared to 118 million stock options. This is especially impressive when you realize that nearly all this trading is confined to a handful of index option contracts, as compared to several hundred stock option contracts.

In early 1987, there were nine stock market index options available:

- S&P 500 index (traded on CBOE)
- S&P 100 index (CBOE)
- NYSE index (NYSE)
- NYSE beta index (NYSE)
- Value Line index (Philadelphia Exchange)
- National OTC index (Philadelphia Exchange)
- Major Market index (AMEX)
- Institutional index (AMEX)
- Financial News composite index (Pacific Exchange)

Thus the options cover not only the popular S&P and NYSE indexes but also the Value Line index of 1,700 stocks tracked by Value Line Investment Service; an index of 100 large, actively traded OTC stocks (the National OTC index); and an index based on the 75 stocks most favored by institutional investors (the Institutional index). While the most popular index of them all, the Dow Jones industrial average, has refused to be the basis for an index option, the AMEX has come up with the Major Market index, which is designed to mimic the Dow.

Both puts and calls are available on index options. They are valued and have characteristics like any other put or call except that they are issued with monthly, rather than quarterly, expiration dates. A put lets a holder profit from a drop in the market: when the underlying market index goes down, the value of a put goes up. In contrast, a call enables the holder to profit from a rising market.

## PUTTING A VALUE ON INDEX OPTIONS

The market price of index options is a function of the difference between the striking price on the option, stated in terms of the underlying index, and the latest published stock market index. To illustrate, consider the highly popular S&P 100 index, traded on the CBOE. (This option contract is by far the most actively traded of all listed options.)

As the accompanying index option quotes reveal, on a day when this index closed at 225.42, there was a January call on the index that carried a striking price

# INDEX OPTIONS

## Chicago Board

**S&P 100 INDEX**

| Strike Price | Calls–Last Nov | Calls–Last Dec | Calls–Last Jan | Puts–Last Nov | Puts–Last Dec | Puts–Last Jan |
|---|---|---|---|---|---|---|
| 205 | .... | .... | .... | 1/16 | ¼ | ⅝ |
| 210 | 14 | 15½ | 15⅞ | 1/16 | 9/16 | 1¼ |
| 215 | 10½ | 11½ | 12 | 1/16 | 1⅛ | 2¼ |
| 220 | 5⅞ | 8 | 8¼ | ⅛ | 2⅜ | 3¾ |
| 225 | 1 11/16 | 4¾ | 6½ | 1⅛ | 4¼ | 6 |
| 230 | 3/16 | 2⅜ | 4¼ | 4⅝ | 7⅛ | 8¾ |
| 235 | 1/16 | 1 1/16 | 2¼ | 9⅝ | 11 | 13¼ |
| 240 | 1/16 | ⅜ | 1 3/16 | 14½ | 15 | 16¾ |
| 245 | .... | ⅛ | ⅝ | 21⅜ | .... | .... |
| 250 | .... | 1/16 | .... | .... | .... | .... |

Total call volume 240,058 Total call open int. 611,869
Total call volume 358,523 Total call open int. 868,088
The index: High 225.79; Low 222.94; Close 225.42, +1.61

**S&P 500 INDEX**

| Strike Price | Calls–Last Nov | Calls–Last Dec | Calls–Last Mar | Puts–Last Nov | Puts–Last Dec | Puts–Last Mar |
|---|---|---|---|---|---|---|
| 215 | .... | 22⅝ | .... | 1/16 | 3/16 | 1 15/16 |
| 220 | .... | 17⅜ | .... | 1/16 | ½ | 2½ |
| 225 | .... | 13¼ | .... | .... | 1 1/16 | 4 |
| 230 | 7⅜ | 8½ | 12½ | 1/16 | 2 | 5¾ |
| 235 | 3½ | 5⅜ | 9¾ | 9/16 | 3⅝ | 7¾ |
| 240 | 9/16 | 3¾ | 7⅞ | 2 3/16 | 5⅜ | 10 |
| 245 | ⅛ | 1 11/16 | 6¼ | 8⅜ | 10 | .... |
| 250 | .... | 1 | 4½ | 13¾ | 13¼ | .... |
| 255 | .... | 5/16 | 3 | .... | 19 | .... |
| 260 | .... | ⅛ | 2 5/16 | .... | .... | .... |
| 265 | .... | 1/16 | 1½ | .... | .... | .... |

Total call volume 6,846 Total call open int. 87,464
Total put volume 7,071 Total put open int. 74,046
The index: High 237.94; Low 235.51; Close 237.66, +0.90

## N.Y. Stock Exchange

**NYSE INDEX OPTIONS**

| Strike Price | Calls–Last Nov | Calls–Last Dec | Calls–Last Jan | Puts–Last Nov | Puts–Last Dec | Puts–Last Jan |
|---|---|---|---|---|---|---|
| 125 | .... | .... | 11¾ | .... | 3/16 | ⅝ |
| 127½ | .... | .... | .... | .... | ⅝ | .... |
| 130 | .... | .... | .... | 1/16 | ⅝ | 15/16 |
| 132½ | 3⅞ | .... | .... | 1/16 | 1 7/16 | .... |
| 135 | 2⅛ | 3¾ | 4¾ | 5/16 | 1⅞ | 3 |
| 137½ | ½ | 2 7/16 | .... | 1⅜ | 3⅛ | .... |
| 140 | 1/16 | 1 5/16 | 2⅜ | 3⅜ | 4½ | 5¾ |
| 142½ | .... | ¾ | .... | 6¾ | 7 | .... |
| 145 | .... | 5/16 | 15/16 | 9¼ | 8½ | 9½ |
| 147½ | .... | 3/16 | .... | .... | .... | .... |
| 150 | .... | ⅛ | 5/16 | .... | .... | .... |

Total call volume 6,591. Total call open int. 30,512.
Total put volume 9,923. Total put open int. 40,898.
The index: High 136.73; Low 135.64; Close 136.62, +0.14

**NYSE BETA INDEX**

| Strike Price | Calls–Last Nov | Calls–Last Dec | Calls–Last Jan | Puts–Last Nov | Puts–Last Dec | Puts–Last Jan |
|---|---|---|---|---|---|---|
| 275 | .... | .... | .... | .... | ⅞ | .... |
| 280 | .... | .... | .... | .... | .... | 3½ |
| 285 | 8¾ | .... | 14⅞ | ⅛ | 2⅞ | 4⅝ |
| 290 | 3 | 8⅛ | .... | 1 | 4⅝ | 7½ |
| 295 | 1¾ | 4⅞ | .... | 1⅝ | 7⅛ | .... |
| 300 | ¼ | 3½ | .... | 6½ | 10¼ | 12¼ |
| 305 | 1/16 | 2⅜ | .... | 10⅞ | 14 | .... |
| 310 | .... | 1⅝ | 3¼ | 15⅞ | .... | .... |
| 315 | .... | .... | 2¼ | .... | .... | .... |
| 320 | .... | .... | 1½ | .... | .... | .... |

Total call volume 274. Total call open int. 956.
Total put volume 846. Total put open int. 1,669.
The index: High 297.81; Low 291.88; Close 294.15, −3.66

*Source: The Wall Street Journal.*

of 220. Since a stock index call has a value as long as the underlying index exceeds the index striking price (just the opposite is true of puts), the intrinsic value of this call is: 225.42 − 220 = 5.42.

Now, this call was trading at 8¼, some 2.83 points above the call's underlying true value. The difference is due to the investment premium. As a rule, the amount of investment premium in an index option tends to increase with the length of the option (note the difference between the November and January options) and with the volatility of market conditions. Returning to our example, if the S&P 100 index were to go up to 240 by late January (the expiration date on the call) this option would be quoted at 240 − 220 = 20. Since all index options are valued in multiples of $100, this option would then be worth $2,000. Thus, if you were fortunate enough to buy this security at 8¼, or $825 (8.25 × $100), in 2 months your profit would be: $2,000 − $825 = $1,175. Index options are valued according to what the market (and market index) is expected to do in the future. Calls are more highly valued if the market is expected to go up, while puts are more highly valued in falling markets.

## HOW TO INVEST IN INDEX OPTIONS

Index options can be used for both speculating and hedging. Given their effectiveness for both purposes, it's little wonder they have become so popular with investors. But a word of caution is in order; for while trading index options appears quite simple and seems to provide high rates of return, they are in reality high-risk trading vehicles subject to considerable price volatility and should *not* be used by amateurs. True, there's only so much you can lose with these options. The trouble is, it's very easy to do just that. Attractive profits are, indeed, available from these securities, but they're not investments you can buy and then forget until they expire. With the wide market swings we've been experiencing lately, these securities have to be closely monitored on a daily basis.

*Speculating.* As a speculative vehicle, index options give you the opportunity to play the market with a relatively small amount of capital. For example, if you think the market is about to climb, you can buy a call on one of the market indexes. Let's say the S&P 500 index is at 235 and you feel confident that it will move to around 250 within the next couple of months. You buy three 60-day calls on the S&P 500 with striking prices of 235, quoted at 2½. Since each call costs $250 (2½ × $100), you are able to speculate on the market with just $750. If the market does indeed take off and the S&P 500 rises to, say, 248.5 by the expiration date on the calls, your profit will be $3,300. That is:

| | |
|---|---:|
| Value of each call at expiration (market price − strike price = 248.5 − 235.0) | 13.5 |
| Less: cost of the call | − 2.5 |
| | 11.0 |
| Cash value | × $100.00 |
| Total profit made on each call | $1,100.00 |
| Number of calls held | × 3 |
| Total profit | $3,300.00 |

Since this profit was made from an investment of just $750 (which is also the most you can lose in this transaction), the holding period return on this transaction amounts to an extremely attractive 440 percent ($3,300/$750). Your risk meanwhile is limited to the $750 you paid to buy the options.

*Hedging.* Index options are equally effective as hedging vehicles. For instance, one way to protect a portfolio of common stocks against an adverse market is to buy puts on one of the market indexes. If you think the market's heading down and you hold a portfolio of, say, a dozen different stocks, you can protect your capital by selling all your stocks. But that could become very expensive, especially if you plan on getting back into the market after it drops. One way to have your cake and eat it too is to hedge your stock portfolio with a stock index put. In this way, if the market does go down, you'll make money on your puts—which can then be used to buy more stocks at the lower, "bargain" prices. On the other hand, if the market doesn't retreat, but instead continues to go up, you'll be out only the cost of the puts, which could well be more than offset by the increased value of your stock holdings (which presumably will benefit from an increasing market). Thus, you can make money no matter which way the market goes.

Hedging with index options is exactly like hedging with stock options except that with index options, you're trying to protect a whole portfolio of stocks rather than individual stocks. There is one important point to keep in mind, however: the amount of profit you make, or protection you obtain, depends, in large part, on how closely the behavior of your stock portfolio matches the behavior of the index option you use in the hedge. Unfortunately, there is no guarantee that the two will behave in the same way. Thus, you should be careful to select the index option that most closely reflects the nature of the stocks in your portfolio. If, for example, you hold a lot of OTC stocks, you might select the National OTC index as the hedging vehicle. If you hold mostly blue chips, consider using the Major Market index. While you'll probably be hard pressed to get dollar-for-dollar portfolio protection (that is, a $1 drop in the value of the portfolio offset by an equal increase in the value of the option), the closer the match, the better the hedge.

## RISK MODIFIERS: OTHER TYPES OF OPTIONS

While options on stocks and stock indexes account for over 90 percent of the market activity in listed options, put and call options can also be obtained on selected industries, debt instruments, and foreign currencies. These options are used primarily by professional and institutional traders as so-called risk modifiers—hedging vehicles used to protect a position in stocks, debt securities, or foreign currencies. For one reason or another, they just haven't caught on much among individual investors; even so, they do provide some interesting investment opportunities.

### INDUSTRY OPTIONS

Industry options are like index options, except that they are written on a smaller segment of the market. Specifically, an industry option (or subindex option, as it's also called) is written on a portfolio of stocks representing a specific industry. For example, the AMEX has industry options on computer technology stocks and oil stocks. These options are written against a portfolio of stocks that are supposed to reflect the average price performance of all stocks in those industries. Thus, underlying the AMEX's computer technology options is an index composed of 30 computer stocks, weighted by their respective market values. As it moves up or down—in conjunction with the weighted average market price of the stocks that make up the index—the option premium moves accordingly. When the industry index goes up, the value of a call increases; when the index goes down, the value of a put goes up. Index options can be used for speculation or hedging. They provide the opportunity to invest in a whole industry with a relatively small amount of capital.

## INTEREST RATE OPTIONS

Puts and calls on fixed income (debt) securities are known as interest rate options. Specific Treasury securities (Treasury notes and bonds) underlie these options. As the prices of these securities move up or down in the market, the values of the puts and calls respond accordingly. A call, for example, enables the holder to buy a certain amount (usually $100,000) of a specific Treasury bond or note; a put gives the holder the right to sell. Interest rate options are written on quarterly cycles with 3- and 6-month expiration dates; no 9-month options are available. Trading in interest rate options is conducted on the CBOE and the AMEX. At the end of 1986, options on the following Treasury securities were traded:

- 7¼% Treasury note of 1996
- 9¼% Treasury bond of 2016
- 7½% Treasury bond of 2016
- 7¼% Treasury bond of 2016
- 6½% Treasury note of 1991
- 7⅜% Treasury note of 1996

As a rule, unless the debt security is considered to be a benchmark issue (one that's closely followed in the marketplace), once the initial 3- and 6-month options have expired, no more puts and calls are written on it. The reason for this is that after the initial life of the T-bond or note, there is not enough secondary trading in the security to support an active options market. Thus, new options are constantly coming out on new government security issues. The market for interest rate options is relatively small since most professional and institutional traders tend to use interest rate futures contracts rather than interest rate options. (These will be described in Chapter 28.)

With interest rate options, the price of a call increases when the yield or interest rate on the underlying debt security *decreases*. Just the reverse occurs with puts. This is because such interest rate behavior will cause the underlying debt security to increase or decrease in value. Since an option should reflect the market behavior of the underlying security, the same valuation principle applies with options as with the securities themselves. If the market yield on Treasury notes and bonds drops, the market value of these securities *and* the price of calls on them will go up together, while the value of puts will decline.

Interest rate options are appealing because of their limited exposure to loss, as well as the attractive leverage they offer—which can lead to substantial capital gains and very high rates of return. They also provide an effective yet inexpensive way to hedge a position in fixed income securities. For example, you might buy a put option on a Treasury bond to protect your bond portfolio against a decline in value. This hedge would work just like a stock hedge: if interest rates go up, the value of the put will increase and, in so doing, offset all or part of the decline in the value of the bond portfolio.

Interest rate options can be used not only for hedging but also for speculating, for option writing, and for spreading—just as stock options can. For example, if you want to speculate on interest rate movements you have two choices: you can buy fixed income securities or put or call options on debt securities. The basic advantage of the latter choice is that it gives you just as much price action but at reduced risk. For instance, if you think interest rates are going to fall in the near future, you can buy Treasury bond calls at a very modest cost; then if rates do fall, the value of the calls will shoot up and you'll enjoy a substantial rate of return on your investment. In contrast, if you think market rates are headed up, you can buy puts and reap similar benefits. Clearly, the ability to forecast interest rates (which is *not* an easy task) lies at the heart of this trading strategy. On the other hand, because of their limited loss exposure, interest rate options will at least lessen the impact of faulty judgment. In other words, if you are wrong, there's only so much you can lose with calls, which is not the case when you speculate directly in bonds.

Because of the pervasive effects that the underlying debt securities have on the price behavior of interest rate options, these securities should be used only by knowledgeable and experienced investors who fully understand the mechanics of interest rates and the behavior of debt securities.

## CURRENCY OPTIONS

Foreign currency options, or currency options as they're more commonly known, allow you to speculate on foreign exchange rates or to hedge foreign currency holdings. These options are traded on the CBOE and Philadelphia Exchange, and include the currencies of most of our major trading partners:

- British pound
- Swiss franc
- West German mark
- Canadian dollar
- Japanese yen
- French franc
- Australian dollar

Puts and calls on these currencies give holders the right to sell or buy large amounts of the currency at a specified price within a specified period. Unlike stock options, which are all keyed to 100-share round lots, the unit of trading in the foreign exchange markets varies (see the table on the next page).

| Underlying Currency* | SIZE OF ONE CONTRACT | |
| --- | --- | --- |
| | CBOE | Philadelphia Exchange |
| British pound | 25,000 pounds | 12,500 pounds |
| Swiss franc | 125,000 francs | 62,500 francs |
| West German mark | 125,000 marks | 62,500 marks |
| Canadian dollar | 100,000 dollars | 50,000 dollars |
| Japanese yen | 12,500,000 yen | 6,250,000 yen |
| French franc | 250,000 francs | 125,000 francs |
| Australian dollar | 50,000 dollars | N.A. |

*The British pound, Swiss franc, West German mark, Canadian dollar, and Australian dollar are all quoted in full cents; the French franc in 10ths of a cent; and the Japanese yen in 100ths of a cent.

Currency options are traded in cents per unit of the underlying currency. Thus, if a put or call on the British pound (from the Philadelphia Exchange) is quoted at, say, 6.40 (read as "6.4 cents"), it is valued at $800, since 12,500 British pounds underlie this option on the Philadelphia Exchange ($.064 × 12,500 = $800). Note that contracts on the CBOE are twice the size of contracts on the Philadelphia Exchange.

The value of a currency option is linked to the exchange rate between the U.S. dollar and the underlying foreign currency. For example, if the Canadian dollar becomes stronger *relative to the U.S. dollar,* causing the exchange rates to go up, the price of a call option on the Canadian dollar will increase, while the price of a put will decline. Thus, you can use currency options to speculate on exchange rates. The striking price of a currency option is stated in terms of exchange rates. As a result, a striking price of 150 implies that each unit of the foreign currency is worth 150 cents, or $1.50, in U.S. dollars. If you held a 150 call on this foreign currency, you would make money if the foreign currency strengthened relative to the U.S. dollar causing the exchange rate to rise to, say, 155. In contrast, if you held a 150 put, you would profit from a decline in the exchange rate to, say, 145.

Let's use a put on the British pound to illustrate what happens. Say you could buy a 150 put at a premium of 1.50. This means the put would cost you $187.50 (.0150 × 12,500). Now if the exchange rate actually dropped to 145 before the put expired, the put would be worth the difference between the prevailing exchange rate and the exchange rate stipulated in the striking price. In our example, the puts would be trading at 5.00, and each one would be worth $625.00 (.05 × 12,500). For each put you held, your profit would be $437.50 ($625.00 − $187.50 = $437.50), which would generate a holding period return of $625.00 − $187.50/$187.50 = 233.3 percent. Success in forecasting movements in foreign exchange rates is obviously essential to a profitable foreign currency options program.

# 27

## THE FAST TRACK
## OF COMMODITIES TRADING

———

Coffee, corn, and soybeans—foodstuffs, but also investment vehicles traded on the futures market. These and dozens of other commodities offer the potential for enormous profit—if you can stand the risk. You'll lose your shirt in commodities if you don't know what you're doing, so we'll warn you in advance to stay away unless you have a stomach of iron and a deep cash reserve. But if you succeed, your payoffs may be nothing short of phenomenal.

### THE FUTURES MARKET

The amount of futures trading in the United States has mushroomed over the past 10 to 15 years as an increasing number of investors have turned to the futures market for highly competitive rates of return. It has not been the traditional commodities contracts that have drawn many of these investors, however, but rather the new investment vehicles being offered. For a major reason behind the growth in the volume of futures trading has been the big jump in the number and variety of contracts available for trading. In addition to such traditional commodities as grains and metals, markets also exist for live animals, processed commodities, crude oil and gasoline, foreign currencies, money market securities, mortgage interest rates, U.S. Treasury notes and bonds, Eurodollar securities, the consumer price index, and common stocks (via stock market indexes). Indeed, even put and call options are available on a select but growing list of futures contracts. All these commodities and financial assets are traded in what is known as the futures market.

## HOW THE FUTURES MARKET WORKS

When a bushel of wheat is sold, the transaction takes place in the *cash market.* That is, the bushel changes hands in exchange for a cash price paid to the seller. The total transaction is complete at that point. Although most traditional securities are traded in this type of market, commodities are also traded in what is known as a *futures market.* In this case, the seller does not actually deliver the wheat until a mutually agreed-upon date in the future. As a result, the transaction is not completed for some time. The seller receives partial payment for the bushel of wheat at the time the agreement is made, and the balance on delivery. The buyer, in turn, owns a highly liquid futures contract that can be held and presented for delivery or traded in the futures market. No matter what the buyer does with the contract, as long as it is outstanding, the seller has a legal and binding obligation to *make* delivery of a stated quantity of wheat on a specified date, and the buyer has a similar obligation to *take* delivery of the underlying commodity.

Futures contracts are like call options in that both involve the future delivery of an item at an agreed-upon price. But a futures contract involves an *obligation* to buy or sell a specified amount of a given commodity at a stated price on or before a stated date—unless the contract is canceled or liquidated before it expires. An option involves only the *right* to buy or sell a specific amount of a real or financial asset at a specific price over a specified period of time. Just as important, the risk of loss with an option is limited to the price paid for it, while there is no such limit on a futures contract. As you will see, a futures contract is more like a share of stock—the amount of profit or loss that you make depends on whether, and to what extent, the price of the contract goes up or down.

*Major exchanges.* The first organized commodity exchange in the United States was the Chicago Board of Trade, which opened its doors in 1848. Today, futures trading is conducted on 12 North American exchanges, all but one in the United States. These include:

- Chicago Board of Trade
- Chicago Mercantile Exchange
- Chicago Rice and Cotton Exchange
- Commodities Exchange of New York
- Kansas City Board of Trade
- Mid-America Commodities Exchange
- Minneapolis Grain Exchange
- New York Coffee, Sugar, and Cocoa Exchange
- New York Cotton Exchange
- New York Futures Exchange (a NYSE subsidiary)
- New York Mercantile Exchange
- Winnipeg Grain Exchange

Trading activity on these exchanges has reached the trillion dollar level, making the commodities market a serious rival to the stock market in terms of trading volume.

Each exchange deals in a variety of futures contracts, but some are more limited in their activities than others. For example, while the New York Cotton Exchange deals in just two types of contracts, the Chicago Mercantile Exchange deals in over a dozen, ranging from wheat and gold to U.S. Treasury bonds and stock market indexes. The table on the next two pages shows where the major commodities, financial futures, and futures options are traded. Note that many commodities are traded on more than one exchange, including gold, which is traded on four separate exchanges.

*Futures contracts.*   A futures contract is a commitment to deliver a certain amount of a specified item at a specified date in the future. The seller of the contract agrees to make the specified future delivery, and the buyer agrees to accept it. Each exchange establishes its own contract specifications, which include not only the quantity and quality of the item, but the delivery procedure and delivery month as well. For example, the Chicago Board of Trade specifies that each of its soybean contracts will involve 5,000 bushels of USDA grade No. 2 yellow soybeans; delivery months include January, March, May, July, August, September, and November. The delivery month for a futures contract is much like the expiration date of put and call options; it specifies when the commodity must be delivered and thus defines the life of the contract.

The maximum life of a futures contract is usually 1 year or less, although some commodities and financial instruments have lives as long as 3 years. Whatever the lifespan, futures contracts always involve extremely large quantities of the underlying commodity or financial instrument, as shown on page 334. Nevertheless, the amount of capital required to deal in these investments is rather small, since all trading is done on margin.

# WHERE FUTURES ARE TRADED

| | Chicago Board of Trade (CBOT) | Chicago Mercantile Exchange (MERC) | Kansas City Board of Trade (KCBT) | Mid-America Commodities Exchange (MIDAM) | Minneapolis Grain Exchange | Chicago Rice and Cotton Exchange | New York Coffee, Sugar & Cocoa Exchange (NYSCTE) | New York Cotton Exchange | Commodities Exchange—New York (COMEX) | New York Futures Exchange (NYFE) | New York Mercantile Exchange (NYMERC) |
|---|---|---|---|---|---|---|---|---|---|---|---|
| Certificates of deposit | | X | | | | | | | | | |
| Foreign currencies | | X | | | | | | | | | |
| Eurodollar futures | | X | | | | | | | | | |
| GNMAs | X | | | | | | | | | | |
| Gold | X | X | | X | | | | | X | | |
| Standard & Poor's Index—futures | | X | | | | | | | | | |
| Value Line Composite Average Stock Index—futures | | | X | | | | | | | | |
| NYSE Composite Index—futures | | | | | | | | | | X | |
| Silver | X | | | X | | | | | X | | |
| U.S. Treasury bills (90-day) | | X | | X | | | | | | | |
| 10-Year Treasury notes | X | | | | | | | | | | |
| U.S. Treasury bonds | X | | | X | | | | | | X | |
| Copper | | | | | | | | | X | | |
| Cocoa | | | | | | | X | | | | |
| Cattle | | X | | | | | | | | | |
| Live cattle | | X | | X | | | | | | | |
| Corn | X | | | X | | X | | | | | |
| Cotton | | | | | | X | | X | | | |
| Leaded gasoline | | | | | | | | | | | X |
| Heating oil | | | | | | | | | | | X |
| Unleaded gasoline | | | | | | | | | | | |
| Hogs | | X | | X | | | | | | | |

TAKING CHANCES—TAX SHELTERS, OPTIONS, COMMODITIES, AND FINANCIAL FUTURES

| | Chicago Board of Trade (CBOT) | Chicago Mercantile Exchange (MERC) | Kansas City Board of Trade (KCBT) | Mid-America Commodities Exchange (MIDAM) | Minneapolis Grain Exchange | Chicago Rice and Cotton Exchange | New York Coffee, Sugar & Cocoa Exchange (NYSCTE) | New York Cotton Exchange | Commodities Exchange—New York (COMEX) | New York Futures Exchange (NYFE) | New York Mercantile Exchange (NYMERC) |
|---|---|---|---|---|---|---|---|---|---|---|---|
| Lumber | | X | | | | | | | | | |
| Oats | X | | | | | | | | | | |
| Orange juice | | | | | | | | X | | | |
| Platinum | | | | X | | | | | | | X |
| Plywood | X | | | | | | | | | | |
| Pork bellies | | X | | | | | | | | | |
| Potatoes | | | | | | | | | | | X |
| Milled and rough rice | | | | | | X | | | | | |
| Soybeans | X | | | X | | X | | | | | |
| Soybean meal | X | | | | | | | | | | |
| Soybean oil | X | | | | | | | | | | |
| Sugar | | | | X | | | X | | | | |
| Wheat | X | | X | X | X | | | | | | |
| Broilers | | X | | X | | | | | | | |
| Eggs | | X | | | | | | | | | |
| Value Line—options | | | X | | | | | | | | |
| Gold Futures—option contracts | | | | | | | | | X | | |
| U.S. T-Bonds futures—options | X | | | | | | | | | | |
| Sugar futures—options | | | | | | | X | | | | |
| 2-Year Treasury note futures | X | | | | | | | | | | |
| Crude oil | | | | | | | | | | | X |
| Coffee | | | | | | | X | | | | |
| Palladium | | | | | | | | | | | X |

# FUTURES CONTRACT DIMENSIONS

| Contract | Size of a Contract* | Market Value of One Contract in Early 1987 |
|---|---|---|
| Corn | 5,000 bu | $ 8,400 |
| Wheat | 5,000 bu | 14,300 |
| Live cattle | 40,000 lb | 24,400 |
| Pork bellies | 40,000 lb | 28,000 |
| Coffee | 37,500 lb | 55,500 |
| Cotton | 50,000 lb | 24,000 |
| Gold | 100 troy oz | 39,400 |
| Copper | 25,000 lb | 14,500 |
| Japanese yen | 12.5 million yen | 76,840 |
| Treasury bills | $1 million | 947,200 |
| Treasury bond | $100,000 | 98,500 |
| S&P 500 Stock Index | 500 times the index | 118,500 |

*Size of the contract may vary depending on the exchange on which the item is traded; e.g., the trading unit for copper is 25,000 pounds on the COMEX but only 12,500 pounds on the Mid-America Exchange.

## FUTURES TRADING

The futures market contains two types of traders: hedgers and speculators. The hedgers are the producers and processors (including financial institutions and corporate money managers) who use futures contracts to protect their interest in the underlying commodity. For example, ranchers who think the price of cattle will drop in the near future act as hedgers by selling futures contracts on cattle in the hope of locking in as high a price as possible for their herds. In effect, the hedgers provide the underlying strength of the futures market and represent the reason for its existence. *Speculators*, on the other hand, give the market liquidity. They trade futures contracts not because of a need to protect a position in the underlying commodity, but simply to earn a profit on expected swings in the price of futures contracts. They are the risk-takers, the individual investors who have no interest in the commodity other than its price action and potential capital gains.

*Trading mechanics.* Once futures contracts are created, they can readily be traded in the market. Like common stocks and other traditional investment vehicles, futures contracts are bought and sold through local brokerage offices. Most firms have at least one or two people in each office who specialize in futures contracts. In addition, a number of commodity firms deal exclusively in futures contracts. Except for the need to set up a special commodity trading account, there is little difference between trading futures and dealing in stocks or bonds. The same types of orders are used, and the use of margin is similar. Any investor can buy or sell any contract, with any delivery month, at any time, as long as it is currently being traded on one of the exchanges.

Buying a contract is referred to as *taking a long position*. Selling one is known as *taking a short position*. These terms have exactly the same connotation as they do in, say, the stock market: the long investor wants the price to rise, while the short seller wants it to drop. Both long and short positions can be liquidated by executing an offsetting transaction. If you are a short seller, for example, you can cover your position by buying an equal amount of the contract. In general, less than 1 percent of all futures contracts are settled by delivery; the rest are offset prior to the delivery month.

*Margin trading.* All futures contracts are traded on margin; it is the normal way of trading in this market. You will recall from Chapter 10 that when you buy on margin you have to put up only a fraction of the total price of the investment, which is the amount of equity that goes into the deal. However, margin trading in the commodities market has a slightly different meaning than it does in the securities market. Here, margin is the deposit made to guarantee fulfillment of the futures contract. As such, there is no borrowing required on the part of the margin trader to finance the unmargined amount of the contract. Rather, the margin deposit simply represents security to cover any loss in the market value of the contract that may result from adverse price movements. It is not a partial payment for the commodity, nor is it in any way related to the value of the product or item underlying the contract.

The margin required for commodity trading usually ranges from about 2 to 10 percent of the value of the contract, which is extremely low compared to the margin required for stocks. The specific size of the required margin deposit, stated as a dollar amount, varies with the type of contract and, in some cases, the exchange. Following are some examples:

### MARGIN REQUIREMENTS FOR SOME COMMODITIES AND FINANCIAL FUTURES IN EARLY 1987

|  | Initial Margin Deposit | Maintenance Margin Deposit |
| --- | --- | --- |
| Corn | $1,000 | $ 750 |
| Wheat | 1,500 | 1,200 |
| Live cattle | 1,500 | 1,200 |
| Pork bellies | 1,500 | 1,200 |
| Coffee | 3,500 | 2,600 |
| Cotton | 1,500 | 1,200 |
| Gold | 3,500 | 2,600 |
| Copper | 1,600 | 1,200 |
| Japanese yen | 1,800 | 1,400 |
| Treasury bills | 2,000 | 1,500 |
| Treasury bond | 2,000 | 1,500 |
| S&P 500 Stock Index | 6,000 | 4,500 |

As you can see from this list, there are two different kinds of margin requirements: an initial margin deposit and a maintenance margin deposit. The *initial deposit* specifies the amount of capital you must deposit with your broker at the time of the transaction. It represents the amount of money required to make a given investment. After the investment is made, the market value of a contract will rise and fall along with the quoted price of the underlying commodity. This market behavior will cause the amount of margin required for the deposit to change. To be sure that an adequate margin is always on hand, investors are required to meet a second type of margin requirement, the *maintenance deposit.* It is somewhat less than the initial deposit and establishes the minimum amount of margin that must be kept in the account at all times.

For instance, say you invest in a corn contract requiring a $1,000 initial deposit and a $750 maintenance deposit. As long as the market value of the contract does not fall by more than $250 (the difference between the contract's initial and maintenance margins), you'll have no problems. But if the market moves against you and the value of your contract drops by more than the allowed amount, you will receive a *margin call,* which means that you must deposit enough cash to bring your account back to the initial margin level.

Your margin position is checked daily by a procedure known as *mark-to-the-market.* That is, the gain or loss in a contract's value is determined at the end of each session, at which time the brokerage house debits or credits your account accordingly. If the market price of your commodity moves up, your account goes up in value. In a falling market, however, the value of your account drops, and you could well receive margin calls, even on a daily basis. If you do not meet these margin calls, your broker has no choice but to close out your position.

## TRADING COMMODITIES

Physical commodities such as grains, metals, wood, and meat make up a major portion of the futures market. They have been actively traded in the United States for well over a century and still account for a significant portion of all trading activity.

Various types of physical commodities are found on nearly all of the 12 North American futures exchanges. In fact, 6 of them deal only in commodities. The market for commodity contracts is divided into the following 5 major segments: grains and oilseeds, livestock and meat, food and fiber, metals and petroleum, and wood. This segmentation does not affect trading mechanics and procedures but provides a convenient way of categorizing commodities into groups based on similar underlying characteristics. Certainly, these groups indicate the diversity of the commodities market and, as the list on the next page shows, the wide range of kinds of contracts available. In 1987 investors had some 40 different commodities from which to choose, including a number, like soybeans and wheat, that are available in several different forms or grades.

# MAJOR CLASSES OF COMMODITIES

## GRAINS AND OILSEEDS

Corn
Oats
Soybeans
Wheat
Barley
Flaxseed
Rapeseed
Sorghum
Rye
Rice

## LIVESTOCK AND MEAT

Cattle
Hogs and pork bellies
Broilers
Turkeys

## FOOD AND FIBER

Cocoa
Coffee
Cotton
Orange juice
Sugar
Eggs
Potatoes
Butter

## METALS AND PETROLEUM

Aluminum
Copper
Gold
Platinum
Silver
Palladium
Mercury
Gasoline
Heating oil
Crude oil
Propane

## WOOD

Lumber
Plywood
Stud lumber

## OTHER

Rubber
Silver coins
Gold coins

## HOW PRICES BEHAVE

When you buy commodities contracts, you are dealing in such enormous trading units as 40,000 pounds of pork bellies and 5,000 bushels of corn. Because of the size of these contracts, even a rather modest price change can have an appreciable impact on the market value of a contract and therefore on investor returns or losses. For example, if the price of corn goes up or down by just 20 cents a bushel, the value of a single contract will change by $1,000. Since a corn contract can be bought with a $1,000 initial margin deposit, it is easy to see the effect this kind of price behavior can have on investor return. This potential for sizable price fluctuation is the reason speculators invest in commodities.

Although the volatile price swings of commodities contracts draw investors to commodities, the exchanges try to put lids on price fluctuations by imposing daily price limits and maximum daily price ranges. The *daily price limit* restricts the amount of change allowed in the price of the underlying commodity from day to day. For example, the price of corn can change by no more than 10 cents a bushel and the price of copper by no more than 3 cents a pound from one day to the next. Despite these limits, investors still have plenty of room to turn a quick profit. The daily price limit on corn and copper allows a change of $500 a day for just one corn contract and $750 for one copper contract. The *maximum daily price range,* in contrast, limits the amount the price can change *during* the day and is usually equal to twice the daily limit restrictions. For example, if the daily price limit on corn is 10 cents a bushel, its maximum daily range is 20 cents a bushel.

## HOLDING PERIOD RETURN

Futures contracts have only one source of return: capital gains. High capital gains are possible because of the volatile nature of commodities prices and because of leverage. The fact that all futures trading is done on margin means that it takes only a small amount of money to control a large investment position. Of course, leverage also means that you can be wiped out in one or two bad days.

   You can calculate your investment return by using a variation of the standard holding period return formula that is based on the amount of money invested in a contract, rather than on the value of the contract itself. This formula, which measures *return on invested capital,* is used because commodities are so highly leveraged. It can be used for both long and short transactions and is computed in the following way:

$$\text{return on invested capital} = \frac{\substack{\text{selling price of} \\ \text{commodity contract}} - \substack{\text{purchase price of} \\ \text{commodity contract}}}{\text{amount of margin deposit}}$$

   To see how it works, assume you bought two September corn contracts at 245 ($2.45 per bushel) by depositing the required initial margin of $2,000 (or $1,000 for each contract). Even though your investment amounts to only $2,000, you control 10,000 bushels of corn worth $24,500 at the time of purchase. Assume September corn closes at 259 (the selling price of the corn contract is now $25,900) and you decide to take your profit. Your return on invested capital would be:

$$\begin{aligned}
\text{return on invested capital} &= \frac{\$25,900 - \$24,500}{\$2,000} \\
&= \frac{\$1,400}{\$2,000} \\
&= \underline{70.0\%}
\end{aligned}$$

Clearly, this high rate of return is due not only to the increase in the price of the commodity, but also, and perhaps most importantly, to the low margin. In this case, the initial margin equaled only about 6 percent of the value of the contract.

## TRADING STRATEGIES

You can use commodities for speculating, spreading, or hedging.

***Speculating.*** Speculators are in the market for one reason: they expect the price of a commodity to go up or down, and they hope to capitalize on these price swings by going long or short. As you can see in the figure below, these price swings can be dramatic and rapid.

To gain an appreciation of the enormous profit potential available from commodities speculation, consider the kind of profit you would make if you went long in a futures contract, expecting the price of the commodity to rise. For example, suppose you buy a February silver contract at 533½ by depositing the required initial margin of $1,000. Since one silver contract involves 5,000 troy ounces, the market value of this contract is $26,675 (that is, $5.33½ × 5,000 ounces). Assume that by January, 1 month before the contract expires, the price of the contract has risen to 552. You then liquidate your position, earning a profit of 18½ cents an ounce (552 − 533½), or $925, from an investment of just $1,000. In this case, your return on invested capital is a whopping 92.5 percent. Of course, instead of rising, the price of silver could have dropped by 18½ cents an ounce. In that case you would have lost just about all your original investment ($1,000 − $925 leaves only $75, out of which would have to come a round trip commission of $50). But the drop in price would be just what short sellers were after. Here's why: they sell (short) the February silver at 533½ and buy it back later at 515. Clearly, the difference between the selling price and purchase price is the same 18½ cents, but in this case it is *profit*, since the selling price exceeds the purchase price.

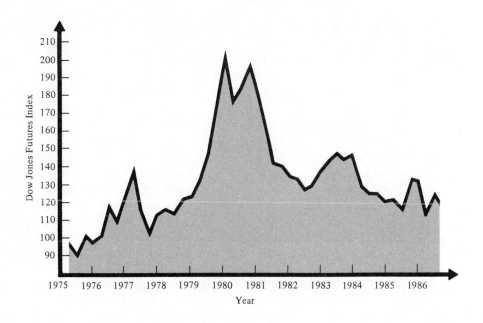

*Spreading.*   Instead of attempting to speculate on the price behavior of a futures contract, you might choose to follow a more conservative tactic, a strategy known as spreading. The principles of spreading futures contracts are much like those for stock options. The idea is to combine two or more different contracts into one investment position that offers the potential for generating a modest amount of profit, while restricting exposure to loss. One very important reason for their use in the commodities market is that, unlike the case of put and call options, there is no limit to the amount of loss that can occur with a futures contract.

You set up a spread by buying one contract and simultaneously selling another. Although one side of the transaction will lead to a loss, you are obviously hoping that the profit earned from the other side will be more than enough compensation, and that the net result will be at least a modest amount of profit. If you are wrong, the spread will serve to limit (but not eliminate) any losses.

Here is a simplified version of how a spread might work: Suppose you buy contract A at 533½ and at the same time short sell contract B for 575½. Some time later you close out your interest in contract A by selling it at 542 and simultaneously cover your short position in B by purchasing a contract at 579. Although you made a profit of 8½ points on the long position, contract A (542 − 533½), you lost 3½ points on the contract that you shorted, B (575½ − 579). The net effect is a profit of 5 points, which, if you were dealing in cents per pound, would mean a profit of $250 on a 5,000-pound contract. Most commodity spreads are highly sophisticated and require specialized skills.

*Hedging.*   A hedge is an approach to commodity trading used by producers and processors to protect a position in a product or commodity. For example, a wheat farmer would use a commodity hedge to obtain as high a price as possible for wheat. In contrast, the processor or manufacturer who uses the commodity would hedge to obtain the goods at as low a price as possible. A successful hedge, in effect, means added income to producers and lower costs to processors.

This example will show how hedging works and why it is used. Suppose a manufacturer uses platinum as a raw material in the production of catalytic converters. It is early in the year and platinum is selling for $380 an ounce, but it is expected to shoot up in price by the end of the year. To protect against future price increases, our manufacturer decides to buy a platinum futures contract, now trading at $405 an ounce. Assume that 8 months later the price of platinum has indeed gone up to $480 an ounce, but so has the price of the futures contract, which is now trading at $525 an ounce. The manufacturer has made $120 an ounce on the 50-ounce futures contract, and is $6,000 ahead on the transaction—a gain that will be used to offset the increase in the cost of platinum. As it turns out, the gain on the futures contract is $1,000 more than the increased cost of 50 ounces of platinum on the open market, for the cost of platinum rose by only $100 an ounce and the cost of 50 ounces of platinum went up by only $5,000. This hedge was successful for the manufacturer because it kept the cost of the raw material in check, at least for the time being. Technically, the manufacturer could take delivery of the contracted platinum—at an effective cost of $405 an ounce, the price at which the futures contract was purchased—but that is unlikely in this case, since in order to do so, the manufacturer would have to forego the $1,000 incremental profit made on the futures contract.

## SHOULD YOU INVEST?

Commodities are appealing because of their high rates of return and their ability to act as an inflation hedge, during periods of rapidly rising consumer prices. During periods of double-digit inflation, traditional investments seldom if ever provide the type of return you need to keep ahead. In these circumstances, commodities are especially attractive since their prices tend to reflect the spiraling inflation rate.

Commodities can play an important role in your investment portfolio as long as you understand the risks you are taking and, equally important, as long as you understand the principles and mechanics of commodities trading. The quickest way to lose money in the commodities market is to jump in without knowing what you are doing. Because of the price volatility and very low margin requirements, the potential for loss is enormous—a fact that makes most investors rightfully wary. Unfortunately, in the long run, most investors wind up losing money in commodities.

If you decide to invest, prepare yourself mentally for the risk and financially for the possibility of loss. You'll need a ready supply of cash on hand to meet margin calls and to absorb any losses. To reduce the risk, it is a good idea to put only a portion of your total portfolio into commodities.

You can invest directly in the commodities market or you can buy put and call options on a number of the actively traded futures contracts. Alternatively, you can take an indirect route by buying commodity mutual funds or by putting your money into a limited partnership commodity pool. The latter two approaches are especially appropriate if you're certain you want to invest in commodities but you also recognize that you lack the time and/or expertise to manage your own commodities investments. Remember, however, that although these approaches offer professional management, they certainly do not guarantee profits; they can only reduce some of the more obvious risks.

*Commodity pools.* Commodity pools are a lot like mutual funds, except that they're set up as limited partnerships. These pools are typically made up of the contributions of a number of individual investors, who are *limited partners* in the pool. These investors hand their money over to the fund's *general partners* who are professional commodities traders and who use the money to speculate in futures. That is, the general partners invest in and provide ongoing management of a portfolio of commodities. They are also the people who organize the pool. As a limited partner, your responsibility for loss is limited to the amount you invest, which is generally a minimum of $5,000

Your earnings from pool investments are likely to be highest when the market is strong. When it is weak, pools generally do not perform very well. It is important to take a look at a fund's track record before you invest, since rates of return vary tremendously. In 1986, for example, the 12-month returns for the top 10 performers ranged from 46 percent to 110 percent. Even if you find a successful fund, however, you probably won't be able to buy a partnership unit, since these units generally are not available after an offer has been sold out.

If a fund is profitable, you'll either receive a cash distribution or your profits will be added to the cash available for trading. Some commodities pools allow you to choose between these two options. Since fund values fluctuate sharply, your profits depend, in large part, on exactly when you buy into the fund and when you get out. If you want to sell your shares in a commodities pool, you'll have to sell them back to the fund's general partners, since virtually no secondary market exists for these investments.

# 28

---

# TRADING IN FINANCIAL FUTURES

---

Instead of trading futures contracts on pork bellies or plywood, you can trade in financial futures, which are futures contracts on a variety of financial instruments. Financial futures were created for much the same reason as commodity futures; they are traded in the same market; their prices behave a lot like those of commodities; and they have common investment merits. Yet in spite of all these similarities, financial futures are a unique kind of investment vehicle.

---

## THE MARKET FOR FINANCIAL FUTURES

Even though the financial futures market has only been around for a little more than a decade, it is now a dominant force in the futures market and has reached a level of trading activity which rivals—and often exceeds—that of the traditional commodities market. Indeed, as the table on the next page shows, not only is the best-selling futures contract a financial future (the Chicago Board of Trade's U.S. Treasury bond contract), but 11 of the 25 most actively traded contracts are finan-

| Rank | Contract | NUMBER OF CONTRACTS TRADED | |
|------|----------|---------------------------|----|
| | | Jan.–June 1986 | 1985 |
| 1 | T-bonds* | 28,689,271 | 40,448,357 |
| 2 | S&P 500 Index* | 9,912,987 | 15,055,955 |
| 3 | Eurodollar* | 5,272,896 | 8,900,528 |
| 4 | Gold | 3,955,920 | 7,773,834 |
| 5 | Deutsche mark* | 3,608,061 | 6,449,384 |
| 6 | Crude oil | 3,552,053 | 3,980,867 |
| 7 | Soybeans | 3,266,423 | 7,392,128 |
| 8 | Corn | 3,048,893 | 6,392,812 |
| 9 | Live cattle | 2,542,563 | 4,427,327 |
| 10 | Swiss franc* | 2,418,588 | 4,758,159 |
| 11 | Silver (5,000 oz.) | 2,095,545 | 4,821,206 |
| 12 | Soybean oil | 1,600,511 | 3,647,408 |
| 13 | Soybean meal | 1,523,255 | 3,339,268 |
| 14 | T-notes (6½–10 yr.)* | 2,340,994 | 2,860,432 |
| 15 | Sugar #11 | 2,110,823 | 3,012,929 |
| 16 | Japanese yen* | 1,946,674 | 2,415,094 |
| 17 | NYSE Composite Index* | 1,653,549 | 2,833,614 |
| 18 | British pound* | 1,505,239 | 2,799,024 |
| 19 | No. 2 heating oil NY | 1,388,957 | 2,207,733 |
| 20 | Copper | 1,133,381 | 2,444,552 |
| 21 | Wheat | 1,162,634 | 2,127,962 |
| 22 | T-bill (90-day)* | 1,075,263 | 2,413,228 |
| 23 | Major Market Index (Maxi)* | 937,929 | 2,062,083 |
| 24 | Live hogs | 850,269 | 1,719,861 |
| 25 | Platinum | 655,317 | 693,256 |

*A financial futures contract.

cial futures. Even more impressive is the fact that 4 of the 5 best-selling contracts are financial futures, and these 4 contracts alone account for more trading volume than the 25 top-selling commodities contracts combined. Although hedgers and large institutional investors account for much of this trading activity, there is still plenty of opportunity in this market for individual investors. For example, using financial futures, you can speculate on the behavior of interest rates, the stock market, and the foreign currency market.

The financial futures market was established in response to the economic turmoil that beset the United States in the 1970s. The dollar had become unstable on the world market, causing serious problems for multinational firms. Closer to home, volatile interest rates created havoc for corporations, financial institutions, and individual investors, all of whom needed a way to protect themselves. As a result, a market for financial futures was born. Although hedging provided the economic rationale for this market, speculators were quick to jump on board in order to capitalize on the price volatility of these instruments.

Currently, financial futures are traded on 6 exchanges: the New York Futures Exchange, the Kansas City Board of Trade, the MidAmerica Commodities Exchange, the New York Cotton Exchange (through its FINEX subsidiary), the Chicago Mercantile Exchange, and the Chicago Board of Trade.

# FINANCIAL FUTURES COME IN THREE BASIC FORMS

Financial futures contracts are written on foreign currencies, debt securities, and stock indexes.

## FOREIGN CURRENCIES

Trading in foreign currencies, known as *currency futures,* began in 1972, and is currently conducted in the following currencies:

- British pound
- German mark
- Swiss franc
- Canadian dollar
- Japanese yen
- French franc

The United States has strong international trade and exchange ties with each of the countries involved.

## DEBT SECURITIES

In October 1975, the first futures contract on debt securities was established when trading started in GNMA pass-through certificates (a special type of mortgage-backed bond issued by an agency of the U.S. government). These contracts met with immediate success and encouraged the development of other *interest rate futures,* including contracts on:

- U.S. Treasury bills
- U.S. Treasury notes
- U.S. Treasury bonds
- 90-day bank certificates of deposit
- 90-day Eurodollar time deposits

With the exception of the Eurodollar time deposits, which represent dollars deposited in interest-bearing accounts in banks outside the United States, all these contracts are based on domestic debt securities.

## STOCK INDEXES

Introduced in 1982, stock index futures are the newest trading vehicle. These futures contracts are pegged to broad-based measures of stock market performance, including the:

- S&P 500 stock index
- S&P index of 250 OTC stocks
- NYSE composite stock index
- Value Line composite stock index
- NASDAQ 100 index
- Major Market index
- Maxi Stock index

Stock index futures, like index options, enable you to participate in the general movement of the entire stock market. Because the various stock indexes represent weighted portfolios of stocks, investors in stock index futures are able to participate in broad market moves. In fact, these are the same futures contracts many observers claim played a major part in the market collapse of October 19, 1987.

In addition to stock market indexes, index-based futures contracts are available on an index of municipal bonds, the consumer price index (which tracks the rate of inflation), and an index that measures the value of the U.S. dollar against 8 foreign currencies. One futures contract is even based on an index of 27 commodities futures contracts.

---

## FINANCIAL FUTURES CONTRACTS

Financial futures contracts are similar to commodities contracts. They control large sums of the underlying financial instrument and are issued with a variety of delivery months. The following table shows the enormous dimensions of several futures contracts:

### DIMENSIONS OF FUTURES CONTRACTS

|  | Contract Size | Market Value of a Single Contract in Early 1987 |
| --- | --- | --- |
| Japanese yen | 12.5 million yen | $ 76,840 |
| Treasury bills | $1 million | $947,200 |
| Treasury bond | $100,000 | $ 98,500 |
| S&P 500 stock index | $500 times the index | $118,500 |
| West German mark | 125,000 marks | $ 67,740 |
| British pound | 25,000 pounds | $ 39,600 |
| U.S. dollar index | $500 times the index | $ 50,530 |
| Major Market index | $250 times the index | $111,450 |

In general, the sellers of futures contracts are obligated to deliver the underlying security when the contract expires. However, the sellers of stock index futures contracts are an exception. Because of the nature of their underlying issue, they make ultimate delivery in the form of cash. The amount of underlying cash is generally set at either $250 or $500 times the value of the stock index. For example, if the Value Line index stands at 220, the amount of cash underlying a single Value Line stock index futures contract is $500 × 220 = $110,000. The owner of a currency future, in contrast, holds a claim on a certain amount of foreign money. The precise amount ranges from 25,000 British pounds to 12.5 million Japanese yen. In a similar fashion, holders of interest rate futures have a claim on a certain amount of the underlying debt security. This claim is also quite large, amounting to $100,000 worth of GNMA and Treasury notes and bonds and $1 million worth of Eurodollar deposits, Treasury bills, and bank CDs.

The lives of financial futures contracts run from about 18 months or less for stock and currency futures to about 3 years or less for interest rate instruments.

## READING THE PRICE QUOTATIONS

The figure on the next page lists quotes for several foreign currency, interest rate, and stock index futures. All currency futures are quoted in dollars or cents per unit of the underlying foreign currency—for instance, in dollars per British pound, or cents per Japanese yen. Thus, according to the closing settle prices in the figure, one December British pound contract was worth $35,437.50 (25,000 pounds × $1.4175) and a December Japanese yen was valued at $76,837.50 (12,500,000 yen × $0.006147).

Except for contracts on Treasury bills and other short-term securities, the quotes for interest rate futures operate in a similar way. The contracts are priced at a percentage of the par value of the underlying debt instrument. Since the instruments are quoted in increments of $1/32$ of 1 percent, a quote of 96-16 for the settle price on the June Treasury bonds in the figure translates into 96 $16/32$, or 96.5 percent of par. Applying this rate to the par value of the underlying securities, we see that a June Treasury bond contract is worth $96,500 ($100,000 × 0.9650).

Stock index futures are quoted in terms of the underlying index, but as we mentioned earlier, most carry a face value of 250 or 500 times the dollar value of the index.

## INVESTMENT CONSIDERATIONS

Interest rate contracts respond to interest rates exactly like their underlying debt instruments: when interest rates go up, the value of an interest rate futures contract goes down, and vice versa. However, the quote system for all interest rate as well as currency and stock index futures is set up to correspond to the market value of the contract. Thus, when the price or quote of a financial futures contract increases, the investor who is long makes money. In contrast, when the price decreases, the short seller makes money.

Price behavior is the only source of return to speculators, since these contracts have no claim on the dividend and interest income of underlying issues. Even so, big profits (or losses) are possible with financial futures because of the equally large

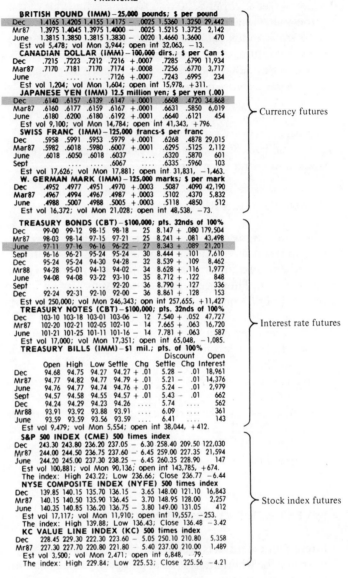

**BRITISH POUND (IMM) – 25,000 pounds; $ per pound**

| | Open | High | Low | Settle | Chg | Lifetime High | Lifetime Low | Open Interest |
|---|---|---|---|---|---|---|---|---|
| Dec | 1.4165 | 1.4205 | 1.4155 | 1.4175 | – .0025 | 1.5360 | 1.3250 | 29,442 |
| Mr87 | 1.3975 | 1.4045 | 1.3975 | 1.4000 | – .0025 | 1.5215 | 1.3725 | 2,142 |
| June | 1.3815 | 1.3850 | 1.3815 | 1.3830 | – .0020 | 1.4660 | 1.3600 | 470 |

Est vol 5,478; vol Mon 3,944; open int 32,063, –13.

**CANADIAN DOLLAR (IMM) – 100,000 dlrs.; $ per Can $**

| | Open | High | Low | Settle | Chg | High | Low | Open Interest |
|---|---|---|---|---|---|---|---|---|
| Dec | .7215 | .7223 | .7212 | .7216 | +.0007 | .7285 | .6790 | 11,934 |
| Mar87 | .7170 | .7181 | .7170 | .7174 | +.0008 | .7256 | .6770 | 3,717 |
| June | .... | .... | .... | .7126 | +.0007 | .7243 | .6995 | 234 |

Est vol 1,204; vol Mon 1,604; open int 15,978, +311.

**JAPANESE YEN (IMM) 12.5 million yen; $ per yen (.00)**

| | Open | High | Low | Settle | Chg | High | Low | Open Interest |
|---|---|---|---|---|---|---|---|---|
| Dec | .6140 | .6157 | .6139 | .6147 | +.0001 | .6608 | .4720 | 34,868 |
| Mar87 | .6160 | .6177 | .6159 | .6167 | +.0001 | .6631 | .5850 | 6,019 |
| June | .6180 | .6200 | .6180 | .6192 | +.0001 | .6640 | .6121 | 454 |

Est vol 9,100; vol Mon 14,784; open int 41,343, +796.

**SWISS FRANC (IMM) – 125,000 francs-$ per franc**

| | Open | High | Low | Settle | Chg | High | Low | Open Interest |
|---|---|---|---|---|---|---|---|---|
| Dec | .5958 | .5991 | .5953 | .5979 | +.0001 | .6268 | .4878 | 29,015 |
| Mar87 | .5982 | .6018 | .5980 | .6007 | +.0001 | .6295 | .5125 | 2,112 |
| June | .6018 | .6050 | .6018 | .6037 | .... | .6320 | .5870 | 601 |
| Sept | .... | .... | .... | .6067 | .... | .6335 | .5960 | 103 |

Est vol 17,626; vol Mon 17,881; open int 31,831, –1,463.

**W. GERMAN MARK (IMM) – 125,000 marks; $ per mark**

| | Open | High | Low | Settle | Chg | High | Low | Open Interest |
|---|---|---|---|---|---|---|---|---|
| Dec | .4952 | .4977 | .4951 | .4970 | +.0003 | .5087 | .4090 | 42,190 |
| Mar87 | .4967 | .4994 | .4967 | .4987 | +.0003 | .5102 | .4370 | 5,832 |
| June | .4988 | .5007 | .4988 | .5005 | +.0003 | .5118 | .4850 | 512 |

Est vol 16,372; vol Mon 21,028; open int 48,538, –73.

Currency futures

**TREASURY BONDS (CBT) – $100,000; pts. 32nds of 100%**

| | Open | High | Low | Settle | Chg | Yield Settle | Yield Chg | Open Interest |
|---|---|---|---|---|---|---|---|---|
| Dec | 99-00 | 99-12 | 98-15 | 98-18 | – 25 | 8.147 | + .080 | 179,504 |
| Mr87 | 98-03 | 98-14 | 97-15 | 97-21 | – 25 | 8.241 | + .081 | 43,498 |
| June | 97-11 | 97-16 | 96-16 | 96-22 | – 27 | 8.343 | + .089 | 21,201 |
| Sept | 96-16 | 96-21 | 95-24 | 95-24 | – 30 | 8.444 | + .101 | 7,610 |
| Dec | 95-24 | 95-24 | 94-30 | 94-28 | – 32 | 8.539 | + .109 | 8,462 |
| Mr88 | 94-28 | 95-01 | 94-13 | 94-02 | – 34 | 8.628 | + .116 | 1,977 |
| June | 94-08 | 94-08 | 93-22 | 93-10 | – 35 | 8.712 | + .122 | 848 |
| Sept | .... | .... | .... | 92-20 | – 36 | 8.790 | + .127 | 336 |
| Dec | 92-24 | 92-31 | 92-10 | 92-00 | – 36 | 8.861 | + .128 | 153 |

Est vol 250,000; vol Mon 246,343; opn int 257,655, +11,427

**TREASURY NOTES (CBT) – $100,000; pts. 32nds of 100%**

| | Open | High | Low | Settle | Chg | Yield Settle | Yield Chg | Open Interest |
|---|---|---|---|---|---|---|---|---|
| Dec | 103-10 | 103-18 | 103-01 | 103-06 | – 12 | 7.540 | + .052 | 47,727 |
| Mr87 | 102-20 | 102-21 | 102-05 | 102-10 | – 14 | 7.665 | + .063 | 16,720 |
| June | 101-21 | 101-25 | 101-11 | 101-16 | – 14 | 7.781 | + .063 | 587 |

Est vol 17,000; vol Mon 17,351; open int 65,048, –1,085.

**TREASURY BILLS (IMM) – $1 mil.; pts. of 100%**

| | Open | High | Low | Settle | Chg | Discount Settle | Discount Chg | Open Interest |
|---|---|---|---|---|---|---|---|---|
| Dec | 94.68 | 94.75 | 94.27 | 94.27 | + .01 | 5.28 | – .01 | 18,961 |
| Mr87 | 94.77 | 94.82 | 94.77 | 94.79 | + .01 | 5.21 | – .01 | 14,376 |
| June | 94.76 | 94.77 | 94.74 | 94.76 | + .01 | 5.24 | – .01 | 2,979 |
| Sept | 94.57 | 94.58 | 94.55 | 94.57 | + .01 | 5.43 | – .01 | 662 |
| Dec | 94.24 | 94.29 | 94.23 | 94.26 | .... | 5.74 | .... | 562 |
| Mr88 | 93.91 | 93.92 | 93.88 | 93.91 | .... | 6.09 | .... | 361 |
| June | 93.59 | 93.59 | 93.56 | 93.59 | .... | 6.41 | .... | 143 |

Est vol 9,479; vol Mon 5,554; open int 38,044, +412.

Interest rate futures

**S&P 500 INDEX (CME) 500 times index**

| | Open | High | Low | Settle | Chg | High | Low | Open Interest |
|---|---|---|---|---|---|---|---|---|
| Dec | 243.30 | 243.80 | 236.20 | 237.05 | – 6.30 | 258.40 | 209.50 | 122,030 |
| Mr87 | 244.00 | 244.50 | 236.75 | 237.60 | – 6.45 | 259.00 | 227.35 | 21,594 |
| June | 244.20 | 245.00 | 237.30 | 238.25 | – 6.45 | 260.35 | 228.90 | 147 |

Est vol 100,881; vol Mon 90,136; open int 143,785, +674.
The index: High 243.22; Low 236.66; Close 236.77 –6.44

**NYSE COMPOSITE INDEX (NYFE) 500 times index**

| | Open | High | Low | Settle | Chg | High | Low | Open Interest |
|---|---|---|---|---|---|---|---|---|
| Dec | 139.85 | 140.15 | 135.70 | 136.15 | – 3.65 | 148.00 | 121.10 | 16,843 |
| Mr87 | 140.15 | 140.50 | 135.90 | 136.45 | – 3.70 | 148.95 | 128.00 | 2,257 |
| June | 140.35 | 140.85 | 136.20 | 136.75 | – 3.80 | 149.00 | 131.05 | 412 |

Est vol 17,117; vol Mon 11,910; open int 19,557, –253.
The index: High 139.88; Low 136.43; Close 136.48 –3.42

**KC VALUE LINE INDEX (KC) 500 times index**

| | Open | High | Low | Settle | Chg | High | Low | Open Interest |
|---|---|---|---|---|---|---|---|---|
| Dec | 228.45 | 229.30 | 222.30 | 223.60 | – 5.05 | 250.10 | 210.80 | 5,358 |
| Mr87 | 227.30 | 227.70 | 220.80 | 221.80 | – 5.40 | 237.00 | 210.00 | 1,489 |

Est vol 3,500; vol Mon 2,471; open int 6,848, –79.
The index: High 229.84; Low 225.53; Close 225.56 –4.21

Stock index futures

Source: *The Wall Street Journal.*

size of the contracts. For instance, if the price of Swiss francs goes up by just 2 cents against the dollar, you are ahead $2,500, since one futures contract covers 125,000 Swiss francs. Similarly, a 3-point drop in the NYSE composite index means a $1,500 loss (3 × 500).

The margin trading rules for commodities contracts apply to financial futures contracts as well. When related to the relatively small initial margin deposit required to make transactions in the financial futures markets, this price activity can mean either a high rate of return or big losses. The following table shows the initial and maintenance margin requirements for financial instruments of several full-service brokers in early 1987:

| | Initial Margin Deposit | Maintenance Margin Deposit |
|---|---|---|
| Japanese yen | $1,800 | $1,400 |
| Treasury bills | $2,000 | $1,500 |
| Treasury bonds | $2,000 | $1,500 |
| S&P 500 stock index | $6,000 | $4,500 |
| West German mark | $2,500 | $1,875 |
| British pound | $2,000 | $1,500 |
| U.S. dollar index | $2,000 | $1,500 |
| Major Market index | $5,000 | $3,750 |

# TRADING IN FINANCIAL FUTURES

Two basic trading strategies are often used by individual investors when dealing in financial futures: speculating and hedging. Although commodities and financial futures may differ, the techniques used with these futures contracts are virtually the same. We will focus here on speculating with currency and interest rate futures and hedging with stock index futures.

## SPECULATING IN FINANCIAL FUTURES

Speculators are especially interested in financial futures because of the large size of the futures contracts. For instance, in early 1987, Canadian dollar contracts were worth almost $72,000, GNMA contracts about $104,000, and Treasury bill contracts nearly $1,000,000. With contracts this large, even small movements in the underlying currency or debt instrument will produce serious price swings and the potential for generous profits.

You can use currency or interest rate futures for just about any speculative purpose. For example, if you expect the dollar to be devalued in relation to the German mark, you can buy mark currency futures, which will go up in value if you are right. If you anticipate a rise in interest rates, you can profit from the drop by short selling interest rate futures.

Because financial futures contracts are so highly leveraged, investment return is measured on the amount of money actually invested rather than on the value of the contract itself. Thus, the return on invested capital formula we introduced in Chapter 27 will enable you to calculate the profitability of your investment. Let's look at an example of a foreign currency contract.

Suppose you believe that the Japanese yen is about to appreciate in value relative to the dollar. As a result, you decide to buy three September yen contracts at .006195. Since each contract is worth $77,438 (12,500,000 × 0.006195), the total market value of the three contracts is $232,314. Despite this huge amount, you have to deposit only $5,400 to acquire this position, since the required initial margin for Japanese yen is only $1,800 a contract. If the price of the yen moves up just a fraction—from .006195 to .006700, for instance—the value of the three contracts will rise to $251,250, providing you with a profit of $18,936; and remember, this is all from an investment of just $5,400. This, in turn, translates into a return on invested capital of some 351 percent:

$$\frac{\text{return on}}{\text{invested capital}} = \frac{\begin{array}{c}\text{selling price of} \\ \text{financial futures contract}\end{array} - \begin{array}{c}\text{purchase price of} \\ \text{financial futures contract}\end{array}}{\text{amount of margin deposit}}$$

$$= \frac{251,250 - 232,314}{5,400}$$

$$= \frac{18,936}{5,400}$$

$$= \underline{351\%}$$

Of course, an even smaller fractional change in the other direction would have wiped out your total investment—a fact that makes financial futures an extremely risky investment.

You can, of course, profit from a drop in security prices by short selling. In fact, speculative short sales are rather common in the financial futures market. For example, suppose you anticipate a sharp rise in long-term interest rates. Because a rise in rates means that interest rate futures contracts will drop in value, you decide to short sell two December GNMA contracts at 87–22. (This quote can also be read as 87 22/32 or 87.6875 percent of par.) Although the two contracts are worth $175,375 ($100,000 × .876875 × 2), you only have to put up $1,500 for each contract to satisfy the initial margin deposit requirements. If interest rates do, in fact, move up, so that the price of GNMA contracts drops to 80, you could cover your short position by buying back the two December GNMA contracts and in the process make a profit of $15,375. This is possible since you originally sold the two contracts at $175,375 and then bought them back at $160,000. Like any investment, the difference between what you pay for a security and what you sell it for is profit. In this case, the return on your invested capital would amount to a whopping 512 percent. Again, this kind of return is due, in no small part, to the very real risk that you'll lose your total investment.

## HEDGING WITH STOCK INDEX FUTURES

One of the most popular trading vehicles in the financial futures market is the stock index futures contract. Because these contracts provide the opportunity to play the market as a whole, they are actively used by speculators looking for a big bang from their money. They are just as popular, however, as hedging vehicles to protect a stock portfolio against an adverse market. Whether speculating or hedging, the key to success is predicting the future course of the stock market. Since you are buying the market as a whole with stock index futures, you must first get a handle on what you think the future direction of the market will be. You can then use this information to formulate a trading or hedging strategy. For example, if you feel strongly that the market is headed up, your strategy would be to buy stock index futures. In contrast, if your market analysis suggests a sharp drop, you could come out ahead by short selling stock index futures.

But rather than dwell on speculative techniques, let's look more closely at the hedging properties of stock index futures. These securities make excellent hedging vehicles because they enable you to protect your stock holdings in a declining market. Although the tactic is not perfect, it gives you a way of buying protection without disturbing your equity holdings. Here's how a short hedge works. Assume you hold a total of 1,000 shares of stock in 15 different companies and that the market value of this portfolio is $75,000. If you think the market is about to undergo a temporary sharp decline, you can sell your shares, short sell your stock against the box or buy puts on each of your stocks. Since these options are either cumbersome or costly, a better way to achieve basically the same result is to short sell stock index futures.

Suppose you short sell one NYSE stock index future at 145.75. Such a contract would provide a close match to the current value of your portfolio, with an approximate value of $73,000, and yet would require an initial margin deposit of only $1,500 (margin deposits are less for hedgers than for speculators). Now if the NYSE composite index does drop to, say, 125.00, you will make a profit from the short sale transaction of some $10,000—that is, since the index fell 20.75 points (145.75 − 125.00), the total profit will be: $20.75 \times \$500 = \$10,375$. Ignoring taxes, this profit can be added to the portfolio (additional shares of stock can be purchased at their new lower prices), the net result being a new portfolio position that will approximate the value which existed prior to the decline in the market. How well the before and after portfolio positions match will depend on how far the portfolio drops in value. If the average price drops about $10 a share in our example, the positions will closely match. But this does not always happen; the price of some stocks will change more than others and the amount of protection provided by this type of short hedge depends on how sensitive the stock portfolio is to movements in the market. Thus, the type of stocks held in the portfolio is an important consideration in structuring the stock index short hedge. OTC and highly volatile stocks will probably require more protection than stocks that are relatively more price stable or have betas closer to 1.0. In any event, hedging with stock index futures can be a low-cost yet effective way of obtaining protection against loss in a declining stock market.

## PROGRAM TRADING AND THE TRIPLE WITCHING HOUR

It happens four times a year: options and futures contracts expire at the same time. This period, known as the *triple witching hour,* has produced unprecedented sell-offs in the market in the hours and minutes immediately before the expiration. On September 11, 1986, for example, the Dow Jones industrial average dropped 86 points—4.6 percent of its total value. Although this did not compare to the 12.8 percent drop on Black Friday in 1929, nor to the 5.7 percent drop in 1962 when a major economic slowdown was feared, it was the third largest drop in market history—at least up to that time.

The major cause of this volatility is *program trading*—computer-assisted trading strategies that help big institutional traders profit from price differences between options and futures contracts on stock market indexes and the individual stocks that make up these indexes. For example, when futures on Standard & Poor's 500 index trade too far above the value of the underlying stocks, traders sell them short and buy blocks of the stock. Since the futures are paid off at the value of the index when they expire, they will have to fall in price or the stock will have to rise. Either way the traders profit. Similarly, when futures trade for less than the stocks in the index, traders buy the futures and short the stock. The traders keep their stock position and their holdings of options and futures in balance, or hedged. But when option and futures contracts expire, the traders are left with huge unhedged positions in stocks. If the stocks' prices move against them, they will have no offsetting gain in the futures. To eliminate this risk, they generally buy or sell massive amounts of stock—$25 million worth or more at a time—just before the expiration.

Portfolio insurance is another form of program trading and one that can affect the market anytime, not just when futures contracts expire. This strategy attempts to protect large institutional portfolios by selling futures short, thereby creating profits to offset losses on stocks in a decline. Institutional investors using portfolio insurance now control anywhere from $25 billion to $40 billion worth of stock. Because they sell futures when the market starts to fall—and arbitrageurs short stocks when futures trade at a discount—there is a risk that an innocuous market downturn may be greatly magnified.

Although program trading has jolted the market at and before the triple witching hour, these downswings have usually reversed themselves within a few days when the market moves would not otherwise have occurred. Instead of causing a sustained drop in market value, program trading compresses a day's—and sometimes even a week's—market movement into a period as short as 10 minutes—a situation that creates extreme price volatility.

Unfortunately, our luck ran out on October 19, 1987. For on Black Monday the market experienced its biggest crash ever, far surpassing the 1929 dive. Many believe that program trading helped cause the crash, because when prices began to fall, program traders kicked in and drove prices down even further, leading to a landslide. The toll by the end of the day: over half a *billion* shares had been traded and the Dow was off 508 points! Not surprisingly, a clamor followed to severely restrict or even eliminate program trading.

# SHOULD YOU INVEST?

Financial futures are highly volatile securities that have considerable potential for both profit and loss. For instance, in the 9 months from March through December 1986, the S&P 500 futures contract fluctuated in price from a low of 209.50 to a high of 258.4. This range of nearly 49 points for a single contract translated into a profit or loss of some $24,500 from an initial investment of only $6,000.

Unfortunately, your potential for loss is as great as your potential for profit. In order to come out ahead—financially as well as mentally—you must thoroughly understand what you are doing *before* you invest and clearly recognize the tremendous risks involved. If you are realistic about this investment, you'll realize that losses are almost inevitable—and you'll prepare yourself for them. One way to minimize the potentially devastating impact of price volatility is to diversify your investments, putting only a small part of your money in financial futures. On the whole, although investing in financial futures may seem like the investment world's equivalent of walking a tightrope, they can provide generous returns if you know how to use them.

# FIVE
## WHERE YOU GO FROM HERE

# 29

## DEFINING YOUR
## INVESTMENT PORTFOLIO

A portfolio is a collection of investment vehicles assembled to meet a common investment goal. The goal of a growth-oriented portfolio, for example, is long-term price appreciation. An income-oriented portfolio, on the other hand, stresses current dividend and interest return. Achieving your investment objectives depends on the balance between risk and return in the individual securities that make up your portfolio.

The success of your portfolio depends in large part on how clearly you define your portfolio objectives. Coming up with a clear idea of what you want is not always easy since there are often trade-offs to be made between risk and return as well as between potential price appreciation and current income. Your decisions will be influenced in part by how much risk you're willing to take, by your need for current income, and by your tax situation.

# DIVERSIFY TO REDUCE RISK

Normally, a portfolio will contain two or more investments and will strive for diversification, or the inclusion of a variety of investment vehicles for the purpose of reducing risk.

## ALL RISK IS NOT THE SAME

As noted in Chapter 5, the securities you buy are subject to two kinds of risk: Diversifiable (or unsystematic) risk is the business and financial risk unique to a particular investment. Nondiversifiable risk is the risk, associated with every investment vehicle, that general market movements will alter a security's return. Unless you're lucky, there's no getting around nondiversifiable risk. You can expect the value of your securities to decline if the market as a whole drops and to rise if the market rises. Thus, you can only hope to reduce diversifiable risk through portfolio management.

Studies have shown that high levels of diversifiable risk do not result in equally high levels of return. Since you get nothing back from bearing this risk, you should try to minimize it in your portfolio.

## HOW TO DO IT

Diversification minimizes diversifiable risk by balancing the poor return from one vehicle against the good return from another. The best way to accomplish this is to invest in securities from a wide variety of industries. It's not a good idea, for example, to include Ford, General Motors, and Chrysler common stock in your portfolio, since these companies face similar business and financial risks. In contrast, by investing in IBM, General Motors, and General Foods, you may achieve the diversification you need. The cyclical changes in the automobile industry will probably not affect the fortunes of IBM or General Foods. Similarly, when high-tech stocks are out of favor, automobile and food stocks may boom.

How many investment vehicles do you need for adequate diversification? The figure on the next page depicts the two types of risk as they relate to the number of securities in your portfolio. As you can see, the level of nondiversifiable risk remains constant. Diversifiable risk declines markedly, however, as the number of securities in the portfolio rises. If your portfolio includes 8 to 20 securities, you have eliminated most of your diversifiable risk. After 20, you get little risk reduction from increasing the number of issues you hold.

Thus, if your goal is to reduce diversifiable risk as much as you can, you should include between 8 and 20 issues in your portfolio. Since the benefits of further diversification are questionable, owning additional securities may actually cost you money because of the high transaction costs involved in trading these securities.

WHERE YOU GO FROM HERE

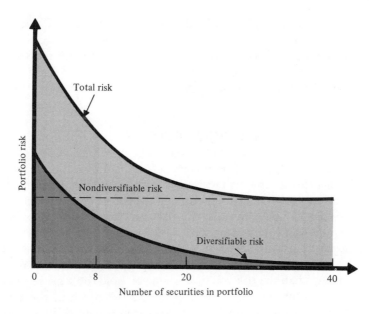

Number of securities in portfolio

## USE BETA TO DETERMINE RISK

Beta, which was explained in Chapter 5, gives you a way of measuring nondiversifiable risk. If a portfolio has a beta of 1.0, the portfolio experiences changes in its rate of return equal to changes in the market's rate of return. The 1.0 beta portfolio would tend to experience a 10 percent increase in return if the stock market as a whole experienced a 10 percent increase in return. Conversely, if the market return fell by 6 percent, the return on the 1.0 beta portfolio would also tend to fall by 6 percent. Here are the expected returns for three portfolio betas in two situations each:

| Portfolio Beta | Change in Return on Market | Change in Expected Return on Portfolio |
|---|---|---|
| +2.0 | +10.0% | +20.0% |
| | −10.0 | −20.0 |
| + .5 | +10.0 | + 5.0 |
| | −10.0 | − 5.0 |
| −1.0 | +10.0 | −10.0 |
| | −10.0 | +10.0 |

When the market experiences an increase in return of 10 percent and a decrease in return of 10 percent, the 2.0 beta portfolio is twice as volatile as the market. When the market return increases by 10 percent, the portfolio return increases by 20 percent. Conversely, the portfolio's return falls by 20 percent when the market declines 10 percent. This would be considered a relatively high-risk, high-return portfolio. A .5 beta portfolio is considered to be a relatively low-risk, low-return, conservative portfolio. The .5 beta portfolio is half as volatile as the market. A beta of $-1.0$ indicates that the portfolio moves in a direction opposite to that of the market. A bearish investor would probably want to own a negative beta portfolio, because this type of investment tends to rise in value when the stock market declines, and vice versa. Finding securities with negative betas is difficult, however, since most securities have positive betas.

## CREATING AN EFFICIENT PORTFOLIO

The ultimate goal of risk diversification is the creation of an efficient portfolio, one that provides the highest return for a given level of risk or has the lowest risk for a given level of return. When given the choice between two equally risky investments offering different returns, the obvious choice is the one with the highest return. Similarly, if you have a choice of two investments with the same return but different levels of risk, the clear choice is the vehicle with the lower risk.

The risk you take when you hold a single security in your portfolio is always greater than the risk you take when you hold the same security in combination with other securities. And the greater the difference in the return behaviors of two securities, the greater the risk reduction achieved through diversification.

Assume, for example, that you hold two equally priced securities in your portfolio that vary greatly in their return behavior. That is, when the return of one security is high, the return of the other is low and vice versa. While, with a risk level of 5, security A is somewhat risky, with a risk level of 10, security B is extremely risky. When the two investments are combined, the resulting risk may be less than 5 and may even approach zero. Thus, a security's risk is always less when viewed in the context of a portfolio rather than in isolation. In fact, if the returns on two securities fluctuate in equal amounts in exactly opposite directions, the portfolio return created by combining them will be stable.

Looking at the other side of the coin, how are returns affected by viewing a security as part of a portfolio rather than in isolation? Interestingly, while risk is reduced through diversification, return is basically unaffected. For example, assume that the returns on securities A and B are 8 and 12 percent, respectively. If a portfolio consists of one share of each, the portfolio return will be 10 percent [(.50 × 8%) + (.50 × 12%) = 10%]. Thus, the returns on these securities remain the same, and the portfolio return is a simple weighted average of the individual returns. (Note that the portfolio consists of equal parts—50 percent—of each security.) The message is clear: since risk can be reduced through portfolio diversification without sacrificing return, it pays to diversify.

## BUILDING A PORTFOLIO

How do you build your portfolio? Your basic construction tools are knowledge of your personal finances and your personal objectives.

## START WITH YOUR OWN CHARACTERISTICS

Your starting point in formulating your portfolio strategy is your personal financial and family situation, including:

- Your level and stability of income
- Your family size and responsibilities (Are your children starting preschool or college? Does your spouse work? Do you own your own home?)
- Your net worth
- Your age and experience as an investor
- Your disposition toward risk

In order for your portfolio to work, it must be tailored to meet your personal and family financial needs. For example, while a relatively young investor with no family responsibilities and a high personal income can take an aggressive investment approach, a middle-income investor with young children should be far more cautious and should not invest at all until the family has a measure of financial security, with ample savings and insurance protection. In general, a single investor with no family responsibilities is better able to handle risk than an individual with a family. When you apply this to your own situation, keep in mind this common-sense principle: the risks you take when you invest should not exceed your ability to bear these risks.

Let's look at some specifics. How much you earn and your degree of job security will affect your portfolio strategy. The more secure your job, the more likely you are to take investment risks. If you are in job jeopardy, your goal should be to put money into highly liquid, short-term instruments that involve little or no risk, and to stay out of the stock market.

Your portfolio strategy is also shaped by taxes. The higher your income, the more important the tax ramifications of your investment program become. For example, municipal bonds normally yield about three-quarters the annual interest of corporate bonds, because the interest income on municipal bonds is tax-free. On an after-tax basis, however, municipal bonds may provide a superior return if you are in the top (33 percent) tax bracket.

Your investment experience also comes into play. Most investors assume increasingly higher levels of investment risk over time. It is best to get your investment feet wet by starting with low-risk investments and gradually increasing the risk as you become more comfortable with the investment process. If your initial investment is too risky and you lose money, you may be so scarred by the experience that you consider even appropriate levels of risk to be too high. Worse yet, you may never invest again.

## STATE YOUR OBJECTIVES

Once you have developed a personal financial profile, you must then ask yourself, "What do I want from my portfolio?" Although we would all like to double our money every year with little risk, the realities of the highly competitive investment environment make this outcome unlikely. Realistically, we can primarily earn current income or capital gains, but not both.

Your needs will determine which avenue you choose. If you are retired and depend on the income from your portfolio to meet your day-to-day living expenses, you'll probably choose a low-risk, current-income–oriented investment approach. If you're financially secure, you're likely to accept higher risk in the hope of improving your worth. A young investor with a secure job is less concerned about current income and better able to bear risk than an older investor. The young investor is likely to be interested in speculative investments that have the potential for significant capital gains. As an investor approaches age 60, income becomes more important than capital gains. At this age, most people are less willing to take risks. They want to consolidate their finances in income-producing investments so they have a steady source of funds during their retirement years.

## STRUCTURE YOUR PORTFOLIO

How do you choose the kinds of securities to include in your portfolio? Basically, you must decide what you need from your investments in each of the following areas:

- Current income
- Capital preservation
- Capital growth
- Taxes

One or more of these factors will probably be more important to you than the others. These choices will change along with your life situation. What is critical at age 30 may not be relevant at age 60.

In general, the goals of current income and capital preservation produce low-risk, conservative investment strategies. Portfolios with these objectives generally contain low-beta (low-risk) securities. On the other hand, if your objective is capital growth, you're willing to risk more and accept a reduced level of current income. High-risk growth stocks, options, commodity and financial futures, and other speculative investment vehicles may be suitable in this case.

Taxes will have an enormous impact on your portfolio strategy. If you have a high income, for example, your portfolio strategy may be to defer as much of your tax burden as possible and earn investment returns in the form of capital gains. You can do this by investing in vehicles such as high-growth common stocks that reinvest rather than pay out earnings and are expected to appreciate in value. If you are in a lower tax bracket, these types of tax concerns will have little effect on your investment choices. If an investment such as a highly rated corporate bond offers high current income, you will have no reason to avoid it as long as it is consistent with your overall portfolio needs.

# SOME SAMPLE PORTFOLIOS

The following four portfolios—developed to meet four entirely different investment objectives—show that no single portfolio is right for every investor: *individualization is the key to success.*

## CAROL NAKAMURA: YOUNG, SINGLE, AND PROSPEROUS

At 28 years of age, Carol Nakamura has done well for herself. She has built a $300,000 investment portfolio consisting of investment real estate in Honolulu, Hawaii, and a holding in a money market mutual fund. Ms. Nakamura is currently employed as the controller of Kamehameha Management, a real estate management firm in Honolulu. She is a CPA, and her income from salary and property rentals is $55,000 a year, putting her in a 35 percent marginal income tax bracket (federal and Hawaii state income tax combined). Ms. Nakamura is not married, and her only debts are secured by her properties.

Carol Nakamura has decided to diversify her portfolio. Most of her net worth consists of rental condominiums located in the Waikiki area of Honolulu. Clearly, diversification is needed to reduce her risk exposure and to increase her overall investment return. The Hawaii real estate market is somewhat unpredictable, and Ms. Nakamura wishes to lessen her risk exposure in that market. She is currently selling one of her properties, and with the funds in her money market mutual fund she will have $75,000 to invest in stocks. She asks her investment advisor, Marjorie Wong, to develop a securities portfolio for her. Because of her relatively young age and her strong future earning capacity, Ms. Nakamura can bear the risks of a speculative investment program. Her portfolio of stocks will emphasize issues that have a strong price appreciation potential.

Ms. Nakamura's securities portfolio is presented in the table. It consists of eight stocks, all of which have above-average risk-return potential. The betas of the issues range from 1.13 to 2.31; the portfolio's beta is approximately 1.61, indicating an above-average risk exposure. (The beta for a portfolio can be calculated as a weighted average of the individual security betas within the portfolio.) The portfolio is diversified across industry lines, with a fairly diverse mix of securities, all selected for their above-average price appreciation potential. Altuna Airlines, an interisland carrier in Hawaii, was chosen because of the expected increase in the number of visitors to Hawaii. Betta Computer is a fast-growing personal computer manufacturer. Easy Work is a retailer that services the growing do-it-yourself home improvement market. Gomez Industries is a rapidly expanding glass manufacturer and photo processor. Hercules is a growing brewer. Jama Motor, based in Japan, provides a measure of international diversification for the portfolio. Karl Lewis Enterprises is an expanding fast-food operator based in California. Ranch Petroleum is a small oil company with refining and oil production interests.

Most of the securities Ms. Wong selected for Ms. Nakamura are not household names. Rather, they are firms with exciting growth potential at the time of purchase. The portfolio should fluctuate in value at a rate approximately 1.6 times greater than the stock market as a whole. The dividend yield on the portfolio is a relatively low 0.6 percent. Most of the return Ms. Nakamura anticipates from this portfolio is in the form of price appreciation. She anticipates holding the stocks for at least a year in order to realize anticipated appreciation. Given Ms. Nakamura's marginal income tax bracket, it seems preferable for her to defer taxes and earn returns in the form of capital gains.

## CAROL NAKAMURA'S PORTFOLIO
### Objective: Speculative Growth (High-Risk, High-Return Potential)

| Number of Shares | Company | Dividend per Share | Dividend Income | Price per Share | Total Cost (including commission) | Beta | Dividend Yield |
|---|---|---|---|---|---|---|---|
| 1,200 | Altuna Airlines | $— | $— | $ 7 | $ 8,480 | 1.75 | —% |
| 300 | Betta Computer | — | — | 30 | 9,090 | 1.87 | — |
| 400 | Easy Work Tile | — | — | 25 | 10,090 | 1.59 | — |
| 300 | Gomez Industries | 0.36 | 108 | 30 | 9,090 | 1.19 | 1.2 |
| 300 | Hercules Brewing | 0.80 | 240 | 32 | 9,700 | 1.27 | 2.5 |
| 300 | Jama Motor ADR | 0.35 | 105 | 33 | 10,000 | 1.13 | 1.1 |
| 500 | Karl Lewis Enterprises | — | — | 20 | 10,100 | 1.79 | — |
| 1,300 | Ranch Petroleum | — | — | 6 | 7,880 | 2.31 | — |
| | Total | | $453 | | $74,430 | | 0.6% |

Portfolio beta = 1.61

## MARTIN AND NANCY JACOB: LOTTERY WINNERS

Martin Jacob, a professor of political science at the University of West Bay City in Michigan, and his wife, Nancy, are very lucky people. After buying a $1 Michigan State Lottery Ticket at a local tavern, Professor Jacob won the $275,000 prize. After paying income taxes on the prize and spending a small amount for personal needs, Martin and Nancy had $210,000 remaining. Because of their philosophy of saving any windfalls and not spending accumulated capital on day-to-day living expenses, they chose to invest these funds (in contrast with many lottery winners, who simply blow their winnings on fast living).

The Jacobs have two children. Martin is 37 years of age and has a secure teaching position. His salary is approximately $35,000 a year. In addition, he earns approximately $15,000 a year from book royalties and several other small sources. Professor Jacob's tax bracket (federal and state) is approximately 30 percent. His life insurance protection of approximately $70,000 is provided by the university. Nancy Jacob is a librarian. She currently is at home with the children and is not expected to be a source of steady income for several years. The Jacobs own (free and clear) their home in the Banks area of Bay City. In addition, they have a $16,000 money market account at a local savings and loan association. They have no outstanding debts.

Professor Jacob asked his investment advisor, Fred Craves, to develop an investment portfolio for them. Together, they decided on the following strategy. First, the professor and his wife tend to be somewhat risk-averse; that is, they do not wish to risk much loss. Second, the Jacobs indicated that they would enjoy some increase in spendable income. Given these facts, Mr. Craves suggested the portfolio presented in the following table. The emphasis in the portfolio is long-term growth at an average risk level, with a moderate dividend return. The portfolio consists of nine issues. There appears to be sufficient diversification. The portfolio's beta is 1.05, indicating a level of nondiversifiable risk approximately equal to that of the stock market as a whole. The portfolio's dividend yield is about 4.9 percent, which approximates the average dividend return for the entire stock market. The betas of individual securities in the portfolio vary somewhat. However, the portfolio's overall risk is moderate.

## MARTIN AND NANCY JACOB'S PORTFOLIO
### Objective: Long-Term Growth (Average Risk, Moderate Dividends)

| Number of Shares | Company | Dividend per Share | Dividend Income | Price per Share | Total Cost (including commission) | Beta | Dividend Yield |
|---|---|---|---|---|---|---|---|
| 1,000 | Bancorp West, Inc. | $1.20 | $ 1,200 | $22 | $ 22,200 | .86 | 5.4% |
| 600 | BST, Inc. | 2.80 | 1,680 | 40 | 24,200 | 1.00 | 6.9 |
| 1,000 | Florida Southcoast Banks | 1.20 | 1,200 | 23 | 23,200 | .84 | 5.2 |
| 1,000 | Kings | 1.60 | 1,600 | 25 | 25,300 | .88 | 6.3 |
| 500 | Light Newspapers | 0.92 | 460 | 46 | 23,200 | 1.12 | 2.0 |
| 600 | Miller Foods | 1.88 | 1,128 | 37 | 22,400 | 1.07 | 5.0 |
| 800 | State Oil of California | 1.00 | 800 | 27 | 21,800 | 1.30 | 3.7 |
| 600 | Vornox | 2.28 | 1,368 | 40 | 24,200 | 1.04 | 5.7 |
| 600 | Woodstock | 1.30 | 780 | 36 | 21,800 | 1.32 | 3.6 |
| | Total | | $10,216 | | $208,300 | | 4.9% |

Portfolio beta = 1.05

The Jacob portfolio consists of stocks from a wide range of American businesses. All the companies have above-average growth potential and none faces technological obsolescence or heavy foreign competition. Two banking stocks were selected, Bancorp West, Inc., and Florida Southcoast Banks. The former is a well-managed bank holding company that owns the largest bank in California. The latter is a growing bank holding company located on the south coast of Florida. Both regions are experiencing rapid population and economic growth. BST, Inc. appears to be well positioned in the growing communications industry. Kings is a food processor with a solid future. Light Newspapers is a large newspaper chain with many Sunbelt papers. Miller Foods is expanding as well, helped by the 1987 acquisition of Denton Companies, a superbly managed supermarket chain. The portfolio has two natural resource stocks, State Oil and Woodstock. These companies are well positioned in their respective industries. Vornox is a major drug firm that should benefit from the aging demographic mix of America. All these are well-managed companies with growth potential. The portfolio has a moderate risk level and provides an average dividend yield. With this portfolio, the Jacobs will have potential price appreciation coupled with a steady dividend income.

## ART AND HELEN BRANDT: RETIREES

Having just sold their family business and liquidated their real estate investment property, the Brandts are eager to begin their retirement. At age 60, both have worked hard for 35 years building the successful business they recently sold. In addition, they made some successful real estate investments over the years. The sale of their business and real estate holdings netted them $600,000 after taxes. They wish to invest these funds and have asked their investment advisor, Jane Tuttle, to develop a portfolio for them. The relevant financial information about the Brandts is as follows: They own their home free and clear and have a $300,000 bond portfolio that yields them yearly income of $25,000. In addition, they have $20,000 in a money market account, which they do not wish to invest but want to hold as a ready cash reserve. Mr. Brandt has a $200,000 whole life insurance policy on his life, with Mrs. Brandt the designated beneficiary.

Now that they are retired, neither of the Brandts plans to seek employment. They do have a small pension plan that will begin paying an income of $4,000 a year in five years. However, their main source of income will be their investment portfolio. During their last few working years, their combined yearly income was approximately $80,000. Their standard of living is rather high, and they do not wish to significantly change their lifestyle. They do not plan to spend any of their investment capital on living expenses, since they wish to keep their estate intact for their two children. Thus, the Brandts' basic investment objective is current income with some capital appreciation potential. The Brandts do not wish to reinvest in real estate, but rather have asked Ms. Tuttle to develop a $600,000 securities portfolio for them. Their $300,000 bond portfolio will be left undisturbed.

The portfolio developed for the Brandts is shown in the table. It contains nine stocks, with approximately $65,000 invested in each issue. The emphasis is on quality, with low-risk, high-yield issues and diversification. The portfolio's beta is approximately .80—a risk level below that of the general stock market. It is expected that a large portion of the portfolio's total return (dividends plus price appreciation) will be in the form of dividend income. The portfolio has a current dividend yield of approximately 8.7 percent, which is above average. Dividend income totals over $52,000, which added to the bond income and the money market account interest will provide the Brandts with a gross income of about $80,000. The Brandts' after-tax income will equal their working years' income; thus, they will not have to alter their lifestyle.

## ART AND HELEN BRANDT'S PORTFOLIO
Objective: Current Income (Low-Risk, High-Yield)

| Number of Shares | Company | Dividend per Share | Dividend Income | Price per Share | Total Cost (including commission) | Beta | Dividend Yield |
|---|---|---|---|---|---|---|---|
| 3,000 | Alaska Bancorp, Inc. | $1.20 | $ 3,600 | $22 | $ 66,600 | .86 | 5.4% |
| 2,000 | Dallas National Corporation | 2.40 | 4,800 | 30 | 60,600 | .81 | 7.9 |
| 2,500 | Energon | 3.00 | 7,500 | 27 | 68,100 | 1.01 | 11.0 |
| 2,000 | Findly Power and Light | 3.36 | 6,720 | 32 | 64,600 | .63 | 10.4 |
| 2,000 | Geoco | 2.80 | 5,600 | 35 | 70,700 | 1.13 | 7.9 |
| 2,500 | Gulf Gas and Electric | 3.00 | 7,500 | 28 | 70,700 | .53 | 10.6 |
| 4,000 | Public Power Company | 1.76 | 7,040 | 16 | 64,600 | .72 | 10.9 |
| 2,500 | Smith Roberts and Company | 1.36 | 3,400 | 27 | 68,100 | .92 | 5.0 |
| 3,000 | Southwest Utilities | 2.04 | 6,120 | 21 | 63,600 | .60 | 9.6 |
| | Total | | $52,280 | | $597,600 | | 8.7% |

Portfolio beta = .80

Analyzing the individual issues in the portfolio, we can see that four public utility stocks are included. Utility stocks are often suitable for low-risk, current-income–oriented portfolios. High-quality electric and natural gas concerns tend to have moderate growth in earnings and dividends. The four issues in the portfolio, Findly Power and Light, Gulf Gas and Electric, Public Power Company, and Southwest Utilities, have growing service areas and records of profit and dividend increases. The stocks of two very large American companies, Energon and Smith Roberts, are included in the portfolio. Energon is a large energy company and offers a high dividend yield. Smith Roberts, one of the country's largest retailers, is also diversifying into financial services. Two bank holding company stocks were selected, Alaska Bancorp and Dallas National. Dallas National was selected for its above-average dividend yield and because the firm is well positioned in the Dallas market. Alaska Bancorp offers a top-quality vehicle to participate in Alaska's growth. The company has raised its dividend several times in recent years, and future dividend increases are expected. Geoco is a large company with chemical and other diversified operations. All the issues in the Brandts' portfolio are well-known, relatively large corporations. Stability, low risk, and a relatively high dividend yield with some potential for increase characterize the stocks in this portfolio.

## ELIZABETH BECKETT: WIDOW

In the preceding example, a portfolio was developed for a fairly affluent retired couple. Most retirees are less fortunate than the Brandts. Elizabeth Beckett, age 70, was recently widowed. Between the estate of her late husband, her personal assets, and their jointly owned assets, Elizabeth has approximately $350,000 in liquid assets, all of it in savings and money market accounts. Elizabeth owns her home free and clear. Other than the interest on her savings, her income consists of $600 a month from Social Security. Unfortunately, her husband's employer did not have a pension plan. She has turned to her investment advisor, Charles Puckett, to discuss strategy and to develop an investment policy.

Between Social Security and interest earned on her savings and money market accounts, Mrs. Beckett's current income is approximately $35,000 annually. She wishes to increase that income, if possible, while only minimally raising her risk exposure. Mr. Puckett recommended the investment portfolio presented in the following table. The portfolio's objective is to maximize current income while keeping risk at a low level. Approximately $296,000 is invested in high-quality corporate bonds. The balance of $54,000 is placed in a money market account at the local savings and loan to provide a substantial contingency reserve. Through the bond portfolio, Mrs. Beckett's yearly income will rise from approximately $35,000 to about $47,800 ($7,200 Social Security, $4,000 savings interest, $36,600 bond interest), placing Mrs. Beckett in the 28 percent marginal income tax bracket. Taxable corporate bonds were recommended over municipal bonds for their greater after-tax rate of return.

## ELIZABETH BECKETT'S PORTFOLIO
### Objective: Maximize Current Income (Minimal Risk)

| Par Value | Issue | Standard & Poor's Bond Rating | Interest Income | Price | Total Cost | Yield to Maturity | Current Yield |
|---|---|---|---|---|---|---|---|
| $50,000 | Boise Northern 12⅞% due 2009 | A | $ 6,437.50 | 100 | $ 50,000 | 12.875% | 12.875% |
| 50,000 | Dalston and Company 11½% due 1993 | A | 5,750.00 | 98 | 49,000 | 11.900 | 11.700 |
| 50,000 | Maryland-Pacific 10.70% due 1991 | A | 5,350.00 | 97 | 48,500 | 11.600 | 11.000 |
| 50,000 | Pacific Utilities 12⅞% due 2017 | AA | 6,437.50 | 100 | 50,000 | 12.875 | 12.875 |
| 50,000 | Trans-States Telephone 12.70% due 2023 | A | 6,350.00 | 97 | 48,500 | 13.200 | 13.100 |
| 50,000 | Urban Life 12½% due 1994 | AA | 6,250.00 | 100 | 50,000 | 12.500 | 12.500 |
| | Total | | $ 36,575.00 | | $296,000 | 12.500% | 12.400% |

Turning to the portfolio, we see that there are six corporate bond issues, which cost about $50,000 each. Each issuer is a high-quality company that has a very low risk of default. The portfolio is diversified in several ways. First, it contains a mix of industrial, utility, railroad, and financial issues. The two utility issues are Pacific Utilities and Trans-States Telephone. Both companies are very large and financially secure. The two industrial concerns, Dalston and Maryland-Pacific, are very large as well. Boise Northern is a financially solid railroad, and Urban Life is a large, secure

368                                                                              WHERE YOU GO FROM HERE

insurance company. An added measure of diversification is attained by staggering the bonds' maturities. They mature in six different years: 1991, 1993, 1994, 2009, 2017, and 2023. The shorter term bonds will provide ready cash when they mature, and they generally will fluctuate less in price than the longer term bonds. By switching funds out of her savings and money market accounts into bonds, Mrs. Beckett was able to increase her current income substantially while experiencing only a minimal increase in risk.

# 30

## MONITORING YOUR INVESTMENT PORTFOLIO

---

The final and perhaps most important part of the personal investment process involves continually monitoring and periodically adjusting your investment portfolio in order to achieve the financial goals you're after. Monitoring involves evaluating the actual performance of your investments, comparing your performance to investment goals, assessing your portfolio performance and making needed adjustments, and timing these transactions to achieve maximum benefit.

## EVALUATING THE PERFORMANCE OF INDIVIDUAL SECURITIES

When you choose a particular investment for your portfolio, you probably do so on the basis of expected returns, associated risks, and certain tax considerations that may affect the return. Since the actual outcomes may not necessarily coincide with those you expect, you must measure and compare actual performance with anticipated performance.

## OBTAIN NEEDED DATA

The first step in analyzing investment returns is gathering data that reflect the actual performance of each investment you own. As we pointed out in Chapter 11, a broad range of sources of investment information is available. *The Wall Street Journal* and *Barron's*, for example, contain considerable data that you can use to assess the performance of securities. The same type of information you used to make investment decisions can be used to monitor the performance of your investments. The following two areas require special attention.

*Return data.* In order to analyze your investment returns you'll need to know their current market value. Many publications provide daily price quotations for stocks, bonds, and other securities. By regularly recording price and return data (dividends, interest, and other sources of income received), you'll know exactly how much your investments are earning and how their prices are fluctuating in the market. You should also monitor corporate earnings and dividends, since a company's showing in these areas affects its stock price. When you determine total return, be sure to consider both current income and capital appreciation.

*Economic and market activity.* Changes in the economy and market can affect both the market value of your investments and the current income you receive from them. By following economic and market changes, you should be able to assess their potential impact on individual investment returns and on the overall return of your portfolio. As economic and market conditions change you must be prepared to revise your portfolio to respond to new developments. In essence, the more knowledge you have, the more likely you are to profit when times are good and avoid loss when times are bad.

## MEASURE INVESTMENT RETURN

In order to monitor your investment portfolio, you'll need reliable techniques for measuring the performance of each investment vehicle. In particular, the holding period return (HPR) measure, first presented in Chapter 4 (and used in one form or another throughout most of this book) as a measure of an investment's expected return, is also used to determine *actual* return performance from stocks, bonds, mutual funds, and other investments.

Investment holdings need to be evaluated periodically over time—at least once a year. HPR is an excellent way to assess actual return behavior, since it captures *total return* performance and is most appropriate for holding periods of 1 year or less. Total return in this context includes periodic cash income from the investment as well as price appreciation or loss, whether realized or unrealized. When you're dealing with periods of 1 year or longer, you should calculate return in terms of yield, which incorporates the time value of money. Yield can be easily estimated with the approximate yield formula. Since our discussions here will focus on short-term investments, we'll rely on the HPR formula, which is:

$$\text{holding period return (HPR)} = \frac{\text{current income} + \text{capital gain (or loss)}}{\text{beginning investment value}}$$

*Stocks.* The HPR for common and preferred stocks includes both cash dividends received and any price change in the security during the period of ownership. Suppose you purchased 1,000 shares of Dallas National Corporation in May 1987 at a cost of $27,312 (including commissions). After holding the stock for just over a year, you sold it and walked away with a total of $32,040. During the holding period, you received $2,000 in cash dividends and realized a $4,728 capital gain on the sale. The calculated HPR is 24.63 percent as shown here:

Security: Dallas National common stock
Date of purchase: May 1, 1987
Purchase cost: $27,312
Date of sale: May 7, 1988
Sale proceeds: $32,040
Dividends received (May 1987-May 1988): $2,000

$$\text{holding period return} = \frac{\$2,000 + (\$32,040 - \$27,312)}{\$27,312}$$

$$= \underline{+24.63\%}$$

Since you're most concerned with after-tax rates of return, you should calculate the after-tax HPR as well. For example, if you are in the 30 percent tax bracket (federal and state combined), income taxes will reduce the after-tax dividend income to $1,400 [(1−.30) × $2,000] and the after-tax capital gain to $3,310 [(1−.30) × ($32,040−$27,312)]. Thus, the after-tax HPR is ($1,400 + $3,310)/$27,312 or 17.25 percent, a reduction of 7.38 percent. As you can see, both the pretax and after-tax HPR are useful gauges of return.

*Bonds.* The HPR for a bond investment is similar to that for stock. The calculation holds for both straight debt and convertible issues and includes the two components of an investor's return on a bond investment: interest income and capital gain or loss realized upon sale. Calculation of the HPR on a bond investment is:

Security: Phoenix Brewing Company 10% bonds
Date of purchase: June 2, 1987
Purchase cost: $10,000
Date of sale: June 5, 1988
Sales proceeds: $9,704
Interest earned (June 1987-June 1988): $1,000

$$\text{holding period return} = \frac{\$1{,}000 + (\$9{,}704 - \$10{,}000)}{\$10{,}000}$$

$$= \underline{+7.04\%}$$

In this case, you purchased the Phoenix Brewing bonds for $10,000, held them for just over 1 year, and then realized $9,704 at the sale. In addition, you earned $1,000 in interest during the period of ownership. The HPR of this investment is 7.04 percent. The HPR is lower than the bonds' current yield of 10 percent ($1,000 interest ÷ $10,000 purchase price) because the bonds were sold at a capital loss. Assuming a 30 percent tax bracket, the after-tax HPR is 4.93 percent: ([(1−.30) × $1,000] + [(1−.30) × ($9,704−$10,000)]) ÷ $10,000—about 2 percent less than the pretax HPR.

*Mutual funds.* There are two basic components of return from a mutual fund investment: dividend income (including any capital gains distribution) plus any change in value. The basic HPR equation for mutual funds is identical to that for stocks. This example assumes that you purchased 1,000 shares of a no-load mutual fund in July 1987 at a NAV of $10.40 a share. Because it is a no-load fund, no commission is charged, so your cost is $10,400. During the 1-year period of ownership, the Beaver State Mutual Fund distributed investment income dividends totaling $270 and capital gains dividends of $320. When you redeemed this fund the NAV was $10.79 a share, giving you a total of $10,790. As you can see, the holding period return before taxes is 9.42 percent:

Security: Beaver State Mutual Fund
Date of purchase: July 1, 1987
Purchase cost: $10,400
Date of redemption: July 3, 1988
Sales proceeds: $10,790
Distributions received
  Investment income dividends: $270
  Long-term capital gains dividends: $320

$$\text{holding period return} = \frac{(\$270 + \$320) + (\$10{,}790 - \$10{,}400)}{\$10{,}400}$$

$$= \underline{+9.42\%}$$

Assuming a 30 percent tax bracket, your after-tax HPR is 6.60 percent: ([(1−.30) × ($270 + $320)] + [(1−.30) × ($10,790−$10,400)]) ÷ $10,400—nearly 3 percent below the pretax HPR.

*Other investment vehicles.* The only source of return on other investment vehicles, such as options, commodities futures, and financial futures, is capital appreciation. Because the return is in the form of capital gains only, the HPR analysis can easily be applied on a pretax or an after-tax basis. No matter what the specific investment vehicle, you can use the same basic procedure for securities that are sold short.

---

## COMPARE PERFORMANCE TO INVESTMENT GOALS

After computing an HPR or yield on an investment, compare it to your investment goal. Keeping track of an investment's performance by periodically computing its return will help you decide which investments you should continue to hold and which have become possible sales candidates. Clearly, an investment holding would be a candidate for sale if: (1) it failed to perform up to expectations and no real change in performance is anticipated; or (2) it has met the original investment objective; or (3) more attractive uses of your funds are currently available through better investment outlets.

*Compare risk and return.*　　Many times in this book we have discussed the basic trade-off between investment risk and return: to earn more return, you must take more risk. Risk is the chance that the actual investment return will be less than expected. In analyzing an investment, you must ask yourself this key question: Am I getting the proper return for the amount of investment risk I am taking?

Nongovernment security and property investments are by nature riskier than investing in U.S. government bonds or insured money market accounts. This fact implies that if you're a rational investor you should invest in risky situations only when the expected rate of return is well in excess of what you could earn from a low-risk investment. Thus, when analyzing investment returns, one benchmark against which to compare them is the rate of return on low-risk investments. If your risky investments fail to outperform low-risk investments, you must carefully examine your entire investment strategy.

*Compare return to market measures.*　　In measuring investment performance, it is often worthwhile to compare your returns with appropriate broad-based market measures, including the Dow Jones industrial average (DJIA), the Standard & Poor's 500 stock composite index (S&P 500), and the New York Stock Exchange composite index (NYSE index).

Despite widespread use of the Dow Jones industrial average by the news media, it is *not* considered the most appropriate comparative gauge of stock price movement. This is because of its narrow coverage and because it excludes many types of stocks from its scope. For example, companies like CBS, Dow Chemical, K-Mart, and Quaker Oats are not included in the DJIA. If your portfolio is composed of a broad range of common stocks, the NYSE composite index is a more appropriate tool. This index consists of stocks that constitute more than 50 percent of all publicly traded stocks, based upon dollar market value. The scope of coverage, as measured by market value, is three times that of the DJIA.

A number of bond market indicators are available for assessing the general behavior of these markets. These indicators consider either bond price behavior or bond yield. The Dow Jones composite bond average is a popular measure of bond price behavior based upon the closing prices of 10 utility and 10 industrial bonds. Like bond quotations, this average reflects the average percentage of face value at which the bonds sell. A variety of sources of bond yield data are also available. These reflect the rate of return you would earn on a bond purchased today and held to maturity. *Barron's* quotes these yields for the Dow Jones composite bond average. Other sources are Standard & Poor's, Moody's Investors Service, and the Federal Reserve. Indices of bond price and bond yield performance can be obtained for specific types of bonds (industrial, utility, and municipal), as well as for a composite of various bonds. In addition, several other indices cover listed options and futures, although there is no widely publicized index or average for mutual funds.

*Isolate problem investments.* A problem investment is one that has not lived up to expectations. It may involve loss or merely an actual return less than what you expected. Many investors try to forget about problem situations, hoping the problem will go away or the investment will turn around by itself. This is a terrible mistake. Problem investments require immediate attention, not neglect. In studying a problem investment, you must make the basic decision of whether or not to continue to hold it. Your question is: Should I take my loss and get out, or should I hang on and hope it turns around? Note that holding on to mediocre investments in the hope they will turn around is a strategy that can backfire and leave you with a portfolio of poor performers.

As you periodically analyze each investment in your portfolio, you should ask two questions: First, has it performed in a manner that could reasonably be expected? Second, if the investment were not currently in the portfolio, would you buy it today? If the answers to both are negative, then the investment probably should be sold. A negative answer to one of the questions qualifies the investment for the problem list, where it should be watched closely. In general, maintaining a portfolio of investments requires constant attention and analysis to insure the best chance of satisfactory returns.

## A RISK-ADJUSTED, MARKET-ADJUSTED RETURN MEASURE (RAR)

A risk-adjusted, market-adjusted return measure is the method of gauging investment performance most suitable for common stocks and for portfolios of common stocks. This measure, called RAR for short, utilizes beta and a broadly based market index. The measure provides you with a tool to gauge investment performance that factors out the influences of general market movements on the portfolio. For instance, if you have a portfolio that earned a rate of return of 15 percent over the past year, that return in and of itself does not provide a true comparative measure of portfolio return. You need to know how the portfolio has performed in relation to other portfolios and in relation to the market in general. The raw return figure alone requires further analysis.

The formula for calculating RAR is:

$$\text{RAR} = \begin{array}{c}\text{return on}\\\text{security or}\\\text{portfolio}\end{array} - \left[\begin{array}{c}\text{risk-free}\\\text{rate}\end{array} + \left[\begin{array}{c}\text{beta of}\\\text{security}\\\text{or portfolio}\end{array} \times \left(\begin{array}{c}\text{return on}\\\text{broad}\\\text{market index}\end{array} - \begin{array}{c}\text{risk-free}\\\text{rate}\end{array}\right)\right]\right]$$

All variables are measured at the same point in time. The return on a security or portfolio is its holding period return. The risk-free rate is the rate of return you can earn on a virtually riskless investment, such as a U.S. Treasury bill. The beta of the security or portfolio is found by methods previously discussed. The return on the broad market index is the total return (dividends plus price change) you could have earned in the given period if you had invested in the market portfolio. The Standard & Poor's 500 stock composite index or the New York Stock Exchange composite index are often used to represent the market portfolio.

For example, if a portfolio earns a 16 percent return when the risk-free rate is 7 percent, its beta is 1.5, and the market return is 13 percent, its RAR is zero: $16\% - (7\% + [1.5 \times (13\% - 7\%)]) = 0$. This portfolio can be said to have performed exactly as it was expected to. If a stock or a portfolio has a positive RAR, it has outperformed the market in general. Conversely, a negative RAR indicates an inferior performance relative to the market.

*Stocks.*    The same calculations can be made for individual stocks. For example, the stock shown below had a beta of .93, was in the portfolio for 1 year, and yielded a holding period return of 16.63 percent. A portfolio assembled in a manner similar to the securities in the NYSE composite index would have earned a return of 18.76 percent over the same time period. The RAR equation tells us that the stock's RAR for the holding period is −1.52 percent:

Security: General Corp. common stock
Holding period: June 20, 1987 to July 1, 1988
Holding period return: +16.63%
Risk-free rate: 10%
Stock beta (May 1, 1987): .93
Return on the NYSE composite index (May 1, 1987–May 7, 1988): 18.76%

$$\begin{aligned}\text{RAR} &= 16.63\% - (10\% + [.93 \times (18.76\% - 10\%)])\\ &= 16.63\% - 18.15\%\\ &= \underline{-1.52\%}\end{aligned}$$

This security performed worse than the market portfolio, earning a return approximately 1.5 percent below that expected during the time period of the analysis. Clearly this stock is a candidate for replacement.

WHERE YOU GO FROM HERE

*Mutual funds.* Beta is more useful for portfolio investment strategy decisions than for individual stocks. This is because a smaller portion of a stock's volatility is related to nondiversifiable risk. Typically, about 90 percent of a diversified portfolio's volatility is due to general stock market fluctuations. Thus, the RAR analysis, while useful for individual stocks, is much more beneficial in the study of portfolio returns. Mutual funds are, of course, portfolios of stocks and bonds, so RAR analysis is particularly useful in the study of mutual fund returns. The beta and the returns on a mutual fund are easy to find and to calculate. Several publications periodically list both the relative fluctuations of fund NAVs and fund dividend distributions. Using this raw data, you can apply RAR analysis to rank the relative performance of mutual fund investment managers.

For instance, consider the no-load Maize and Blue Mutual Fund, described below. It is growth-oriented, as its beta of 1.33 indicates. The fund normally has an above-average amount of nondiversifiable risk. The holding period of analysis is slightly over 1 year, from May 1, 1987, through May 4, 1988. During that time span, the fund paid $.40 a share in investment income dividends and $1.40 a share in capital gains dividends. The fund's NAV rose from $24.12 per share to $26.41 per share. The pretax holding period return for the fund is 16.96 percent:

Security: Maize and Blue Mutual Fund
Holding period: May 1, 1987–May 4, 1988
NAV, May 1, 1987: $24.12
NAV, May 4, 1988: $26.41
Distributions paid out
   Investment income dividends: $.40/share
   Capital gains dividends: $1.40/share
Risk-free rate: 8%
Fund beta (May 1, 1987): 1.33
Return on NYSE composite index (May 1, 1987–May 4, 1988): 12.79%

$$\text{HPR} = \frac{(\$.40 + \$1.40) + (\$26.41 - \$24.12)}{\$24.12}$$

$$= \underline{+16.96\%}$$

In the RAR analysis, it is found that the fund's risk-adjusted, market-adjusted rate of return equals 2.59 percent:

$$\text{RAR} = 16.96\% - (8\% + [1.33 \times (12.79\% - 8\%)])$$

$$= 16.96\% - 14.37\%$$

$$= \underline{+2.59\%}$$

The fund's positive RAR indicates a better-than-expected return performance. A mutual fund whose management consistently earned positive RARs would be an excellent one indeed.

# ASSESSING PORTFOLIO PERFORMANCE

The procedures used to assess portfolio performance are based on many of the procedures used to assess the performance of individual securities. Here we will look at this process, using a hypothetical securities portfolio over a 1-year holding period. As you will see, the holding period return method is an important part of this assessment process.

## MEASURE PORTFOLIO RETURN

On January 1, 1988, the portfolio of Robert K. Hathaway looked like this:

| Number of Shares | Company | Date Acquired | Cost (including commissions) | Cost per Share | Current Price per Share | Current Value |
|---|---|---|---|---|---|---|
| 1,000 | Bancorp West, Inc. | 1/16/86 | $ 21,610 | $21.61 | $30 | $ 30,000 |
| 1,000 | Dallas National Corp. | 5/ 1/87 | 27,312 | 27.31 | 29 | 29,000 |
| 1,000 | Dexter Companies, Inc. | 4/13/82 | 13,704 | 13.70 | 27 | 27,000 |
| 500 | Excelsior Industries | 8/16/85 | 40,571 | 81.14 | 54 | 27,000 |
| 1,000 | Florida Southcoast Banks | 12/16/85 | 17,460 | 17.46 | 30 | 30,000 |
| 1,000 | Maryland-Pacific | 9/27/85 | 22,540 | 22.54 | 26 | 26,000 |
| 1,000 | Moronson | 2/27/85 | 19,100 | 19.10 | 47 | 47,000 |
| 500 | Northwest Mining and Mfg. | 4/17/86 | 25,504 | 51.00 | 62 | 31,000 |
| 1,000 | Rawland Petroleum | 3/12/86 | 24,903 | 24.90 | 30 | 30,000 |
| 1,000 | Vornox | 4/16/86 | 37,120 | 37.12 | 47 | 47,000 |
| | Total | | $249,824 | | | $324,000 |

Mr. Hathaway is 50 years old, a widower, and his children are married. His income is $50,000 per year. His primary investment objective is long-term growth with a moderate dividend return. He selects stocks with two criteria in mind: quality and growth potential. On January 1, 1988, his portfolio consisted of 10 issues, all of good quality. He had been fortunate in his selection process and had approximately $74,000 in unrealized price appreciation in his portfolio.

During 1988, Mr. Hathaway decided to make a change in his portfolio. On May 7, he sold 1,000 shares of Dallas National for $32,040. His holding period return was 24.63 percent as shown in the example on page 372. Using funds from the sale, on May 10, 1988, he acquired 1,000 additional shares of Florida Southcoast Banks. He decided to make the switch because he believed the prospects for the Florida bank holding company were better than those of Dallas National, a Texas-based bank holding company. Florida Southcoast is based in one of the fastest growing counties in terms of population and income in the United States.

*Measure the amount invested.*   You would be wise periodically to list your holdings, as shown for the Hathaway portfolio. List number of shares, acquisition date, cost, and current value for each issue. These data aid in formulating strategy decisions and are also useful for tax purposes. Mr. Hathaway's portfolio does not utilize the leverage of a margin account. If leverage were present, all return calculations would be based on his equity in the account.

Mr. Hathaway's invested capital as of January 1, 1988, is $324,000. No new additions of capital were made in the portfolio during 1988, although he sold one stock, Dallas National, and used the proceeds to buy another stock, Florida Southcoast Banks.

*Measure income.*   There are two sources of return from a portfolio of common stocks: income and capital appreciation. Current income is realized from dividends. Current income from a portfolio of bonds is realized by interest. Investors must report taxable dividends and interest on federal and state income tax returns. Companies are required to furnish income reports (Form 1099-DIV for dividends and Form 1099-INT for interest) to stockholders and bondholders. Many investors maintain logs to keep track of dividend and interest income as received. Mr. Hathaway's dividend income log for calendar 1988 looks like this:

| Number of Shares | Company | Dividends Paid per Share | Dividends Received |
|---|---|---|---|
| 1,000 | Bancorp West, Inc. | $1.20 | $ 1,200 |
| 1,000 | Dallas National Corp.* | .90 | 900 |
| 1,000 | Dexter Companies, Inc. | 1.12 | 1,120 |
| 500 | Excelsior Industries | 2.00 | 1,000 |
| 2,000 | Florida Southcoast Banks** | 1.28 | 1,920 |
| 1,000 | Maryland-Pacific | 1.10 | 1,100 |
| 1,000 | Moronson | — | — |
| 500 | Northwest Mining and Mfg. | 2.05 | 1,025 |
| 1,000 | Rawland Petroleum | 1.20 | 1,200 |
| 1,000 | Vornox | 1.47 | 1,470 |
| | Total | | $ 10,935 |

*Sold May 7, 1988.
**1,000 shares acquired on May 10, 1988.

He received two quarterly dividends of $.45 a share before he sold the Dallas stock, and he received two $.32-a-share quarterly dividends on the additional Florida Southcoast Banks shares he acquired. His total dividend income for 1988 was $10,935.

*Measure appreciation in value.*   An analysis of the change in price of each of the issues in the Hathaway portfolio appears on the next page.

| Number of Shares | Company | Market Value (1/1/88) | Market Price (12/31/88) | Market Value (12/31/88) | Unrealized Appreciation (Loss) | Percentage Change |
|---|---|---|---|---|---|---|
| 1,000 | Bancorp West, Inc. | $ 30,000 | $27 | $ 27,000 | $ (3,000) | −10.0% |
| 1,000 | Dexter Companies, Inc. | 27,000 | 36 | 36,000 | 9,000 | +33.3 |
| 500 | Excelsior Industries | 27,000 | 66 | 33,000 | 6,000 | +22.2 |
| 2,000 | Florida Southcoast Banks* | 62,040 | 35 | 70,000 | 7,960 | +12.8 |
| 1,000 | Maryland-Pacific | 26,000 | 26 | 26,000 | — | — |
| 1,000 | Moronson | 47,000 | 55 | 55,000 | 8,000 | +17.0 |
| 500 | Northwest Mining and Mfg. | 31,000 | 60 | 30,000 | (1,000) | − 3.2 |
| 1,000 | Rawland Petroleum | 30,000 | 36 | 36,000 | 6,000 | +20.0 |
| 1,000 | Vornox | 47,000 | 43 | 43,000 | (4,000) | − 8.5 |
| | Total | $327,040 | | $356,000 | $28,960 | + 8.9% |

*1,000 additional shares acquired on May 10, 1988, at a cost of $32,040. The value listed is the cost plus the market value of the previously owned shares as of January 1, 1988.

For each issue except the additional shares of Florida Southcoast Banks, the January 1, 1988, and December 31, 1988, values are listed. The amounts listed for Florida Southcoast Banks reflect the fact that 1,000 additional shares of the stock were acquired on May 10, 1988, at a cost of $32,040. It can be seen that Mr. Hathaway's current holdings had beginning-of-the-year values of $327,040 (including the additional Florida Southcoast Bank shares at the date of purchase) and are worth $356,000 at year-end. During 1988, the portfolio increased in value by 8.9 percent, or by $28,960 in unrealized capital appreciation. In addition, Mr. Hathaway realized a capital gain in 1988 by selling his Dallas National holding. From January 1, 1988, until its sale on May 7, 1988, the Dallas holding rose in value from $29,000 to $32,040. This is the only sale in 1988; thus, total realized appreciation was $3,040. During 1988, the portfolio had both realized appreciation of $3,040 and unrealized appreciation of $28,960. The total increment in value equals the sum of the two: $32,000.

*Measure the portfolio's holding period return.* To measure the total return of the Hathaway portfolio during 1988, the HPR measurement is used. The basic 1-year HPR formula for portfolios is:

$$\text{HPR for a portfolio} = \frac{\substack{\text{dividends and} \\ \text{interest} \\ \text{received}} + \substack{\text{realized} \\ \text{appreciation}} + \substack{\text{unrealized} \\ \text{appreciation}}}{\substack{\text{initial} \\ \text{equity} \\ \text{investment}} + \left( \substack{\text{new} \\ \text{funds}} \times \frac{\substack{\text{number of} \\ \text{months in} \\ \text{portfolio}}}{12} \right) - \left( \substack{\text{withdrawn} \\ \text{funds}} \times \frac{\substack{\text{number of months} \\ \text{withdrawn} \\ \text{from portfolio}}}{12} \right)}$$

This formula includes both the realized return (income plus appreciation) and unrealized yearly appreciation of the portfolio. Portfolio additions and deletions are time-weighted for the number of months they are in the portfolio.

A detailed change-in-value analysis was shown in the previous table, in which all the issues in the portfolio as of December 31, 1988, are listed. The beginning and year-end values are included for comparison purposes. The crux of the analysis is the HPR calculation for the year:

Portfolio value (1/1/88): $324,000
Portfolio value (12/31/88): $356,000
Realized appreciation: $3,040 (1/1/88 to 5/7/88 when Dallas National was sold)
Unrealized appreciation (1/1/88 to 12/31/88): $28,960
Dividends received: $10,935
New cash invested or withdrawn: None

$$\text{HPR} = \frac{\$10,935 + \$3,040 + \$28,960}{\$324,000}$$

$$= \underline{+13.25\%}$$

All the elements of a portfolio's return are included. Dividends total $10,935. The realized appreciation figure represents the increment in value of the Dallas holding from January 1, 1988, until its sale. During 1988, the portfolio had $28,960 of unrealized appreciation. There were no additions of new funds and no capital was withdrawn. Utilizing the formula for HPR, we find that the portfolio had a total return of 13.25 percent in 1988.

## COMPARE PORTFOLIO RETURN WITH OVERALL MARKET MEASURES

As we discussed earlier, meaningful return comparisons must also consider risk; in this case, Mr. Hathaway should determine the risk-adjusted, market-adjusted return (RAR) to see how his portfolio is doing in comparison to the stock market as a whole. The Standard & Poor's 500 stock composite index or the New York Stock Exchange composite index are acceptable indices for this type of analysis because they are broadly based and appear to represent the stock market as a whole.

Assume that during 1988 the return on the S&P 500 index was +10.7 percent. Assume the comparable NYSE index return was +10.8 percent. These returns include both dividends and price appreciation. The return from Mr. Hathaway's portfolio was 13.25 percent. This compares very favorably with the broadly based indexes: the Hathaway portfolio performed about 20 percent better than these broad indicators of stock market return. Assuming the risk-free rate is 7.50 percent, the beta of Mr. Hathaway's portfolio is 1.20, and the market return is 10.75 percent, the RAR would be:

$$\text{RAR} = 13.25\% - (7.50\% + [1.20 \times (10.75\% - 7.50\%)])$$

$$= 13.25\% - 11.40\%$$

$$= \underline{+1.85\%}$$

During 1988, Mr. Hathaway's portfolio earned an above-average rate of return.

## REVISE THE PORTFOLIO

In this example, one transaction occurred during the year: Mr. Hathaway sold Dallas National and bought Florida Southcoast Banks. He did this because he no longer believed that Dallas National met his portfolio objectives.

This kind of reassessment is important for every investor. You should periodically analyze your portfolio with one basic question in mind: *Does the portfolio contain issues that are best suited to my risk-return needs?* If you systematically study your portfolio, you will almost certainly decide to sell certain issues and to purchase new ones as market and economic conditions change and as your own personal financial situation evolves. It's important to reevaluate your holdings on a regular basis. In today's stock market, timeliness is the essence of profitability.

Look carefully at each of the issues in your portfolio to be sure that its risk-return balance hasn't changed. If it has and your overall objectives are still the same, replace the issue with a better match. In addition, make sure that market and economic changes haven't affected your portfolio's diversification, If they have, buy and sell once again to maintain the diversification you're after.

## TIMING TRANSACTIONS

The essence of timing is to "buy low and sell high." This is the dream of all investors. There is no tried and true way for achieving this goal, but several methods are commonly used to time purchase and sale actions. Among them are formula plans. *Formula plans* are mechanical methods of portfolio management, which try to take advantage of price changes in securities resulting from cyclical price movements. Formula plans are not set up to provide unusually high returns; rather, they are conservative strategies primarily oriented toward investors who do not wish to bear a high level of risk. Following are some common formula plans.

### DOLLAR COST AVERAGING

Dollar cost averaging is a basic type of formula plan. Following this strategy, a fixed dollar amount is invested in a security in each time period. This is a passive buy-and-hold strategy in which a periodic dollar investment is held constant. This plan requires that you have the discipline to invest on a regular basis in order to make the plan work. The hoped-for outcome of a dollar cost averaging program is growth in the value of the security to which the funds are allocated. The price of the investment security will probably fluctuate over time. If the price declines, more shares are purchased; conversely, if the price rises, fewer shares are purchased. As an example of dollar cost averaging assume that you

## TRANSACTIONS

| Month | Net Asset Value (NAV), Month-End | Number of Shares Purchased |
|---|---|---|
| January | $26.00 | 19.23 |
| February | 27.46 | 18.21 |
| March | 27.02 | 18.50 |
| April | 24.19 | 20.67 |
| May | 26.99 | 18.53 |
| June | 25.63 | 19.51 |
| July | 24.70 | 20.24 |
| August | 24.16 | 20.70 |
| September | 25.27 | 19.79 |
| October | 26.15 | 19.12 |
| November | 29.60 | 16.89 |
| December | 30.19 | 16.56 |

### ANNUAL SUMMARY

Total investment: $6,000.00
Total number of shares purchased: 227.95
Average cost per share: $26.32
Year-end portfolio value: $6,881.81

invest $500 a month in the Wolverine Mutual Fund, a growth-oriented no-load mutual fund.

During one year's time you have placed $6,000 in the mutual fund shares. This is a no-load fund, so shares are purchased at net asset value (NAV). As shown in the table above, purchases were made at NAVs ranging from a low of $24.16 to a high of $30.19. At year-end, your holdings in the fund were valued at slightly less than $6,900. While dollar cost averaging is a passive strategy, other formula plans have a more active posture.

## CONSTANT DOLLAR PLAN

A constant dollar plan consists of a portfolio that is divided into two parts. The speculative portion is invested in securities having high promise of capital appreciation. The conservative portion consists of very low-risk investments such as bonds or a money market account. The constant dollar plan basically skims off profits from the speculative portion of the portfolio if it rises a certain percentage or amount in value. These funds are then added to the conservative portion of the portfolio. If the speculative portion of the portfolio declines by a specific percentage or amount, funds are added to it from the conservative portion. The target dollar amount for the speculative portion is constant, and you establish trigger points (upward or downward movement in the speculative portion) where funds are removed from or added to that portion.

If you began with a $20,000 portfolio consisting of a $10,000 portion invested in a high-beta no-load mutual fund and $10,000 deposited in a money market account and decide to rebalance the portfolio every time the speculative portion is worth $2,000 more or $2,000 less than its initial value of $10,000, here is what your plan might look like:

| Mutual Fund NAV | Value of Speculative Portion | Value of Conservative Portion | Total Portfolio Value | Transactions | Number of Shares in Speculative Portion |
|---|---|---|---|---|---|
| $10.00 | $10,000.00 | $10,000.00 | $20,000.00 | | 1,000 |
| 11.00 | 11,000.00 | 10,000.00 | 21,000.00 | | 1,000 |
| 12.00 | 12,000.00 | 10,000.00 | 22,000.00 | | 1,000 |
| →12.00 | 10,000.00 | 12,000.00 | 22,000.00 | Sold 166.67 shares | 833.33 |
| 11.00 | 9,166.63 | 12,000.00 | 21,166.63 | | 833.33 |
| 9.50 | 7,916.64 | 12,000.00 | 19,916.64 | | 833.33 |
| →9.50 | 10,000.00 | 9,916.64 | 19,916.64 | Purchased 219.30 shares | 1,052.63 |
| 10.00 | 10,526.30 | 9,916.64 | 20,442.94 | | 1,052.63 |

If the speculative portion of the portfolio equaled or exceeded $12,000, sufficient shares of the fund were sold to bring its value down to $10,000, and the proceeds from the sale were added to the conservative portion. If the speculative portion declined in value to $8,000 or less, funds were taken from the conservative portion and used to purchase sufficient shares to raise the value of the speculative portion to $10,000.

Two portfolio rebalancing actions were taken here. Initially, $10,000 was allocated to each portion of the portfolio. Then, when the mutual fund's NAV rose to $12.00 so that the speculative portion was worth $12,000, 166.67 shares valued at $2,000 were redeemed and the proceeds added to the money market account. Later, the mutual fund's NAV declined to $9.50 a share, causing the value of the speculative portion to drop below $8,000. This triggered the purchase of sufficient shares to raise the value of the speculative portion to $10,000. Over the long run, if the speculative investment of the constant dollar plan rises in value, the conservative component of the portfolio will increase in dollar value as profits are transferred into it.

## CONSTANT RATIO PLAN

A constant ratio plan establishes a desired fixed *ratio* of the speculative to the conservative portion of the portfolio. When the actual ratio of the two differs by a predetermined amount from the desired ratio, rebalancing occurs; that is, transactions are made in order to bring the actual ratio back to the desired ratio. If you use this plan, you must decide on the appropriate apportionment between speculative and conservative investments. Then, you must make a decision regarding the ratio trigger point at which transactions occur.

A constant ratio plan for an initial portfolio of $20,000 might look like this:

| Mutual Fund NAV | Value of Speculative Portion | Value of Conservative Portion | Total Portfolio Value | Ratio of Speculative Portion to Conservative Portion | Transactions | Number of Shares in Speculative Portion |
|---|---|---|---|---|---|---|
| $10.00 | $10,000.00 | $10,000.00 | $20,000.00 | 1.000 | | 1,000 |
| 11.00 | 11,000.00 | 10,000.00 | 21,000.00 | 1.100 | | 1,000 |
| 12.00 | 12,000.00 | 10,000.00 | 22,000.00 | 1.200 | | 1,000 |
| → 12.00 | 11,000.00 | 11,000.00 | 22,000.00 | 1.000 | Sold 83.33 shares | 916.67 |
| 11.00 | 10,083.00 | 11,000.00 | 21,083.00 | 0.917 | | 916.67 |
| 10.00 | 9,166.70 | 11,000.00 | 20,166.70 | 0.833 | | 916.67 |
| 9.00 | 8,250.00 | 11,000.00 | 19,250.00 | 0.750 | | 916.67 |
| → 9.00 | 9,625.00 | 9,625.00 | 19,250.00 | 1.000 | Purchased 152.77 shares | 1,069.44 |
| 10.00 | 10,694.40 | 9,625.00 | 20,319.40 | 1.110 | | 1,069.44 |

In this case 50 percent of the portfolio is allocated to the speculative high-beta mutual fund and 50 percent to a money market account. Rebalancing will occur when the ratio of the speculative portion to the conservative portion is greater than or equal to 1.20 or less than or equal to .80. As you can see, a sequence of net asset value changes is listed. Initially, $10,000 is allocated to each portion of the portfolio. When the fund NAV reached $12, the 1.20 ratio triggered the sale of 83.33 shares. Then, the portfolio was back to its desired 1.0 ratio. Later, the fund NAV declined to $9, lowering the value of the speculative portion to $8,250. The ratio of the speculative portion to the conservative portion was then .75, below the .80 trigger point. A total of 152.77 shares were purchased to bring the desired ratio back up to 1.0.

The long-run expectation under a constant ratio plan is that the speculative security or securities will rise in value. When this occurs, you can sell these securities to reapportion the portfolio and increase the value of the conservative portion. The philosophy is similar to the constant dollar plan, except that a ratio rather than a dollar value is used as a trigger point.

## VARIABLE RATIO PLAN

A variable ratio plan attempts more aggressively to capture stock market movements to your advantage. It is another plan aimed at timing the market—that is, it tries to buy low and sell high. The ratio of the speculative portion to the conservative portion of the portfolio varies depending upon the movement in value of the speculative securities. When the ratio rises a certain predetermined amount, the amount committed to the speculative segment of the portfolio is reduced. Conversely, if the value of the speculative portion declines significantly in proportion to the whole portfolio, the percentage of commitment in the speculative vehicle is increased.

In implementing a variable ratio plan, you have several decisions to make. First, you must determine the initial allocation between the speculative and conservative portions of the portfolio. Next, you must choose points to trigger buy or sell activity. These points are a function of the ratio between the value of the speculative portion and the value of the *total* portfolio. Finally, you must set the adjustments in that ratio at each trigger point.

A variable ratio plan might look like this:

| Mutual Fund NAV | Value of Speculative Portion | Value of Conservative Portion | Total Portfolio Value | Ratio of Speculative Portion to Total Portfolio | Transactions | Number of Shares in Speculative Portion |
|---|---|---|---|---|---|---|
| $10.00 | $10,000.00 | $10,000.00 | $20,000.00 | 0.50 | | 1,000 |
| 15.00 | 15,000.00 | 10,000.00 | 25,000.00 | 0.60 | | 1,000 |
| →15.00 | 11,250.00 | 13,750.00 | 25,000.00 | 0.45 | Sold 250 shares | 750 |
| 10.00 | 7,500.00 | 13,750.00 | 21,250.00 | 0.35 | | 750 |
| →10.00 | 11,687.50 | 9,562.50 | 21,250.00 | 0.55 | Purchased 418.75 shares | 1,168.75 |
| 12.00 | 14,025.00 | 9,562.50 | 23,587.50 | 0.41 | | 1,168.75 |

Initially, the portfolio is divided equally between the speculative and the conservative portions. The former consists of a high-beta (around 2.0) mutual fund, and the latter is a money market account. It was decided that when the speculative portion was 60 percent of the total portfolio, its portion would be reduced to 45 percent. If the speculative portion of the portfolio dropped to 40 percent of the total portfolio, its proportion would be raised to 55 percent. Thus when the fund moves up in value, profits are taken and the proportion invested in the no-risk money market account is increased. When the fund declines markedly in value, the proportion of funds committed to it is increased.

The table shows a sequence of transactions. When the fund NAV climbed to $15, the 60 percent ratio trigger point was reached and 250 shares of the fund were sold. The proceeds were placed in the money market account, which then represented 55 percent of the value of the portfolio. Later, the fund NAV declined to $10, causing the speculative portion of the portfolio to drop to 35 percent. This triggered a portfolio rebalancing, and 418.75 shares were purchased, moving the speculative portion to 55 percent. When the fund NAV then moved to $12, the total portfolio was worth in excess of $23,500. In comparison, if the initial investment of $20,000 had been allocated equally and no rebalancing was done between the mutual fund and the money market account, the portfolio's value at this time would be only $22,000 ($12 × 1,000 = $12,000 speculative portion plus $10,000 money market account).

WHERE YOU GO FROM HERE

# CONCLUDING COMMENTS

You can now better appreciate the complexity of investment planning and decision-making. You cannot simply put your money into a "hot tip" investment and sit back to reap rewards. You will more likely lose every penny of your investment with that action.

Before you even think about making the first investment, you must analyze your personal lifestyle, family needs, and possibly most important, your financial health. You must insure the essentials for yourself and your family before investing.

Once your essential obligations are fulfilled, you must determine your motivations and intentions for investing and clearly define your objectives. You must then develop your plans and strategies, identify the level of risk you are willing to assume and the returns you desire, and study, analyze, and select the right investments for you that will meet your investment objectives. This entire process takes in every aspect of your financial life.

Eventually, however, you will develop an investment portfolio that meets your needs and goals. But investments do not stand still. They move and fluctuate, sometimes quickly and unexpectedly. Your investment objectives and needs will also change as you pass through life. As a result you may find your investments being selected to meet different requirements. Gradually you will select more conservative investments providing less in the way of capital gains potential and more security as well as current income.

If your portfolio is to continue to meet your objectives, you must monitor it. You must constantly analyze your investments and observe the impact of their movements on your portfolio. You must also make certain that the investments within the portfolio meet your changing objectives and requirements. Adjustments will have to be made. Current investments will need to be sold and new ones purchased. Monitoring your portfolio requires time and effort. But with patience, persistence, and hard work, you can achieve your investment goals, experience the satisfaction such achievement brings, and acquire the financial security you seek. These are the rewards of becoming a knowledgeable investor.

# APPENDIX A

## PUBLICATIONS

GENERAL INFORMATION SOURCES
FINANCIAL PERIODICALS
BOOKS FOR INVESTORS
INVESTMENT ADVISORIES AND NEWSLETTERS
INVESTORS' SUBSCRIPTION SERVICES
MUTUAL FUND DIRECTORIES

## GENERAL INFORMATION SOURCES

| PUBLICATION | PUBLISHER | PRICE | TYPE OF INFORMATION PROVIDED |
|---|---|---|---|
| *Broker-Dealer Directory* | U.S. Securities and Exchange Commission<br>Office of Registration and Reports<br>500 N. Capital Street, NW<br>Washington, DC 20549<br>202-272-7450 | $.20 per page | Listing of all broker-dealers registered with the Securities and Exchange Commission. |
| *Business Information Sources,* rev. ed. | University of California Press<br>2223 Fulton Street<br>Berkeley, CA 94720<br>415-642-4247 | $35.00 | Guide to selected business books and reference sources, with a section on investment sources. |
| *Encyclopedia of Business* | Gale Research Company<br>Book Tower<br>Detroit, MI 48226<br>313-961-2242 | $185.00 | Comprehensive listings and description of business and investment information sources. |

## GENERAL INFORMATION SOURCES *(continued)*

| PUBLICATION | PUBLISHER | PRICE | TYPE OF INFORMATION PROVIDED |
|---|---|---|---|
| *The Fortune Investment Information Directory* | The Dushkin Publishing Group Sluice Dock Guilford, CT 06437 800-243-6532/203-453-4351 | $24.95 | Guide to investing information sources: periodicals, books, courses, recordings, broadcasts, software and databases, and group activities. |
| *Investment Advisor Directory* | U.S. Securities and Exchange Commission 500 N. Capital Street, NW Washington, DC 20549 202-272-7450 | $.20 per page | List of investment advisors registered with the Securities and Exchange Commission. |
| *Money Market Directory* | Money Market Directories, Inc. 300 E. Market Street Charlottesville, VA 22901 800-977-1450 | $485.00 | Information on investment management, including tax-exempt funds, investment services, and research departments of brokerage firms. |
| *Moody's Manuals and Financial Guides* | Moody's Investors Services, Inc. 99 Church Street New York, NY 10007 212-553-0300 | Free | Brochure listing and describing Moody's various services and publications and providing price information. |
| *SIE 1987 Catalog* | Select Information Exchange 2095 Broadway New York, NY 10023 212-874-6408 | Free | Irregularly issued catalog providing a directory to publications and services concerned with business and investment in the U.S. and abroad. |
| *Source Book of Health Insurance Data* | Health Insurance Association 1025 Connecticut Avenue, NW Suite 1200 Washington, DC 20036 202-223-7780 | Free | Compilation and documentation of data on health insurance industry. |
| *Standard and Poor's Catalog of Services and Publications* | Standard and Poor's 25 Broadway New York, NY 10004 212-208-8000 | Free | Brochure listing and describing Standard and Poor's various services and publications, with price information. Also lists addresses of S&P's branch and foreign offices. |
| *Ulrich's International Periodicals Directory* | R. R. Bowker Company Database Services Group 205 E. 42nd Street New York, NY 10017 800-521-8110 | $149.95 | Comprehensive directory of all periodicals published in the U.S. and abroad. |

## FINANCIAL PERIODICALS

| PUBLICATION | YEARLY SUBSCRIPTION RATE | PUBLISHER | TYPE OF INFORMATION PROVIDED |
|---|---|---|---|
| **DAILY** | | | |
| *The Wall Street Journal* | $107.00 | Dow Jones & Co., Inc. 22 Cortlandt Street New York, NY 10007 212-416-2000 | General business, financial, and world news, with market quotations. |

| PUBLICATION | YEARLY SUBSCRIPTION RATE | PUBLISHER | TYPE OF INFORMATION PROVIDED |
|---|---|---|---|
| **WEEKLY** | | | |
| American Stock Exchange Weekly Bulletin | $20.00 | American Stock Exchange 86 Trinity Place New York, NY 10006 212-306-1445 | Summation of exchange activity on a weekly basis. |
| Barron's | $63.00 | Dow Jones & Co., Inc. 22 Cortlandt Street New York, NY 10007 212-416-2000 | Newspaper: financial and investment news; information on commodities, international trading; tables on New York Stock Exchange transactions. |
| Comex Weekly Market Report for Copper, Silver & Gold | $25.00 | Commodity Exchange, Inc. Southeast Plaza Building 4 World Trade Center New York, NY 10048 212-938-2900 | Trading activity and trends in metals, futures markets; statistics. |
| Economist | $75.00 | Economist Newspaper, Ltd. 25 St. James Street London SWIA IHG England | Covers economic and political news and trends. European perspective on U.S. business and political developments. |
| Media General Financial Weekly; Market Digest | $108.00 | Media General Financial 100 E. Broad Street Suite 1050, Box C-32333 Richmond, VA 23293 804-649-6000 | Media General Financial Weekly is a statistical wonderland that publishes exhaustive numbers on thousands of stocks and scores of stock groups and subgroups. It also follows mutual funds and prints detailed excerpts from brokerage firms' research reports, market commentaries, and investment advisory newsletters. |
| National OTC Stock Journal | $79.00 | OTC Stock J., Inc. 1780 S. Bellaire Street Suite 400, Box 24321 Denver, CO 80224 303-758-9131 | National OTC Stock Journal calls itself "America's Financial Weekly for Over-the-Counter Stocks." It's often described as a penny-stock publication, but the paper covers many investing subjects, such as financial planning and investor protection, although many of the featured investments are rather risky. It's a comprehensive paper in a risk-loaded environment. |
| **SEMIMONTHLY** | | | |
| Financial World | $42.00 | Financial World Partners 1450 Broadway New York, NY 60611 212-869-1616 | Investment analysis and forecasts for specific companies and industries as a whole. |
| Forbes | $45.00 | Forbes, Inc. 60 Fifth Avenue New York, NY 10011 212-620-2200 | General economic and financial news; reports on various corporations, executives, stocks, and industries. August issue contains their annual performance review of mutual funds. |
| Fortune | $44.50 | Time, Inc. 541 N. Fairbanks Ct. Chicago, IL 60611 800-621-8200 | Business and economic developments; evaluates specific industries and corporations; notes banking and energy news. |

## FINANCIAL PERIODICALS *(continued)*

| PUBLICATION | YEARLY SUBSCRIPTION RATE | PUBLISHER | TYPE OF INFORMATION PROVIDED |
|---|---|---|---|
| *Real Estate Investment Ideas Letters* | $57.00 | Institute for Business Planning, Inc. Two Concourse Parkway #800 Atlanta, GA 30328 210-368-4680 | Devotes articles to financing ownership and disposition of real estate; includes planning techniques and strategies. |
| **MONTHLY** *Changing Times* | $15.00 | Kiplinger Washington Editors, Inc. 1729 H Street, NW Washington, DC 20006 202-887-6400 | Articles of general consumer interest; tax and personal financial planning. |
| *Commodities: Futures* | $34.00 | Commodities Magazine, Inc. 250 S. Wacker Drive Suite 250 Chicago, IL 60606 312-977-0999 | Charts, illustrations, statistics articles in the areas of commodities and futures trading and markets. |
| *Futures: The Magazine of Commodities and Options* | $34.00 | Futures Magazine, Inc. 250 S. Wacker Drive Suite 950 Chicago, IL 60606 312-977-0999 | *Futures* reports on the developments that affect commodity and options futures prices. The magazine publishes an annual reference guide to futures markets that features listings of more than 500 brokerage firms, advisors, and commodity pool operators. |
| *Inc.* | $21.00 | Inc. Publishing Corp. 38 Commercial Wharf Boston, MA 02110 617-227-4700 | Stresses how-to aspects of financial management, marketing, sales, administration, and operations for small, growing companies. |
| *Money* | $31.95 | Money Time, Inc. Box 2519 Boulder, CO 80322 800-621-8200 | Reports on personal finance: stock market trends, estate planning, taxes, tax shelters, and consumer affairs. |
| *National Real Estate Investor* | $45.00 | Communication Channels Inc. 6255 Barfield Road Atlanta, GA 30328 404-256-9800 | Articles, book reviews, current topics in real estate financing, marketing, partnership offerings, and taxation for professionals and serious real estate investors. |
| *Nation's Business* | $22.00 | Chamber of Commerce of the United States 1615 H Street, NW Washington, DC 20062 202-659-6000 | Forecasts, analyzes, and interprets trends and developments in business and government. |
| *New York Stock Exchange Statistical Highlights* | $3.00 | New York Stock Exchange 11 Wall Street New York, NY 10005 212-623-3000 | Updates on New York Stock Exchange activity. |
| *Open Outcry* | Free | Chicago Mercantile Exchange 30 S. Wacker Drive Chicago, IL 60606 312-930-1000 | Reports on activities of the Chicago Mercantile Exchange. |
| *Sylvia Porter's Personal Finance Magazine* | $19.97 | SPPFM Co. 380 Lexington Avenue New York, NY 10017 212-490-8989 | Sylvia Porter touches on every aspect of an individual's financial life. Article topics range from bargains in auto insurance to pension planning, from coop-education to divorce settlements. |

| PUBLICATION | YEARLY SUBSCRIPTION RATE | PUBLISHER | TYPE OF INFORMATION PROVIDED |
|---|---|---|---|
| *Wealth Building: The Magazine of Personal Financial Planning* | $30.00 | The Investor Group, Inc. 402 W. Interstate 30 Suite 140 Garland, TX 75043 214-226-4333 | Formerly the *National Tax Shelter Digest.* Articles by nationally recognized experts on current investment, tax, and legislative topics. Regular departments on investors' outlook, money management, personal financial planning, what happens in Washington, traditional investing, and tax-advantaged investments. Occasional emphasis on one topic or industry for tax-advantaged investing. |
| **EVERY TWO MONTHS** | | | |
| *Personal Investor* | $11.97 | Plaza Communications Inc. 18188 Teller Avenue Suite 280 Irvine, CA 92715 714-851-2220 | *Personal Investor* features practical information for investors on everything from mutual funds to how to invest in thoroughbreds. The magazine is organized by "Outlook" sections, interest rates, futures, collectibles, and personal finances. |
| **QUARTERLY** | | | |
| *American Stock Exchange Quarterly Report* | Free | American Stock Exchange 86 Trinity Place New York, NY 10006 212-306-1445 | Reports of American Stock Exchange activity on a quarterly basis. |
| *Everybody's Money* | $2.00 | Credit Union National Association Box 431-B Madison, WI 53701 608-231-4000 | A guide to family finance and consumer action. |
| *Journal of Financial Planning Today* | $60.00 | New Directions Publications, Inc. Box 5359 Lake Worth, FL 33461 305-964-8727 | Articles on personal financial management; estate planning, taxes, tax shelters, mutual funds, commodities, stocks and bonds. |
| **ANNUAL** | | | |
| *Action in the Marketplace: Trading Commodity Futures* | Free | Chicago Board of Trade Literature Section 141 W. Jackson Street Chicago, IL 60606 312-435-3535 | Describes activities of the Chicago Board of Trade and the operation of commodity markets. |
| *New York Stock Exchange Fact Book* | $3.70 | New York Stock Exchange 11 Wall Street New York, NY 10005 212-623-3000 | Description of New York Stock Exchange activity. |

# BOOKS FOR INVESTORS

| TITLE AND AUTHOR(S) | PUBLISHER | PRICE | TYPE OF INFORMATION PROVIDED |
|---|---|---|---|
| *Barron's Finance and Investment Handbook* | Barron's Educational Series, Inc.<br>113 Crossways Park Drive<br>Woodbury, NY 11797<br>516-921-8750 | $21.95 | This handbook provides an analysis of investment fundamentals and discusses personal investment alternatives. It explains how to read annual reports and financial news and contains a dictionary of 2,500 key terms. There are listings, including the addresses, of NYSE, AMEX, and NASDAQ (NMS) stocks. There are also directories, with current and historical data, of mutual funds, investment newsletters, and financial institutions. |
| *The Changing Role of the Individual Investor,* Marshall E. Blume and Irwin Friend (1978) | John Wiley & Sons, Inc.<br>605 Third Avenue<br>New York, NY 10158<br>212-850-6000 | $10.95 | This study examines the past, present, and future participation of individual investors in the securities markets. It refutes much of the conventional wisdom about individual investors and presents a great deal of fascinating material on the expectations of investors and their attitudes toward risk and reward. |
| *How to Buy Stocks,* Brendan Boyd and Louis Engel (1983) | Little, Brown Publishers, Inc.<br>34 Beacon Street<br>Boston, MA 02106<br>800-343-9204/617-227-0730 | $15.95 | A classic guide to how the market works and how to deal with brokers and securities firms. |
| *Intelligent Investor,* 4th ed., Benjamin Graham with Warren Buffet (1973) | Harper & Row, Publishers, Inc.<br>10 E. 53rd Street<br>New York, NY 10022<br>800-242-7737 | $18.95 | The late Benjamin Graham was the father of modern security analysis. Stock-picking systems come and go, but Graham's fundamental theories, first published in 1949 and revised several times, are still applicable. |
| *Random Walk Down Wall Street,* Burton G. Malkiel (1985) | W.W. Norton & Co., Inc.<br>500 Fifth Avenue<br>New York, NY 10110<br>212-354-5500 | $9.95 | This publication presents observations on mortgage securities, zero-coupon bonds, and other investment vehicles available in the contemporary markets. It also includes Malkiel's now-classic examination of why stock prices are unpredictable. |
| *Super Hedging,* Thomas Noddings (1986) | Probus Publishing, Inc.<br>118 N. Clinton Street<br>Chicago, IL 60606<br>312-346-7895 | $29.50 | This is the seventh book by a foremost hedging strategist. Noddings describes more than 40 different techniques, from basic put-and-call option strategies for hedging common stock positions to using index options to protect profits in convertible bonds. |

# INVESTMENT ADVISORIES AND NEWSLETTERS

| PUBLICATION | YEARLY SUBSCRIPTION RATE | PUBLISHER | TYPE OF INFORMATION PROVIDED |
|---|---|---|---|
| **DAILY**<br>*American Banker* | $460.00 | American Banker, Inc.<br>1 State Street Plaza<br>New York, NY 10004<br>212-943-6000 | Daily news and features to meet the working needs of bankers in the U.S. |

| PUBLICATION | YEARLY SUBSCRIPTION RATE | PUBLISHER | TYPE OF INFORMATION PROVIDED |
| --- | --- | --- | --- |
| **WEEKLY** | | | |
| *Commodity Service* | $150.00 | Dunn & Hargitt, Inc. 22 N. 2nd Street Box 1100 Lafayette, IN 47902 317-423-2624 | The service charts 34 of the most actively traded commodities. Includes buy and sell recommendations. |
| *Dow Theory Forecasts* | $163.00 | Dow Theory Forecasts, Inc. 7412 Calumet Avenue Hammond, IN 46324-2692 219-931-6480 | Forecasts of stock market based on Dow theory. List of their stock choices, generally blue chips. |
| *Dunn & Hargitt's* | $195.00 | Dunn & Hargitt, Inc. 22 N. 2nd Street Box 1100 Lafayette, IN 47902 317-423-2624 | This market guide provides investment advice on stocks and options based on analyses of 1,000 leading stocks. |
| *Kiplinger Washington Letter* | $48.00 | Kiplinger Washington Editors, Inc. 1729 H Street, NW Washington, DC 20006 202-887-6400 | Newsletter with briefings on business trends and pertinent government policies and information on employment, investments, and interest rates. |
| *R.M.H. Survey of Warrants, Options & Low-Price Stocks* | $155.00 | RMH Associates, Inc. 172 Forest Avenue Glen Cove, NY 11542 516-759-2904 | Investment advice on warrants, call and put options, and low-priced stocks. Tables and charts. |
| *United Business & Investment Report* | $170.00 | United Business Service Company 210 Newbury Street Boston, MA 02116 617-267-8855 | Weekly newsletter evaluating stock market and other investment trends. Notes related federal developments, tables. |
| *Value Line Investment Survey* | $495.00 | Value Line, Inc. 711 Third Avenue New York, NY 10017 212-687-3965 | Weekly looseleaf booklet covering the business activities of corporations in a variety of industries. Charts and graphs. |
| *Value Line Options & Convertibles* | $595.00 | Value Line Options & Convertibles Value Line, Inc. 711 Third Avenue New York, NY 10017 212-687-3915 | Evaluation and analysis of hundreds of convertible bonds, warrants, and options. Probably the preeminent source of this information for active investors. |
| *Weekly Insider Report* | $85.00 | Stock Research Corp. 50 Broadway New York, NY 10004 212-482-8300 | Information on stock transactions of 500 or more shares by corporate officers, directors, and 10% holders who buy or sell shares in their own companies. |
| **SEMIMONTHLY** | | | |
| *The Babson Staff Letter* | $14.50 | David L. Babson & Co. One Boston Place Boston, MA 02108 617-723-7450 | From one of the nation's oldest money-management firms comes an attractively presented, educational essay on some facets of the market, such as how high is high or confusion in the computer industry. |

## INVESTMENT ADVISORIES AND NEWSLETTERS *(continued)*

| PUBLICATION | YEARLY SUBSCRIPTION RATE | PUBLISHER | TYPE OF INFORMATION PROVIDED |
|---|---|---|---|
| *The Cabot Market Letter* | $100.00— 6 months $175.00— 1 year | The Cabot Market Letter PO Box 3044 Salem, MA 01970 617-745-5532 | Model portfolios, trend lines, recommended stocks, and market commentary in a concise and readable form. Also discusses mutual funds. |
| *Consensus of Insiders* | $147.00 | Consensus of Insiders PO Box 24349 Fort Lauderdale, FL 33307 305-562-6827 | Data on selling and buying of stocks by company officials, plus weekly "market-timing modules" that measure indicators such as short selling. |
| *Contrary Investor* | $85.00 | Fraser Management Assoc. Box 494 Burlington, VT 05402 802-658-0322 | Newsletter espousing the "contrary opinion" theory of investing that reviews and comments on recommendations and trends in the traditional investment community. Broad market timing recommendations. |
| *Grant's Interest Rate Observer* | $295.00 | Grant's Interest Rate Observer 233 Broadway Suite 4008 New York, NY 10279 212-608-7994 | In this literary magazine of financial comings and goings, former Barron's writer James Grant presents wonderfully creative indexes and statistics and gives pithy advice on fixed-income investments. |
| *Growth Stock Outlook; Junior Growth Stock Outlook* | $175.00; $115.00 | Growth Stock Outlook, Inc. 4405 E-W Highway Box 9911 Bethesda, MD 20814 301-654-5205 | Reports on selected stocks with vigorous growth. *Growth Stock Outlook* gives specific buy-sell recommendations while *Junior Growth Stock Outlook* does not. |
| *Holt Investment Advisory* | $225.00 | T. J. Holt & Co, Inc. 290 Post Road West Westport, CT 06880 203-226-8911 | Discusses the economy and stock market for investors concerned with long-term capital growth. |
| *The Insiders* | $100.00 | The Insiders The Institute for Econometric Research 3471 N. Federal Highway Fort Lauderdale, FL 33306 305-583-9000 | Another publication based on the idea that company officials and directors who trade in their own stock know something. Collects and translates SEC data on buying and selling by insiders and makes recommendations. |
| *InvesTech Market Letter* | $185.00 | InvesTech Market Letter 522 Crestview Drive Kalispell, MT 59901 406-755-8527 | Summarizes and reacts to other letter editors' views. Clear technical analysis and stock and mutual fund choices. |
| *Investment Horizons* | $195.00 | Investment Horizons Investment Information Services 205 W. Wacker Drive Chicago, IL 60606 312-750-9300 | Gerald Perritt follows small companies that aren't extensively watched by professional analysts. For example, one issue explained why small utilities can be better buys than large ones. A well-done letter for intellectual investors. |

| PUBLICATION | YEARLY SUBSCRIPTION RATE | PUBLISHER | TYPE OF INFORMATION PROVIDED |
|---|---|---|---|
| *Investors Intelligence* | $84.00 | Chartcraft, Inc. 1 West Avenue Larchmont, NY 10538 914-834-5181 | Evaluates stock market trends, recommends specific stocks, summarizes various investment advisory services' recommendations, and notes insider transactions. |
| *Market Logic* | $200.00 | Market Logic The Institute for Econometric Research 3471 N. Federal Highway Fort Lauderdale, FL 33306 305-563-9000 | The flagship publication of the institute, this is a concise, thorough and multifaceted stock market guide. Predicts market movements and recommends trades. Full of indicators and other research tools. |
| *Pension Investing Strategies* | $98.00 | Pension Investing Strategies PO Box 509 Ridgewood, NJ 07451 201-447-0681 | Updates on legislative, tax, and investment developments affecting people with Keoghs or IRAs, or pension plan managers. |
| *Realty Stock Review* | $264.00 | Realty Stock Review Audit Investments, Inc. 136 Summit Avenue Montvale, NJ 07645 212-661-1710 | The authority on real estate investment trusts and other real estate stocks. Securities are rated and there's plenty of company news. |
| *Technical Digest* (20 per year plus twice weekly *HOTLINE*) | $125.00 | Technical Digest Woodland Road New Vernon, NJ 07976 201-822-3315 | A regular stock and bond market letter for investors, includes commentary, charts, statistics, recommendations, and summaries of other major market letters. |
| *The Value Line New Issues* | $30.00 | The Value Line New Issues Service 711 Third Avenue New York, NY 10017 212-687-3965 | Each issue is a package: a summary, a review of initial public new offerings, and detailed recommendations on several new stocks. Covers penny and junk stocks and higher-quality issues, at prices from one cent and up. |
| *Value Line OTC Special Situations Service* | $300.00 | Value Line, Inc. 711 Third Avenue New York, NY 10017 212-687-3965 | Loose-leaf newsletter contains information for investors on stocks traded over-the-counter. |

EVERY THREE WEEKS

| PUBLICATION | YEARLY SUBSCRIPTION RATE | PUBLISHER | TYPE OF INFORMATION PROVIDED |
|---|---|---|---|
| *The Astute Investor* | $197.00 | Investor's Analysis, Inc. PO Box 988 Paoli, PA 19301 215-296-2411 | Robert Nurock of *Wall Street Week* writes about the stock market, covering both technical and fundamental developments. One of the best letters for intellectually minded stock market fans. |
| *Income Investor Perspectives* | $119.00 | Income Investor Perspectives 3907 N. Green Bay Avenue Milwaukee, WI 53206 | Updates on tax-advantaged and income-oriented investments, such as utility stocks and real estate investment trusts. Useful for safety-and-yield shoppers. |

| PUBLICATION | YEARLY SUBSCRIPTION RATE | PUBLISHER | TYPE OF INFORMATION PROVIDED |
|---|---|---|---|
| **MONTHLY** | | | |
| *Alan Shawn Feinstein Insiders Report* | $36.00 | Alan Shawn Feinstein and Associates 41 Alhambra Circle Cranston, RI 02905 401-467-5155 | Reports on special investment opportunities, inside tips, new or unusual opportunities. |
| *America's Fastest Growing Companies* | $124.00 | John S. Herold, Inc. 35 Mason Street Greenwich, CT 06830 203-869-2585 | A useful agglomeration of model portfolios, company profiles, and ratings and statistics on small companies and emerging industries. Does not make specific buy-and-sell calls. |
| *Better Investing Magazine* | $12.00 | National Association of Investors Clubs 1515 E. 11 Mile Road Royal Oak, MI 48067 313-543-0612 | Guidelines and advice on investment techniques for investment clubs. Investment education: one company analyzed each month. General articles on investment topics. |
| *Brennan Reports: on Tax Shelters and Tax Planning* | $184.00 | Brennan Reports, Inc. Valley Forge Office Colony PO Box 882, Suite 200 Valley Forge, PA 19482 215-783-0647 | Report of 4 to 8 pages discussing timely topics on tax planning, recent tax legislation, and court decisions affecting tax-advantaged investments. Reviews and summarizes the key features, risks, and rewards of 2 or 3 tax-advantaged publicly offered limited partnership offerings each month with primary emphasis on real estate, oil and gas, equipment leasing, and agricultural programs. |
| *Brennan's IRA Adviser* | $184.00 | Brennan Reports, Inc. Valley Forge Office Colony PO Box 882, Suite 200 Valley Forge, PA 19482 215-783-0647 | Discusses the ins and outs of unusual IRA investments, such as income real estate limited partnerships. |
| *Dines Letter* | $150.00 | James Dine & Company Box 22 Belvedere, CA 94920 415-435-5458 | Combines important technical, psychological, and business indicators concerning the markets. |
| *Forbes Special Situation Survey* | $395.00 | Forbes Investors Advisory Institute, Inc. 60 Fifth Avenue New York, NY 10011 212-620-2200 | Monthly loose-leaf report discusses and recommends the purchase of one speculative equity security in each issue. |
| *Forecasts & Strategies* | $95.00 | Forecasts & Strategies Phillips Publishing, Inc. 7811 Montrose Road Potomac, MD 20854 301-340-2100 | Mark Skousen's common sense on investments, taxes, and "financial privacy," with an emphasis on tax avoidance and keeping the government and others out of your financial affairs. Analyses of new products, such as single-premium variable life insurance. |

| PUBLICATION | YEARLY SUBSCRIPTION RATE | PUBLISHER | TYPE OF INFORMATION PROVIDED |
|---|---|---|---|
| *The Gourgues Report* | $125.00 | Harold Gourgues Co., Inc.<br>P.O. Box 81668<br>Atlanta, GA 30305<br>404-261-1713 | Practical investment advice and information directed towards noninstitutional investors. |
| *High Technology Growth Stocks* | $165.00 | High Technology Growth Stocks<br>14 Nason Street<br>Maynard, MA 01754<br>617-897-9422 | Recently redesigned and beefed up, this is one of several well-researched guides to tech stocks to buy and avoid. |
| *Income & Safety* | $100.00 | Income & Safety<br>The Institute for Econometric Research<br>3471 N. Federal Highway<br>Fort Lauderdale, FL 33306<br>305-563-9000 | A guide to safe places to save and invest for income, concentrating on money-market funds, bank accounts, and tax-free income funds. |
| *The Investor's Guide to Closed-End Funds* | $200.00 | The Investor's Guide to Closed-End Funds<br>Thomas J. Herzfeld Advisors, Inc.<br>7800 Red Road<br>South Miami, FL 33143<br>305-665-6500 | From the only brokerage firm specializing in closed-end investment companies comes an update and recommendations on these overlooked funds, including foreign ones. |
| *Investor's Strategist* | $95.00 | Investor's Strategist<br>82 Wall St., Suite 1105<br>New York, NY 10005 | A newsletter that discusses long-term tax-advantaged investments, such as cable-TV partnerships and numismatic coins. |
| *Johnson Survey* | $94.00 | John S. Herold, Inc.<br>35 Mason Street<br>Greenwich, CT 06830<br>203-869-2585 | Data and comment on fast-growing over-the-counter stocks. Also displays charts. |
| *Limited Partners Letter* | $197.00 | Prologue Press<br>Box 1146<br>Menlo Park, CA 94026<br>415-321-9110 | Report that analyzes important tax, legal, and practical aspects of private and public partnership investments. Emphasis on the primary shelter areas of real estate, oil and gas, equipment leasing, and research and development. |
| *The McKeever Strategy Letter* | $195.00 | The McKeever Strategy Letter<br>PO Box 4130<br>Medford, OR 97501<br>503-826-9279 | James McKeever is one of the more respected letter writers, and he leads off his longer-than-average letters with essays on economic or market topics, before giving advice on stocks, bonds, metals, and currencies. |
| *News Bulletin* | Included in AARP membership fee | AARP Headquarters<br>1909 K Street<br>Washington, DC 20049<br>202-662-4842 | To stimulate persons 50 years old or older, retired or otherwise, toward active retirement, independence, and purpose, improving every aspect of living for older people—health, community service, travel articles. |

# INVESTMENT ADVISORIES AND NEWSLETTERS *(continued)*

| PUBLICATION | YEARLY SUBSCRIPTION RATE | PUBLISHER | TYPE OF INFORMATION PROVIDED |
|---|---|---|---|
| *Real Estate Investing Letter* | $79.00 | HBJ Newsletter, Inc.<br>Harcourt, Brace & Jovanovich, Inc.<br>545 Fifth Avenue<br>New York, NY 10017<br>212-503-2900 | Monthly newsletter covers real estate investments, including tax strategies, depreciation, and real estate syndication. |
| *Robert Kinsman's Low-Risk Growth* | $155.00 | Robert Kinsman's Low-Risk Growth Letter<br>70 Mitchell Boulevard<br>San Rafael, CA 94903 | Recommended investments and model portfolios for income-oriented readers. A lot of common-sense educational materials as well. |
| *Stanger Register— Partnership Profiles* | $225.00 | Robert A. Stanger and Company<br>PO Box 7490<br>1129 Broad Street<br>Shrewsbury, NJ 07701<br>201-389-3600 | Investment information, listings and ranking on public and private partnerships; financial planning ideas, investment product ideas, and articles and features on various investment products, concepts, and strategies. |
| *The Stranger Report: A Guide to Partnership Investing* | $325.00 | Robert A. Stanger and Company<br>1129 Broad Street<br>Shrewsbury, NJ 07701<br>201-389-3600 | Ten-page monthly newsletter with tax-planning ideas and news and views related to limited partnership ventures and other tax shelter investments. |
| *Tax Angles* | $60.00 | Kephart Communications<br>1300 N. 17th Street<br>Suite 1660<br>Arlington, VA 22209<br>804-276-7100 | A monthly newsletter of tax-saving ideas, strategies, and techniques and reviews of pending tax legislation of importance for personal tax and financial planning. |
| *Tax Shelter Insider* | $177.00 | Export Newsletter Assn.<br>Box 3007<br>Boca Raton, FL 33431<br>305-483-2600 | Eight-page newsletter with 8 topic areas: shelter rulings—recent court cases; shelter strategy—tax planning strategies; shelter news—new tax shelter ideas; shelter profile—key features of a current offering; shelter digest—topics in tax shelter financing and legislation; and shelter forum—answering readers' queries. |
| *Tax Shelter Investment Review* | $177.00 | Leland Publishing Co.<br>81 Canal Street<br>Boston, MA 02114<br>617-227-9314 | Reports on currently available publicly offered tax shelter investments, primarily in the major shelter industries of oil and gas, real estate, and leasing. Presents an investment outlook on these industries and provides advice on how to evaluate shelters from experts and practitioners in the shelter field. |

| PUBLICATION | YEARLY SUBSCRIPTION RATE | PUBLISHER | TYPE OF INFORMATION PROVIDED |
|---|---|---|---|
| **5–8 ISSUES PER YEAR** | | | |
| *BI Research* | $80.00 | BI Research<br>PO Box 133<br>Redding, CT 06875<br>203-938-9170 | Detailed research profiles of high-growth or overlooked stocks, with continuing advice on whether to buy more, hold, or sell. |
| **SEMIANNUAL** | | | |
| *MMI Memo* | Free | Household Finance Corporation<br>Money Management Institute<br>2700 Sanders Road<br>Prospect Heights, IL 60070<br>312-564-5000 ext. 5368 | Newsletter on consumer and personal finance topics. |

## INVESTORS' SUBSCRIPTION SERVICES

Active investors need the most current information available to stay on top of the market. As you gain more experience and greater confidence in planning and monitoring your portfolio, you might consider subscribing to some of the many subscription services provided by the industry giants, Standard & Poor's and Moody's Investors Services. Both offer a variety of daily, weekly, and monthly subscriptions on many important investment topics. Each offers current research delivered to you on a regular basis. These services are far from inexpensive, ranging from less than $100 a year to more than $2,000. What you are buying is the latest research findings and continually updated analysis on specific aspects of the financial marketplace. Only you can decide which, if any, of these services you need.

The following list provides an overview of some of the products offered by Standard & Poor's and Moody's Investors Services. Call or write for current subscription prices and further information.

### Standard & Poor's, 345 Hudson Street, New York, NY 10014

| PUBLICATION | FREQUENCY OF PUBLICATION | SUBSCRIPTION PRICE | TYPE OF INFORMATION PROVIDED |
|---|---|---|---|
| *Corporation Records* | Daily revisions | $2,136.00 | Comprehensive reference library on corporations in 6 loose-leaf binders. |
| *Dividend Record* | Daily<br>Weekly<br>Quarterly | $610.00<br>$305.00<br>$120.00 | Authority on dividend details. |
| *Called Bond Record* | Semiweekly | $800.00 | Reports calls and tenders, sinking-fund proposals, defaulted issues, forthcoming redemptions, etc. |
| *Creditweek* | Weekly | $1,238.00 | Comments on trends and outlook for fixed-income securities, including money market instruments and corporate and government bonds. Money market rates, bond yields, federal figures, new offerings, credit analyses. |

# INVESTORS' SUBSCRIPTION SERVICES: STANDARD & POOR'S *(continued)*

| PUBLICATION | FREQUENCY OF PUBLICATION | SUBSCRIPTION PRICE | TYPE OF INFORMATION PROVIDED |
|---|---|---|---|
| *Daily Action Stock Charts* | Weekly | $447.00 | Numerous stocks plotted on a daily basis. |
| *The Outlook* | Weekly | $219.00 | Specific advice on individual stocks. Analyzes and projects business trends. Advice and articles on special situations, stock groups, economics, industries, options, and subjects of concern to investors. |
| *Registered Bond Interest Record* | Weekly | $1,900.00 | Weekly cumulative record of information relating to interest payment on registered bonds. |
| *Review of Financial Services Regulation* | Semimonthly | $1,900.00 | Practical analysis of regulation affecting the banking and insurance industries. Covers a broad spectrum—banks offering brokerage services; financial planning; insurance companies offering financial services; consumer credit. |
| *Bond Guide* | Monthly | $145.00 | Descriptive and statistical data on 3,000 corporate bonds. Nearly 10,000 state, municipal, general obligation, and revenue bonds, over 650 convertibles, and more than 200 foreign bonds. |
| *Current Market Perspectives* | Monthly | $157.00 | Books of charts on 100 issues shows Hi-Lo-Close for five years. |
| *Stock Guide* | Monthly | $88.00 | Data and reviews on over 5,100 common and preferred stocks listed and OTC. Also, special section on performance of over 380 mutual funds. |
| *OTC Chart Manual* | Every two months | $129.00 | Charts the most active over-the-counter stocks. |
| *Daily Stock Price Record* | 3 quarterly | $268.00 ASE $282.00 NYSE $340.00 OTC | Three sets of volumes, each set devoted to one market—NYSE, ASE, or OTC. NYSE volumes cover over 2,400 issues; ASE volumes cover more than 1,000; OTC volumes cover over 4,000 issues, including more than 500 mutual funds and 3,500 NASDAQ bank, insurance, and industrial companies. |
| *Growth Stocks Handbook* | Semiannual update | $57.00 | Facts and figures on over 300 stocks with accelerated earnings growth over the past 5 years. |
| *Oil and Gas Stocks Handbook* | Semiannual update | $57.00 | Over 250 stock reports on international and domestic oil companies; crude oil and gas producers; coal companies; refining companies, exploration and gathering companies; oil well service companies; off-shore drilling companies; and marine construction companies. Special editorial appraising energy situation. |
| *OTC Handbook* | Semiannual update | $57.00 | Individual stock reports on over 526 important OTC stocks; the biggest, most actively traded; the fastest growing OTC stocks; low-priced stocks and selected banks and insurance companies. |

| PUBLICATION | FREQUENCY OF PUBLICATION | SUBSCRIPTION PRICE | TYPE OF INFORMATION PROVIDED |
|---|---|---|---|
| *Analyst's Handbook* | Annual (monthly updates) | $605.00 | Per-share data on various industries and S&P's industrials. |
| *Industry Surveys* | Annual (with 2 supplements) | $995.00 | Surveys 65 leading industries under 32 headings. Trends and projections. Better that forecasts industry and economic trends; earnings supplement. |
| *Register of Corporate Directors and Executives* | Annual (with supplements) | $425.00 | Directory of executive personnel. |
| *Stock Summary* | Annual | $43.50 | Condensed information on widely traded stocks, editorial features highlighting industries of current interest to investors and S&P's. Rapid growth stocks feature focusing on companies with high 5-year growth rates. |
| *ASE Stock Reports* | Periodically revised | $660.00 | Data on American Exchange issues, financial aspects, current items, etc. |
| *NYSE Stock Reports* | Periodically revised | $820.00 | Data on numerous NYSE issues, including financial data, latest developments, etc. |
| *OTC Stock Reports* | Periodically revised | $660.00 | Regional and over-the-counter stocks surveyed. |

## Moody's Investors Services, Inc., 99 Church Street, New York, NY 10007

| PUBLICATION | FREQUENCY OF PUBLICATION | SUBSCRIPTION PRICE | TYPE OF INFORMATION |
|---|---|---|---|
| *Dividend Record* | Twice weekly and annual year-end issue | $345.00 | Dividend information on various issues. |
| *Bond Survey* | Weekly | $895.00 | Comments and recommendations on issues in various bond categories. |
| *International Manual* | Every two weeks | $1,280.00 | Business/financial information on over 3,000 major corporations and multinational institutions in 95 countries. |
| *Bond Record* | Monthly | $125.00 | Issues, current prices, call prices, ratings, and other statistics on numerous bonds. |
| *Handbook of Common Stocks* | Quarterly | $145.00 | Statistics and background on common stocks. |
| *Moody's Bank and Finance News Reports* | Yearly (supplement twice weekly) | $895.00 | Facts and figures on financial enterprises. |
| *Moody's Industrial Manual* | Yearly (supplement twice weekly) | $895.00 | Information on industrial stocks, history, management, financial data. |
| *Moody's Municipal and Governments Manual* | Yearly (supplement twice weekly) | $1,175.00 | Information and ratings on governments, municipals, foreign bonds. |
| *Moody's Public Utility Manual* | Yearly (supplement twice weekly) | $780.00 | Information on public utilities, plus special studies on market areas. |
| *Moody's Transportation Manual* | Yearly (supplement twice weekly) | $750.00 | Information on transportation companies such as air, rail, bus, oil pipelines, tunnel and bridge companies, trucking. |
| *OTC Industrial Manual* | Yearly (supplement twice weekly) | $815.00 | Reference source for over 2,700 OTC issues. |
| *OTC Unlisted Manual* | Yearly (supplement weekly) | $750.00 | Detailed information on 2,000 hard-to-find, emerging companies not listed on any of the major or regional exchanges and not reported on the NASDAQ National Market System. |

# MUTUAL FUNDS DIRECTORIES

| PUBLICATION | YEARLY SUBSCRIPTION RATE | PUBLISHER | TYPE OF INFORMATION PROVIDED |
|---|---|---|---|
| **TWICE PER WEEK** | | | |
| *Mutual Fund Guide* | $415.00 | Commerce Clearing House Inc. 4025 W. Peterson Avenue Chicago, IL 60646 312-583-8500 | Covers federal and state rules governing mutual funds. |
| **SEMIMONTHLY** | | | |
| *United Mutual Fund Selector* | $103.00 | United Business Service Company 210 Newbury Street Boston, MA 02116 617-267-8855 | This report evaluates mutual funds, including bond and municipal bond funds. Reports industry developments; includes tables and charts. |
| **MONTHLY** | | | |
| *Fundline* | $97.00 | Fundline Box 663 Woodland Hills, CA 91365 818-346-5637 | Monthly report on no-load mutual funds with buy-sell recommendations. |
| *Growth Fund Guide* | $85.00 | Growth Fund Research Box 6600 Rapid City, SD 57709 605-341-1971 | Twenty-four-page publication tracking solidly proven funds. Ranks funds by the volatility of stock portfolio. |
| *Mutual Fund Chartist* | $85.00 | Growth Fund Research Box 6600 Rapid City, SD 57709 605-341-1971 | Chart book for no-load and low-load fund investors. |
| *Mutual Fund Forecastor* | $100.00 | Institute for Econometric Research 3471 N. Federal Highway Fort Lauderdale, FL 33306 305-563-9000 | Forecasts performance for more than 300 mutual funds and rates best buys. A directory of mutual funds is included in which performance data, one-year profit projections, and risk ratings are presented. |
| *Mutual Fund Performance Monitor* | $240.00 | Monitored Assets Corp. Box 7740 Des Moines, IA 50322-1111 515-270-1111 | Computer studies and performance data. |
| *Mutual Fund Specialist* | $79.00 | Mutual Fund Specialist Box 1025 Eau Claire, WI 54701 | Tracks and ranks some 50 groups or families of funds, pinpointing top equity fund in each family. Ranks 200 money market funds as well. |
| *No-Load Fund Investor* | $79.00 | Box 283 Hastings-on-the-Hudson, NY 10706 914-478-2381 | Complete performance statistics, news, views, recommendations, and forecasts for no-load mutual funds. |
| *No-Load Fund X* | $95.00 | No-Load Fund X 235 Montgomery Street Suite 662 San Francisco, CA 94104 415-866-7979 | Ranks over 300 no-load funds. Provides switching advice for movement of investments among fund families. |
| *Switch Fund Advisory* | $135.00 | Switch Fund Advisory 8943 Shady Grove Ct. Gaithersburg, MD 20877 301-840-0301 | Letter profiling certain funds and recommending buy or no-buy decisions or switches among fund families. |

| PUBLICATION | YEARLY SUBSCRIPTION RATE | PUBLISHER | TYPE OF INFORMATION PROVIDED |
|---|---|---|---|
| *Telephone Switch* | $117.00 | Telephone Switch Newsletter 5772 Bolsa Avenue Suite 100 Huntington Beach, CA 92647 714-898-2588 | Provides specific market timing investment fund switching advice. Includes a telephone hotline to inform subscribers of changes in recommendations. |
| *Wiesenberger's Current Performance* | $66.00 | Warren, Gorham & Lamont 210 South Street Boston, MA 02111 617-423-2020 | A supplement to *Wiesenberger Services, Inc., Investment Companies,* providing detailed data on mutual fund performance. |
| **EVERY TWO MONTHS** *Donoghue's Money Letter* | $87.00 | Donoghue's Money Letter Box 540 Holliston, MA 01746 617-420-5930 | Reports exclusively on money market mutual funds: performance portfolio composition, management, current yields. |
| **ANNUAL** *Donoghue's Money Fund Almanac* | $23.00 | Donoghue's Money Fund Almanac Box 540 Holliston, MA 01746 617-429-5930 | Statistical review of 10-year performance of over 850 mutual funds. |
| *Investors' Directory: Your Guide to No-Load Funds* | $6.00 | No-Load Mutual Fund 11 Penn Plaza New York, NY 10001 212-563-4540 | Lists by type of fund (growth, income, balanced) the names and addresses of no-load funds that are members of the association. |
| *Mutual Fund Investing* | $145.00 | Phillips Publishing Co. 7811 Montrose Road Potomac, MD 20854 301-340-2100 | Investment advice designed for mutual fund investors' goals. |
| *Wiesenberger Services, Inc., Investment Companies* | $295.00 | Warren, Gorham & Lamont 211 South Street Boston, MA 02111 617-423-2020 | The publication considered by many in the investment community to be the bible on mutual funds and investment companies. Gives background, management policy, and financial record for all leading U.S. and Canadian investment companies. Published annually with quarterly updatings, this publication is available for reference in most public and college libraries. |

# APPENDIX B

## A SAMPLING OF MUTUAL FUNDS

### LOAD MUTUAL FUNDS

Some investment professionals believe load funds provide greater returns on an investment than no-loads. Their contention is that because of the load, these funds often have lower management and operational charges. It is their belief that when all charges are totaled and compared to those involved with a no-load fund, the load fund has lower overall costs, therefore returning a greater portion of its earnings to the investor.

This is, of course, a matter of discussion and disagreement among individuals involved in the investment community. And there does not appear to be the possibility of a final resolution in the near future.

The following pages present listings of some of the more prominent load funds. Both equity and debt-instrument funds are listed. The lists include telephone numbers, initial and subsequent purchase requirements, and the applied loads. The funds are also grouped by type. For example, the equity funds are categorized as maximum capital gains funds, growth funds, equity income funds, balanced funds, to name just a few. Bond funds include high-yield corporate funds, high-grade corporate funds, mortgage-backed securities funds, high-yield tax-exempt bond funds, etc.

# LOAD MUTUAL FUNDS

| FUND | PURCHASE REQUIREMENTS | | LOAD* |
| | Initial | Subsequent | |
|---|---|---|---|
| **Maximum Capital Gains Funds** | | | |
| ABT Emerging Growth<br>700 Dixie Terminal Building<br>Cincinnati, OH 45202<br>800-354-0436 | $1,000 | $50 | 4¾ |
| Constellation Growth Fund<br>331 Madison Avenue<br>New York, NY 10017<br>212-557-8784 | $1,000 | $100 | 4¾ |
| Pacific Horizon Aggregate<br>3550 Wilshire Boulevard<br>Suite 1408<br>Los Angeles, CA 90010<br>800-645-3515 | $1,000 | $100 | 4½ |
| Putnam Voyager<br>One Post Office Square<br>Boston, MA 02109<br>800-225-1581/617-292-1000 | $500 | $50 | 8½ |
| Weingarten Equity Fund<br>331 Madison Avenue<br>New York, NY 10017<br>212-557-8787 | $1,000 | $100 | 4¾ |
| **Growth Funds** | | | |
| Fidelity Magellan<br>82 Devonshire Street<br>Boston, MA 02109<br>800-225-6190/617-570-7000 | $1,000 | $250 | 3 |
| Franklin Equity<br>777 Mariner Island Boulevard<br>San Nateo, CA 94401<br>415-570-3000 | $100 | $25 | 4 |
| Guardian Park Avenue<br>201 Park Avenue, South<br>New York, NY 10003<br>212-598-8259 | $300 | $50 | 8½ |
| IDS New Dimensions<br>1000 Roanoke Building<br>Minneapolis, MN 55402<br>800-328-8300/612-372-2897 | $2,000 | $100 | 5 |
| New England Life Growth Fund<br>501 Boylston Street<br>Boston, MA 02109<br>800-343-7104 | $250 | $25 | 6½ |

*Stated as a percentage of investment purchase.

| FUND | PURCHASE REQUIREMENTS | | LOAD* |
| | Initial | Subsequent | |
| --- | --- | --- | --- |
| **Growth and Income Funds** | | | |
| Eaton Vance Total Return<br>24 Federal Street<br>Boston, MA 02110<br>800-225-6265/617-482-8260 | $1,000 | $20 | 4¾ |
| Fundamental Investors<br>Four Embarcadero Center<br>San Francisco, CA 94111-4125<br>415-421-9360 | $250 | $50 | 8½ |
| Investment Co. of America<br>333 S. Hope Street<br>Los Angeles, CA 90071<br>800-421-9900/213-486-9500 | $250 | $50 | 8½ |
| Seligmann Common Stock<br>One Banker Trust Plaza<br>New York, NY 10006<br>800-221-7844/212-432-4180 | No min. | None | 4¾ |
| Sentinel Common Stock<br>National Life Drive<br>Montpelier, VA 05602<br>800-233-4332/802-229-3333 | $250 | $25 | 8½ |
| **Equity Income** | | | |
| Decatur I<br>Ten Penn Center Plaza<br>Philadelphia, PA 19103<br>800-523-4640/215-988-1333 | $25 | $25 | 8½ |
| Fidelity Equity Income<br>82 Devonshire Street<br>Boston, MA 02109<br>800-544-6666/617-523-1919 | $1,000 | $250 | 2 |
| National Total Income<br>605 Third Avenue<br>New York, NY 10016<br>800-223-7757/212-661-3000 | $250 | $25 | 7¼ |
| United Income Fund<br>20 N. Meridian Street<br>Indianapolis, IN 46204<br>800-862-7283/317-634-3301 | $500 | $25 | 8½ |
| Venture Retirement Plan of America—Equity<br>309 Johnson Street<br>Santa Fe, NM 87501<br>800-545-2098 | $1,000 | $25 | 5 |
| **Balanced Funds** | | | |
| Alliance Balanced Shares<br>140 Broadway<br>New York, NY 10005<br>800-221-5672/212-902-4160 | $250 | $50 | 5½ |
| IDS Mutual Fund<br>1000 Roanoke Building<br>Minneapolis, MN 55402<br>800-328-3000/612-373-3131 | $2,000 | $100 | 5 |

*Stated as a percentage of investment purchase.

| FUND | PURCHASE REQUIREMENTS | | LOAD* |
| | Initial | Subsequent | |
| --- | --- | --- | --- |
| Kemper Total Return<br>120 S. LaSalle Street<br>Chicago, IL 60603<br>800-621-1048/312-781-1121 | $1,000 | $100 | 8½ |
| Phoenix Balanced Fund<br>One American Row<br>Hartford, CT 06114<br>800-243-4361/203-278-8050 | $500 | $50 | 8½ |
| United Continental Income<br>One Crown Center<br>PO Box 1341<br>Kansas City, MO 64141<br>816-283-4000 | $500 | $25 | 8½ |

**Small Company Growth Funds**

| FUND | Initial | Subsequent | LOAD* |
| --- | --- | --- | --- |
| Fairfield Fund<br>605 Third Avenue<br>New York, NY 10158<br>800-223-7757/212-661-3000 | $500 | $50 | 8½ |
| Nicholas II<br>312 E. Wisconsin Avenue<br>Milwaukee, WI 53202<br>412-272-6133 | $1,000 | $20 | 1** |
| OTC Securities Fund<br>510 Pennsylvania Avenue<br>Suite 325, PO Box 1537<br>Ft. Washington, PA 19034<br>800-523-2478/214-643-2510 | $500 | $25 | 8 |
| Putnam OTC Emerging Growth Fund<br>One Post Office Square<br>Boston, MA 02109<br>800-225-1581/617-292-1000 | $500 | $50 | 6¾ |
| United New Concepts<br>One Crown Center<br>PO Box 1343<br>Kansas City, MO 64141<br>816-283-4000 | $500 | $25 | 8½ |

**Sector Funds**

| FUND | Initial | Subsequent | LOAD* |
| --- | --- | --- | --- |
| Alliance Technology<br>140 Broadway<br>New York, NY 10005<br>800-221-5672/212-902-4160 | $250 | $50 | 5½ |
| Fidelity Select—Financial Services<br>82 Devonshire Street<br>Boston, MA 02109<br>800-544-6666/617-523-1919 | $1,000 | $250 | 2 & 1** |
| Fidelity Select—Health Care<br>82 Devonshire Street<br>Boston, MA 02109<br>800-544-6666/617-523-1919 | $1,000 | $250 | 2 & 1** |
| Pru-Bache—Utilities<br>One Seaport Plaza<br>New York, NY 10292<br>800-872-7787/212-214-1214 | $1,000 | $100 | 5 |

*Stated as a percentage of investment purchase. **Back-end load.

A SAMPLING OF MUTUAL FUNDS

| FUND | PURCHASE REQUIREMENTS | | LOAD* |
|------|--------|------------|-------|
| | Initial | Subsequent | |
| Putnam Health Sciences Trust<br>One Post Office Square<br>Boston, MA 02109<br>800-225-1581/617-292-1000 | $500 | $50 | 8½ |
| **Gold and Precious Metals Funds** | | | |
| IDS Precious Metals<br>1000 Roanoke Building<br>Minneapolis, MN 55402<br>800-328-8300/612-372-2987 | $2,000 | $100 | 5 |
| International Investors<br>122 E. 42nd Street<br>New York, NY 10168<br>800-221-2220/212-687-5200 | $1,000 | $100 | 8½ |
| Keystone Precious Metals<br>99 High Street<br>Boston, MA 02104<br>800-225-2618/614-338-3200 | $1,000 | $100 | 4 |
| Oppenheimer Gold and Special Metals<br>Two Broadway<br>New York, NY 10004<br>800-525-7048/212-668-5055 | $2,500 | $25 | 8½ |
| Strategic Investments<br>2030 Royal Lane<br>Dallas, TX 75229<br>800-527-5027/214-484-1326 | $500 | $100 | 8½ |
| **Global Funds** | | | |
| Dean Witter World Wide Investments Trust<br>One World Trade Center<br>New York, NY 10048<br>800-221-2685/212-938-4554 | $1,000 | $100 | 5 |
| New Perspective Fund<br>333 S. Hope Street<br>Los Angeles, CA 90071<br>800-421-9900/213-486-9200 | $250 | $50 | 8½ |
| Oppenheimer Global<br>Two Broadway<br>New York, NY 10004<br>800-525-7048/212-668-5055 | $1,000 | $25 | 8½ |
| Paine Webber Atlas<br>1221 Avenue of the Americas<br>New York, NY 10020<br>800-544-9300/212-730-8625 | $1,000 | $100 | 8½ |
| Putnam International Equities<br>One Post Square<br>Boston, MA 02109<br>800-225-1581/617-292-1000 | $500 | $50 | 8½ |
| **International Funds** | | | |
| Fidelity Overseas<br>82 Devonshire Street<br>Boston, MA 02109<br>800-225-6190/617-570-7000 | $1,000 | $250 | 3 |

*Stated as a percentage of investment purchase.

APPENDIX B

| FUND | PURCHASE REQUIREMENTS | | LOAD* |
| | Initial | Subsequent | |
| --- | --- | --- | --- |
| IDS International<br>1000 Roanoke Building<br>Minneapolis, MN 55402<br>800-328-8300/612-372-2987 | $2,000 | $100 | 4½ |
| Kemper International<br>120 S. LaSalle Street<br>Chicago, IL 60603<br>800-621-1048/312-781-1121 | $1,000 | $100 | 8½ |
| Merrill Lynch Pacific<br>PO Box 9011<br>Princeton, NJ 68543-0911<br>609-282-2800 | $250 | $50 | 6½ |
| Templeton Foreign Fund<br>405 Central Avenue, PO Box 3942<br>St. Petersburg, FL 33371<br>800-237-0738/FL: 800-282-0106 | $500 | $25 | 8½ |
| United International Growth Fund<br>One Crown Center<br>PO Box 1341<br>Kansas City, MD 64141<br>816-283-4000 | $500 | $25 | 8½ |

**High-Yield Corporate Bonds**

| | | | |
| --- | --- | --- | --- |
| Cigna High Yield Fund, Inc.<br>N-73<br>Hartford, CT 06152<br>800-225-5151/203-726-6000 | $500 | $50 | 6½ |
| Colonial High Yield Securities<br>One Financial Center<br>Boston, MA 02111<br>617-426-3750 | $250 | $25 | 4¾ |
| Delchester Bond Fund<br>Ten Penn Center Plaza<br>Philadelphia, PA 19103<br>800-523-4640/215-298-1333 | $25 | $25 | 6¾ |
| Kemper High Yield Fund<br>120 S. LaSalle Street<br>Chicago, IL 60603<br>800-621-1048/312-781-1121 | $1,000 | $100 | 5½ |
| Pacific Horizon High Bond Fund<br>3550 Wilshire Boulevard, Suite 1408<br>Los Angeles, CA 90010<br>800-645-3515 | $1,000 | $100 | 4½ |

**High-Grade Corporate Bonds**

| | | | |
| --- | --- | --- | --- |
| Bond Fund of America<br>333 S. Hope Street<br>Los Angeles, CA 90071<br>800-421-9900/213-486-9651 | $1,000 | $50 | 4¾ |
| Hutton Investment Series—Bond and Income<br>One Battery Park Plaza<br>New York, NY 10004<br>800-334-2626/212-742-5000 | $500 | $250 | 5** |

*Stated as a percentage of investment purchase. **Back-end load.

| FUND | PURCHASE REQUIREMENTS | | LOAD* |
| | Initial | Subsequent | |
| --- | --- | --- | --- |
| Sigma Income Shares<br>Greenville Center C-200<br>3801 Kennett Pike<br>Wilmington, DE 19807<br>800-441-9490/302-652-3091 | No min. | None | 8½ |
| UMB Bond Fund, Inc.<br>2440 Pershing Road, G-15<br>Kansas City, MO 64108<br>800-821-5591 | $1,000 | $100 | 6 |
| United Bond Fund<br>One Crown Center<br>PO Box 1343<br>Kansas City, MO 64141<br>816-283-4000 | $500 | $25 | 8½ |
| **U.S. Government Securities Funds** | | | |
| AMEV U.S. Government Fund<br>Box 64284<br>St. Paul, MN 55164<br>800-872-2638/612-738-4000 | $250 | $25 | 4½ |
| Carnegie Government Securities—High Yield<br>1331 Euclid Avenue<br>Cleveland, OH 44115<br>800-321-2322/216-781-4440 | $1,000 | $50 | 4¾ |
| Hancock (John) U.S. Government Security Fund<br>Hancock Place, PO Box 111<br>Boston, MA 02117<br>800-225-5291/617-421-4506 | $500 | $25 | 8½ |
| Lord Abbett U.S. Government Securities<br>63 Wall Street<br>New York, NY 10005<br>800-223-4224/212-424-8720 | $500 | None | 5 |
| U.S. Government Guaranteed Securities<br>333 S. Hope Street<br>Los Angeles, CA 90071<br>800-421-9900/213-486-9200 | $1,000 | $50 | 4¾ |
| **Mortgage-backed Securities Funds** | | | |
| Alliance Mortgage Securities, Inc.<br>140 Broadway<br>New York, NY 10005<br>800-221-5672/212-902-4160 | $1,000 | $25 | 5½ |
| Colonial Enhance Mortgage Trust<br>One Financial Center<br>Boston, MA 02111<br>617-426-3750 | $250 | $25 | 4¾ |
| Franklin U.S. Government Series<br>77 Mariner Island Boulevard<br>San Mateo, CA 94401<br>800-632-2180/415-570-3000 | $100 | $25 | 4 |
| Kemper U.S. Government Securities<br>120 S. LaSalle Street<br>Chicago, IL 60603<br>800-621-1048/312-781-1121 | $1,000 | $100 | 4½ |

*Stated as a percentage of investment purchase.

| FUND | PURCHASE REQUIREMENTS | | LOAD* |
| | Initial | Subsequent | |
|---|---|---|---|
| United Government Securities<br>One Crown Center<br>PO Box 1343<br>Kansas City, MO 64141<br>816-283-4000 | $500 | $25 | 4 |

**High-Yield Tax-exempt Bond Funds**

| FUND | Initial | Subsequent | LOAD* |
|---|---|---|---|
| IDS High Yield Tax Exempts<br>1000 Roanoke Building<br>Minneapolis, MN 55402<br>800-328-8300/612-372-2897 | $2,000 | $100 | 5 |
| Merrill Lynch Bond Fund<br>PO Box 9011<br>Princeton, NJ 68543-0911<br>609-282-2800 | $1,000 | $100 | 4½ |
| MFS Managed High Yield<br>200 Berkeley Street<br>Boston, MA 02116<br>617-423-3500 | No min. | None | 4¾ |
| Pru-Bach High Yield<br>One Seaport Plaza<br>New York, NY 10292<br>800-872-7787/212-214-1214 | $1,000 | $100 | 5 |
| Seligmann California Tax-exempt—High Yield<br>One Banker Trust Plaza<br>New York, NY 10006<br>800-221-7844/212-432-4180 | No min. | None | 4½ |

**High-Grade Tax-exempt Bond Funds**

| FUND | Initial | Subsequent | LOAD* |
|---|---|---|---|
| DMC Tax-free Trust—U.S.A. Series<br>Ten Penn Center Plaza<br>Philadelphia, PA 19103<br>215-988-1200 | $1,000 | $25 | 4¾ |
| Hutton National Muni Bond<br>One Battery Park<br>New York, NY 10004<br>800-334-2626/212-742-5000 | $500 | $50 | 4 |
| Kemper Muni Bond Fund<br>120 S. LaSalle Street<br>Chicago, IL 60603<br>800-621-1048/312-781-1121 | $1,000 | $100 | 4¾ |
| Mutual of Omaha Tax-free Inc.<br>10235 Regency Circle<br>Omaha, NE 68114<br>800-228-9011/NE:800-642-8112<br>402-397-8555 | $1,000 | $50 | 8 |
| United Municipal Bond Fund<br>One Crown Center<br>PO Box 1343<br>Kansas City, MO 64141<br>816-283-4000 | $500 | $25 | 4 |

*Stated as a percentage of investment purchase.

## NO-LOAD MUTUAL FUNDS

The following is a list of no-load mutual funds. The list is not all-inclusive but does contain pertinent information (addresses, telephone numbers, and purchase requirements) for nearly 150 of the more prominent funds. The funds are grouped by type, such as growth funds, funds that seek maximum capital gains, income funds, balanced funds, bond funds, and money funds.

| FUND | PURCHASE REQUIREMENTS | |
| --- | --- | --- |
| | Initial | Subsequent |
| **Growth Funds** | | |
| American Investors<br>777 W. Putnam Avenue<br>Box 2500<br>Greenwich, CT 06836<br>800-243-5353/203-531-5000 | $400 | $20 |
| Boston Company Capital Appreciation<br>One Boston Place<br>Box 2537<br>Boston, MA 02106<br>800-343-6324/617-722-7250 | $1,000 | None |
| Bull and Bear Capital Growth<br>11 Hanover Square, 11th floor<br>New York, NY 10005<br>800-523-9250/212-785-0900 | $1,000 | $100 |
| Fidelity Contrafund<br>82 Devonshire Street<br>Boston, MA 02109<br>800-225-6190/617-570-7000 | $1,000 | $250 |
| Fidelity Trend<br>82 Devonshire Street<br>Boston, MA 02109<br>800-225-6190/617-570-7000 | $1,000 | $250 |
| Founders Growth<br>810 Cherry Creek<br>National Bank Building<br>3033 E. First Avenue<br>Denver, CO 80206<br>800-525-2440/303-394-4404 | $1,000 | $100 |
| Invest Fund<br>Box 2600<br>Valley Forge, PA 19482<br>800-523-7125/215-964-2600 | $500 | $50 |
| Ivy Fund<br>40 Industrial Park Road<br>Hingham, MA 02043<br>800-235-3322/617-749-1416 | $1,000 | $100 |
| Lehman Capital<br>55 Water Street<br>New York, NY 10041<br>800-221-5350/212-558-2031 | $1,000 | $100 |
| Lindner Fund<br>200 South Berniston Avenue<br>St. Louis, MO 63105<br>314-727-5305 | $2,000 | $100 |

| FUND | PURCHASE REQUIREMENTS | |
| --- | --- | --- |
| | Initial | Subsequent |
| Mathers Fund<br>125 S. Wacker Drive<br>Chicago, IL 60606<br>312-236-8215 | $1,000 | $200 |
| W. L. Morgan Growth<br>Box 2600<br>Valley Forge, PA 19482<br>800-523-7025/215-964-2600 | $1,500 | $50 |
| Mutual Shares Corporation<br>26 Broadway<br>New York, NY 10004<br>800-221-7864/212-908-4047 | $1,000 | None |
| Nicholas Fund<br>312 E. Wisconsin Avenue<br>Milwaukee, WI 53202<br>414-272-6133 | $500 | $100 |
| Partners Fund<br>342 Madison Avenue<br>New York, NY 10173<br>800-225-1596/212-850-8336 | $500 | $50 |
| Penn Square Mutual<br>2650 Westview Drive<br>Wyomessing, PA 19610<br>800-523-8440/215-670-1031 | $500 | $100 |
| T. Rowe Price Growth Stock<br>100 E. Pratt Street<br>Baltimore, MD 21202<br>800-638-5660/301-547-2308 | $1,000 | $100 |
| T. Rowe Price New Era<br>100 E. Pratt Street<br>Baltimore, MD 21202<br>800-638-5660/301-547-2308 | $1,000 | $100 |
| Scudder Capital Growth<br>175 Federal Street<br>Boston, MA 02110<br>800-225-2470/617-482-3990 | $1,000 | None |
| Scudder Common Stock<br>175 Federal Street<br>Boston, MA 02110<br>800-225-2470/617-482-3990 | $1,000 | None |
| Steinroe and Farnham Capital Opportunities<br>PO Box 1143<br>Chicago, IL 60609<br>800-621-0320/312-368-7800 | $2,500 | $100 |
| Steinroe and Farnham Stock<br>PO Box 1143<br>Chicago, IL 60690<br>800-621-0320/312-368-7800 | $2,500 | None |
| Steinroe Universe<br>PO Box 1143<br>Chicago, IL 60690<br>800-621-0320/312-368-7800 | $2,500 | $100 |

| FUND | Initial | Subsequent |
| --- | --- | --- |
| Twentieth Century Select<br>Box 200<br>Kansas City, MO 64141<br>816-531-5575 | None | None |
| USAA Mutual Growth<br>880 Fredericksburgh Road<br>San Antonio, TX 78288<br>800-531-8181/512-690-6062 | $1,000 | $25 |
| **Funds That Seek Maximum Capital Gains** | | |
| Acorn Fund<br>120 S. LaSalle Street<br>Room 1330<br>Chicago, IL 60603<br>312-621-0603 | $1,000 | $200 |
| Constellation Growth<br>331 Madison Avenue<br>New York, NY 10017<br>212-557-8784 | $1,000 | $100 |
| Explorer<br>Box 2600<br>Valley Forge, PA 19482<br>800-523-7125/215-964-2600 | $3,000 | $50 |
| Financial Dynamics<br>Box 2040<br>Denver, CO 80201<br>800-525-8085/303-779-1233 | $1,000 | $100 |
| 44 Wall Street Fund<br>One State Street Plaza<br>New York, NY 10004<br>800-221-7836/212-344-4224 | $1,000 | $100 |
| Founders Special<br>810 Cherry Creek<br>National Bank Building<br>3033 E. First Avenue<br>Denver, CO 80206<br>800-525-2440/303-394-4404 | $1,000 | $100 |
| Hartwell Leverage<br>515 Madison Avenue, 31st floor<br>New York, NY 10022<br>212-308-3355 | $2,000 | $50 |
| Janus<br>100 Fillmore Street, Suite 300<br>Denver, CO 80206<br>800-525-3713/303-837-1810 | $1,000 | $50 |
| North Star Stock<br>1100 Dain Tower<br>Box 1160<br>Minneapolis, MN 55440<br>612-371-7780 | $1,000 | $100 |
| Pennsylvania Mutual<br>1414 Avenue of the Americas<br>New York, NY 10019<br>800-221-4268/212-486-1445 | $1,000 | $50 |

| FUND | PURCHASE REQUIREMENTS | |
| :--- | :---: | :---: |
| | Initial | Subsequent |
| T. Rowe Price New Horizons<br>100 E. Pratt Street<br>Baltimore, MD 21202<br>800-638-5660/301-547-2308 | $1,000 | $100 |
| Scudder Development<br>175 Federal Street<br>Boston, MA 02110<br>800-225-2470/617-482-3990 | $1,000 | None |
| Steinroe Special Fund<br>PO Box 1143<br>Chicago, IL 60690<br>800-621-0320/312-368-7800 | $1,000 | $100 |
| Tudor<br>One New York Plaza<br>New York, NY 10004<br>800-223-3332/212-908-9582 | $1,000 | $50 |
| Twentieth Century Growth<br>Box 200<br>Kansas City, MO 64141<br>816-531-5575 | None | None |
| Twentieth Century Ultra<br>Box 200<br>Kansas City, MO 64141<br>816-531-5575 | None | None |
| Value Line Leveraged Growth<br>711 Third Avenue<br>New York, NY 10017<br>800-223-0818/212-687-3965 | $250 | $25 |
| Value Line Special Situations<br>711 Third Avenue<br>New York, NY 10017<br>800-223-0818/212-687-3965 | $250 | $25 |
| Weingarten Equity<br>331 Madison Avenue<br>New York, NY 10017<br>212-557-8787 | $1,000 | $100 |

**Income Funds**

| FUND | Initial | Subsequent |
| :--- | :---: | :---: |
| Babson Income Trust<br>2440 Pershing Road<br>G-15<br>Kansas City, MO 64108<br>800-821-5591/816-471-5200 | $500 | $50 |
| Boston Co. Government Income Fund<br>One Boston Place<br>Boston, MA 02106<br>800-343-6324/617-722-7250 | $1,000 | None |
| Dreyfus A Bonds Plus<br>767 Fifth Avenue<br>New York, NY 10005<br>800-645-6561/212-715-6000 | $2,500 | $100 |

| FUND | PURCHASE REQUIREMENTS | |
| --- | --- | --- |
| | Initial | Subsequent |
| Fidelity Corporate Bond<br>82 Devonshire Street<br>Boston, MA 02109<br>800-225-6190/617-570-7000 | $2,500 | $250 |
| Fidelity Equity Income<br>82 Devonshire Street<br>Boston, MA 02109<br>800-225-6190/617-570-7000 | $1,000 | $250 |
| Financial Industrial Income<br>Box 2040<br>Denver, CO 80201<br>800-525-8085/CO: 800-525-9769<br>303-779-1233 | $1,000 | $100 |
| Mutual Qualified Income<br>26 Broadway<br>New York, NY 10004<br>800-221-7864/212-908-4047 | $1,000 | None |
| Northeast Investors T<br>50 Congress Street<br>Boston, MA 02109<br>800-225-6704/617-523-3588 | $500 | None |
| North Star Bond<br>110 Dain Tower<br>Box 1160<br>Minneapolis, MN 55440<br>612-371-7780 | $1,000 | $100 |
| T. Rowe Price New Income<br>100 E. Pratt Street<br>Baltimore, MD 21202<br>800-638-5660/301-547-2308 | $1,000 | $100 |
| Pro Income<br>5 Sentry Parkway, W<br>Suite 120<br>PO Box 1111<br>Blue Bell, PA 19422<br>800-523-0864/215-836-0400 | $300 | None |
| Qualified Dividend<br>Portfolio I<br>Box 2600<br>Valley Forge, PA 19482<br>800-523-7025/215-964-2600 | $3,000 | $50 |
| Safeco Special Bond<br>Safeco Plaza<br>Seattle, WA 98185<br>800-426-6730/206-545-5530 | $200 | $25 |
| Scudder Income<br>175 Federal Street<br>Boston, MA 02110<br>800-225-2470/617-482-3990 | $1,000 | None |
| Steadman Associated<br>1730 K Street, NW<br>Washington, DC 20006<br>800-424-8570/202-223-1000 | $100 | $25 |

| FUND | PURCHASE REQUIREMENTS | |
|---|---|---|
| | Initial | Subsequent |
| Steinroe Bond<br>PO Box 1143<br>Chicago, IL 60690<br>800-621-0320/312-368-7800 | $2,500 | $100 |
| Value Line Income<br>711 Third Avenue<br>New York, NY 10017<br>800-223-0818/212-687-3965 | $250 | $25 |
| Vanguard GNMA Portfolio<br>Box 2600<br>Valley Forge, PA 19482<br>800-523-7025/215-964-2600 | $3,000 | $100 |
| Vanguard High Yield Bond<br>Box 2600<br>Valley Forge, PA 19482<br>800-523-7025/215-964-2600 | $3,000 | $100 |
| Wellesley Income<br>Box 2600<br>Valley Forge, PA 19482<br>800-523-7025/215-964-2600 | $1,500 | $50 |

**Balanced Funds**

| FUND | Initial | Subsequent |
|---|---|---|
| Babson Investment Fund<br>2440 Pershing Road<br>Kansas City, MO 64108<br>800-821-5591/816-471-5200 | $500 | $50 |
| Drexel Burnham Fund<br>60 Broad Street<br>New York, NY 10004<br>212-480-6000 | $1,000 | $25 |
| Dreyfus Fund<br>767 Fifth Avenue<br>New York, NY 10005<br>800-645-6561/212-715-6000 | $2,500 | $100 |
| Fidelity Fund<br>82 Devonshire Street<br>Boston, MA 02109<br>800-225-6190/617-570-7000 | $1,000 | $50 |
| Financial Industrial Fund<br>Box 2040<br>Denver, CO 80201<br>800-525-8085/CO: 800-525-9769<br>303-779-1233 | $1,000 | $100 |
| Guardian Mutual<br>342 Madison Avenue<br>New York, NY 10173<br>800-225-1596/212-850-8336 | $500 | $50 |
| Loomis-Sayles Mutual<br>PO Box 449<br>Back Bay Annex<br>Boston, MA 02117<br>800-225-7670/617-267-6600 | $250 | $50 |

| FUND | PURCHASE REQUIREMENTS | |
|---|---|---|
| | Initial | Subsequent |
| One William Street<br>55 Water Street<br>New York, NY 10041<br>800-221-5350/212-558-3288 | $500 | $50 |
| T. Rowe Price Growth and Income<br>100 E. Pratt Street<br>Baltimore, MD 21202<br>800-638-5660/301-547-2308 | $1,000 | $100 |
| Steinroe and Farnham Balanced<br>PO Box 1143<br>Chicago, IL 60690<br>800-621-0320/312-368-7800 | $2,500 | $100 |
| Value Line Fund<br>711 Third Avenue<br>New York, NY 10017<br>800-223-0818/212-687-3965 | $250 | $25 |
| Vanguard Index Trust<br>Box 2600<br>Valley Forge, PA 19482<br>800-523-7025/215-964-2600 | $1,500 | $100 |
| Wellington Fund<br>Box 2600<br>Valley Forge, PA 19482<br>800-523-7025/215-946-2600 | $1,500 | $100 |
| Windsor Fund<br>Box 2600<br>Valley Forge, PA 19482<br>800-523-7025/215-964-2600 | $500 | $50 |

**Municipal Bond Funds**

| FUND | Initial | Subsequent |
|---|---|---|
| Babson Tax-free Fund—Long Term<br>2440 Pershing Road<br>Kansas City, MO 64108<br>800-821-5591/816-471-5200 | $1,000 | $50 |
| Calvert Tax-free Reserve—Ltd. Term Port.<br>1700 Pennsylvania Ave., NW<br>Washington, DC 20006<br>800-368-2748/301-951-4820 | $2,000 | $250 |
| Composite Tax-exempt Bond Fund<br>Sea First Financial Center, 9th floor<br>Spokane, WA 99201<br>800-541-0830/509-624-4101 | $1,000 | $100 |
| Dreyfus Tax-exempt Bond Fund<br>767 Fifth Avenue<br>New York, NY 10005<br>800-645-6561/212-715-6000 | $2,500 | $100 |
| Federated Short-Intermediate Muni Trust<br>421 Seventh Avenue<br>Pittsburgh, PA 15219<br>800-245-4270/412-288-1979 | $25,000 | None |

| FUND | PURCHASE REQUIREMENTS | |
|---|---|---|
| | Initial | Subsequent |
| Fidelity High Yield Municipal<br>82 Devonshire Street<br>Boston, MA 02109<br>800-225-6190/617-570-7000 | $2,500 | $250 |
| Fidelity Municipal Bond Fund<br>82 Devonshire Street<br>Boston, MA 02109<br>800-225-6190/617-570-7000 | $2,500 | $250 |
| Nuveen Municipal Bond Fund<br>333 W. Wacker Drive<br>Chicago, IL 60606<br>312-621-3184 | $2,500 | $250 |
| T. Rowe Price Tax-free Income Fund<br>100 E. Pratt Street<br>Baltimore, MD 21202<br>800-638-5660/301-547-2308 | $1,000 | $100 |
| Safeco Municipal Bond Fund<br>Safeco Plaza<br>Seattle, WA 98185<br>800-426-6730/206-545-5530 | $2,500 | $250 |
| Scudder Managed Municipal Bonds<br>175 Federal Street<br>Boston, MA 02110<br>800-225-2470/617-482-3990 | $1,000 | None |
| Steinroe Tax-exempt Bond Fund<br>PO Box 1143<br>Chicago, IL 60690<br>800-621-0320/312-368-7800 | $2,500 | $100 |
| Vanguard Municipal Bond—Intermediate<br>Box 2600<br>Valley Forge, PA 19482<br>800-523-7025/215-965-2600 | $3,000 | $100 |
| Vanguard Municipal Bond—Long Term<br>Box 2600<br>Valley Forge, PA 19482<br>800-523-7025/215-964-2600 | $3,000 | $100 |

**Money Market Funds**

| FUND | PURCHASE REQUIREMENTS | |
|---|---|---|
| | Initial | Subsequent |
| Cash Equivalent Fund-MM Portfolio<br>120 S. LaSalle Street<br>Chicago, IL 60603<br>312-845-1811 | $1,000 | $100 |
| Current Investment Fund<br>333 Clay Street<br>Suite 4300<br>Houston, TX 77002<br>713-751-2400 | $1,000 | $100 |
| Daily Cash Accumulation Fund<br>PO Box 300<br>Denver, CO 80201<br>303-671-3568 | $500 | $25 |

| FUND | PURCHASE REQUIREMENTS | |
|---|---|---|
| | Initial | Subsequent |
| DBL Cash Fund-MM Portfolio<br>60 Broad Street<br>New York, NY 10004<br>212-480-6000 | $1,000 | $100 |
| Delaware Cash Reserve Fund<br>10 Penn Center Plaza<br>Philadelphia, PA 19103<br>215-988-1200 | $1,000 | $25 |
| Dreyfus Liquid Assets<br>767 Fifth Avenue<br>New York, NY 10005<br>800-645-6561/212-715-6000 | $2,500 | $100 |
| Fidelity Cash Reserves<br>82 Devonshire Street<br>Boston, MA 02109<br>800-225-6190/617-570-7000 | $1,000 | $250 |
| IDS Cash Management Fund<br>1000 Roanoke Building<br>Minneapolis, MN 55402<br>800-437-4332/612-372-2897 | $1,000 | $100 |
| Kemper Money Market Fund<br>120 S. LaSalle Street<br>Chicago, IL 60603<br>312-845-1121 | $1,000 | $100 |
| Liquid Capital Income Fund<br>1331 Euclid Avenue<br>Cleveland, OH 44115<br>800-231-2322/216-781-4440 | $1,000 | $250 |
| Merrill Lynch Ready Assets<br>PO Box 9011<br>Princeton, NJ 68543-0911<br>609-282-2800 | $5,000 | $1,000 |
| Moneymart Assets<br>One Seaport Plaza<br>New York, NY 10001<br>800-221-7984/212-214-1226 | $1,000 | $100 |
| National Liquid Reserves<br>333 W. 34th Street<br>New York, NY 10001<br>212-613-2619 | $1,000 | $100 |
| Paine Webber Cash Fund<br>1221 Avenue of the Americas<br>New York, NY 10020<br>212-730-8625 | $5,000 | $500 |
| T. Rowe Price Prime Reserves Fund<br>100 E. Pratt Street<br>Baltimore, MD 21202<br>800-628-5660/301-547-2308 | $1,000 | $100 |
| Reserve Fund-Primary Portfolio<br>810 Seventh Avenue<br>New York, NY 10019<br>800-223-2213/212-246-3550 | $1,000 | $1,000 |

| | PURCHASE REQUIREMENTS | |
|---|---|---|
| FUND | Initial | Subsequent |
| Scudder Cash Investment Trust<br>175 Federal Street<br>Boston, MA 02110<br>800-225-2470/617-482-3990 | $1,000 | None |
| Shearson Daily Dividend<br>Two World Trade Center<br>New York, NY 10048<br>212-577-5794 | $2,500 | $1,000 |
| Vanguard Money Market Trust–Prime Portfolio<br>Box 2600<br>Valley Forge, PA 19482<br>800-523-7025/215-964-2600 | $1,000 | $100 |
| Webster Cash Reserve<br>20 Exchange Place<br>New York, NY 10005<br>212-510-5041 | $1,500 | $500 |

**Money Market Funds—U.S. Government Securities Only**

| FUND | Initial | Subsequent |
|---|---|---|
| AARP U.S. Government Money Market Trust<br>421 Seventh Avenue<br>Pittsburgh, PA 15219<br>412-392-6300 | $500 | $100 |
| Capital Preservation Fund<br>755 Page Mill Road<br>Palo Alto, CA 94303<br>800-227-8380/CA: 800-982-6150 | $1,000 | $100 |
| Capital Preservation Fund II<br>755 Page Mill Road<br>Palo Alto, CA 94304<br>800-227-8380/CA: 800-982-6150 | $1,000 | $100 |
| Dreyfus Money Market Instruments—Government Series<br>767 Fifth Avenue<br>New York, NY 10005<br>800-645-6561/212-715-6000 | $2,500 | $100 |
| Fund for Government Investors<br>4022 Fairmont Avenue<br>Bethesda, MD 20814<br>301-657-1510 | $2,500 | None |
| Merrill Lynch Government Fund<br>125 High Street<br>Boston, MA 02110<br>800-225-1576/617-357-1460 | $5,000 | $1,000 |
| Shearson Government and Agencies Fund<br>Two World Trade Center<br>New York, NY 10048<br>212-577-5794 | $5,000 | $1,000 |
| Trust for Short-Term Federal Securities/Federal Funds<br>Suite 204, Webster Building<br>3411 Silverside Road<br>Wilmington, DE 19810<br>800-441-7450/CA: 800-323-7712 | $1,000 | None |

| | PURCHASE REQUIREMENTS | |
|---|---|---|
| FUND | Initial | Subsequent |
| U.S. Treasury Securities Fund-MM<br>PO Box 29467<br>San Antonio, TX 78229<br>800-531-5771/512-696-1234 | $500 | $50 |

**Tax-exempt Money Market Funds**

| | | |
|---|---|---|
| Calvert Tax-free Reserve—MM Portfolio<br>1700 Pennsylvania Avenue, NW<br>Washington, DC 20006<br>800-368-2748/301-951-4820 | $2,000 | $250 |
| Carnegie Tax-free Income Trust<br>1331 Euclid Avenue<br>Cleveland, OH 44115<br>800-321-2322/216-781-4400 | $5,000 | $500 |
| Daily Tax-free Income Fund<br>100 Park Avenue<br>New York, NY 10017<br>212-370-1110 | $5,000 | $500 |
| Fidelity Tax-exempt Money Market Trust<br>82 Devonshire Street<br>Boston, MA 02109<br>800-225-6190/617-570-7000 | $10,000 | $500 |
| Municipal Bond for Temporary Investments<br>PO Box 7488<br>Wilmington, DE 19803<br>800-441-7450/302-792-8833<br>NY: 212-323-7712 | $1,000 | None |
| Nuveen Tax-free Reserves<br>333 W. Wacker Drive<br>Chicago, IL 60606<br>312-621-3184 | $1,000 | $100 |
| T. Rowe Price Tax-exempt Money Fund<br>100 E. Pratt Street<br>Baltimore, MD 21202<br>800-638-5660/301-547-2308 | $1,000 | $100 |
| Scudder Tax-free Money<br>175 Federal Street<br>Boston, MA 02110<br>800-225-2470/617-482-3990 | $1,000 | None |
| Tax-exempt Money Market Fund<br>120 S. LaSalle Street<br>Chicago, IL 60603<br>800-621-1048/312-845-1811 | $1,000 | $100 |
| Tax-free Money Fund<br>1345 Avenue of the Americas<br>New York, NY 10105<br>212-613-2631 | $5,000 | $100 |

**Specialty Funds**

| | | |
|---|---|---|
| Analytical Optioned Equity<br>2222 Martin Street<br>Suite 230<br>Irvine, CA 92715<br>714-833-0294 | $25,000 | $1,000 |

| FUND | PURCHASE REQUIREMENTS | |
|---|---|---|
| | Initial | Subsequent |
| Century Shares Trust<br>50 Congress Street<br>Boston, MA 02109<br>800-225-6704/617-523-6844 | $500 | $25 |
| Energy and Utilities Shares<br>Box 550<br>Blue Bell, PA 19422<br>215-542-8025 | $1,000 | $100 |
| Energy Fund<br>342 Madison Avenue<br>New York, NY 10173<br>800-225-1596/212-850-8300 | $500 | $50 |
| Gateway Option Income<br>1120 Carew Tower<br>Cincinnati, OH 45202<br>513-621-7774 | $500 | $100 |
| Golcanda Investors<br>11 Hanover Square<br>New York, NY 10005<br>800-523-9250/212-785-0900 | $1,000 | $100 |
| G. T. Pacific<br>601 Montgomery Street<br>Suite 1400<br>San Francisco, CA 94111<br>800-824-1580/415-392-6181 | $500 | $100 |
| Lexington Goldfund<br>PO Box 1515<br>Englewood Cliffs, NJ 07632<br>800-526-4791/201-845-7300 | $1,000 | $50 |
| Medical Technology Fund<br>5 Sentry Parkway, W<br>PO Box 19423<br>Blue Bell, PA 19422<br>800-523-0864/215-836-0400 | $1,000 | None |
| National Aviation and Tech. Corp.<br>50 Broad Street<br>New York, NY 10004<br>212-482-8100 | $500 | None |
| Precious Metals Holdings<br>One Post Office Square<br>Boston, MA 02109<br>617-338-4420 | $1,000 | $250 |
| T. Rowe Price International<br>100 E. Pratt Street<br>Baltimore, MD 21202<br>800-638-5660/301-547-2308 | $1,000 | $100 |
| Scudder International<br>175 Federal Street<br>Boston, MA 02110<br>800-225-2470/617-482-3990 | $1,000 | None |
| United Services Gold Shares<br>9800 Fredericksburgh Road<br>San Antonio, TX 78228<br>800-531-8181/512-690-6062 | $500 | $50 |

## PROMINENT INDEPENDENT MUTUAL FUND ORGANIZATIONS AND THEIR SWITCHING POLICIES*

| Company Name | Headquarters | Telephone | Funds Managed | Switching Policies |
|---|---|---|---|---|
| American Capital | Houston, TX | 800-231-3638 | 40 | There is no limit. The load is applied if a switch is made from a no-load to a load fund, or the load is changed if switching is made among load funds. |
| Capital Research & Management | Los Angeles, CA | 213-486-9200 | 18 | No limit or fee is applied. |
| Dreyfus | New York, NY | 800-645-6561 | 24 | No limit or fee is applied. |
| Federated | Pittsburgh, PA | 800-245-5000 | 47 | No limits to switching are in effect. |
| Fidelity | Boston, MA | 617-570-4810 | 103 | There are charges on select funds, and only five switches per year are permitted. |
| First | New York, NY | 212-825-7900 | 14 | Switching is permitted among government funds but not allowed among the other funds. |
| Franklin | San Mateo, CA | 800-632-2180 | 33 | No switching limit is in effect, but a $5 fee is applied. |
| IDS | Minneapolis, MN | 800-328-8300 | 23 | No limit or fee is applied. |
| Kemper | Chicago, IL | 800-621-1148 | 20 | No change is permitted after having been involved with any fund for six months or more. |
| Keystone | Boston, MA | 800-225-1587 | 11 | Five switches per year are permitted with a $5 fee. |
| Massachusetts Financial Service | Boston, MA | 617-423-3500 | 30 | No switching limit is in effect, but a $5 fee is applied. |
| T. Rowe Price | Baltimore, MD | 800-225-2465 | 23 | Limited switching among stock funds is permitted. |
| Provident Institutional Management | Wilmington, DE | 800-441-7450 | 8 | No switching limit has been established. |
| Putnam | Boston, MA | 800-225-2465 | 32 | No switching limit is in effect, but a $5 fee is applied. |
| Scudder, Stevens and Clark | Boston, MA | 800-225-2470 | 23 | No switching limit has been established. |
| Stein-Roe Farnham, Inc. | Chicago, IL | 800-621-0320 | 13 | No switching limit has been established. |
| Templeton Investment Council | St. Petersburg, FL | 800-237-0738 | 5 | Switching permitted among the funds. |
| Vanguard Group | Valley Forge, PA | 800-662-7447 | 45 | No charge is applied, but frequent switching is discouraged. |
| Waddell and Reed | Kansas City, MO | 816-283-4000 | 14 | Generally, switching is permitted, but certain funds are excluded. |
| Wellington Management | Boston, MA | 800-523-7025 | 16 | No limit on switching has been established. |

*This information current as of January 30, 1987

# INDEX

intrinsic value of stock, 156, 175, 184
inventories, 163
investment, 4–11, 13, 61; advisors,
    86–89; short-term securities, 15–16
investment bankers, 66
investment clubs, 89
*Investment Companies,* 277
investment premium of options, 308,
    323
investment trusts, 216, 261–63
investment value, 47, 140; of
    convertible securities, 237
*Investor's Daily,* 123
IRAs. *See* Individual Retirement
    Accounts
ITS (Intermarket Trading System), 70

Japanese yen futures, 334, 335
joint accounts, 85
*Journal of Commerce,* 123
junior bonds, 205
junk bonds, 5, 217

Kansas City Board of Trade (KCBT),
    332–33, 344
Kemper Growth Fund, 101
Keogh plans, 30–33
Keystone International Fund, 102
*Kiplinger Washington Letter,* 124

labor relations, 161
leaded gasoline futures, 332
leverage, 108–16, 168; futures market,
    338; options, 300, 301, 309, 315,
    326
liabilities, 163, 164, 165
life cycle, and investment, 13
limited partnership commodity pools,
    341–42
limit orders, 78–79
liquidation, 140, 244
liquidity, 14–23, 55, 167; common
    stocks, 145; futures market, 334;
    institutional bonds, 215; money
    market funds, 268; municipal
    bonds, 211; mutual funds, 258;
    Treasury bonds, 208
listed bonds, 208
listed options, 303–6
livestock, 337
load mutual funds, 101, 258, 261,
    263–64, 268
loan from life insurance policy,
    298–99
long-term assets, 164–65
long-term debt, 165
long-term growth, 153, 265, 364–66
long trading, 107–8; futures market,
    334–35
low-coupon bonds. *See* discount
    bonds
low-load funds, 263
low-risk, high-yield portfolio, 366–67
lumber futures, 333

maintenance margin, 112
Major Market index options, 322
makers of options, 301–2

margin call, 112
margin trading, 86, 108–16, 228, 252;
    futures, 331, 335–36, 349; short
    selling, 118–19; warrants, 317
market, 11, 73–74; averages, 127–29;
    indexes, 127; and portfolio
    performance, 374–75, 381–82; and
    stock prices, 189–90; volume,
    192–93
market-makers, 71–72, 80–81, 83
market multiples, 179
market orders, 79
market portfolio, 376
market price, 145; dividends and, 141;
    option value, 306–7
market ratios, 170
market risk, 55–56; mutual fund, 282;
    and return rate, 185–86
market value, 136, 140
mark-to-the-market, 336
maturity date of bond, 203, 222; and
    price, 224
maximization of current income,
    367–69
maximum capital gains funds, 265
maximum daily price range, 338
MBIA (Municipal Bond Insurance
    Association), 211
measurement of returns, 47–52
*Media General Financial Weekly,* 123
MERC (Chicago Mercantile
    Exchange), 331, 332–33, 344
Merrill Lynch, Pierce, Fenner &
    Smith, 68, 83
metals futures, 332–35
Mid-America Commodities Exchange
    (MIDAM), 332–33, 344
minimum guaranteed interest rate of
    annuity, 293
Minneapolis Grain Exchange, 332–33
models of stock valuation, 184–87
monetary policy, 159
*Money,* 124, 277
money funds. *See* money market
    mutual funds
money market, 12, 65; deposit
    accounts (MMDAs), 15, 19, 23;
    mutual funds (MMMFs), 15, 19–20,
    23, 267–68, 276
Moody's Investors Services, 125, 131,
    375; bond ratings, 219; preferred
    stock ratings, 249–50
*Moody's Manuals,* 125
mortgage-backed securities, 216–17;
    bonds, 205; REITs, 262
Municipal Bond Insurance Association
    (MBIA), 211
municipal bonds, 96, 99, 210–13, 230,
    361; margin trading, 109; taxes on,
    286–87; yields, 221, 222
mutual funds, 4, 11, 100–102, 145,
    255–82; holding period return, 373;
    RAR analysis, 377

naked options, 313–14
NASDAQ. *See* National Association
    of Securities Dealers Automated
    Quotation

National Association of Investors
    Corporation (NAIC), 89
National Association of Securities
    Dealers (NASD), 73
National Association of Securities
    Dealers Automated Quotation
    (NASDAQ), 72, 76, 80–81, 83;
    indexes, 130; price quotations,
    91–92
National Market Issues, 91–92
National Market System (NMS), 72, 80
National Securities Clearing
    Corporation, 78
*Nation's Business,* 124
net asset value (NAV), 100–101;
    mutual funds, 260, 279–80;
    preferred stock, 249
net earnings, 166
net profit margin, 169
new building permits, 158
newspapers, 123; price quotations, 127
New York Coffee, Sugar & Cocoa
    Exchange (NYSCTE), 332–33
New York Cotton Exchange, 331,
    332–33; financial futures, 344
New York Futures Exchange (NYFE),
    71, 332–33, 344
New York Mercantile Exchange
    (NYMERC), 332–33
New York Stock Exchange (NYSE),
    67, 68–69, 75–79; bond statistics,
    132; indexes, 130, 374–75; options
    trading, 303; price quotations, 91
*The New York Times* averages, 131
no-load annuities, 295
no-load mutual funds, 102, 261,
    263–64, 268; holding period return,
    373
noncallable bonds, 204, 221
noncontributory retirement plans, 28
nondiversifiable risk, 56–59, 358
not-for-profit organizations, annuities,
    294
NOW accounts, 16, 17, 18, 23

OARS (Opening Automated Report
    Service), 77
oats futures, 333
odd-lot trading, 77–78, 193–94;
    transaction fees, 93
open-end mutual funds, 260, 261, 263,
    278–82
Opening Automated Report Service
    (OARS), 77
opening of accounts, 85–86
operating expenses, 166
opportunity cost, 44
options, 4, 102–5, 300–320;
    exchanges, 70; futures, 333; stock
    index, 321–25
options spreads, 314–15
orange juice futures, 333
ordinary annuities, 43
organized labor, 161
OTC (over-the-counter) market,
    71–73, 83; bonds, 208; margin
    requirements, 111; options, 303;
    price quotations, 91

## ABOUT THE AUTHORS

**Lawrence J. Gitman** is professor of finance at Wright State University. Dr. Gitman is both a Certified Financial Planner (CFP) and a Certified Cash Manager (CCM). He has published widely in finance journals such as *Journal of Financial Research* and *Real Estate Review* and serves as a consulting editor of the *Review of Business and Economic Research* and the *Journal of Financial Education.* In addition, Dr. Gitman has written a number of bestselling finance textbooks. He resides in Dayton, Ohio, with his family.

**Michael D. Joehnk** is professor of finance at Arizona State University. He is a Chartered Financial Analyst (CFA) who is active in research and consulting. His articles on investments and finance have appeared in numerous professional journals, including *Financial Management* and the *Journal of Portfolio Management.* Dr. Joehnk is also a coauthor of two best-selling finance textbooks and is a member of the editorial advisory board of and contributor to the *Handbook of Fixed Income Securities.* He lives in Scottsdale, Arizona, with his wife and two sons.